THE

LAND-WAR IN IRELAND

KENNIKAT PRESS SCHOLARLY REPRINTS

Ralph Adams Brown, Senior Editor

Series In

IRISH HISTORY AND CULTURE

Under the General Editorial Supervision of
Gilbert A. Cahill
Professor of History, State University of New York

THE

LAND-WAR IN IRELAND

A HISTORY FOR THE TIMES

BY

JAMES GODKIN

KENNIKAT PRESS
Port Washington, N. Y./London

THE LAND-WAR IN IRELAND

First published in 1870
Reissued in 1970 by Kennikat Press
Library of Congress Catalog Card No: 72-102605
SBN 8046-0782-6

Manufactured by Taylor Publishing Company   Dallas, Texas

KENNIKAT SERIES IN IRISH HISTORY AND CULTURE

PREFACE.

IT WOULD BE DIFFICULT to name any subject so much discussed during the last half century as 'the condition of Ireland.' There was an endless diversity of opinion; but in one thing all writers and speakers agreed: the condition was morbid. Ireland was always sick, always under medical treatment, always subject to enquiries as to the nature of her maladies, and the remedies likely to effect a cure. The royal commissions and parliamentary committees that sat upon her case were innumerable, and their reports would fill a library. Still the nature of the disease, or the complication of diseases, was a mystery. Sundry 'boons' were prescribed, by way of experiment; but, though recommended as perfect cures, they did the patient no good. She was either very low and weak, or so dangerously strong and violent that she had to be put under restraint. Whenever this crisis arrived, she arrested the special attention of the state doctors. Consultations were held, and it was solemnly determined that something should be done. Another effort should be made to discover the *fons malorum*, and dry it up if possible.

A diseased nation, subject to paroxysms of in-
sanity, and requiring 30,000 keepers, was a dangerous
neighbour, as well as a serious financial burden. Yet
many contended that all such attempts were useless.
It was like trying different kinds of soap to whiten
the skin of a negro. The patient was incurable.
Her ailment was nothing but natural perversity,
aggravated by religious delusions; and the root of
her disorder could never be known till she was subjected to a *post mortem* examination, for which it
was hoped emigration, and the help of improving
landlords, would soon afford an opportunity. In
the meantime, the strait waistcoat must be put on,
to keep the patient from doing mischief.

But at length a great physician arose, who declared
that this state of things should not continue; the
honour, if not the safety, of England demanded that
the treatment should be reversed. Mr. Gladstone
understands the case of Ireland, and he has courage
to apply the proper remedies. Yet the British
public do not understand it so well; and he will
need all the force of public opinion to sustain him
and his cabinet in the work of national regeneration
which they have undertaken. It is not enough for a
good physician to examine the symptoms of his patient.
He must have a full and faithful history of the case.
He must know how the disease originated, and how it
was treated. If injuries were inflicted, he must know
under what circumstances, how they affected the
nervous system, and whether there may not be sur-

rounding influences which prevent the restoration of health, or some nuisance that poisons the atmosphere.

Such a history of the case of Ireland the author has endeavoured to give in the following pages. It it is no perfunctory service. He resolved to do it years ago, when he finished his work on the Irish Church Establishment, and it has been delayed only in consequence of illness and other engagements. He does not boast of any extraordinary qualifications for the work. But he claims the advantage of having studied the subject long and earnestly, as one in which he has been interested from his youth. He has written the history of the country more or less fully three times. During his thirty years' connexion with the press, it has been his duty to examine and discuss everything that appeared before the public upon Irish questions, and it has always been his habit to bring the light of history to bear upon the topics of the day. Twenty years ago he was an active member of the Irish Tenant League, which held great county meetings in most parts of the island; and was enthusiastically supported by the tenant farmers, adopting resolutions and petitions on the land question almost identical with those passed by similar meetings at the present time. Then Mr. Sharman Crawford was the only landlord who joined in the movement; now many of the largest proprietors take their stand on the tenant-right platform. And after a generation of sectarian division and religious dissension in Ulster, stimulated by the landed gentry, for political purposes, the Catholic priests and the Presbyterian clergy have again united to advocate the demands of the people for the legal protection of their industry and their property.

There is scarcely a county in Ireland which the author of this volume has not traversed more than once, having always an eye to the condition of the population, their mode of living, and the relations of the different classes. During the past year, as special commissioner of the *Irish Times*, he went through the greater part of Ulster, and portions of the south, in order to ascertain the feelings of the farmers and the working classes, on the great question which is about to engage the attention of Parliament.

The result of his historical studies and personal enquiries is this:—All the maladies of Ireland, which perplex statesmen and economists, have arisen from injuries inflicted by England in the wars which she waged to get possession of the Irish land. Ireland has been irreconcilable, not because she was conquered by England, not even because she was persecuted, but because she was robbed of her inheritance. If England had done everything she has done against the Irish nation, omitting the *confiscations*, the past would have been forgotten and condoned long ago, and the two nations would have been one people. Even the religious wars resolve themselves into efforts to retain the land, or to recover the forfeited estates. And the banished chiefs never could have rallied the nation to arms, as they so often did against overwhelming odds, if the people had not been involved in the ruin of their lords. All that is really important in the history of the country for the last three centuries is, the fighting of the two nations for the possession of the soil. The Reformation was in reality nothing but a special form of the land war. The oath of supremacy was simply a lever for evicting the owners of the land. The process was simple. The king demanded spiritual allegiance; refusal was high treason; the punishment of high treason was forfeiture of estates, with death or banishment to the recusants. Any other law they might have obeyed, and retained their inheritance. This law fixed its iron grapples in the conscience, and made obedience impossible, without a degree of baseness that rendered life intolerable. Hence Protestantism was detested, not so much as a religion, as an instrument of spoliation.

The agrarian wars were kept up from generation to generation, Ireland always making desperate efforts to get back her inheritance, but always crushed to the earth, a victim of famine and the sword, by the power of England.

The history of these wars, then, is the history of the case of the Irish patient. Its main facts are embodied in the general history of the country. But they have recently been brought out more distinctly by authors who have devoted years to the examination of the original state papers, in which

the actors themselves described their exploits and
recorded their motives and feelings with startling
frankness.   When a task of this kind has been performed by a capable and conscientious historian, it
would be a work of supererogation for another en-
quirer to undergo the wearisome toil, even if he
could.   I have, therefore, for the purpose of my
argument, freely availed myself of the materials given
to the public by Mr. Froude, the Rev. C. P. Meehan,
and Mr. Prendergast, not, however, without asking
their permission, which was in each case most readily
and kindly granted.

The ancient state of Ireland, and especially of
Ulster, is so little known in England, that I was
glad to have the facts vouched for by so high an
authority as Mr. Froude, and a writer so full of the
instinctive pride of the dominant nation; the more
so as I have often been obliged to dissent from his
views, and to appeal against his judgments.   Be-
guiled by the beauty of his descriptions, I am afraid
I have drawn too largely on his pages, in proving
and illustrating my case; but I feel confident that no
one will read these extracts without more eagerly
desiring to possess the volumes of his great work
from which they are taken.

I have similar acknowledgments to make to
Father Meehan and Mr. Prendergast, both of whom
are preparing new editions of their most valuable
works.   The royal charters, and other documents
connected with the Plantation of Ulster, are printed in

the ' Concise View of the Irish Society,' compiled from their records, and published by their authority in 1832. Whenever I have been indebted to other writers, I have acknowledged my obligation in the course of the work. In preparing it, I have had but one object constantly in view: to present to the public a careful collection and an impartial statement of facts on the state of Ireland, for the right government of which the British people are now more than ever responsible. I shall be thankful if my labours should contribute in any measure, however humble, to the new conquest of Ireland ' by justice ' of which Mr. Bright has spoken. His language is suggestive. It is late (happily not ' too late ') to commence the reign of justice. But the nation is not to be despised which requires nothing more than *that* to win its heart, while its spirit could not be conquered by centuries of injustice. Nor should it be forgotten by the people of England that some atonement is due for past wrongs, not the least of which is the vilification and distrust from which the Irish people have suffered so much. ' The spirit of a man may sustain his infirmity; but a wounded spirit who can bear?' Some manifestation of Christian magnanimity just now would greatly help the work of national reconciliation. The time is favourable. The Government enjoys the prestige of an unparalleled success. The only Prime Minister that ever dared to do full justice to Ireland, is the most powerful that England has had for nearly a century. He has in his Cabinet the only Chief Secretary of Ireland that ever thoroughly sympathised with the nation, not excepting Lord Morpeth; the great tribune of the English people, who has been one of the most eloquent advocates of Ireland; an Ex-Viceroy who has pronounced it felony for the Irish landlords to avail themselves of their legal rights, although he put down a rebellion which that felony mainly provoked; another Ex-Governor, who was one of the most earnest and conscientious that ever filled the vice-regal throne, and who returned to Parliament to be one of the ablest champions of the country he had ruled so well; not to mention other members of commanding ability, who are solemnly pledged to the policy of justice. In these facts there is great promise. He understands little of ' the signs of the times,' who does not see the dangers that hang on the non-fulfilment of this promise.

J. G.

London: *January* 20, 1870.

CONTENTS.

THE

LAND-WAR IN IRELAND.

CHAPTER I.

INTRODUCTION.

As the hour approaches when the legislature must deal with
the Irish Land question, and settle it, like the Irish Church
question, once for all, attempts are redoubled to frighten
the public with the difficulties of the task. The alarmists
conjure up gigantic apparitions more formidable than those
which encountered Bunyan's Pilgrim. Monstrous figures
frown along the gloomy avenue that leads up to the Egyptian temple in which the divinity, PROPERTY, dwells in mysterious darkness. To enter the sanctuary, we are solemnly
assured, requires all the cardinal virtues in their highest
state of development—the firmest faith, the most vivid hope,
and the charity that never faileth. But this is not the only
country that has had a land question to settle. Almost every
nation in Europe has done for itself what England is now
called upon to do for Ireland. In fact, it is a necessary
process in the transition from feudalism to constitutional
self-government. Feudalism gave the land to a few whom
it made princes and lords, having forcibly taken it from the
many, whom it made subjects and serfs. The land is the
natural basis of society. The Normans made it the artificial
basis of a class. Society in nearly every other country has

B

reverted back to its original foundations, and so remains
firm and strong without dangerous rents or fissures. No
doubt, the operation is difficult and critical. But what has
been done once may be done again; and as it was England
that kept Irish society so long rocking on its smaller end, it
is her duty now to lend all her strength to help to seat it on
its own broad foundations. Giving up the Viceroy's dreams
that the glorious mission of Ireland was to be a kitchen
garden, a dairy, a larder for England, we must come frankly
to the conclusion that the national life of the Irish people,
without distinction of creed or party, increases in vigour with
their intelligence, and is now invincible. Let the imperial
legislature put an end for ever to such an unnatural state of
things—thus only can they secure the harmonious working
and cordial union of the two nations united together in one
State—thus only can they insure for the landlords themselves
all the power and all the influence that can be retained by
them in consistency with the industrial rights and political
freedom of the cultivators of the soil. These now complain
of their abject dependence, and hopeless bondage, under
grinding injustice. They are alleged to be full of discontent,
which must grow with the intelligence and manhood of the
people who writhe under the system. Their advocates affirm
that their discontent must increase in volume and angry force
every year, and that, owing to the connection of Ireland with
the United States, it may at any time be suddenly swollen
with the fury of a mountain torrent, deeply discoloured by
a Republican element.

It must be granted, I fear, that the Celts of Ireland feel
pretty much as the Britons felt under the ascendency of the
Saxons, and as the Saxons in their turn felt under the
ascendency of the Normans. In the estimation of the
Christian Britons, their Saxon conquerors, even after the
conversion of the latter, were ' an accursed race, the children
of robbers and murderers, possessing the fruits of their
fathers' crimes.' ' With them,' says Dr. Lingard, ' the
Saxon was no better than a pagan bearing the name of a

Christian. They refused to return his salutation, to join in prayer with him in the church, to sit with him at the same table, to abide with him under the same roof. The remnant of his meals and the food over which he had made the sign of the cross they threw to their dogs or swine; the cup out of which he had drunk they scoured with sand, as if it had contracted defilement from his lips.'

It is not the Celtic memory only that is tenacious of national wrong. The Saxon was doomed to drink to the dregs the same bitter cup which he administered so unmercifully to the Briton. His Teutonic blood saved him from no humiliation or insult. The Normans seized all the lands, all the castles, all the pleasant mansions, all the churches and monasteries. Even the Saxon saints were flung down out of their shrines and trampled in the dust under the iron heel of the Christian conqueror. Everything Saxon was vile, and the word ' Englishry ' implied as much contempt and scorn as the word ' Irishry ' in a later age. In fact, the subjugated Saxons gradually became infected with all the vices and addicted to all the social disorders that prevailed among the Irish in the same age; only in Ireland the anarchy endured much longer from the incompleteness of the conquest and the absence of the seat of supreme government, which kept the races longer separate and antagonistic. Perhaps the most humiliating notice of the degrading effects of conquest on the noble Saxon race to be found in history, is the language in which Giraldus Cambrensis, the reviler of the Irish Celt, contrasts them with his countrymen, the Welsh. ' Who dare,' he says, ' compare the English, the most degraded of all races under heaven, with the Welsh? In their own country they are the serfs, the veriest slaves of the Normans. In ours whom else have we for our herdsmen, shepherds, cobblers, skinners, cleaners of our dog kennels, ay, even of our privies, but Englishmen? Not to mention their original treachery to the Britons, that hired by them to defend them they turned upon them in spite of their oaths and engagements, they are to this day given to treachery and murder.'

The lying Saxon was, according to this authority, a proverbial expression.

The Saxon writers lamented their miserable subjection in a monotonous wail for many generations. So late as the seventeenth century an English author speaks in terms of compassion of the disinherited and despoiled families who had sunk into the condition of artisans, peasants, and paupers. ' This,' says M. Thierry, ' is the last sorrowful glance cast back through the mist of ages on that great event which established in England a race of kings, nobles, and warriors of foreign extraction. The reader must figure to himself, not a mere change of political rule, not the triumph of one of two competitors, but the intrusion of a nation into the bosom of another people which it came to destroy, and the scattered fragments of which it retained as an integral portion of the new system of society, in the *status* merely of personal property, or, to use the stronger language of records and deeds, *a clothing of the soil.* He must not picture to himself on the one hand the king and despot; on the other simply his subjects, high and low, rich and poor, all inhabiting England, and consequently all English. He must bear in mind that there were two distinct nations—the old Anglo-Saxon race and the Norman invaders, dwelling intermingled on the same soil; or, rather, he might contemplate two countries—the one possessed by the Normans, wealthy and exonerated from public burdens, the other enslaved and oppressed with a land tax—the former full of spacious mansions, of walled towns, and moated castles—the latter occupied with thatched cabins, and ancient walls in a state of dilapidation. This peopled with the happy and the idle, with soldiers, courtiers, knights, and nobles—that with miserable men condemned to labour as peasants and artisans. On the one side he beholds luxury and insolence, on the other poverty and envy—not the envy of the poor at the sight of opulence and men born to opulence, but that malignant envy, although justice be on its side, which the despoiled cannot but entertain on looking upon the spoilers. Lastly, to complete the picture, these two countries are in some sort interwoven with each other—they meet at every point, and yet they are more distinct, more completely separated, than if the ocean rolled between them.'

Does not this picture look very like Ireland? To make it more like, let us imagine that the Norman king had lived in Paris, and kept a viceroy in London—that the English parliament were subordinate to the French parliament, composed exclusively of Normans, and governed by Norman undertakers for the benefit of the dominant State—that the whole of the English land was held by ten thousand Norman proprietors, many of them absentees—that all the offices of the government, in every department, were in the hands of Normans—that, differing in religion with the English nation, the French, being only a tenth of the population, had got possession of all the national churches and church property, while the poor natives supported a numerous hierarchy by voluntary contributions—that the Anglo-Norman parliament was bribed and coerced to abolish itself, forming a union of England with France, in which the English members were as one to six. Imagine that in consequence of rebellions the land of England had been confiscated three or four times, after desolating wars and famines, so that all the native proprietors were expelled, and the land was parcelled out to French soldiers and adventurers on condition that the foreign ' planters' should assist in keeping down ' the mere English' by force of arms. Imagine that the English, being crushed by a cruel penal code for a century, were allowed to reoccupy the soil as mere tenants-at-will, under the absolute power of their French landlords. If all this be imagined by English legislators and English writers, they will be better able to understand the Irish land question, and to comprehend the nature of 'Irish difficulties,' as well as the justice of feeble, insincere, and baffled statesmen in casting the blame of Irish misery and disorder on the unruly and barbarous nature of Irishmen. They will recollect that the aristocracy of Ireland are the high-spirited descendants of conquerors, with the

instinct of conquest still in their blood. The parliament
which enacted the Irish land laws was a parliament composed
almost exclusively of men of this dominant race. They
made all political power dependent on the ownership of land,
thus creating for themselves a monopoly which it is not in
human nature to surrender without a struggle.

The possession of this monopoly, however, fully accounts
for two things—the difficulty which the landlords feel in
admitting the justice of the tenant's claims for the legal
recognition of the value which his labour has added to the
soil, and the extreme repugnance with which they regard any
legislation on the subject. Besides, the want of sympathy
with the people, of earnestness and courage in meeting the
realities of the case, is conspicuous in all attempts of the
kind during the last half-century. Those attempts have
been evasive, feeble, abortive—concessions to the demand
that *something* must be done, but so managed that nothing
should be done to weaken the power of the eight thousand
proprietors over the mass of the nation dependent on the
land for their existence. Hence has arisen a great amount
of jealousy, distrust, and irritability in the landlord class
towards the tenantry and their advocates.

The Irish race, to adopt Thierry's language, are full of
' malignant envy ' towards the lords of the soil; not because
they are rich, but because they have the people so completely in their power, so entirely at their mercy for all
that man holds most dear. The tenants feel bitterly when
they think that they have no legal right to live on their
native land. They have read the history of our dreadful
civil wars, famines, and confiscations. They know that
by the old law of Ireland, and by custom from times far
beyond the reach of authentic history, the clans and tribes
of the Celtic people occupied certain districts with which
their names are still associated, and that the land was
inalienably theirs. Rent or tribute they paid, indeed,
to their princes, and if they failed the chiefs came with
armed followers and helped themselves, driving away

cows, sheep, and horses sufficient to meet their demand, or more if they were unscrupulous, which was 'distress' with a vengeance. But the eviction of the people even for non-payment of rent, and putting other people in their place, were things never heard of among the Irish under their own rulers. The chief had his own mensal lands, as well as his ribute, and these he might forfeit. But as the clansmen could not control his acts, they could never see the justice of being punished for his misdeeds by the confiscation of their lands, and driven from the homes of their ancestors often made doubly sacred by religious associations.

History, moreover, teaches them that, as a matter of fact, the government in the reign of James I.—and James himself in repeated proclamations—assured the people who occupied the lands of O'Neill and O'Donnell at the time of their flight that they would be protected in all their rights if they remained quiet and loyal, which they did. Yet they were nearly all removed to make way for the English and Scotch settlers.

Thus, historical investigators have been digging around the foundations of Irish landlordism. They declare that those foundations were cemented with blood, and they point to the many wounds still open from which that blood issued so profusely. The facts of the conquest and confiscation were hinted at by the Devon Commissioners as accounting for the peculiar difficulties of the Irish land question, and writers on it timidly allude to 'the historic past' as originating influences still powerful in alienating landlords and tenants, and fostering mutual distrust between them. But the time for evasion and timidity has passed. We must now honestly and courageously face the stern realities of this case. Among these realities is a firm conviction in the minds of many landlords that they are in no sense trustees for the community, but that they have an absolute power over their estates—that they can, if they like, strip the land clean of its human clothing, and clothe it with sheep or cattle instead, or lay it bare and desolate, let it lapse into a

wilderness, or sow it with salt. That is in reality the
terrific power secured to them by the present land code,
to be executed through the Queen's writ and by the
Queen's troops—a power which could not stand a day if
England did not sustain it by overwhelming military force.

Another of the realities of the question is the no less
inveterate conviction in the tenants' mind that the absolute
power of the landlord was originally a usurpation effected
by the sword. Right or wrong, they believe that the confiscations were the palpable violation of the natural rights of
the people whom Providence placed in this country. With
bitter emphasis they assert that no set of men has any
divine right to root a nation out of its own land. Painful
as this state of feeling is, there is no use in denying that it
exists. Here, then, is the deep radical difference that is to
be removed. Here are the two conflicting forces which are
to be reconciled. This is the real Irish land question. All
other points are minor and of easy adjustment. The people
say, and, I believe, sincerely, that they are willing to pay
a fair rent, according to a public valuation—not a rent
imposed arbitrarily by one of the interested parties, which
might be raised so as to ruin the occupier. The feelings of
these two parties often clash so violently, there is such
instinctive distrust between them, the peace and prosperity
of the country depend so much on their coming to terms
and putting an end to their long-standing feud, that it is still
more imperatively necessary than in the Church question,
that a third party, independent, impartial, and authoritative,
should intervene and heal the breach.

There was one phrase constantly ringing in the ears of the
Devon Commissioners, and now, after nearly a generation
has passed away, it is ringing in the ears of the nation louder
than ever—' the want of tenure.' All the evidence went to
show that the want of security paralysed industry and impeded social progress. It seems strange that any evidence
should be thought necesary to prove that a man will not
sow if he does not hope to reap, and that he will not build

houses for strangers to enjoy. This would be taken as an axiom anywhere out of Ireland. Of all the people in Europe, the Irish have suffered most from the oppression of those who, from age to age, had power in the country. Whoever fought or conquered, they were always the victims; and it is a singular fact that their sufferings are scarcely ever noticed by the contemporary annalists, even when those annalists were ecclesiastics. The extent to which they were slaughtered in the perpetual wars between the native chiefs, and in the wars between those chiefs and the English, is something awful to contemplate, not to speak of the wholesale destruction of life by the famines which those wars entailed. On several occasions the Celtic race seemed very nearly extinct. The penal code, with all its malign influence, had one good effect. It subdued to a great extent the fighting propensities of the people, and fused the clans into one nation, purified by suffering. Since that time, in spite of occasional visitations of calamity, they have been steadily rising in the social scale, and they are now better off than ever they were in their whole history. When we review the stages by which they have risen, we cannot but feel at times grieved and indignant at the opportunities for tranquillising and enriching the country which were lost through the ignorance, apathy, bigotry, and selfishness of the legislature. There was no end of commissions and select committees to inquire into the condition of the agricultural population, whenever Parliament was roused by the prevalence of agrarian outrages. They reported, and there the matter ended. There were always insuperable difficulties when the natives were to be put in a better position. Between 1810 and 1814, for example, a commission reported four times on the condition of the Irish bogs. They expressed their entire conviction of the practicability of cultivating with profit an immense extent of land lying waste. In 1819, in 1823, in 1826, and in 1830, select committees inquired into and reported on drainage, reclamation of bogs and marshes, on roads, fisheries, emigration, and other schemes for giving employment to the redundant population that had been encouraged to increase and multiply in the most reckless manner, while 'war prices' were obtained for agricultural produce, and the votes of the forty-shilling freeholders were wanted by the landlords. When, by the Emancipation Act in 1829, the forty-shilling franchise was abolished, the peasant lost his political value. After the war, when the price of corn fell very low, and, consequently, tillage gave place to grazing, labourers became to the middleman an encumbrance and a nuisance that must be cleared off the land, just as weeds are plucked up and flung out to wither on the highway. Then came Lord Devon's Land Commission, which inquired on the eve of the potato failure and the great famine. The Irish population was now at its highest figure—between eight and nine millions. Yet, though there had been three bad seasons, it was clearly proved at that time that by measures which a wise and willing legislature would have promptly passed, the whole surplus population could have been profitably employed.

In this great land controversy, on which side lies the truth? Is it the fault of the people, or the fault of the law, that the country is but half cultivated, while the best of the peasantry are emigrating with hostile feelings and purposes of vengeance towards England? As to the landlords, as a class, they use their powers with as much moderation and mercy as any other class of men in any country ever used power so vast and so little restrained. The best and most indulgent landlords, the most genial and generous, are unquestionably the old nobility, the descendants of the Normans and Saxons, those very conquerors of whom we have heard so much. The worst, the most harsh and exacting, are those who have purchased under the Landed Estates Court—strangers to the people, who think only of the percentage on their capital. We had heard much of the necessity of capital to develope the resources of the land. The capital came, but the development consists in turning tillage lands into pasture, clearing out the labouring population and sending them to the poorhouse, or shipping them off at a few pounds per head to keep down the rates. And yet is it not possible to set all our peasantry to work at the profitable cultivation of their native land? Is it not possible to establish by law what many landlords act upon as the rule of their estates—namely, the principle that no man is to be evicted so long as he pays a fair rent, and the other principle, that whenever he fails, he is entitled to the market value by public sale of all the property in his holding beyond that fair rent? The hereditary principle, rightly cherished among the landlords, so conservative in its influence, ought to be equally encouraged among the tenants. The man of industry, as well as the man of rank, should be able to feel that he is providing for his children, that his farm is at once a bank and an insurance office, in which all his minute daily deposits of toil and care and skill will be safe and productive. This is the way to enrich and strengthen the State, and to multiply guarantees against revolution— not by consolidation of farms and the abandonment of tillage, not by degrading small holders into day labourers, levelling the cottages and filling the workhouses.

If the legislature were guided by the spirit that animates Lord Erne in his dealings with his tenantry, the land question would soon be settled to the satisfaction of all parties. ' I think,' said his lordship, ' as far as possible, every tenant on my estate may call his farm his castle, as long as he conducts himself honestly, quietly, and industriously; and, should he wish to leave in order to find a better landlord, I allow him to sell his farm, provided he pleases me in a tenant. Therefore, if a man lays out money on his farm judiciously, he is certain to receive back the money, should he wish to go elsewhere.' He mentioned three cases of sale which occurred last year. One tenant sold a farm of seventy acres in bad order for 570*l.*, another thirty acres for 300*l.*, and a third the same number of acres in worse condition for 200*l.* The landlord lost nothing by these changes. His rent was paid up, and in each case he got a good tenant for

a bad one.   Lord Erne is a just man, and puts on no more
than a fair rent.   But all landlords are not just, as all
tenants are not honest.   Even where tenant-right is admitted in name, it is obvious that the rent may be raised
so high as to make the farm worth nothing in the market.
To give to the tenant throughout the country generally the
pleasant feeling that his farm is his castle, which he can
make worth more money every day he rises, there must be
a public letting valuation, and this the State could easily
provide.   And then there should be the right of sale to the
highest solvent bidder.

This might be one way of securing permanent tenure, or
stimulating the industry and sustaining the thrift of the
farmer.   But the nature of the different tenures, and the
effect of each in bracing up or relaxing the nerves of industry, will be the object of deliberation with the Government and the legislature.   It is said that, in the hands of
small farmers, proprietorship leads to endless subdivision;
that long leases generally cause bad husbandry; that tenants-
at-will often feel themselves more secure and safe than a
contract could make them; that families have lived on the
same farm for generations without a scrape of a pen except
the receipt for rent.   On the other hand, there is the general cry of ' want of tenure; ' there is the custom of serving
notices to quit, sometimes for other reasons than non-payment
of rent; there are occasional barbarities in the levelling of
villages, and dragging the aged and the sick from the old
roof-tree, the parting from which rends their heart-strings;
and, above all, there is the feeling among the peasantry
which makes them look without horror on the murder of a
landlord or an agent who was a kind and benevolent neighbour; and, lastly, the paramount consideration for the legislature, that a large portion of the people are disaffected to
the State, and ready to join its enemies, and this almost
solely on account of the state of the law relating to land.
Hence the necessity of settling the question as speedily as
possible, and the duty of all who have the means to con-

tribute something towards that most desirable consummation, which seems to be all that is wanted to make Irishmen
of every class work together earnestly for the welfare of
their country. It is admitted that no class of men in the
world has improved more than the Irish landlords during
the last twenty years. Let the legislature restore confidence between them and the people by taking away all
ground for the suspicion that they wish to extirpate the
Celtic race.

Nor was this suspicion without cause, as the following
history will too clearly prove. A very able English writer
has said : ' The policy of all the successive swarms of settlers
was to extirpate the native Celtic race, but every effort
made to break up the old framework of society failed, for
the new-comers soon became blended with and undistinguish-
able from the mass of the people—being obliged to ally
themselves with the native chieftains, rather than live
hemmed in by a fiery ring of angry septs and exposed to
perpetual war with everything around them. Merged in the
great Celtic mass, they adopted Irish manners and names, yet
proscribed and insulted the native inhabitants as an inferior
race. Everything liberal towards them is intercepted in its
progress.

' The past history of Ulster is but a portion of Scottish
history inserted into that of Ireland—a stone in the Irish
mosaic of an entirely different quality and colour from the
pieces that surround it.

' Thus it came to pass that, through the confiscation of
their lands and the proscription of their religion, popery
was worked by a most vehement process into the blood and
brain of the Irish nation.'

It has been often said that the Irish must be an inferior
race, since they allowed themselves to be subjugated by
some thousands of English invaders. But it should be recol-
lected, first, that the conquest, commenced by Henry II. in
the twelfth century, was not completed till the seventeenth
century, when the King's writ ran for the first time through

the province of Ulster, the ancient kingdom of the O'Neills ;
in the second place, the weakness of the Celtic communities was not so much the fault of the men as of their institutions, brought with them from the East and clung to with
wonderful tenacity.   So long as they had boundless territory
for their flocks and herds, and could always move on ' to
pastures new,' they increased and multiplied, and allowed the
sword and the battle-axe to rest, unless when a newly elected
chief found it necessary to give his followers ' a hosting'—
which means an expedition for plunder.   Down to the seventeenth century, after five hundred years' contact with the
Teutonic race, they were essentially the same people as they
were when the ancient Greeks and Romans knew them.
They are thus described by Dr. Mommsen in his ' History of
Rome :'—' Such qualities—those of good soldiers and of bad
citizens—explain the historical fact that the Celts have
shaken all States and have *founded none.*   Everywhere we
find them ready to rove, or, in other words, to march, preferring movable property to landed estate, and gold to
everything else; following the profession of arms as a
system of organised pillage, or even as a trade for hire,
and with such success that even the Roman historian,
Sallust, acknowledges that the Celts bore off the prize from
the Romans in feats of arms.   They were the true ' soldiers of fortune' of antiquity, as pictures and descriptions
represent them, with big but sinewy bodies, with shaggy
hair and long moustaches—quite a contrast to the Greeks
and Romans, who shaved the upper lip—in the variegated
embroidered dresses which in combat were not unfrequently
thrown off, with a broad gold ring round their neck, wearing
no helmets and without missile weapons of any sort, but
furnished instead with an immense shield, a long ill-tempered
sword, a dagger and a lance, all ornamented with gold, for
they were not unskilful in working in metals.   Everything
was made subservient to ostentation—even wounds, which
were often enlarged for the purpose of boasting a broader
scar.   Usually they fought on foot, but certain tribes on

horseback, in which case every free man was followed by two attendants, likewise mounted. War-chariots were early in use, as they were among the Libyans and Hellenes in the earliest times. Many a trait reminds us of the chivalry of the middle ages, particularly the custom of single combat, which was foreign to the Greeks and Romans. Not only were they accustomed in war to challenge a single enemy to fight, after having previously insulted him by words and gestures; in peace also they fought with each other in splendid equipments, as for life or death. After such feats carousals followed in due course. In this way they led, whether under their own or a foreign banner, a restless soldier life, constantly occupied in fighting and in their so-called feats of heroism. They were dispersed from *Ireland* and Spain to Asia Minor, but all their enterprises melted away like snow in spring, and they nowhere created a great state or developed a distinctive culture of their own.' Such were the people who once almost terminated the existence of Rome, and were afterwards with difficulty repulsed from Greece, who became masters of the most fertile part of Italy and of a fair province in the heart of Asia Minor, who, after their Italian province had been subdued, inflicted disastrous blows on successive Roman generals, and were only at last subjugated by Cæsar himself in nine critical and sometimes most dangerous campaigns, B.C. 51.

Niebuhr observes that at that time the form of government was everywhere an hereditary monarchy, which, when Cæsar went into Gaul, had been swallowed up, as had the authority of the Senate, in the anarchy of the nobles. Their freedom was lawlessness; an inherent incapacity of living under the dominion of laws distinguishes them as barbarians from the Greeks and Italians. As individuals had to procure the protection of some magnate in order to live in safety, so the weaker tribes took shelter under the patronage of a more powerful one. For they were a disjointed multitude; and when any people had in this manner acquired an extensive sovereignty, they exercised it arbitrarily until its abuses became intolerable, or their subjects were urged by blind hatred of their power to fall off from them, and gather round some new centre. The sole bond of union was the Druidical hierarchy which, at least in Cæsar's time, was common to both nations. Both of them paid obedience to its tribunal, which administered justice once a year—an institution which probably was not introduced till long after the age of migrations, when the expulsion of the vanquished had ceased to be regarded as the end of war, and which must have been fostered by the constant growth of lawlessness in particular states—being upheld by the *ban*, which excluded the contumacious from all intercourse in divine worship and in daily life with the faithful. The huge bodies, wild features, and long shaggy hair of the men, gave a ghastliness to their aspect. This, along with their fierce courage, their countless numbers, and the noise made by an enormous multitude of horns and trumpets, struck the armies arrayed against them with fear and amazement. If these, however, did not allow their terror to overpower them, the want of order, discipline, and perseverance would often enable an inferior number to vanquish a vast host of the barbarians. Besides, they were but ill equipped. Few of them wore any armour; their narrow shields, which were of the same height with their bodies, were weak and clumsy; they rushed upon their enemies with broad thin battle-swords of bad steel, which the first blow upon iron often notched and rendered useless. Like true savages, they destroyed the inhabitants, the towns, and the agriculture of the countries they conquered. They cut off the heads of the slain, and tied them by the hair to the manes of their horses. If a skull belonged to a person of rank, they nailed it up in their houses and preserved it as an heirloom for their posterity, as the nobles in rude ages do stag-horns. Towns were rare amongst them; the houses and the villages, which were very numerous, were mean, the furniture wretched—a heap of straw covered with skins served both for a bed and a seat. They did not cultivate

corn save for a very limited consumption, for the main part
of their food was the milk and the flesh of their cattle.
These formed their wealth. Gold, too, they had in abundance, derived partly from the sandy beds of their rivers,
partly from some mines which these had led them to
discover. It was worn in ornaments by every Gaul of rank.
In battle he bore gold chains on his arms and heavy gold
collars round his neck, even when the upper part of his body
was in other respects quite naked. For they often threw
off their parti-coloured chequered cloaks, which shone with
all the hues of the rainbow, like the picturesque dress of
their kinspeople the Highlanders, who have laid aside the
trousers of the ancient Gauls. Their duels and gross revels
are an image of the rudest part of the middle ages. Their
debauches were mostly committed with beer and mead ; for
vines and all the plants of southern regions were as yet total
strangers to the north of the Alps, where the climate in those
ages was extremely severe ; so that wine was rare, though
of all the commodities imported it was the most greedily
bought up.

Ulster was known in ancient times as one of the five
Irish 'kingdoms,' and remained unconquered by the English till the reign of James I., when the last prince of the
great house of O'Neill, then Earl of Tyrone, fled to the
Continent in company with O'Donel, Earl of Tyrconnel,
head of another very ancient sept. Up to that period the
men of Ulster proudly regarded themselves as ' Irish of the
Irish and Catholic of the Catholics.' The inhabitants were
of mixed blood, but, as in the other provinces of the island,
the great mass of the people, as well as the ruling classes,
were of Celtic origin. Those whom ethnologists still
recognise as aborigines, in parts of Connaught and in some
mountainous regions, an inferior race, are said to be the
descendants of the Firbolgs, or Belgæ, who formed the
third immigration. They were followed and subdued by the
Tuatha de Danans—men famed for their gigantic power and
supernatural skill—a race of demigods, who still live in the

national superstitions.   The last of the ancient invasions was
by the Gael or Celt, known as the Milesians and Scoti.
The institutions and customs of this people were established over the whole island, and were so deeply rooted in
the soil that their remnants to this day present the greatest
obstacles to the settlement of the land question according to
the English model, and on the principles of political economy,
which run directly counter to Irish instincts.   It is truly
wonderful how distinctly the present descendants of this
race preserve the leading features of their primitive character.   In France and England the Celtic character was
moulded by the power and discipline of the Roman Empire.
To Ireland this modifying influence never extended; and
we find the Ulster chiefs who fought for their territories with
English viceroys 280 years ago very little different from
the men who followed Brennus to the sack of Rome, and
encountered the legions of Julius Cæsar on the plains of
Gaul.

Mr. Prendergast observes, in the introduction to his 'Cromwellian Settlement' that when the companions of Strongbow
landed in the reign of Henry II. they found a country such
as Cæsar had found in Gaul 1200 years before.   A thousand
years had passed over the island without producing the
slightest social progress—'the inhabitants divided into tribes
on the system of the clansmen and chiefs, without a common
Government, suddenly confederating, suddenly dissolving,
with Brehons, Shaunahs, minstrels, bards, and harpers, in all
unchanged, except that for their ancient Druids they had
got Christian priests.   Had the Irish remained honest pagans,
Ireland perhaps had remained unconquered still.   Round
the coast strangers had built seaport towns, either traders
from the Carthaginian settlements in Spain, or outcasts from
their own country, like the Greeks that built Marseilles.
At the time of the arrival of the French and Flemish
adventurers from Wales, they were occupied by a mixed
Danish and French population, who supplied the Irish with
groceries, including the wines of Poitou, the latter in such
abundance that they had no need of vineyards.'

If vineyards had been needed, we may be sure they would
not have been planted, for the Irish Celts planted nothing.
Neither did they build, except in the simplest and rudest
way, improving their architecture from age to age no more
than the beaver or the bee. Mr. Prendergast is an able,
honest, and frank writer; yet there is something amusingly
Celtic in the flourish with which he excuses the style of
palaces in which the Irish princes delighted to dwell.
' Unlike England,' he says, ' then covered with castles on
the heights, where the French gentlemen secured themselves
and their families against the hatred of the churls and
villains, as the English peasantry were called, the dwellings
of the Irish chiefs were of wattles or clay. It is for robbers
and foreigners to take to rocks and precipices for security;
for native rulers, there is no such fortress *as justice and
humanity.*' This is very fine, but surely Mr. Prendergast
cannot mean that the Irish chiefs were distinguished by their
justice and humanity. The following touch is still grander :—
' The Irish, like the wealthiest and highest of the present
day, loved detached houses surrounded by fields and woods.
Towns and their walls they looked upon as tombs or
sepulchres, &c.' As to fields, there were none, because the
Irish never made fences, their patches of cultivated land
being divided by narrow strips of green sod. Besides, they
lived in villages, which were certainly surrounded by woods,
because the woods were everywhere, and they furnished
the inhabitants with fuel and shelter, as well as materials
for building their huts.

But further on this able author expresses himself much
more in accordance with the truth of history, when he states
that the ' Irish enemy' was no *nation* in the modern sense of
the word, but a race divided into many nations or tribes,
separately defending their lands from the English barons in
the immediate neighbourhood. There had been no ancient
national government displaced, no dynasty overthrown;
the Irish had *no national flag,* nor any capital city as the
metropolis of their common country, nor any common

administration of law.' He might have added that they had no *mint*. There never was an Irish king who had his face stamped on a coin of his realm. Some stray pieces of money found their way into the country from abroad, but up to the close of the sixteenth century the rudest form of barter prevailed in Ulster, and accounts were paid not in coins but in cows. Even the mechanical arts which had flourished in the country before the arrival of the Celts had gradually perished, and had disappeared at the time of the English invasion. Any handy men could build a house of mud and wattles. Masons, carpenters, smiths, painters, glaziers, &c., were not wanted by a people who despised stone buildings as prisons, and abhorred walled towns as sepulchres. Spinning and weaving were arts cultivated by the women, each household providing materials for clothing, which was little used in warm weather, and thrown off when fighting or any other serious work was to be done.

I should be sorry to disparage the Celtic race, or any other race, by exaggerating their bad qualities or suppressing any reliable testimony to their merits. But with me the truth of history is sacred. Both sides of every case should be fairly stated. Nothing can be gained by striving to hide facts which may be known to every person who takes the trouble to study the subject. I write in the interest of the people—of the toiling masses; and I find that they were oppressed and degraded by the ruling classes long before the Norman invader took the place of the Celtic chief. And it is a curious fact that when the Cromwellians turned the Catholic population out of their homes and drove them into Connaught, they were but following the example set them by the Milesian lords of the soil centuries before.

The late Mr. Darcy Magee, a real lover of his country, in his Irish history points out this fact. The Normans found the population divided into two great classes—the free tribes, chiefly if not exclusively Celtic, and the unfree tribes, consisting of the descendants of the subjugated races, or of clans once free, reduced to servitude by the sword, and the offspring of foreign mercenary soldiers. 'The unfree tribes,' says Mr. Darcy Magee, 'have left no history. Under the despotism of the Milesian kings, it was high treason to record the actions of the conquered race, so that the Irish Belgæ fared as badly in this respect at the hands of the Milesian historians as the latter fared in after times from the chroniclers of the Normans. We only know that such tribes were, and that their numbers and physical force more than once excited the apprehension of the children of the conquerors. One thing is certain—the jealous policy of the superior race never permitted them to reascend the plane of equality from which they had been hurled at the very commencement of the Milesian ascendency.'

Mr. Haverty, another Catholic historian, learned, accurate, and candid, laments the oppression of the people by their native rulers. 'Those who boasted descent from the Scytho-Spanish hero would have considered themselves degraded were they to devote themselves to any less honourable profession than those of soldiers, *ollavs*, or physicians; and hence the cultivation of the soil and the exercise of the mechanic arts were left almost exclusively to the *Firbolgs* and the *Tuatha-de-Danans*—the former people, in particular, being still very numerous, and forming the great mass of the population in the west. These were ground down by high rents and the exorbitant exactions of the dominant race, *in order to support their unbounded hospitality* and defray the expenses of costly assemblies; but this oppression must have caused perpetual discontent, and the hardworking plebeians, as they were called, easily perceived that their masters were running headlong to destruction, and that it only required a bold effort to shake off their yoke.' Then follows an account of a civil war, one of the leaders of the revolution being elected king at its termination. Carbry reigned five years, during which time there was no rule or order, and the country was a prey to every misfortune. 'Evil was the state of Ireland during his reign; fruitless her corn, for there used to be but one

grain on the stalk; and fruitless her rivers; her cattle
without milk; her fruit without plenty, for there used to be
but one acorn on the oak.'

Dr. Lynch, author of *Cambrensis Eversus*, expresses
his astonishment at the great number of ancient Irish
kings, most of whom were cut off by a violent death, each
hewing his way to the throne over the body of his predecessor.
But upon applying his mind to the more profound consideration of the matter, he found nothing more wonderful in the
phenomenon 'than that the human family should proceed
from one man—the overflowing harvest from a few grains
of seed, &c.' His learned translator, the Rev. Matthew
Kelly, of Maynooth, sees proof of amendment in the fact
that between 722 and 1022 twelve Irish kings died a natural death. This candid and judicious writer observes in
a note—' It appears from the Irish and English annals that
there was perpetual war in Ireland during more than 400
years after the invasion. It could not be called a war of
races, except perhaps during the first century, for English
and Irish are constantly found fighting under the same
banner, according to the varying interests of the rival lords
and princes of both nations. This was the case even from
the commencement.' *

Many persons have wondered at the success of small bands
of English invaders. Why did not the Irish nation rise *en
masse*, and drive them into the sea? The answer is easy.
There was no Irish nation. About half a million of people
were scattered over the island in villages, divided into
tribes generally at war with one another, each chief ready
to accept foreign aid against his adversary—some, perhaps,
hoping thereby to attain supremacy in their clans, and
others, who were pretenders, burning to be avenged of those
who had supplanted them. It was religion that first gave
the Irish race a common cause. In the very year of the
English invasion (1171) there were no fewer than twenty predatory excursions or battles among the Irish chiefs themselves,

* Vol. i. p. 216.

exclusive of contests with the invaders. Hence the Pope said—' *Gens se interimit mutua cæde.*' The Pope was right.

The clergy exerted themselves to the utmost in trying to exorcise the demon of destruction and to arrest the work of extermination. Not only the *Bashall Isa,* or ' the staff of Jesus,' but many other relics were used with the most solemn rites, to impress the people with a sense of the wickedness of their clan-fights, and to induce them to keep the peace, but in vain. The King of Connaught once broke a truce entered into under every possible sanction of this kind, trampling upon all, that he might get the King of Meath into his clutches. Hence the Rev. Mr. Kelly is constrained to say—' It is now generally admitted by Catholic writers that however great the efforts of the Irish clergy to reform their distracted country in the eleventh and twelfth centuries, the picture of anarchy drawn by Pope Adrian is hardly overcharged.' Indeed, some Catholic writers have confessed that the anarchy would never have been terminated except by foreign conquest establishing a strong central government. This, however, was not accomplished till after a struggle of centuries, during which, except in brief intervals, when a strong prince was able to protect his people, the national demoralisation grew worse and worse. An Oxford priest, who kept a school at Limerick, writing so late as 1566 of the Irish nobles, says—' Of late they spare neither churches nor hallowed places, but thence also they fill their hands with spoil—yea, and sometimes they set them on fire and kill the men that there lie hidden.'

Mr. Froude, following the Irish MSS. in the Rolls House, has presented graphic pictures of the disorders of the Irishry in the reign of Queen Mary. 'The English garrison,' he says, 'harassed and pillaged the farmers of Meath and Dublin; the chiefs made forays upon each other, killing, robbing, and burning. When the war broke out between England and France, there were the usual conspiracies and uprisings of nationality; the young Earl of Kildare, in reward to the Queen who had restored him to his rank, appearing as the natural leader of the patriots. Ireland was thus happy in the gratification of all its natural tendencies. The Brehon law readvanced upon the narrow limits to which, by the exertions of Henry VIII., the circuits of the judges had been extended. And with the Brehon law came anarchy as its inseparable attendant.'

The correctness of this view is too well attested by the records which the learned historian brings to light, adopting the quaint and expressive phraseology of the old writers whom he quotes. For example :—

' The lords and gentiles of the Irish Pale that were not governed under the Queen's laws were compelled to keep and maintain a great number of idle men of war to rule their people at home, and exact from their neighbours abroad— working everyone his own wilful will for a law—to the spoil of his country, and decay and waste of the common weal of the same. The idle men of war ate up altogether; the lord and his men took what they pleased, destroying their tenants, and themselves never the better. The common people, having nothing left to lose, became as idle and careless in their behaviour as the rest, stealing by day and robbing by night. Yet it was a state of things which they seemed all equally to enjoy, and high and low alike were always ready to bury their own quarrels, to join against the Queen and the English.'

At the time when the crown passed to Elizabeth the qualities of the people were thus described by a correspondent of the council, who presents the English view of the Irishry at that time :—

' The appearance and outward behaviour of the Irish showeth them to be fruits of no good tree, for they exercise no virtue and refrain and forbear from no vice, but think it lawful to do every man what him listeth. They neither love nor dread God, nor yet hate the devil. They are worshippers of images and open idolaters. Their common oath they swear is by books, bells, and other ornaments which they do use as holy religion. Their chief and solemnest oath is by their lord or master's hand, which whoso forsweareth is sure to pay a fine or sustain a worse turn. The Sabbath-day they rest from all honest exercises, and the week days they are not idle, but worse occupied. They do not honour their father and mother as much as they do reverence strangers. For every murder that they commit they do not so soon repent, for whose blood they once shed, they lightly never cease killing all that name. They do not so commonly commit adultery; not for that they profess or keep chastity, but for that they seldom or never marry, and therefore few of them are lawful heirs, by the law of the realm, to the lands they possess. They steal but from the strong, and take by violence from the poor and weak. They know not so well who is their neighbour as who they favour; with him they will witness in right and wrong. They covet not their neighbours' good, but command all that is their neighbours' as their own. Thus they live and die, and there is none to teach them better. There are no ministers. Ministers will not take pains where there is no living to be had, neither church nor parish, but all decayed. People will not come to inhabit where there is no defence of law.'

After six years of *discipline and improvement* Sir Henry Sidney, in 1566, described the state of the four shires, the Irish inhabitants, and the English garrison, in the following terms :—' The *English Pale* is overwhelmed with vagabonds —stealth and spoil daily carried out of it—the people miserable—not two gentlemen in the whole of it able to lend 20*l*. They have neither horse nor armour, nor apparel, nor victual. The soldiers be so beggerlike as it would abhor a general to look on them; yet so insolent as to be intolerable to the people, so rooted in idleness as there is no hope by correction to amend them, yet so allied with the Irish, I dare not trust them in a forte, or in any dangerous service.'

A sort of ' special correspondent ' or ' commissioner,' as we should call him now, furnished to Cecil a detailed account of

the social condition of the people, which of course he viewed
with English eyes.   He found existing among them a
general organisation wherever the Irish language was spoken
—the remnants of a civilisation very ancient, but now fast
tending to ruin.   Next to the chiefs were the priesthood, and
after them came a kind of intellectual hierarchy, consisting
of four classes of spiritual leaders and teachers, which were
thus described.   The first was called the Brehon, or the
judge.   These judges took ' pawns ' of both the parties, and
then judged according to their own discretion.   Their property was neutral, and the Irishmen would not prey upon
them.   They had great plenty of cattle, and they harboured
many vagabonds and idle persons.   They were the chief
maintainers of rebels, but when the English army came to
their neighbourhood they fled to the mountains and woods
' because they would not succour them with victuals and
other necessaries.'   The next sort was called *Shankee*, who
had also great plenty of cattle wherewith they succoured the
rebels.   They made the ignorant men of the country believe
that they were descended from Alexander the Great, or
Darius, or Cæsar, ' or some other notable prince, which made
the ignorant people run mad, and care not what they did.'
This, the correspondent remarked, ' was very hurtful to the
realm.'   Not less hurtful were the third sort called *Denisdan*,
who not only maintained the rebels, but caused those that
would be true to become rebellious—' thieves, extortioners,
murderers, raveners, yea, and worse if it was possible.'   These
seem to have been the historians or chroniclers of the tribe.
If they saw a young man, the descendant of an O' or a Mac,
with half a dozen followers, they forthwith made a rhyme
about his father and his ancestors, numbering how many
heads they had cut off, how many towns they had burned, how
many virgins they had deflowered, how many notable murders they had done, comparing them to Hannibal, or Scipio,
or Hercules, or some other famous person—' wherewithal
the poor fool runs mad, and thinks indeed it is so.'   Then he
will gather a lot of rascals about him, and get a fortune-teller

to prophesy how he is to speed. After these preliminaries he betakes himself with his followers at night to the side of a wood, where they lurk till morning. And when it is daylight, then will they go to the poor villages, not sparing to destroy young infants and aged people; and if a woman be ever so great with child, her will they kill, burning the houses and corn, and ransacking the poor cots; then will they drive away all the kine and plough-horses, with all the other cattle. Then must they have a bagpipe blowing before them, and if any of the cattle fortune to wax weary or faint they will kill them rather than it should do the owner good; and if they go by any house of friars, or religious house, they will give them two or three beeves, and they will take them and pray for them, yea, and praise their doings, and say, ' His father was accustomed so to do, wherein he will rejoice.' The fourth class consisted of ' poets.' These men had great store of cattle, and ' used all the trade of the others with an addition of prophecies. They were maintainers of witches and other vile matters, to the blasphemy of God, and to the impoverishing of the commonwealth.'

These four septs were divided in all places of the four quarters of Ireland, and some of the islands beyond Ireland, as Aran, the land of the Saints, Innisbuffen, Innisturk, Innismain, and Innisclare. These islands, he added, were under the rule of O'Neill, and they were ' very pleasant and fertile, plenty of wood, water, and arable ground, pastures, and fish, and a very temperate air.' On this description Mr. Froude remarks in a note—' At present they are barren heaps of treeless moors and mountains. They yield nothing but scanty oat crops and potatoes, and though the seas are full of fish as ever, there are no hands to catch them. *The change is a singular commentary upon modern improvements.*' There were many branches belonging to the four septs, continues the credulous reporter, who was evidently imposed upon, like many of his countrymen in modern times with better means of information. For example, ' there was the branch of Gogath, the glutton, of which one man would eat half a sheep at a sitting.   There was another called the Carrow, a gambler, who generally went about naked, carrying dice and cards, and he would play the hair off his head.   Then there was a set of women called Goyng women, blasphemers of God, who ran from country to country, sowing sedition among the people.' *

Mr. Froude says that this ' picture of Ireland' was given by some half Anglicised, half Protestantised Celt, who wrote what he had seen around him, careless of political philosophy, or of fine phrases with which to embellish his diction.   But if he was a Celt, I think his description clearly proves that he must have been a Celt of some other country than the one upon whose state he reports.   Judging from internal evidence, I should say that he could not be a native; for an Irishman, even though a convert to Anglicanism, and anxious to please his new masters, could scarcely betray so much ignorance of the history of his country, so much bigotry, such a want of candour and discrimination.   If Mr. Froude's great work has any fault, it is his unconscious prejudice against Ireland.   He knows as well as anyone the working of the feudal system and the clan system in Scotland in the same age.   He knows with what treachery and cruelty murders were perpetrated by chiefs and lairds, pretenders and usurpers—how anarchy, violence, and barbarism reigned in that land; yet, when he is dealing with a similar state of things in Ireland, he uniformly takes it as proof of an incurable national idiosyncrasy, and too often generalises from a few cases.   For example, in speaking of Shane O'Neill, who killed his half-brother, Matthew Kelly, Baron of Dungannon, in order to secure the succession for himself, he says—' *They manage things strangely in Ireland.* The old O'Neill, instead of being irritated, saw in this exploit a proof of commendable energy.   He at once took Shane into favour, and, had he been able, would have given him his dead brother's rights.'

* Froude's History, of England, vol. viii. chap. vii.

CHAPTER II.

THE RULE OF THE O'NEILLS.

SHANE O'NEILL was a man of extraordinary ability and tremendous energy, as the English found to their cost. He was guilty of atrocious deeds; but he had too many examples in those lawless times encouraging him to sacrifice the most sacred ties to his ambition. He resolved to seize the chieftainship by deposing his father and banishing him to the Pale, where, after passing some years in captivity, he died. He was, no doubt, urged to do this, lest by some chance the son of the baron of Dungannon should be adopted by England as the rightful heir, and made Earl of Tyrone. This title he spurned, and proclaimed himself the O'Neill, the true representative of the ancient kings of Ulster, to which office he was elected by his people, taking the usual oath with his foot upon the sacred stone. This was an open defiance of English power, and he prepared to abide the consequences. He thought the opportunity a favourable one to recover the supremacy of his ancestors over the O'Donels. He accordingly mustered a numerous army, and marched into Tyrconnel, where he was joined by Hugh O'Donel, brother of Calvagh, the chief, with other disaffected persons of the same clan. O'Donel had recourse to stratagem. Having caused his cattle to be driven out of harm's way, he sent a spy into the enemy's camp, who mixed with the soldiers, and returning undiscovered, he undertook to guide O'Donel's army to O'Neill's tent, which was distinguished by a great watch-fire, and guarded by six galloglasses on one side and as many Scots on the other. The

camp, however, was taken by surprise in the dead of night,
and O'Neill's forces, careless or asleep, were slaughtered
and routed without resistance.   Shane himself fled for his
life, and, swimming across three rivers, succeeded in reaching
his own territory.   This occurred the year before he cast
off his allegiance to England.   He was required to appear
before Elizabeth in person to explain the grounds on which
he had claimed the chieftainship.   He consented, on condition that he got a safe-conduct and money for the expenses
of his journey.   At the same time he sent a long letter to
the Queen, complaining of the treatment he had received,
and defending his pretensions.   The letter is characteristic
of the man and of the times.   He said : ' The deputy has
much ill-used me, your Majesty ; and now that I am going
over to see you, I hope you will consider that I am but rude
and uncivil, and do not know my duty to your Highness,
nor yet your Majesty's laws, but am one brought up in wild-
ness, far from all civility.   Yet have I a good will to the
commonwealth of my country ; and please your Majesty to
send over two commissioners that you can trust, that will
take no bribes, nor otherwise be imposed on, to observe what
I have done to improve the country, and hear what my
accusers have to say; and then let them go into the Pale,
and hear what the people say of your soldiers, with their
horses, and their dogs, and their concubines.   Within this
year and a half, three hundred farmers are come from the
English Pale to live in my country, where they can be
safe.

' Please your Majesty, your Majesty's money here is not
so good as your money in England, and will not pass current
there.   Please your Majesty to send me three thousand
pounds in English money to pay my expenses in going over
to you, and when I come back I will pay your deputy
three thousand pounds Irish, such as you are pleased to
have current here.   Also I will ask your Majesty to marry
me to some gentlewoman of noble blood meet for my voca-
tion.   I will make Ireland all that your Majesty wishes for

you. I am very sorry your Majesty is put to such expense.
If you will trust it to me, I will undertake that in three
years you will have a revenue, where now you have continual loss.'

Shane suspected evil designs on the part of the English,
and not without reason. The object of the summons to
England was to detain him there with 'gentle talk' till
Sussex could return to his command with an English army
powerful enough to subjugate Ulster. For this purpose
such preparations were made by the English Government
in men and money, 'that rebellion should have no chance;
and,' says Mr. Froude, 'so careful was the secresy which
was observed, to prevent Shane from taking alarm, that a
detachment of troops sent from Portsmouth sailed with
sealed orders, and neither men nor officers knew that Ireland was their destination till they had rounded the Land's
End.' The English plans were well laid. Kildare, whom
Elizabeth most feared, had accepted her invitation to go to
London, and thus prevented any movement in the south,
while O'Donel was prepared to join the English army on its
advance into Ulster; and the Scots, notwithstanding their
predilection for Mary Stuart, were expected to act as
Argyle and his sister should direct. But Shane had a
genius for intrigue as well as Elizabeth, and he was far
more rapid than her generals in the execution of his plans.
By a master-stroke of policy he disconcerted their arrangements. He had previously asked the Earl of Argyle to
give him his daughter in marriage, in order that he might
strengthen his alliance with the Ulster Scots. It is true
that she had been already married to his rival, O'Donel;
but that was a small difficulty in his way. The knot was
tied, but he had no hesitation in cutting it with his sword.
'The countess' was well educated for her time. She was
also a Protestant, and the government had hopes that her influence would be favourable to 'civility and the Reformation'
among the barbarians of the north. But whatever advantages the presence of the fair Scottish missionary might bring,

Shane O'Neill did not see why they should not be all his own, especially as he had managed somehow to produce a favourable impression on her heart. Accordingly he made a dash into Tyrconnel, and carried off both the lady and her husband to his stronghold, Shane's Castle, on the banks of Lough Neagh. Her Scotch guard, though fifteen hundred strong, had offered no resistance. O'Donel was shut up in a prison, and his wife became the willing paramour of the captor. ' The affront to McConnell was forgiven or atoned for by private arrangement, and the sister of the Earl of Argyle—an educated woman for her time, not unlearned in Latin, speaking French and Italian, counted sober, wise, and no less subtle—had betrayed herself and her husband. The O'Neills, by this last manœuvre, became supreme in Ulster. Deprived of their head, the O'Donels sank into helplessness. The whole force of the province, such as it was, with the more serious addition of several thousand Scotch marauders, was at Shane's disposal, and thus provided, he thought himself safe in defying England to do its worst.' *

Meantime, Sussex had arrived in Dublin preceded by his English forces. He made a rapid preliminary movement to the north, and seized the Cathedral of Armagh, in order to make it a fortified depôt for his stores. He then fell back into Meath, where he was joined by Ormond with flying companies of galloglasses. Soon after a singular attack was made on the English garrison at Armagh. Seeing a number of kernes scattered about the town, the officer in command sallied out upon them, when O'Neill suddenly appeared, accompanied by the Catholic Archbishop, on a hill outside the walls. ' The English had but time to recover their defences when the whole Irish army, led by a procession of monks, and every man carrying a fagot, came on to burn the cathedral over their heads. The monks sang a mass; the primate walked three times up and down the lines, willing the rebels to go forward, for God was on their side. Shane swore a great oath not to turn his back

* Froude, Ibid.

while an Englishman was alive; and with scream and yell his men came on. *Fortunately there were no Scots among them.* The English, though out-numbered ten to one, stood steady in the churchyard, and, after a sharp hand-to-hand fight, drove back the howling crowd. The Irish retired into the friars' houses outside the cathedral close, set them on fire, and ran for their lives.'

' So far,' adds Mr. Froude, ' all was well. After this there was no more talk of treating, and by the 18th, Sussex and Ormond were themselves at Armagh with a force—had there been skill to direct it—sufficient to have swept Tyrone from border to border.'

The English historian exults in the valour of the small garrison of his countrymen, well-disciplined and sheltered behind a strong wall, in resisting the assault of a howling multitude of mere Irish, and he observes significantly, that ' fortunately there were no *Scots* among them.' But he is obliged immediately after to record an Irish victory so signal that, according to the lord deputy himself, ' the fame of the English army so hardly gotten, was now vanished.' Yet Mr. Froude does not, in this, lay the blame of defeat upon the *nationality* of the vanquished. It is only the Irish nation that is made the scape-goat in such cases.

It was July, but the weather was wet, the rivers were high, Ormond was ill, Sussex would not leave his friend, and so the English army stayed in town doing nothing till the end of the month, when their failing provisions admonished them that an Irish hosting would be desirable. O'Neill, who seems to have been aware of the state of things, presented the appropriate temptation. Spies brought the lord deputy word that in the direction of Cavan there were herds of cows, which an active party might easily capture. These spies, with ardent professions of loyalty, offered to guide the English troops to the place where the booty would be found, their object being to draw them among bogs and rivers where they might be destroyed. The lord deputy did not think it necessary to accompany this host,

which consisted of 200 horse, 500 men-at-arms, and some
hundreds of the loyal Irish of the Pale.   Shane intended to
attack them the first night while resting on their march.
But they escaped by an alteration of the route.   Next
morning they were marching on the open plain, miles from
any shelter of hill or wood, when the Irish chief, with less
than half their number, pursued them, and fell upon the
cavalry in the rear, with the cry, '*Laundarg Aboo*—the Bloody
Hand—Strike for O'Neill!' The English cavalry commanded
by Wingfield, seized with terror, galloped into the ranks of
their own men-at-arms, rode them down, and extricated
themselves only to fly panic-stricken from the field to the
crest of an adjoining hill.   Meantime, Shane's troopers rode
through the broken ranks, cutting down the footmen on all
sides.   The yells and cries were heard far off through the
misty morning air.   Fitzwilliam, who had the chief command,
was about a mile in advance at the head of another body of
cavalry, when a horseman was observed by him, galloping
wildly in the distance and waving his handkerchief as a signal.
He returned instantly, followed by his men, and flung himself into the *mêlée*.   Shane receiving such a charge of those
few men, and seeing more coming after, ran no farther risk,
blew a recall note, and withdrew unpursued.   Fitzwilliam's
courage alone prevented the army from being annihilated.
Out of 500 English 50 lay dead, and 50 more were badly
wounded.   The survivors fell back to Armagh ' so *dismayed*
as to be unfit for farther service.'   Pitiable were the lamen-
tations of the lord deputy to Cecil on this catastrophe.
It was, said he, ' by cowardice the dreadfullest beginning
that ever was seen in Ireland.   Ah! Mr. Secretary, what
unfortunate star hung over me that day to draw me, that
never could be persuaded to be absent from the army at any
time—to be then absent for a little disease of another man?
The rearward was the best and picked soldiers in all this land.
If I or any stout man had been that day with them, we
had made an end of Shane—which is now further off
than ever it was.   Never before durst Scot or Irishman look

on Englishmen in plain or wood since I was here; and now Shane, in a plain three miles away from any wood, and where I would have asked of God to have had him, hath, with 120 horse, and a few Scots and galloglasse, *scarce half in numbers,* charged our whole army, and by the cowardice of one wretch whom I hold dear to me as my own brother, was like in one hour to have left not one man of that army alive, and after to have taken me and the rest at Armagh. The fame of the English army, so hardly gotten, is now vanished, and I, wretched and dishonoured, by the vileness of other men's deeds.'

This is real history that Mr. Froude has given us. It places the actors before us, enables us to discern their characters, tells us who they are and what they have done. It shows also the value and the necessity of documentary evidence for establishing the truth of history. How different from the vague, uncertain, shadowy representations derived from oral tradition, or mere reports, though contemporary, circulated from mouth to mouth, and exaggerated according to the interests of one party or the other. Let us for illustration compare Mr. Froude's vivid picture of this battle, so disastrous to the English, with the account given of the same event by the Annalists called the Four Masters. These writers had taken great pains to collect the most authentic records of the various Irish tribes from the invasion by Henry II. to the period of which we are writing. They were intensely Irish, and of course glad of any opportunity of recording events creditable to the valour of their countrymen. They lived in Donegal, under the protection of O'Donel, but they showed themselves quite willing to do full justice to his great rival O'Neill. The presence of the lord deputy, the Earl of Ormond, and other great men at Armagh, with a select English army, would naturally have roused their attention, and when that army was encountered and vanquished in the open field by the Irish general, we should have expected that the details of such a glorious event

would have been collected with the greatest care from the
accounts of eye-witnesses. The bards and historiographers
should have been on the alert to do justice to their country
on so great an occasion. They were on the spot, they were
beside the victors, and they had no excuse whatever for
ignorance. Yet here is the miserably cold, *jejune*, feeble,
and imperfect record which we find in the Annals of the Four
Masters : —' The Lord Justice of Ireland, namely Thomas
Fitzwalter (Sussex), marched into Tyrone to take revenge for
the capture of Caloach O'Donel, and also for his own
quarrels with the country. He encamped with a great army
at Armagh, and constructed deep entrenchments and impregnable ramparts about the great church of Armagh,
which he intended to keep constantly guarded. O'Neill, *i.e.*
John, having received intelligence of this, sent a party of
his faithful men and friends with Caloach O'Donel to guard
and keep him from the Lord Justice, and they conveyed
him from one island to another, in the recesses and se-
questered places of Tyrone. After some time the Lord
Justice sent out from the camp at Armagh, a number of
his captains with 1000 men to take some prey and plunder
in Oriel. O'Neill, having received private information and
intelligence of those great troops marching into Oriel, proceeded privately and silently to where they were, and came
up to them after they had collected their prey; a battle
ensued in which many were slain on both sides ; and finally
the preys were abandoned, and fell into the hands of their
original possessors on that occasion.'

That is the whole account of the most signal victory over
the English that had crowned the arms of Ulster during
those wars ! Not a word of the disparity of the forces, or
the flight of the English cavalry, or the slaughter of
the Englishmen-at-arms, or the humiliation and disabled
condition of the garrison at Armagh. Equally unsatisfactory
is the record of the subsequent march through Tyrone by
Sussex, in the course of which his army slaughtered 4000
head of cattle, which they could not drive away. Of this

tremendous destruction of property the Four Masters do not say a word. Such omissions often occur in their annals, even when dealing with contemporary events. Uncritical as they were and extremely credulous, how can we trust the records which they give of remote ages?

CHAPTER III.

O'NEILL, SOVEREIGN OF ULSTER.

THE moral atmosphere of Elizabeth's court was not favourable to public virtue. Strange to say at this time Lord Pembroke seemed to be the only nobleman connected with it whose patriotism could be depended on; and, according to Cecil, there was not another person, ' no not one' who did not either wish well to Shane O'Neill, or so ill to the Earl of Sussex as ' rather to welcome the news than regret the English loss!' It would be difficult to find ' intriguing factiousness' baser than this even in barbarous Ireland. The success of O'Neill, however, had raised him high in the opinion of the Queen, who proposed, through the Earl of Kildare, to leave him in possession of all his territories, and let him govern the Irish ' according to Irish ideas' if he would only become her vassal. Sussex had returned to Dublin with the remnant of his army, while Fitzwilliam was dispatched to London to explain the disaster, bearing with him a petition from the Irish Council, that the troops who had been living in free quarters on the tenants of the Pale should be recalled or disbanded. ' Useless in the field and tyrannical to the farmer, they were a burden on the English exchequer, and answered no purpose but to make the English name detested.'

To O'Neill the Queen sent a pardon, with a safe conduct to England, if he could be prevailed on to go. In the meantime Shane sent a message to the lord deputy, demanding the removal of the garrison from Armagh. One of his messengers, Neill Grey communicated secretly with Lord

Sussex, affecting to dislike rebellion, and intimating that he might help the English to get rid of his master. The lord deputy, without the least scruple or apparent consciousness of the criminality or disgrace of the proceeding, actually proposed to this man that he should murder O'Neill. This villanous purpose he avows in his letter to the Queen. 'In fine,' said he, ' I breake with him to kill Shane ; and bound myself by my oath to see him have a hundred marcs of land by the year to him, and to his heirs, for his reward. He seemed desirous to serve your Highness, and to have the land; but fearful to do it, doubting his own escape after with safety, which he confessed and promised to do by any means he might, escaping with his life. What he will do I know not, but I assure your Highness he may do it without danger if he will. And if he will not do that he may in your service, there will be done *to him* what others may. God send your Highness a good end.'

This English nobleman was, it seems, pious as well as honourable, and could mingle prayers with his plots for assassination. Mr. Froude suggests extenuating circumstances : 'Lord Sussex, it appears, regarded Shane as a kind of wolf, whom having failed to capture in fair chase he might destroy by the first expedient that came to his hand.' And ' English honour, like English coin, lost something of its purity in the sister island.' Of course; it was the Irish atmosphere that did it all. But Sussex was not singular in this mode of illustrating English honour. A greater than he, the chivalrous Sir Walter Raleigh, wrote to a friend in Munster, recommending the treacherous assassination of the Earl of Desmond, as perfectly justifiable. And this crime, for which an ignorant Irishman would be hanged, was deliberately suggested by the illustrious knight whilst sitting quietly in his English study.* But what perplexes the historian most of all is that the Queen of England showed no resentment at the infamous proposal of Sussex. 'It is most sadly certain, however, that Sussex was continued

* See Life of Sir Walter Raleigh.

in office, and inasmuch as it will be seen that he repeated
the experiment a few months later, his letter could not have
been received with any marked condemnation.' Yet Elizabeth was never in Ireland.

Fitzwilliam, however, returned with reinforcements of
troops from Berwick, with which the deputy resolved to repair the credit of the English arms, and to set the Irish an
example of civilised warfare. How did he do this? Dis-
patching provisions by sea to Lough Foyle, he succeeded
this time in marching through Tyrone, ' and in destroying
on his way 4,000 cattle, which he was unable to carry away.
He had left Shane's cows to rot where he had killed them;
and thus being without food, and sententiously and charac-
teristically concluding that man by his policy might propose,
but God at His will did dispose; Lord Sussex fell back by
the upper waters of Lough Erne, sweeping the country
before him.' When the Irish peasantry saw the carcasses of
their cattle rotting along the roads, while their children were
famished for want of milk, they must have been most favour-
ably impressed with the blessings of British rule! Shane,
instead of encountering the deputy on his own territory,
amused himself burning villages in Meath. Neither of those
rulers—those chief protectors of the people—seems to have
been conscious that he was doing anything wrong in destroying the homes and the food of the wretched inhabitants,
whom they alternately scourged. On the contrary, the
extent of devastation which they were able to effect was
supposed to put them in a better position for meeting together, and treating as honourable and gallant representatives of their respective nations.

In accordance with the desire of the Queen, Shane, fresh
from the work of destruction in the Pale, was invited to a
conference with Kildare. They met at Dundalk, and the
Irish chief consented to wait upon Elizabeth in London,
being allowed to name his own conditions. In doing so
he implied ' that he was rather conferring a favour than
receiving one, and that he was going to England as a

victorious enemy permitting himself to be conciliated.' He
demanded a safe-conduct so clearly worded that, whatever
was the result of his visit, he should be free to return; he
required ' a complete amnesty for his past misdeeds, and he
stipulated that Elizabeth should pay all expenses for himself
and his retinue; the Earls of Ormond, Desmond, and Kildare
must receive him in state at Dundalk, and escort him to
Dublin; Kildare must accompany him to England; and,
most important of all, Armagh Cathedral must be evacuated.
He did not anticipate treachery; and either he would persuade Elizabeth to recognise him, and thus prove to the Irish
that rebellion was the surest road to prosperity and power,
or, at worst, by venturing into England, and returning unscathed, he would show them that the Government might be
defied with more than impunity.'*

These terms, so humiliating to English pride, were advo-
cated in the Council ' for certain secret respects;' and even
Sir William Cecil was not ashamed to say, ' that, in Shane's
absence from Ireland,' *something might be cavilled against
him or his,* for non-observing the covenants on his side; and
so the pact being infringed, the matter might be used as
should be thought fit. With this understanding Elizabeth
wrote, making all the ignominious concessions demanded,
save one, the evacuation of the cathedral. Shane replied in
lofty terms that, although for the Earl of Sussex he would
not mollify one iota of his agreement, yet he would consent
at the request of her Majesty. ' Thus,' says Mr. Froude,
' with the Earl of Kildare in attendance, a train of galloglasse, 1,000*l.* in hand, and a second 1,000*l.* awaiting for him
in London, the champion of Irish freedom sailed from
Dublin, and appeared on the second of January at the
English court.'

It is stated that Cecil, Pembroke, and Bacon, received
him privately on his arrival, instructed him how to behave
in the royal presence, gave him the promised money, and
endeavoured to impress upon him the enormity of his

* Froude.

offences. But, to every appeal made to his conscience, Shane answered by a counter appeal about money; 2,000*l.* was a poor present from so great a Queen; he was sure their honours would give him a few more hundreds. He agreed, however, to make a general confession of his sins in Irish and English; and, thus tutored, Elizabeth received him in state on January 6, 1562, attended by the Council, the peers, the foreign ambassadors, bishops, aldermen, dignitaries of all kinds, who gazed ' as if at the exhibition of some wild animal of the desert.' The scene is very graphically described by Mr. Froude: ' O'Neill stalked in, his saffron mantle sweeping round and round him, his hair curling on his back, and clipped short below the eyes, which gleamed from under it with a grey lustre, frowning, fierce, and cruel. Behind him followed his galloglasse, bare-headed and fair-haired, with shirts of mail which reached their knees, a wolf-skin flung across their shoulders, and short broad battle-axes in their hands. At the foot of the throne the chief paused, bent forward, threw himself on his face upon the ground, and then, rising upon his knees, spoke aloud in Irish!' Camden says he ' confessed his crime and rebellion with howling,' and Mr. Froude adds that, to his hearers, the sound of the words ' was as the howling of a dog.' He said:—

' Oh! my most dread sovereign lady and queen, like as I Shane O'Neill, your Majesty's subject of your realm of Ireland, have of long time desired to come into the presence of your Majesty to acknowledge my humble and bounden subjection, so am I now here upon my knees by your gracious permission, and do most humbly acknowledge your Majesty to be my sovereign lady and Queen of England, France, and Ireland; and I do confess that, for lack of civil education, I have offended your Majesty and your laws, for the which I have required and obtained your Majesty's pardon. And for that I most humbly, from the bottom of my heart, thank your Majesty, and still do with all humbleness require the continuance of the same; and I faithfully promise here before Almighty God and your Majesty, and in presence of all these your nobles, that I intend, by God's grace, to live hereafter in the obedience of your Majesty as a subject of your land of Ireland.

'And because this my speech, being Irish, is not well understanded, I have caused this my submission to be written in English and Irish, and thereto have set my hand and seal; and to these gentlemen, my kinsmen and friends, I most humbly beseech your Majesty to be merciful and gracious.'

Camden remarks that the bare-headed galloglasse, with long dishevelled hair, crocus-dyed shirts, wide sleeves, short jackets, shaggy cloaks, &c., were objects of great wonder to the Londoners; while the hauteur of the Irish prince excited the merriment of the courtiers, who styled him 'O'Neill the Great, cousin to St. Patrick, friend to the Queen of England, enemy to all the world besides.' Notwithstanding Shane's precautions with respect to the safe-conduct, English artifice outdid Irish cunning. With all their horror of the Jesuits, Elizabeth's ministers in this case practised mental reservation. True, the Government had promised to permit him to return to Ireland, but then the time of his stay had not been specified. Various pretexts were invented to detain him. He must be recognised as his father's heir; the cause must be pleaded before the English judges; the young Baron of Dungannon must come over and be heard on the other side. O'Neill was told that he had been sent for, while Cecil wrote privately to Fitzwilliam to keep him safe in Ireland. While the prince was thus humoured with vain excuses, he was occupied in pleading his own cause by flattering communications to the Queen, 'whose fame was spoken of throughout the world.' He wished to study the wisdom of her government, that he might know better how to order himself in civil polity. He was most urgent that her Majesty would give him 'some noble English lady for a wife, with augmentation of living suitable.' If she would give him his father's earldom, he

would make her the undisputed sovereign of willing subjects
in Ulster; he would drive away all her enemies, save her
from all further expense, and secure for her a great increase
of revenue. He begged in the meantime, that he might be
allowed to attend her favourite, Lord Robert Cecil, in order
to learn ' to ride after the English fashion, to run at the tilt,
to hawk, to shoot, and use such other good exercises as the
said good lord was most apt unto.' Thus month after month
passed away, and Shane was still virtually a prisoner. ' At
length,' says Mr. Froude, ' the false dealing produced its
cruel fruit, the murder of the boy who was used as the pretext for the delay. Sent for to England, yet prevented
from obeying the command, the young Baron of Dungannon
was waylaid at the beginning of April in a wood near
Carlingford by Turlogh O'Neill. He fled for his life, with
the murderers behind him, till he reached the bank of a deep
river, which he could not swim, and there he was killed.'

This event brought matters to a crisis, and Shane's cause
was triumphant. By articles entered into between him and
the Queen it was agreed that he was to be constituted
captain or governor of Tyrone 'in the same manner as
other captains of the said nation called O'Nele's had right-
fully executed that office in the time of King Henry VIII.
And, moreover, he was to enjoy and have the name and title
of O'Nele, with the like authority as any other of his
ancestors, with the service and homage of all the lords and
captains called *urraughts*, and other nobles of the said nation
of O'Nele.' All this was upon the condition 'that he and his
said nobles should truly and faithfully, from time to time,
serve her Majesty, and, where necessary, wage war against
all her enemies in such manner as the Lord Lieutenant
for the time being should direct.' The title of O'Neill,
however, was to be contingent on the decision of Parliament as to the validity of the letters-patent of Henry VIII.
Should that decision be unfavourable, he was to enjoy his
powers and prerogatives under the style and title of the
Earl of Tyrone, with feudal jurisdiction over the northern

counties. The Pale was to be no shelter to any person whom he might demand as a malefactor. If any Irish lord or chief did him wrong, and the deputy failed within twenty-one days to exact reparation, Shane might raise an army and levy war on his private account. An exception was made on behalf of the loyal O'Donel, whose cause was to be submitted to the arbitration of the Irish earls. The 'indenture' between the Queen and O'Neill was signed by the high contracting parties, and bears date April 30, 1562. The English historian indignantly remarks : ' A rebel subject treating as an equal with his sovereign for the terms on which he would remain in his allegiance was an inglorious spectacle; and the admission of Shane's pretensions to sovereignty was one more evidence to the small Ulster chiefs that no service was worse requited in Ireland than fidelity to the English crown. The Maguires, the O'Reillys, the O'Donels—all the clans who had stood by Sussex in the preceding summer—were given over to their enemy bound hand and foot. But Elizabeth was weary of the expense, and sick of efforts which were profitless as the cultivation of a quicksand. True it was that she was placing half Ireland in the hands of an adulterous, murdering scoundrel, but the Irish liked to have it so, and she forced herself to hope that he would restrain himself for the future within the bounds of decency.' *

In that hope she was soon disappointed. Shane with his galloglasse returned in glory, his purse lined with money and honour wreathed about his brows. He told the northern chiefs that he had gone to England not to lose but to win, and that they must henceforth submit to his authority, or feel his power. The O'Donels, relying on English promises, dared to refuse allegiance to the O'Neill, whereupon, without consulting the lord deputy, 'he called his men to arms and marched into Tyrconnel, killing, robbing, and burning in the old style through farm and castle.' The Irish historians, however, make excuses for O'Neill, affirming that he

* Froude.

was released from his obligations by the bad faith of the lord deputy. He it was who gave him a safe conduct to Dublin, that he might take the oath of allegiance according to promise; but the document was so ingeniously worded that its meaning might be twisted so as to make him a prisoner. He was informed of this treachery, and, as Mr. Froude remarks, ' Shane was too cunning a fish, and had been too lately in the meshes, to be caught again in so poor a snare.' A most attractive bait was provided by Sussex in the person of his sister, who had been brought over to Dublin, and who might be won by the great northern chief if he would only come up to the viceregal court to woo her. ' Shane glanced at the tempting morsel with wistful eyes. Had he trusted himself in the hands of Sussex he would have had a short shrift for a blessing and a rough nuptial knot about his neck. At the last moment a little bird carried the tale to his ear. He had been advertized out of the Pale that the lady was brought over only to entrap him, and if he came to the deputy he should never return.' He therefore excused himself by alleging that his duty to the Queen forbade him to leave the province while it was in such a disturbed condition, the disturbance being caused chiefly by his own predatory excursions into the territories of the O'Donels and Maguires.

Shane took charge of the affairs of the Church as well as of the State. The Catholic primate refusing to acknowledge Elizabeth as the head of the Church, the see was declared vacant, and a *congé d'élire* was sent down for the appointment of 'Mr. Adam Loftus,' an Englishman, who came over as the lord deputy's chaplain. The answer returned and reported by Sussex to the Queen was ' that the chapter there, whereof the greater part were Shane O'Neill's horsemen, were so sparkled and out of order that they could by no means be assembled for the election. In the meantime the lord deputy began to apprehend that O'Neill aspired, not without some hope of success, to the sovereignty of the whole island. It was found that he was in correspondence with the Pope, and the Queen of Scots, and the King of Spain. No greater danger, wrote Sussex, had ever been in Ireland. He implored the Queen not to trifle with it, declaring that he wished some abler general to take the command, not from any want of will, 'for he would spend his last penny and his last drop of blood for her Majesty.' Right and left Shane was crushing the petty chiefs, who implored the protection of the Government. Maguire requested the deputy to write to him in English, not in Latin, because the latter language was well known, and but few of the Irish had any knowledge of the former, in which therefore the secrets of their correspondence would be more safe. Here is a specimen of his English : ' I know well that within these four days the sayed Shan will come to dystroy me contrey except your Lordshypp will sette some remedy in the matter.' He did indeed go down into Fermanagh with ' a great hoste.' As Maguire refused to submit, Shane 'bygan to wax mad, and to cawsse his men to bran all his corn and howsses.' He spared neither church nor sanctuary; three hundred women and children were piteously murdered, and Maguire himself, clean banished, as he described it, took refuge with the remnant of his people in the islands on the lake, whither Shane was making boats to pursue him. 'Help me, your lordship,' the hunted wretch cried, in his despair, to Sussex. 'Ye are lyke to make hym the strongest man of all Erlond, for every man wyll take an exampull by the gratte lostys; take hyd to yourself by thymes, for he is lyke to have all the power from this place thill he come to the wallys of Gallway to rysse against you.' *

It is the boast of the Irish that when Shane had subdued all his opponents, he ruled Tyrone for some time with such order, ' that if a robbery was committed within his territory, he either caused the property to be restored, or reimbursed the loser out of his own treasury.' †

* Wright's Elizabeth, vol. i. p. 73.
† Haverty's History of Ireland, p. 390.

The perplexity of the Government In this critical emergency is vividly described by Mr. Froude: ' Elizabeth knew not which way to turn. Force, treachery, conciliation had been tried successively, and the Irish problem was more hopeless than ever. In the dense darkness of the prospects of Ulster there was a solitary gleam of light. Grown insolent with prosperity, Shane had been dealing too peremptorily with the Scots; his countess, though compelled to live with him, and to be the mother of his children, had felt his brutality and repented of her folly, and perhaps attempted to escape. In the daytime, when he was abroad marauding, she was coupled like a hound to a page or a horse-boy, and only released at night when he returned to his evening orgies. The fierce Campbells were not men to bear tamely these outrages from a drunken savage on the sister of their chief, and Sussex conceived that if the Scots, by any contrivance, were separated from Shane, they might be used as a whip to scourge him.'

At length Sussex, determined to crush the arch-rebel, marched northward in April, 1563, with a mixed force of English and Irish, ill-armed, ill-supplied, dispirited and almost disloyal. The diary of the commander-in-chief is, perhaps, the funniest on record: ' April 6: The army arrived at Armagh. April 8: The army marches back to Newry to bring up stores and ammunition left behind. April 11: The army advances again to Armagh, where it waits for galloglasse and kerne from the Pale. April 14: The commander-in-chief answers a letter from James M'Connell. April 15: The army goes upon Shane's cattle, of which it takes enough to serve it, but would have taken more if it had had galloglasse.' Next day it returns to Armagh. There it waits three days for the galloglasse, and then sends back for them to Dublin. On April 20, again writes M'Connell, because he did not come according to promise. April 21: The army surveys the Trough mountains. April 22: The pious commander winds up the glorious record in these words:

'To Armagh with the spoil taken which would have been much more if we had had galloglasse, and because St. George even forced me, her Majesty's lieutenant, to return to divine service that night. April 23: Divine service.' Subsequently his lordship's extreme piety caused him the loss of 300 horses, which he naïvely confesses thus: 'Being Easter time, and he having travelled the week before, and Easter day till night, thought fit to give Easter Monday to prayer, and in this time certain churls stole off with the horses.' To this Mr. Froude adds the pertinent remark: 'The piety which could neglect practical duty for the outward service of devotion, yet at the same time could make overtures to Neil Greg to assassinate his master, requires no very lenient consideration.'

In connexion with the Irish Church Disestablishment Bill Lord Elcho proposed Solomon's plan of settling the dispute of the two mother Churches about Ireland. He would cut the country in two, establishing Protestantism in the north and Catholicism in the south. When an experienced member of the House of Commons makes such a proposition in this age, we should not be surprised that Sir Thomas Cusack in the year 1563 proposed to Queen Elizabeth that Ireland should be divided into four provinces, each with a separate president, either elected by the people or chosen in compliance with their wishes. O'Neill was to have the north, the Clanrickards the west, the O'Briens or Desmonds the south, and thus the English might be allowed the undisturbed enjoyment of the Pale. This notable scheme for settling the Irish question was actually adopted by the Queen, and she wrote to Sussex, stating that, as his expedition to the north had resulted only in giving fresh strength to the enemy, she 'had decided to come to an end of the war of Ulster by agreement rather than by force.' To Shane she was all compliance. He had but to prove himself a good subject, and he might have any pre-eminence which her Majesty could grant without doing any other person wrong. 'If he desired to have a council established at Armagh, he should himself be the president of that council, if he wished to drive the Scots out of Antrim, her own troops would assist in the expulsion; if he was offended with the garrison in the cathedral, she would gladly see peace maintained in a manner less expensive to herself. To the primacy he might name the person most agreeable to himself, and with the primacy, as a matter of course, even the form of maintaining the Protestant Church would be abandoned also. In return for these concessions the Queen demanded only that Shane, to save her honour, should sue for them as a favour instead of demanding them as a right. The rebel chief consented without difficulty to conditions which cost him nothing, and after an interview with Cusack, O'Neill wrote a formal apology to Elizabeth, and promised for the future to be her Majesty's true and faithful subject. Indentures were drawn up on December 17, in which the Ulster sovereignty was transferred to him in everything but the name, and the treaty required only Elizabeth's signature, when a second dark effort was made to cut the knot of the Irish difficulty.'[*]

This second 'dark effort' was nothing less than an attempt to murder O'Neill by means of poison. He could not be conquered; he could not be out-manœuvred; he could not be assassinated in the ordinary way. But the resources of Dublin Castle, and of English ingenuity, were not exhausted. The lord deputy was of course delighted with the reconciliation which had been effected with the Ulster prince. What could be more natural than to send him a present of the choicest wine from the viceregal cellars? certainly few presents could be more agreeable. Shane and his household quaffed the delicious beverage freely enough we may be sure, without the slightest suspicion that there was death in the cup. But the wine was mingled with poison. Those who drank it were quickly at the point of death. O'Neill might thank his good constitution for his recovery from an illness almost mortal. The crime was traced to an Englishman named Smith, who, if employed

* Froude, vol. viii. p. 48.

by Lord Sussex, did not betray the guilty secret. Mr. Froude admits that the suspicion cannot but cling to him that this second attempt at murder was not made without his connivance; 'nor,' he adds, 'can Elizabeth herself be wholly acquitted of responsibility. She professed the loudest indignation, but she ventured no allusion to his previous communication with her, and no hint transpires of any previous displeasure when the proposal had been made openly to herself. The treachery of an English nobleman, the conduct of the inquiry, and the anomalous termination of it, would have been incredible even in Ireland, were not the original correspondence extant, in which the facts are not denied.'

O'Neill of course complained loudly to the Queen, whereupon she directed that a strict investigation should take place, in order that the guilty parties should be found out and punished, 'of what condition soever the same should be.' In writing to the lord deputy she assumed that Smith had been committed to prison and would be brought to condign punishment. That person, after many denials, at length confessed his guilt, and said that his object was to rid his country of a dangerous enemy. This motive was so good in the eye of the Government that it saved the life of the culprit. Sir Thomas Cusack, writing to Cecil, March 22, 1564, says, 'I persuaded O'Neill to forget the matter, whereby no more talk should grow of it; seeing there is no law to punish the offender other than by discretion and imprisonment, which O'Neill would little regard except the party might be executed by death, and that the law doth not suffer. So as the matter be wisely pacified, it were well done to leave it.' Shane was probably aware that Smith was but an instrument, who would be readily sacrificed as a peace-offering.

The sketch which Mr. Froude gives of Ulster and its wild sovereign at this time is admirably picturesque. 'Here then, for the present, the story will leave Shane safely planted on the first step of his ambition, in all but the

title, sole monarch of the North.   He built himself a fort on
an island in Lough Neagh, which he called *Foogh-ni-gall*,
or, Hate of Englishmen, and grew rich on the spoils of his
enemies, the only strong man in Ireland.   He administered
justice after a paternal fashion, permitting no robbers but
himself; when wrong was done he compelled restitution, or
at his own cost redeemed the harm " to the loser's con-
tentation."   Two hundred pipes of wine were stored in his
cellars; 600 men-at-arms fed at his table, as it were his
janissaries; and daily he feasted the beggars at his gate,
saying, it was meet to serve Christ first.   Half wolf, half
fox, he lay couched in his Castle of Malepartuis, with his
emissaries at Rome, at Paris, and at Edinburgh.   In the
morning he was the subtle pretender to the Irish throne;
in the afternoon, when the wine was in him, he was a dissolute savage, revelling in sensuality with his unhappy countess,
uncoupled from her horseboy to wait upon his pleasure.   He
broke loose from time to time to keep his hand in practice.
At Carlingford, for example, he swept off one day 200
sheep and oxen, while his men violated sixty women in the
town; but Elizabeth looked away and endeavoured not to
see.   The English Government had resolved to stir no
sleeping dogs in Ireland till a staff was provided to chastise
them if they would bite.   Terence Daniel, the dean of those
rough-riding canons of Armagh, was installed as primate;
the Earl of Sussex was recalled to England; and the new
archbishop, unable to contain his exultation at the blessed
day which had dawned upon his country, wrote to Cecil to
say how the millennium had come at last, glory be to God!'

   As a picture of Irish savage life this is very good.   But the
historian has presented a companion picture of English civilised life, which is not at all inferior.   Sir Thomas Wroth
and Sir Nicholas Arnold were sent over to reform the Pale.
They were stern Englishmen, impatient of abuses among
their own countrymen, and having no more sympathy for
Irishmen than for wolves.   In the Pale they found that
peculation had grown into a custom; the most barefaced

frauds had been converted by habit into rights ; and a captain's commission was thought ill-handled if it did not yield, beyond the pay, 500*l.* a year. They received pay for each hundred men, when only sixty were on the roll. The soldiers, following the example of their leaders, robbed and ground the peasantry. In fact, the Pale was ' a weltering sea of corruption—the captains out of credit, the soldiers mutinous, the English Government hated ; every man seeking his own, and none that which was Christ's.' The purification of the Pale was left to Arnold, ' a hard, iron, pitiless man, careful of things and careless of phrases, untroubled with delicacy, and impervious to Irish enchantments. The account books were dragged to light, where iniquity in high places was registered in inexorable figures. The hands of Sir Henry Ratcliffe, the brother of Sussex, were not found clean. Arnold sent him to the Castle with the rest of the offenders. Deep, leading drains were cut through the corrupting mass. The shaking ground grew firm, and honest healthy human life was again made possible. With the provinces beyond the Pale, Arnold meddled little, save where, taking a rough view of the necessities of the case, he could help the Irish chiefs to destroy each other.'

To Cecil, Arnold wrote thus : ' I am with all the wild Irish at the same point I am at with bears and ban-dogs ; when I see them fight, so they fight earnestly indeed, and tug each other well, I care not who has the worst.' ' Why not, indeed ? ' asks Mr. Froude ; ' better so than hire assassins ! Cecil, with the modesty of genius, confessed his ignorance of the country, and his inability to judge ; yet, in every opinion which he allowed himself to give, there was always a certain nobility of tone and sentiment.' Nobility was scarcely necessary to induce a statesman to revolt against the policy of Arnold. A little Christianity, nay a slight touch of humanity, would have sufficed for that purpose. Sussex was a nobleman, and considered himself, no doubt, a very godly man, but everyone must admit that, in all heroic qualities, he was incomparably beneath the uncul-

tured Shane O'Neill, while in baseness and wickedness he
was not far behind his northern foe, 'half wolf, half fox.'
Cecil, however, was a man of a very different stamp from
Sussex. Evidently shocked at the prevailing English notions about the value of Irish life, he wrote to Arnold:
' You be of that opinion which many wise men are of, from
which I do not dissent, being an Englishman ; but being, as
I am, a Christian man, I am not without some perplexity to
enjoy of such cruelties.'

The work of reform, however, did not prove so easy a
task. Arnold's vigour was limited by his powers. The pay-
masters continued to cheat the Government by false returns.
The Government allowed the pay to run in arrear, the
soldiers revenged themselves by oppressing and plundering
the people ; and ' so came to pass this wonderful phenomenon,
that *in O'Neill's country* alone in Ireland—defended as it
was from attacks from without, and enriched with the
plunder of the Pale—*were the peasantry prosperous, or life
or property secure.*' This fact might suggest to the English
historian that the evils of Ireland do not all proceed from
blood or race ; and that the Saxon may be placed in circumstances which make him as false, as dishonest, as lazy,
as disordered, as worthless as the Celt, and that even men
of ' gentle blood ' may become as base as their most plebeian
servants. Nor did zeal for religious reformation redeem
the defects of the Anglo-Irish rulers. The Protestant
bishops were chiefly agitated by the vestment controversy.
' Adam Loftus, the titular primate, to whom,' says Mr.
Froude, ' sacked villages, ravished women, and famine-
stricken skeletons crawling about the fields, were matters
of everyday indifference, shook with terror at the mention
of a surplice.' Robert Daly wrote in anguish to Cecil, in
dismay at the countenance to ' Papistry,' and at his own
inability to prolong a persecution which he had happily
commenced. An abortive ' devise for the better government of Ireland ' gives us some insight into the condition of
the people. ' No poor persons should be *compelled* any more

to work or labour by the day, or otherwise, without meat, drink, wages, or some other allowance during the time of their labour; no earth tillers, nor any others inhabiting a dwelling, under any lord, should be distrained or punished, in body or goods, for the faults of their landlord; nor any honest man lose life or lands without fair trial by parliamentary attainder, according to the ancient laws of England and Ireland.' Surely it was no proof of incurable perversity of nature, that the Irish peasantry were discontented and disaffected, under the horrid system of oppression and slavery here laid before the English Government.

As remedial measures, it was proposed that a true servant of God should be placed in every parish, from Cape Clear to the Giant's Causeway; that the children should be taught the New Testament and the Psalms in Latin, 'that they, being infants, might savour of the same in age as an old cask doth;' that there should be a university for the education of the clergy, 'and such godly discipline among them that there should be no more pluralities, no more abuse of patronage, no more neglect, or idleness, or profligacy.' Mr. Froude's reflection upon this projected policy is highly characteristic:—

'Here was an ideal Ireland painted on the retina of some worthy English minister; but the real Ireland was still the old place. As it was in the days of Brian Boroihme and the Danes, so it was in the days of Shane O'Neill and Sir Nicholas Arnold; and the Queen, who was to found all these fine institutions, cared chiefly to burden her exchequer no further in the vain effort *to drain the black Irish morass*, fed as it was from the perennial fountains of Irish NATURE.' *

The Queen, however, thought it more prudent to let Shane have his way in Ulster. To oblige him, she would remove the Protestant primate, Loftus, to Dublin, and appoint his own nominee and friend, Terence Daniel. The Pope had sent a third archbishop for the same see, named Creagh;

* Vol. viii. p. 377.

but, when passing through London, he was arrested, and
incarcerated in the Tower, ' where he lay in great misery,
cold, and hunger, without a penny, without the means of
getting his single shirt washed, and without gown or hose.'
At last he made his escape by gliding over the walls into
the Thames. The events of 1565 made the English Government more than ever anxious to come to terms with
the chieftain ' whom they were powerless to crush.' Since
the defeat of the Earl of Sussex, continues Mr. Froude,
' Shane's influence and strength had been steadily growing.
His return unscathed from London, and the fierce attitude
which he assumed on the instant of his reappearance in
Ulster, convinced the petty leaders that to resist him longer
would only ensure their ruin. O'Donel was an exile in
England, and there remained unsubdued in the North only
the Scottish colonies of Antrim, which were soon to follow
with the rest. O'Neill lay quiet through the winter. With
the spring and the fine weather, when the rivers fell and
the ground dried, he roused himself out of his lair, and with
his galloglasse and kerne, and a few hundred harquebuss-
men, he dashed suddenly down upon the Red-shanks, and
broke them utterly to pieces. Six or seven hundred were
killed in the field, James M'Connell and his brother, Sorleyboy, were taken prisoners, and, for the moment, the whole
colony was swept away. James M'Connell, himself badly
wounded in the action, died a few months later, and Shane
was left undisputed sovereign of Ulster.'

Primate Daniel announced to the Queen this ' glorious
victory over a malicious and dangerous people ' who were
gradually fastening on the country; and Sir Thomas Cusack
urged that now was the time to make O'Neill a friend for
ever, an advice which was backed up by the stern Arnold.
' For what else could be done? The Pale,' he pleaded, ' is poor
and unable to defend itself. If he do fall out before the beginning of next summer, there is neither outlaw, rebel, murderer, thief, nor any lewd nor evil-disposed person—of whom
God knoweth there is plenty swarming in every quarter

among the wild Irish, yea and in our own border too—which would not join to do what mischief they might.'

But Shane did not wait for further royal overtures. He saw that with the English Government might was right, and that the justice of his cause shone out more brightly in proportion to the increase of his power. Thus encouraged in his course of aggression and conquest, he seized the Queen's Castles of Newry and Dundrum. He then marched into Connaught, demanding the tribute due of old time ' to them that were kings in that realm.' He exacted pledges of obedience from the western chiefs, and spoiled O'Rourke's country, and returned to Tyrone driving before him 4,000 head of cattle. While proceeding at this rate he wrote soothing and flattering words to the Queen. It was for her majesty he was fighting; he was chastising her enemies and breaking stiff-necked chiefs into her yoke; and he begged that she would not credit any stories which his ill-willers might spread abroad against him. On the contrary he hoped she would determine his title and rule without delay, and grant him, in consideration of his good services, some augmentation of living in the Pale. Elizabeth, however, excused his conduct, saying ' we must allow something for his wild bringing-up, and not expect from him what we should expect from a perfect subject. If he mean well he shall have all his reasonable requests granted.'

But there was among Elizabeth's advisers a statesman who felt that this sort of policy would never do. Sir Henry Sidney, on being requested to take charge of the Government of Ireland, urged the absolute necessity of a radical change. The power of O'Neill, and such rulers as he, must be utterly broken, and that by force, at whatever cost. And this, he argued, would not only be sound policy but true economy. The condition of Ireland was unexampled; free from foreign invasion, the sovereignty of the Queen not denied, yet the revenue so mean and scanty that ' great yearly treasures were carried out of the realm of England to satisfy the stipends of the officers and soldiers required for the

governance of the same.' He must have 10,000*l.* or 12,000*l.*
to pay out-standing debts and put the army in proper condition. As for his own remuneration, the new viceroy, as he
could expect nothing from the Queen, would be content
with permission to export six thousand kerseys and clothes,
free of duty.

Sir Henry Sidney struck out the only line of policy by
which the English government of Ireland could be made
successful or even possible. He said: 'To go to work by
force will be chargeable, it is true; but if you will give the
people justice and minister law among them, and exercise
the sword of the sovereign, and put away the sword of the
subject, *omnia hæc adjicientur vobis*—you shall drive the
now man of war to be an husbandman, and he that now
liveth like a lord to live like a servant, and the money now
spent in buying armour, and horses, and waging of war,
shall be bestowed in building of towns and houses. By
ending these incessant wars ere they be aware, you shall
bereave them both of force and beggary, and make them
weak and wealthy. Then you can convert the military service due from the lords into money ; then you can take up
the fisheries now left to the French and the Spaniards ; then
you can open and work your mines, and the people will be
able to grant you subsidies.'* When the lord deputy arrived in Ireland he found a state of things in the Pale far
worse than he could have imagined. It was ' as it were overwhelmed with vagabonds; plunder and spoils daily carried
out of it; the people miserable ; not two gentlemen in the
whole of it able to lend 20*l.* ; without horse, armour, apparel,
or victual. The soldiers were worse than the people : so
beggarlike as it would abhor a general to look on them ;
never a married wife among them, and therefore so allied
with Irishwomen that they betrayed secrets, and could not be
trusted on dangerous service ; so insolent as to be intolerable ;
so rooted in idleness as there was no hope by correction to
amend them.' In Munster a man might ride twenty or

* Opinions of Sir H. Sidney, Irish MSS., Rolls House; Froude, p. 385.

thirty miles and find no houses standing in a country which
he had known as well inhabited as many counties in England.
' In Ulster,' Sidney wrote, ' there tyrannizeth the prince of
pride ; Lucifer was never more puffed up with pride and
ambition than that O'Neill is ; he is at present the only
strong and rich man in Ireland, and he is the dangerest man
and most like to bring the whole estate of this land to sub-
version and subjugation either to him or to some foreign
prince, that ever was in Ireland.' He invited this Lucifer
to come into the Pale to see him, and Shane at first agreed
to meet him at Dundalk, but on second thoughts he politely
declined, on the ground that the Earl of Sussex had twice
attempted to assassinate him, and but for the Earl of Kildare
would have put a lock upon his hands when he was passing
through Dublin to England. Hence his ' timorous and mis-
trustful people' would not trust him any more in English
hands. In fact O'Neill despised any honours the Queen
could confer upon him. ' When the wine was in him he
boasted that he was in blood and power better than the best
of their earls, and he would give place to none but his
cousin of Kildare, because he was of his own house. They
had made a wise earl of M'Carthymore, but Shane kept as
good a man as he. Whom was he to trust? Sussex gave
him a safe-conduct and then offered him the courtesy of a
handlock. The Queen had told him herself that, though he
had got a safe-conduct to come and go, the document did not
say when he was to go ; and, in order to get away from
London, he was obliged to agree to things against his honour
and profit, and he would never perform them while he lived.'
That treachery drove him into war. ' My ancestors,' he
said, ' were kings of Ulster; and Ulster is mine, and shall
be mine. O'Donel shall never come into his country, nor
Bagenal into Newry, nor Kildare into Dundrum, or Lecale.
They are now mine. With this sword I won them, with
this sword I will keep them.' Sidney, indignant at these
pretensions, wrote thus to Leicester : ' No Atila nor Yotila,
no Vandal nor Goth that ever was, was more to be

dreaded for over-running any part of Christendom, than
this man is for over-running and spoiling of Ireland.   If
it be an angel of heaven that will say that ever O'Neill
will be a good subject till he be thoroughly chastised, believe
him not, but think him a spirit of error.   Surely if the
queen do not chastise him in Ulster, he will chase all hers
out of Ireland.   Her majesty must make up her mind to the
expense, and chastise this cannibal.'   He therefore demanded
money that he might pay the garrison and get rid of the idle,
treacherous, incorrigible soldiers which were worse than none.
Ireland, he said, would be no small loss to the English crown.
It was never so likely to be lost as then, and he would
rather die than that it should be lost during his government.
The queen, however, sent money with the greatest possible
reluctance, and was strangely dissatisfied with this able and
faithful servant, even when his measures were attended with
signal success.

In the meantime O'Neill zealously espoused the cause of
Mary Queen of Scots.   His friendship with Argyle grew
closer, and he proposed that it should be cemented by a
marriage.   ' The countess' was to be sent away, and Shane
was to be united to the widow of James M'Connell, whom
he had killed—who was another half-sister of Argyle, and
whose daughter he had married already and divorced.
Sidney wrote, that was said to be the earl's practice ; and
Mr. Froude, who has celebrated the virtues of Henry VIII.,
takes occasion from this facility of divorce to have another
fling at ' Irish nature.'   He says:—' The Irish chiefs, it
seemed, three thousand years behind the world, retained the
habits and the moralities of the Greek princes in the tale of
Troy, when the bride of the slaughtered husband was the
willing prize of the conqueror; and when only a rare Andro-
mache was found to envy the fate of a sister

Who had escaped the bed of some victorious lord.'

After a brief and brilliant campaign, in which Shane
' swept round by Lough Erne, swooped on the remaining

cattle of Maguire, and struck terror and admiration into the Irishry,' he wrote a letter to Charles IX. of France, inviting his co-operation in expelling the heretics, and bringing back the country to the holy Roman see. The heretic Saxons, he said, were the enemies of Almighty God, the enemies of the holy Church of Rome, the King's enemies, and his. 'The time is come when we all are confederates in a common bond to drive the invader from our shores, and we now beseech your Majesty to send us 6,000 well-armed men. If you will grant our request there will soon be no Englishmen left alive among us, and we will be your Majesty's subjects ever more.' This letter was intercepted, and is now preserved among the Irish MSS.

Sidney resolved to adopt a new plan of warfare. His campaigns would not be mere summer forays, mere inroads of devastation during the few dry weeks of August and September. He would wait till the harvest was gathered in, place troops in fortresses, and continue hostilities through the winter. He adopted this course because 'in the cold Irish springs, the fields were bare, the cattle were lean, and the weather was so uncertain that neither man nor horse could bear it, whereas in August *food everywhere was abundant,* and the soldiers would have time to become hardened to their work.' They could winter somewhere on the Bann; harry Tyrone night and day without remission, and so break Shane to the ground and ruin him. There was no time to be lost. Maguire had come into Dublin, reporting that his last cottage was in ashes, and his last cow driven over the hill into Shane's country; while Argyle, with the whole disposable force of the western isles, was expected to join him in summer. O'Neill himself, after an abortive attempt to entrap Sidney at Dundalk, made a sudden attack on that town in July; but his men were beaten back, 'and eighteen heads were left behind to grin hideously over the gates.' He then returned to Armagh and burned the cathedral to the ground, to prevent its being again occupied by an English garrison. He next sent a swift messenger to Desmond,

calling for a rising in Munster. 'Now was the time or
never' to set upon the enemies of Ireland. If Desmond
failed, or turned against his country, God would avenge it
on him. But Desmond's reply was an offer to the deputy
'to go against the rebel with all his power. The Scots also
held back.' Shane offered them all Antrim to join him, all
the cattle in the country, and the release of Sorleyboy from
captivity; but Antrim and its cattle they believed that they
could recover for themselves, and James M'Connell had left
a brother Allaster, who was watching with eager eyes for an
opportunity to revenge the death of his kinsman, and the
dishonour with which Shane had stained his race.

In the meantime troops and money came over from
England, and on September 17, Colonel Randolph was at
the head of an army in Lough Foyle; and the lord deputy
took the field accompanied by Kildare, the old O'Donel,
Shane Maguire, and O'Dogherty. So that this war against
O'Neill was waged for the dispossessed Irish chiefs as well
as for England. Armagh city they found a mere heap of
blackened stones. Marching without obstruction to Ben
brook, one of O'Neill's best and largest houses, which they
found 'utterly burned and razed to the ground,' thence
they went on towards Clogher, 'through pleasant fields, and
villages so well inhabited as no Irish county in the realm
was like it.' The Bishop of Clogher was out with Shane in
the field. 'His well-fattened flock were devoured by Sidney's
men as by a flight of Egyptian locusts.' 'There we stayed,'
said Sidney, 'to destroy the corn; we burned the country for
124 miles compass, and we found by experience that now
was the time of the year to do the rebel most harm.' But
he says not a word of the harm he was doing to the poor
innocent peasantry, whose industry had produced the crops,
to the terrified women and children whom he was thus consigning to a horrible lingering death by famine. This was
a strange commencement of his own programme to treat the
people with justice.

The lord deputy expected to meet Randolph at Lifford;

but struck with the singular advantages presented by Derry,
then an island, for a military position, he pitched his tents
there, and set the troops to work in erecting fortifications.
Nothing then stood on the site of the present city, save a de-
crepid and deserted monastery of Augustine monks, which
was said to have been built in the time of St. Columba.

Sidney stayed a few days at Derry, and then, leaving
Randolph with 650 men, 350 pioneers, and provisions for
two months, he marched on to Donegal. This was once a
thriving town, inhabited by English colonists. At the time
of Sidney's arrival it was a pile of ruins, 'in the midst of
which, like a wild beast's den, strewed round with mangled
bones, rose the largest and strongest castle which he had
seen in Ireland. It was held by one of O'Donel's kinsmen,
to whom Shane, to attach him to his cause, had given his
sister to wife. At the appearance of the old chief with the
English army, it was immediately surrendered. O'Donel
was at last rewarded for his fidelity and sufferings ; and the
whole tribe, with eager protestations of allegiance, gave
sureties for their future loyalty.' Sidney next directed his
march to Ballyshannon, and on by the coast of Sligo.
Passing over the bogs and mountains of Mayo, they came
into Roscommon, and then, ' leaving behind them as fruitful
a country as was in England or Ireland all utterly waste,'
the army crossed the Shannon at Athlone, swimming
' for lack of a bridge.' The results of this progress are thus
summed up by Mr. Froude. ' Twenty castles had been
taken as they went along and left in hands that could be
trusted. In all that long and painful journey Sidney was
able to say that there had not died of sickness but three
persons ; men and horses were brought back in full health
and strength, while her majesty's honour was re-established
among the Irishry, and grown to no small veneration—" an
expedition comparable only to Alexander's journey into
Bactria," wrote an admirer of Sidney to Cecil—revealing
what to Irish eyes appeared the magnitude of the difficulty,
and forming a measure of the effect which it produced. The

English deputy had bearded Shane in his stronghold, burned his houses, pillaged his people, and had fastened a body of police in the midst of them, to keep them waking in the winter nights. He had penetrated the hitherto impregnable fortresses of mountain and morass; the Irish who had been faithful to England were again in safe possession of their lands and homes. The weakest, maddest, and wildest Celts were made aware that, when the English were once roused to effort, they could crush them as the lion crushes the jackal.' *

O'Neill had followed the lord deputy to Lifford, and then marched on to the Pale, expecting to retaliate upon the invaders with impunity. But he was encountered by Warren St. Leger, lost 200 men, and was at first hunted back over the border. He again returned, however, with ' a main army,' burned several villages, and in a second fight with St. Leger, compelled the English to retire, ' for lack of more aid; ' but they held together in good order, and Shane, with the Derry garrison in his rear, durst not follow far from home in pursuit. ' Before he could revenge himself on Sidney, before he could stir against the Scots, before he could strike a blow at O'Donel, he must pluck out the barbed dart which was fastened in his unguarded side.'

In order to accomplish this object, he hovered cautiously about the Foyle, watching for an opportunity to attack the garrison. But Randolph fell upon him by surprise, and after a short sharp action, the O'Neills gave way. O'Dogherty with his Irish horse chased the flying crowd of his countrymen, killing every person he caught; and Shane lost 400 men, the bravest of his warriors. The English success was dearly bought, for Randolph leading the pursuit, was struck by a random shot, and fell dead from his horse.

Before the Irish chief could recover from this great disaster, Sidney ' struck in again beyond Dundalk, burning his farms and capturing his castles. The Scots came in

* Vol. viii. p. 407.

over the Bann, wasting the country all along the river side. Allaster M'Connell, like some chief of Sioux Indians, sent to the captain of Knockfergus an account of the cattle that he had driven, and *the wives and bairns* that he had slain. Like swarms of angry hornets, these avenging savages drove their stings in the now maddened and desperate Shane on every point where they could fasten; while in December the old O'Donel came out over the mountains from Donegal, and paid back O'Neill with interest for his stolen wife, his pillaged country, and his own long imprisonment and exile. The tide of fortune had turned too late for his own revenge : worn out with his long sufferings, he fell from his horse, at the head of his people, with the stroke of death upon him ; but before he died, he called his kinsmen about him, and prayed them to be true to England and their queen, and Hugh O'Donel, who succeeded to his father's command, went straight to Derry, and swore allegiance to the English crown.

'Tyrone was now smitten in all its borders. Magennis was the last powerful chief who still adhered to Shane's fortunes; the last week in the year Sidney carried fire and sword through his country, and left him not a hoof remaining. It was to no purpose that Shane, bewildered by the rapidity with which disasters were piling themselves upon him, cried out now for pardon and peace; the deputy would not answer his letter, and nothing was talked of but his extirpation by war only.' *

The war, however, was interrupted by a singular calamity that befel the Derry garrison. By the death of their commander left ' a headless people,' they suffered from want of food and clothing. They also became the prey of a mysterious disease, against which no precautions could guard, which no medicine could cure, and by which strong men were suddenly struck dead. By the middle of November ' the flux was reigning among them wonderfully ; ' many of the best men went away because there was none to stay them. The

* Froude, p. 413.

F

secret of the dreadful malady something like the cholera—was discovered in the fact that the soldiers had built their sleeping quarters over the burial-ground of the abbey, ' and the clammy vapour had stolen into their lungs and poisoned them.' The officer who succeeded to the command applied the most effectual remedy. He led the men at once into the pure air of the enemies' country, and they returned after a few days driving before them 700 horses and 1,000 cattle. He assured Sidney, that with 300 additional men, he could so hunt the rebel, that ere May was passed, he should not show his face in Ulster. But the ' Black Death' returned after a brief respite ; and, says Mr. Froude, in the reeking vapour of the charnel-house, it was indifferent whether its victims returned in triumph from a stricken field, or were cooped within their walls by hordes of savage enemies. By the middle of March there were left out of 1,100 but 300 available to fight. Reinforcements had been raised at Liverpool, but they were countermanded when on the point of sailing. The English council was discussing the propriety of removing the colony to the Bann, when accident finished the work which the plague had begun, and spared them the trouble of deliberation. The huts and sheds round the monastery had been huddled together for the convenience of fortification. At the end of April, probably after a drying east wind, a fire broke out in a blacksmith's forge, which spread irresistibly through the entire range of buildings. The flames at last reached the powder magazine : thirty men were blown to pieces by the explosion, and the rest, paralysed by this last addition to their misfortunes, made no more effort to extinguish the conflagration. St. Loo, with all that remained of that ill-fated party, watched from their provision boats in the river the utter destruction of the settlement which had begun so happily, and then sailed drearily away to find a refuge in Knockfergus. Such was the fate of the first efforts for the building of Londonderry ; and below its later glories, as so often happens in this world, lay the bones of many a hundred gallant men who lost their lives in laying its foundations. Elizabeth, who in the immediate pressure of calamity resumed at once her noble nature, ' perceiving the misfortune not to come of treason, but of God's ordinance,' bore it well; she was willing to do that should be wanting to repair the loss; and Cecil was able to write cheerfully to Sidney, telling him to make the best of the accident and let it stimulate him to fresh exertions.' *

In the meantime Shane O'Neill, hard pressed on every side, earnestly implored the cardinals of Lorraine and Guise, in the name of their great brother the duke, to bring the *Fleur-de-lys* to the rescue of Ireland from the grasp of the ungodly English. ' Help us,' he cried, blending *Irish-like* flattery with entreaty : ' when I was in England, I saw your noble brother, the Marquis d'Elbœuf, transfix two stags with a single arrow. If the most Christian king will not help us, move the pope to help us. I alone in this land sustain his cause.' To propitiate his holiness, Primate Daniel was dismissed to the ranks of the army, and Creagh received his crosier, and was taken into O'Neill's household.

' All was done,' says the English historian, ' to deserve favour in earth and heaven, but all was useless. The Pope sat silent or muttering his anathemas with bated breath. The Guises had work enough on hand at home to heed the *Irish wolf,* whom the English, having in vain attempted to trap or poison, were driving to bay with more lawful weapons.' His own people, divided and dispirited, began now to desert the failing cause. In May, by a concerted movement, the deputy with the light horse of the Pale overran Tyrone, and robbed the farmers of 3,000 cattle, while the O'Donels mustered their forces for a great contest with Shane, now struggling, almost hopelessly, to maintain his supremacy. The O'Neills and O'Donels met on the banks of the Foyle near Lifford. The former were superior in number, being about 3,000 men. After a brief fight ' the

* Page 416.
F 2

O'Neills broke and fled; the enemy was behind them, the river was in front ; and when the Irish battle cries had died away over moor and mountain, but 200 survived of those fierce troopers, who were to have cleared Ireland for ever from the presence of the Saxons. For the rest, the wolves were snarling over their bodies, and the seagulls whirling over them with scream and cry, as they floated down to their last resting-place beneath the quiet waters of Lough Foyle. Shane's foster-brethren, faithful to the last, were all killed ; he himself with half-a-dozen comrades rode for his life, pursued by the avenging furies. His first desperate intention was to throw himself at Sidney's feet, *with a slave's collar upon his neck* ; but his secretary, Neil M'Kevin, persuaded him that his cause was not yet absolutely without hope. Sorleyboy was still a prisoner in the castle at Lough Neagh, the Countess of Argyle had remained with her ravisher through his shifting fortunes, had continued to bear him children, and notwithstanding his many infidelities, was still attached to him. M'Kevin told him that for their sakes, or at their intercession, he might find shelter and perhaps help among the kindred of the M'Connells.'

Acting on this advice, O'Neill took his prisoner, ' the countess, his secretary, and fifty men to the camp of Allaster M'Connell, in the far extremity of Antrim. He was received with dissembled gratulatory words.' For two days all went on well, and an alliance was talked of. But the vengeance of his hosts was with difficulty suppressed. The great chief who was now in their power, had slain their leaders in the field, had divorced James M'Connell's daughter, had kept a high-born Scottish lady as his mistress, and had asked Argyle to give him for a wife M'Connell's widow, who, to escape the dishonour, had remained in concealment at Edinburgh. On the third evening, Monday June 2, when the wine and the whiskey had gone freely round, and the blood in Shane's veins had warmed, Gilespie M'Connell, who had watched him from the first with an ill-boding eye, turned round upon M'Kevin, and asked scornfully, ' whether it was he who had bruited abroad that the lady his aunt did offer to come from Scotland to Ireland to marry with his master ? '

M'Kevin meeting scorn with scorn said, that if his aunt was Queen of Scotland she might be proud to match with the O'Neill. ' It is false,' the fierce Scot shouted ; ' my aunt is too honest a woman to match with her husband's murderer.'

' Shane, who was perhaps drunk, heard the words, and forgetting where he was, flung back the lie in Gilespie's throat. Gilespie sprung to his feet, ran out of the tent, and raised the slogan of the Isles. A hundred dirks flashed into the moonlight, and the Irish, wherever they could be found, were struck down and stabbed. Some two or three found their horses and escaped, all the rest were murdered ; and Shane himself, gashed with fifty wounds, was wrapped in a kern's old shirt, and flung into a pit, dug hastily among the ruined arches of Glenarm. Even there, what was left of him was not allowed to rest. Four days later, Piers, the captain of Knockfergus, hacked the head from the body, and carried it on a spear's point through Drogheda to Dublin, where, staked upon a pike, it bleached on the battlements of the castle, a symbol to the Irish world of the fate of Celtic heroes.' *

Mr. Froude might have added: Celtic heroes struck down by Celtic hands. No lord deputy could boast of a victory over Shane O'Neill in the field. Irish traitors in English pay, Irish clans moved by vengeance, did the work of England in the destruction of the great principality of the O'Neills, and it was by *their* swords, not by English valour, that Sidney ' recovered Ireland for the crown of Elizabeth.' Whatever may have been the faults of Shane O'Neill, and no doubt they were very great, though not to be judged of by the morality of the nineteenth century, his talents, his force of character, his courage and capacity

---

* Froude, p. 418, &c.

as a general, deserved more favourable notice from Mr. Froude, who, in almost every sentence of his graphic and splendid descriptions, betrays an animosity to the Celtic race, very strange in an author so enlightened, and evincing, with this exception, such generous sympathies. After so often reviling the great Irish champion by comparing him to all sorts of wild beasts, the historian thus concludes:— ' So died Shane O'Neill, one of those champions of Irish nationality, who under varying features have repeated themselves in the history of that country with periodic regularity. At once a *drunken ruffian,* and a keen and fiery patriot, the representative in his birth of the line of the ancient kings, the ideal in his character of all which Irishmen most admired, regardless in his actions of the laws of God and man, yet the devoted subject in his creed of the holy Catholic Church; with an eye which could see far beyond the limits of his own island, and a tongue which could touch the most passionate chords of the Irish heart; the like of him has been seen many times in that island, and the like of him may be seen many times again till the Ethiopian has changed his skin, and the leopard his spots. Numbers of his letters remain, to the Queen, to Sussex, to Sidney, to Cecil, and to foreign princes; far-reaching, full of pleasant flattery and promises which cost him nothing, but showing true ability and insight. Sinner though he was, he too in his turn was sinned against; in the stained page of Irish misrule there is no second instance in which an English ruler stooped to treachery, or to the infamy of attempted assassination; and it is not to be forgotten that Lord Sussex, who has left under his own hand the evidence of his own baseness, continued a trusted and favoured councillor of Elizabeth, while Sidney, who fought Shane and conquered him in the open field, found only suspicion and hard words.'

CHAPTER IV.

EXTERMINATING WARS.

MR. FROUDE'S magnificent chapter on Ireland, in the eleventh volume of his history, just published, ought to be studied by every member of the legislature before parliament meets. If a nation has a conscience, England must feel remorse for the deeds done in her name in Ireland; and ought to make amends for them, if possible. The historian has well described the policy of Queen Elizabeth. She was at times disposed to forbearance, but ' she made impossible the obedience she enjoined. Her deputies and her presidents, too short-sighted to rule with justice, were driven to cruelty in spite of themselves. It was easier to kill than to restrain. Death was the only gaoler which their finances could support, while the Irish in turn lay in wait to retaliate upon their oppressors, and atrocity begat atrocity in hopeless continuity.'

Whenever there was a failing in any enterprise, the queen conceived ' a great misliking of the whole matter;' but success covered a multitude of sins. When the Irish were powerful, and the colony was in danger, she thought it ' a hard matter to subvert the customs of the people which they had enjoyed, to be ruled by the captains of their own nation. Let the chiefs sue for pardon, and submit to her authority, and she would let them have their seignories, their captaincies, their body-guards, and all the rest of their dignities, with power of life and death over their people. But,' says Mr. Froude, 'it was the curse of the English rule that it never could adhere consistently to any

definite principle. It threatened, and failed to execute its
threats. It fell back on conciliation, and yet immediately,
by some injustice or cruelty, made reliance on its good faith
impossible.'

Essex seemed to understand well the nature and motive
of the queen's professions, and he resolved to make some
bold attempts to win back her favour. He had made a
sudden attack on Sir Brian O'Neill of Clandeboye, with
troops trained in the wars of the Low Countries, and in a
week he brought him to abject submission, which he
expressed by saying that 'he had gone wickedly astray,
wandering in the wilderness like a blind beast.' But it was
the misfortune of Sir Brian, or M'Phelim, that he still
held his own territory, which had been granted by the
queen to Essex. 'The attempt to deprive him had been
relinquished. He had surrendered his lands, and the queen,
at Essex's own intercession, had reinstated him as tenant
under the crown. It seems, however, as if Essex had his
eye still upon the property.' Under such circumstances, it
was easy to assume that O'Neill was still playing false. So
he resolved that he should not be able to do so any longer.
' He determined to make sure work with so fickle a people.'
He returned to Clandeboye, as if on a friendly visit. Sir
Brian and Lady O'Neill received him with all hospitality.
The Irish Annalists say that they gave him a banquet.
They not only let him off safe, but they accompanied him to
his castle at Belfast. There he was very gracious. A high
feast was held in the hall; and it was late in the night when
the noble guest and his wife retired to their lodging outside the walls. When they were supposed to be asleep, a
company of soldiers surrounded the house and prepared to
break the door. ' The O'Neills flew to arms. The cry rang
through the village, and the people swarmed out to defend
their chief; but surprised, half-armed, and outnumbered, they
were overpowered and cut to pieces. Two hundred men were
killed. The Four Masters add that the women were slain.
The chieftain's wife had female attendants with her, and

no one was knowingly spared. The tide being out, a squadron of horse was sent at daybreak over the water into the " Ardes," from which, in a few hours, they returned with 3,000 of Sir Brian's cattle, and with a drove of stud mares, of which the choicest were sent to Fitzwilliam. Sir Brian himself, his brother, and Lady O'Neill, were carried as prisoners to Dublin, where they were soon after executed.'*

Essex did not miscalculate the probable effect of this exploit. It raised him high in the estimation of the Anglo-Irish of the Pale. ' The taint of the country was upon him; he had made himself no better than themselves, and was the hero of the hour.' The effect of such conduct and such a spirit in the rulers, may be imagined. A few weeks later, Sir Edward Fitton wrote : ' I may say of Ireland, that it is quiet; but if universal oppression of the mean sort by the great; if murder, robberies, burnings make an ill commonwealth, then I cannot say we are in a good case. . . Public sentiment in Dublin, however, was unanimous in its approbation. Essex was the man who would cauterize the long-standing sores. There was a soldier in Ireland at last who understood the work that was to be done, and the way to set about it. Beloved by the soldiers, admirable alike for religion, nobility, and courtesy, altogether the queen's, and not bewitched by the factions of the realm, the governor of Ulster had but to be armed with supreme power, and the long-wished-for conquest of Ireland would be easily and instantly achieved.'

These feelings were not unnatural to the party in Dublin, now represented by the men who recently declared that they rejoiced in the election of a Fenian convict in Tipperary, and declared that they would vote for such a candidate in preference to a loyal man. But how did Queen Elizabeth receive the news of the treacherous and atrocious massacre at Belfast? She was not displeased. ' Her occasional disapprobation of severities of this kind,' says Mr. Froude, ' was confined to cases to which the attention of Europe

* Froude, vol. xi. p. 179.

happened to be especially directed. She told Essex that he
was a great ornament of her nobility, she wished she had
many as ready as he to spend their lives for the benefit of
their country.'

Thus encouraged by his sovereign, and smarting under
the reproach of cowardice cast on him by Leicester, Essex
determined to render his name illustrious by a still more
signal deed of heroism. After an unprovoked raid on the
territories of O'Neill in Tyrone, carrying off cattle and
slaughtering great numbers of innocent people whom his
soldiers hunted down, he perpetrated another massacre,
which is certainly one of the most infamous recorded in
history. A great number of women and children, aged and
sick persons, had fled from the horrors that reigned on the
mainland, and taken refuge in the island of Rathlin. The
story of their tragic fate is admirably told by Mr. Froude:—
' The situation and the difficulty of access had thus long
marked Rathlin as a place of refuge for Scotch or Irish fugitives, and, besides its natural strength, it was respected as a
sanctuary, having been the abode at one time of St. Columba.
A mass of broken masonry, on a cliff overhanging the sea, is
a remnant of the castle in which Robert Bruce watched the
leap of the legendary spider. To this island, when Essex
entered Antrim, M'Connell and other Scots had sent their
wives and children, their aged and their sick, for safety. On
his way through Carrickfergus, when returning to Dublin,
the earl ascertained that they had not yet been brought
back to their homes. The officer in command of the English
garrison (it is painful to mention the name either of him,
or of any man concerned in what ensued) was John Norris,
Lord Norris's second son, so famous afterwards in the Low
Countries, grandson of Sir Henry Norris, executed for
adultery with Anne Boleyn. Three small frigates were in the
harbour. The summer had been hot and windless; the sea
was smooth, there was a light and favourable air from the
east ; and Essex directed Norris to take a company of soldiers
with him, cross over, and——'

What ? Bring those women and children, those sick and aged folk, back to their homes ? Essex had made peace by treaty with the O'Neill. He had killed or chased away every man that could disturb the peace ; and an act of humanity like this would have had a most conciliatory effect, and ought to recommend the hero to the queen, who should be supposed to have the heart as well as the form of a woman.

No ; the order was, to go over ' *and kill whatever he could find !* ' Mr. Froude resumes : ' The run of the Antrim coast was rapidly and quietly accomplished. Before an alarm could be given, the English had landed, close to the ruins of the church which bears St. Columba's name. Bruce's castle was then standing, and was occupied by a score or two of Scots, who were in charge of the women. But Norris had brought cannon with him. The weak defences were speedily destroyed, and after a severe assault, in which several of the garrison were killed, the chief who was in command offered to surrender, if he and his people were allowed to return to Scotland. The conditions were rejected. The Scots yielded at discretion, and every living creature in the place, except the chief and his family (who were probably reserved for ransom), was immediately put to the sword. Two hundred were killed in the castle. It was then discovered that several hundred more, chiefly mothers and their little ones, were hidden in the caves about the shore. There was no remorse, nor even the faintest shadow of perception that the occasion called for it. They were hunted out as if they had been seals or otters, and all destroyed. Sorleyboy and other chiefs, Essex coolly wrote, had sent their wives and children into the island, " which be all taken and executed to the number of six hundred. Sorleyboy himself," he continued, "stood upon the mainland of the Glynnes and saw the taking of the island, and was likely to have run mad for sorrow, tearing and tormenting himself, and saying that he there lost all that he ever had ! " The impression left upon the mind by this horrible story, is increased by the

composure with which even the news of it was received.
"Yellow-haired Charley," wrote Essex to the queen, "might
tear himself for his pretty little ones and their *dam*," but in
Ireland itself the massacre was not specially distinguished
in the general system of atrocity. Essex described it himself as one of the exploits with which he was most satisfied ;
and Elizabeth, in answer to his letters, bade him tell John
Norris, " the executioner of his well-designed enterprise, that
she would not be unmindful of his services." '

I have transcribed this narrative partly for the sake of the
reflection with which Mr. Froude concludes. He says:
' But though passed over and unheeded at the time, and
lying buried for three hundred years, the bloody stain comes
back to the light again, not in myth or legend, but in the
original account of the nobleman by whose command the
deed was done ; and when the history of England's dealings
with Ireland settles at last into its final shape, that hunt
among the caves at Rathlin will not be forgotten.' * It was
for services like these that Essex got the barony of
Farney, in the county Monaghan. He had mortgaged his
English estates to the queen for 10,000*l.*, and after his
plundering expeditions in Ireland he went home to pay his
debts.

Further on Mr. Froude has another reflection connected
with the death of Essex, supposed to have been poisoned, as
his widow immediately after married Leicester. He says:
' Notwithstanding Rathlin, Essex was one of the noblest of
living Englishmen, and that such a man could have ordered
such a deed, being totally unconscious of the horror of it, is
not the least instructive feature in the dreadful story.' It is
certainly a strange fact that nearly all the official murderers
who ruled in Ireland in those times were intensely religious,
setting to their own class a most edifying example of
piety. Thus, from the first, Protestantism was presented to
the Irish in close connexion with brutal inhumanity and
remorseless cruelty. Essex, when dying, was described by

* History of England, vol. xi. p. 184.

the bystanders as acting 'more like a divine preacher or
heavenly prophet than a man.' His opinion of the religious
character of his countrymen was most unfavourable. ' The
Gospel had been preached to them,' he said, ' but they
were neither Papists nor Protestants —of no religion, but
full of pride and iniquity. There was nothing but infidelity,
infidelity, infidelity!—atheism, atheism!—no religion, no
religion!' What such tiger-like slaughterers of women and
children, such ruthless destroyers, could have meant by
religion is a puzzle for philosophers.

Sidney reluctantly resumed the office of viceroy in 1575.
Tirlogh O'Neill congratulated the Government on his appointment, ' wretched Ireland needing not the sword, but
sober, temperate, and humane administration.' Though it was
winter, the new deputy immediately commenced a progress
through the provinces. Going first to Ulster, he saw
Sorleyboy, and gave him back Rathlin. He paid a
friendly visit to the O'Neill, who gave him an assurance of
his loyalty. Leinster he found for the most part ' waste,
burnt up and destroyed.' He proceeded by Waterford to
Cork. He was received everywhere with acclamation. ' The
wretched people,' says Mr. Froude, how truly!—' sanguine
then, as ever, in the midst of sorrow, looked on his coming as
the inauguration of a new and happier era.' So, in later
times, they looked on the coming of Chesterfield, and
Fitzwilliam, and Anglesey. But the good angel was quickly
chased away by the evil demon—invoked under the name of
the ' Protestant Interest.' The Munster and the Connaught
chiefs all thronged to Sidney's levées, weary of disaffection,
and willing to be loyal, if their religion were not interfered
with, ' detesting their barbarous lives,'—promising rent and
service for their lands. ' The past was wiped out. Confiscation on the one hand, and rebellion on the other,
were to be heard of no more. A clean page was turned.'
Even the Catholic bishops were tractable, and the viceroy
got ' good and honest juries in Cork, and with their help
twenty-four malefactors were honourably condemned and

hanged.' Enjoying an ovation as he passed on to Limerick and Galway, he found many grievances to be redressed— ' plenty of burnings, rapes, murders, besides such spoil in goods and cattle as in number might be counted infinite, and in quantity innumerable.'

Sir William Drury was appointed president of Munster; and he was determined that in his case the magistrate should not bear the sword in vain.   Going round the counties as an itinerant judge, he gleaned the malefactors Sidney had left, and hanged forty-three of them in Cork.   One he pressed to death for declining to plead to his indictment. Two M'Sweenys, from Kerry, were drawn and quartered. At Limerick he hanged forty-two, and at Kilkenny thirty-six, among which he said were ' some good ones,' as a sportsman might say, bagging his game.   He had a difficulty with ' a blackamoor and two witches,' against whom he found no statute of the realm, so he dispatched them ' by natural law.' Although Jeffreys, at the Bloody Assizes, did not come near Drury, the latter found it necessary to apologise to the English Government for the paucity of his victims, saying, ' I have chosen rather with the snail tenderly to creep, than with the hare swiftly to run.'   With the Government in Ireland, as Mr. Froude has well remarked, ' the gallows is the only preacher of righteousness.'

But the gallows was far too slow, as an instrument of reform and civilisation, for Malby, president of Connaught; and as modern evictors in that province and elsewhere have chosen Christmas as the most appropriate season for pulling down dwellings, extinguishing domestic fires, and unhousing women and children, so Malby chose the same blessed season for his ' improvements ' in 1576.   It is such a model for dealing with the Fenians and tenants on the Tory plan, that I transcribe his own report, which Mr. Froude has found among the Irish MSS. ' At Christmas,' he wrote, ' I marched into their territory, and finding courteous dealing with them had like to have cut my throat, I thought good to take another course ; and so with determination *to consume them with fire and sword, sparing neither old nor young*, I entered their mountains. I burnt all their corn and houses, and committed to the sword all that could be found, where were slain at that time above sixty of their best men, and among them the best leaders they had. This was Shan Burke's country. Then I burnt Ulick Burke's country. In like manner I assaulted a castle where the garrison surrendered. I put them to the misericordia of my soldiers. They were all slain. Thence I went on, sparing none which came in my way, which cruelty did so amaze their followers, that they could not tell where to bestow themselves. Shan Burke made means to me to pardon him and forbear killing of his people. I would not hearken, but went on my way. The gentlemen of Clanrickard came to me. I found it was but dallying to win time, so I left Ulick as little corn and as few houses standing as I left his brother; and what people was found had as little favour as the other had. *It was all done in rain and frost and storm*, journeys in such weather bringing them the sooner to submission. They are humble enough now, and will yield to any terms we like to offer them.'

And so Malby and his soldiers enjoyed a merry Christmas; and when Walsingham read his letters, giving an account of his civilising progress, to the Queen, she, too, must have enjoyed a fresh sensation, a new pleasure amidst the festivities and gallantries of her brilliant court. Mr. Froude has rendered a timely service in this Christmas time to the Coercionists, the Martial Law men, and the Habeas Corpus Suspension men of our own day. He has shown them their principles at work and carried out with a vengeance, and with what results! He has admirably sketched the progress of English rule in Ireland up to that time—a rule unchanged in principle to the present hour, though restrained in its operation by the spirit of the age. Mr. Froude says: ' When the people were quiet, there was the rope for the malefactors, and death by the natural law for those whom the law written could not touch. When they broke out,

there was the blazing homestead, and death by the sword
for all, not for the armed kerne only, but for the aged and
infirm, the nursing mother and the baby at her breast.
These, with ruined churches, and Irish rogues for ministers,
—these, and so far *only* these were the symbols of the
advance of English rule; yet even Sidney could not order
more and more severity, and the president of Munster was
lost in wonder at the detestation with which the English
name was everywhere regarded. Clanrickard was sent to
Dublin, and the deputy wished to hang him, but he dared
not execute an earl without consulting his mistress, and
Elizabeth's leniency in Ireland, as well as England, was alive
and active towards the great, although it was dead towards
the poor. She could hear without emotion of the massacres
at Rathlin or Slievh Broughty; but the blood of the nobles,
who had betrayed their wretched followers into the rebellion for which they suffered, was for ever precious in her
sight. She forbade Sidney to touch him.'*

Next came the great Desmond Rebellion, by which
Munster was desolated. The Pope had encouraged an
expedition against the heretics in Ireland, and some Spanish
forces joined in the enterprise. It was organised by an
English ecclesiastic, named Sanders, and an exiled Geral-
dine, named Fitzmaurice of Kerry, both able and energetic
men. The Spaniards landed at Dingle in 1579. In a few
days all Kerry and Limerick were up, and the woods between Mallow and the Shannon 'were swarming with howling kerne.' ' The rebellion,' wrote Waterhouse, ' is the most
perilous that ever began in Ireland. Nothing is to be
looked for but a general revolt.' Malby took the command
against them, joined by one of the Burkes, Theobald, who
when he saw Fitzmaurice struck by a ball and staggering
in his saddle, rode at him and cut him down. The Papal
standard was unfolded in this battle. Malby then burnt
the Desmonds' country, killing all the human beings he met,
up to the walls of Askeaton. When opportunity offered,

* Vol. xi. p. 197.

Desmond retaliated by sacking and burning Youghal For two days the Geraldines revelled in plunder; they violated the women and murdered all who could not escape. At length Elizabeth was roused to the greatness of the danger, her parsimony was overcome. A larger force was drawn into Ireland than had ever been assembled there for a century. Ormond, the hereditary enemy of Desmond, was appointed commander-in-chief; and Burghley, writing to him in the name of the queen, concluded thus: ' So now I will merely say, Butler aboo, against all that cry in the new language—Papa aboo, and God send your hearts' desire to banish and vanquish those cankered Desmonds!' The war now raged, and, as usual, the innocent people, the cultivators of the soil, were the first victims. ' We passed through the rebel countries,' wrote Pelham, ' in two companies, burning with fire *all habitations, and executing the people* wherever we found them.' Mr. Froude says: ' *Alone* of all the English commanders he expressed remorse at the work.' Well, if the creatures they destroyed were horses, dogs, or cats, we should expect a man of ordinary human feelings to be shocked at the wholesale butchery. But the beings slaughtered were men and women and children—Christians found unarmed and defenceless in their dwellings. Let the English imagine such a war carried on in Kent or Yorkshire, by Irish invaders, killing in the name of the Pope. The Irish Annalists say that Pelham and Ormond killed the blind and the aged, women and children, sick and idiots, sparing none.

The English, as usual, had help from an Irish chief in the work of destruction. Ormond had in his train M'Carthymore, ' who, believing Desmond's day to be done, hoped, by making himself useful, to secure a share of the plunder.' Dividing their forces, Pelham marched on to Dingle, ' destroying as he went, with Ormond parallel to him on the opposite side of the bay, the two parties watching each other's course at night across the water by the flames of the burning cottages !'

The fleet was waiting at Dingle. There was a merry

meeting of the officers. ' Here,' says Sir Nicholas White,
' my lord justice and I gathered cockles for our supper.'* The
several hunting parties compared notes in the evening.
Sometimes the sport was bad. On one occasion Pelham reported that his party had hanged a priest in the Spanish dress.
' Otherwise,' he says, ' we took small prey, and killed less
people, though we reached many places in our travel!'
At Killarney they found the lakes full of salmon. In one
of the islands there was an abbey, in another a parish church,
in another a castle, ' out of which there came to them a fair
lady, the rejected wife of Lord Fitzmaurice.' Even the
soldiers were struck with the singular loveliness of the scene.
' A fairer land,' one of them said, ' the sun did never shine
upon—pity to see it lying waste in the hands of traitors.'
Mr. Froude, who deals more justly by the Irish in his last
volumes, replies : ' Yet it was by those traitors that the woods
whose beauty they so admired had been planted and fostered.
Irish hands, unaided by English art or English wealth, had
built Muckross and Innisfallen and Aghadoe, and had
raised the castles on whose walls the modern poet watched the
splendour of the sunset.'

Ormond was the arch-destroyer of his countrymen. In a
report of his services he stated that in this one year 1580, he
had put to the sword ' forty-six captains and leaders, with 800
notorious traitors and malefactors, *and above* 4,000 other
people.' * In that year the great Desmond wrote to Philip
of Spain that he was a homeless wanderer. ' Every town,
castle, village, farm-house belonging to him or his people
had been destroyed. There was no longer a roof standing
in Munster to shelter him.' Hunted like a wolf through
the mountains, he was at last found sleeping in a hut and
killed. In vain his wife pleaded with Ormond, and threw
herself on his protection. Even she was not spared. Mr.
Froude gives an interesting account of Desmond's last hours.
He was hunted down into the mountains between Tralee
and the Atlantic. M'Sweeny had sheltered him and fed him

---

* Carew Papers ; Froude, vol. xi. p. 225.

through the summer, though a large price was set on his head; and when M'Sweeny was gone, killed by an Irish dagger, the earl's turn could not be distant. Donell M'Donell Moriarty had been received to grace by Ormond, and had promised to deserve his pardon. This man came to the captain of Castlemayne, gave information of the hiding-place, a band was sent—half-a-dozen English soldiers and a few Irish kerne, who stole in the darkness along the path which followed the stream—the door was dashed in, and the last Earl of Desmond was killed in his bed.

Ormond had recourse to a horrible device to extinguish the embers of the rebellion. It was carrying out to a diabolical extent the policy of setting one Irishman against another. If the terror-stricken wretches hoped for pardon, they must deserve it, by murdering their relations. Accordingly sacks full of the heads of reputed rebels were brought in daily. Yet concerning him Mr. Froude makes this singular remark: ' To Ormond the Irish were human beings with human rights. To the English they were *vermin, to be cleared from off the earth* by any means that offered.'

Consequently, when it was proposed to make Ormond viceroy, the Pale was in a ferment. How could any man be fit to represent English power in Dublin Castle, who regarded the Irish as human beings! Not less curious is the testimony which the historian bears to the character of the English exterminators. He says, ' They were honourable, high-minded men, full of natural tenderness and gentleness, to every one with whom they were placed in *human relations.* The Irish, unfortunately, they looked upon as savages who had refused peace and protection when it was offered to them, and were now therefore to be *rooted out and destroyed.*' A reformer in 1583, however, suggested a milder policy. He recommended that ' all Brehons, carraghs, bards, rhymers, friars, monks, jesuits, pardoners, nuns, and such-like should be executed by martial law, and that with this clean sweep the work of death might end, and a new era be ushered in with universities and schools, a fixed police, and agriculture, and good government.'

When the English had destroyed all the houses and churches, burnt all the corn, and driven away all the cattle, they were disgusted at the savage state in which the remnant of the peasantry lived. A gentleman named Andrew Trollope gave expression to this feeling thus: 'The common people ate flesh if they could steal it, if not they lived on shamrock and carrion. They never served God or went to church; they had no religion and no manners, but were in all things more barbarous and beast-like than any other people. No governor shall do good here,' he said, 'except he show himself a Tamerlane. If hell were open and all the evil spirits abroad, they could never be worse than these Irish rogues—rather dogs, and worse than dogs, for dogs do but after their kind, and they degenerate from all humanity.' *

The population of Ireland was then by slaughter and famine reduced to about 600,000, one-eighth of the population of England; but far too many, in the estimation of their English rulers. Brabason succeeded Malby in Connaught, and surpassed him in cruelty. The Four Masters say: 'Neither the sanctuary of the saint, neither the wood nor the forest valley, the town nor the lawn, was a shelter from this captain and his people, till the whole territory was destroyed by him.' In the spring of 1582 St. Leger wrote from Cork: 'This country is so ruined as it is well near unpeopled by the murders and spoils done by the traitors on the one side, and by the killing and spoil done by the soldiers on the other side, together with the great mortality in town and country, which is such as the like hath never been seen. There has died by famine only not so few as 30,000 in this province in less than half a year, besides others that are hanged and killed.'

At length the world began to cry shame on England; and Lord Burghley was obliged to admit that the English in Ireland had outdone the Spaniards in ferocious and bloodthirsty persecution. Remonstrating with Sir H. Wallop,

* Froude, vol. xi. p. 246.

ancestor of Lord Portsmouth, he said that the ' Flemings had not such cause to rebel against the oppression of the Spaniards, as the Irish against the tyranny of England.' Wallop defended the Government; the causes of the rebellion were not to be laid at the door of England at all. They were these, ' the great affection they generally bear to the Popish religion, which agreeth with their humour, that having committed murder, incest, thefts, with all other execrable offences, by hearing a mass, confessing themselves to a priest, or obtaining the Pope's pardon, they persuade themselves that they are forgiven, and, hearing mass on Sunday or holyday, they think all the week after they may do what heinous offence soever and it is dispensed withal.' Trollope said they had no religion. Wallop said they had too much religion. But their nationality was worse than their creed. Wallop adds, ' They also much hate our nation, partly through the general mislike or disdain one nation hath to be governed by another; partly that we are contrary to them in religion; and lastly, they seek to have the government among themselves.'

The last was the worst of all. Elizabeth wished to heal the wounds of the Irish nation by appointing Ormond lord deputy. He was a nobleman of Norman descent. His family had been true to England for centuries. He had commanded her armies during this exterminating war, and, being a native of the country, he would be best fitted to carry on the work of conciliation after so much slaughter. But, says Mr. Froude, ' from every English officer serving in the country, every English settler, every bishop of the Anglo-Irish Church, there rose one chorus of remonstrance and indignation; to them it appeared as a proposal now would appear in Calcutta to make the Nizam Viceroy of India.' * Wallop wrote that if he were appointed, there would be ' no dwelling in the country for any Englishman.'

The fear that a merciful policy might be adopted towards Ireland sorely troubled Wallop and Archbishop Loftus; but

* Ibid. p. 252.

they were comforted by a great prize—an archbishop fell
into their hands. Dr. Hurley refused to give information
against others. Walsingham suggested that he should be
put to the torture. To him Archbishop Loftus wrote with
unction. 'Not finding that easy method of examination do
any good, we made command to Mr. Waterhouse and Mr.
Secretary Fenton to put him to the torture, such as your
honour advised us, which was to *toast his feet* against the
fire with hot boots.' He confessed something. They
asked permission to execute him by martial law. The
queen took a month to consider. She recommended an
ordinary trial for high treason, and if the jury did not do
its duty, they might take the shorter way. She wished for
no more torture, but 'for what was past her majesty accepted
in good part their careful travail, and greatly commended
their doings.' The Irish judges had repeatedly decided that
there was no case against Archbishop Hurley; but on June
19, 1584, Loftus and Wallop wrote to Walsingham, ' We
gave warrant to the knight-marshal to do execution upon
him, which accordingly was performed, and thereby the
realm rid of a most pestilent member.'*

This was the last act of these two lords justices. Sir
John Perrot, the new viceroy, made a speech which sent a
ray of hope athwart the national gloom. It was simply that
the people might thenceforth expect a little justice and protection. He told the natives that 'as natural-born subjects
of her majesty she loved them as her own people. He
wished to be suppressed and universally abolished throughout the realm the name of a churle and the crushing of a
churle; affirming that, however the former barbarous times
had desired it and nourished it, yet he held it tyrannous both
in name and manner, and therefore would extirpate it, and
use in place of it the titles used in England, namely, husbandmen, franklins or yeomen.' 'This was so plausible,' wrote
Sir G. Fenton, 'that it was carried throughout the whole realm,
in less time than might be thought credible, if expressed.'

* Froude, vol. xi. p. 264.

The extirpation of the Munster Geraldines, in the right line, according to the theory of the 'Undertakers' and the law of England in general, vested in the queen the 570,000 acres belonging to the late earl. Proclamation was accordingly made throughout England, inviting 'younger brothers of good families' to undertake the plantation of Desmond— each planter to obtain a certain scope of land, on condition of settling thereupon so many families—'none of the native Irish to be admitted.' Under these conditions, Sir Christopher Hatton took up 10,000 acres in Waterford; Sir Walter Raleigh 12,000 acres, partly in Waterford and partly in Cork; Sir William Harbart, or Herbert, 13,000 acres in Kerry; Sir Edward Denny 6,000 in the same county; Sir Warren St. Leger, and Sir Thomas Norris, 6,000 acres each in Cork; Sir William Courtney 10,000 acres in Limerick; Sir Edward Fitton 11,500 acres in Tipperary and Waterford, and Edmund Spenser 3,000 acres in Cork, on the beautiful Blackwater. The other notable Undertakers were the Hides, Butchers, Wirths, Berkleys, Trenchards, Thorntons, Bourchers, Billingsleys, &c. Some of these grants, especially Raleigh's, fell in the next reign to Richard Boyle, the so-called '*great* Earl of Cork'—probably the most pious hypocrite to be found in the long roll of the 'Munster Undertakers.'

CHAPTER V.

AN IRISH CRUSADE.

In 1602, the Lord Deputy Mountjoy, in obedience to instructions from the Government in London, marched to the borders of Ulster with a considerable force, to effect, if he could, the arrest of Hugh O'Neill, Earl of Tyrone, or to bring him to terms. Since the defeat of the Irish and Spanish confederacy at Kinsale, O'Neill comforted himself with the assurance that Philip III. would send another expedition to Ireland to retrieve the honour of his flag, and avenge the humiliation it had sustained, owing to the incompetency or treachery of Don Juan d'Aquila. That the king was inclined to aid the Irish there can be no question; 'for Clement VIII., then reigning in the Vatican, pressed it upon him as a sacred duty, which he owed to his co-religionists in Ireland, whose efforts to free themselves from Elizabeth's tyranny, the pontiff pronounced to be a *crusade* against the most implacable heretic of the day.'*

If Mr. Meehan's authorities may be relied upon, Queen Elizabeth was, in intention at least, a murderer as well as a heretic. He states that while she was gasping on her cushions at Richmond, gazing on the haggard features of death, and vainly striving to penetrate the opaque veil of the future, she commanded Secretary Cecil to charge Mountjoy to entrap Tyrone into a submission, on diminished rank as Baron of Dungannon, and with lessened territory; or if possible, to have his head, before engaging

* Fate and Fortunes of the Earls of Tyrone and Tyrconnell. By the Rev. P. C. Meehan, M.R.I.A.

the royal word. It was to accomplish either of these objects,
that Mountjoy marched to the frontier of the north.
'Among those employed to murder O'Neill in cold blood,
were Sir Geoffry Fenton, Lord Dunsany, and *Henry Oge
O'Neill.* Mountjoy bribed one Walker, an Englishman,
and a ruffian calling himself Richard Combus, to make the
attempt, but they all failed.'* Finding it impossible to
procure the assassination of ' the sacred person of O'Neill,
who had so many eyes of jealousy about him,' he wrote to
Cecil from Drogheda, that nothing prevented Tyrone from
making his submission but mistrust of his personal safety
and guarantee for maintenance commensurate to his princely
rank. The lords of Elizabeth's privy council empowered
Mountjoy to treat with O'Neill on these terms, and to give
him the required securities. Sir Garret Moore and Sir
William Godolphin were entrusted with a commission to
effect this object. But while the lord deputy, with a brilliant
retinue, was feasting at Mellifont, a monastery bestowed
by Henry VIII. on an ancestor of Sir Garret Moore, by
whom it was transformed into a ' fair mansion,' half palace,
half fortress, a courier arrived from England, announcing
the death of the queen. Nevertheless the negotiations were
pressed on in her name, the fact of her decease being carefully concealed from the Irish. Tyrone had already sent
his secretary, Henry O'Hagan, to announce to the lord
deputy that he was about to come to his presence. Accordingly on March 29, he surrendered himself to the two
commissioners at Tougher, within five miles of Dungannon.
On the following evening he reached Mellifont, when, being
admitted to the lord deputy's presence, ' he knelt, as was
usual on such occasions ; ' and made penitent submission to
her majesty. Then, being invited to come nearer to the
deputy, he repeated the ceremony, if we may credit Fynes
Moryson, in the same humiliating attitude, thus :—

'I, Hugh O'Neill, Earl of Tyrone, do absolutely submit
myself to the queen's mercy, imploring her gracious com-

* See Life and Letters of Florence M'Carthy. By D. M'Carthy, Esq.

miseration, imploring her majesty to mitigate her just in dignation against me. I do avow that the first motives of my rebellion were neither malice nor ambition; but that I was induced by fear of my life, to stand upon my guard. I do therefore most humbly sue her majesty, that she will vouchsafe to restore to me my former dignity and living. In which state of a subject, I vow to continue for ever here- after loyal, in all true obedience to her royal person, crown, and prerogatives, and to be in all things as dutifully con- formable thereunto as I or any other nobleman of this realm is bound by the duty of a subject to his sovereign, utterly renouncing the name and title of O'Neill, or any other claim which hath not been granted to me by her majesty. I abjure all foreign power, and all dependency upon any other potentate but her majesty. I renounce all manner of dependency upon the King of Spain, or treaty with him or any of his confederates, and shall be ready to serve her majesty against him or any of his forces or confederates. I do renounce all challenge or intermeddling with the Uriaghts, or fostering with them or other neighbour lords or gentlemen outside my country, or exacting black-rents of any Uriaghts or bordering lords. I resign all claim and title to any lands but such as shall now be granted to me by her majesty's letters patent. Lastly, I will be content to be advised by her majesty's magistrates here, and will assist them in anything that may tend to the advancement of her service, and the peaceable government of this kingdom, the abolishing of barbarous customs, the clearing of difficult passes, wherein I will employ the labours of the people of my country in such places as I shall be directed by her majesty, or the lord deputy in her name; and I will en- deavour for myself and the people of my country, to erect civil habitations such as shall be of greater effect to preserve us against thieves, and any force but the power of the state.'

To this act of submission Tyrone affixed his sign manual, and handed it to the deputy, who told him he must write to Philip III. of Spain, to send home his son Henry, who had

gone with Father M'Cawell to complete his studies in
Salamanca. The deputy also insisted that he should reveal
all his negotiations with the Spanish court, or any other
foreign sovereign with whom he maintained correspondence ;
and when the earl assured him that all these requirements
should be duly discharged, the lord deputy in the queen's
name promised him her majesty's pardon to himself and
followers, to himself the restoration of his earldom and blood
with new letters patent of all his lands, excepting the
country possessed by Henry Oge O'Neill, and the Fews
belonging to Tirlough Mac Henry O'Neill, both of whom
had recently taken grants of their lands, to be holden immediately from the queen. It was further covenanted that
Tyrone should give 300 acres of his land to the fort of
Charlmont, and 300 more to that of Mountjoy, as long as it
pleas.d her majesty to garrison said forts. Tyrone assented
to all these conditions, and then received the accolade from
the lord deputy, who, a few months before, had written to
Queen Elizabeth, that he hoped to be able to send her that
ghastliest of all trophies—her great rebel's head !

On April 4, the lord deputy returned to Dublin accompanied by the great vassal whom he fancied he had bound in
inviolable loyalty to the English throne. To make assurance
doubly sure, the day after James was proclaimed, Tyrone
repeated the absolute submission made at Mellifont, the
name of the sovereign only being changed. He also
despatched a letter to the King of Spain stating that he had
held out as long as he could, in the vain hope of being
succoured by him, and finally when deserted by his nearest
kinsmen and followers, he was enforced as in duty bound
to declare his allegiance to James I., in whose service and
obedience he meant to live and die.

The importance of this act of submission will appear from
a manifesto issued by O'Neill three years before, dated
Dungannon, November 16, 1599, and subscribed ' O'Neill.'
This remarkable document has been published for the first
time by Father Meehan.

' *To the Catholics of the towns in Ireland.*

' Using hitherto more than ordinary favour towards all my countrymen, who generally by profession are Catholics, and that naturally I am inclined to affect [esteem] you, I have for these and other considerations abstained my forces from tempting to do you hindrance, and because I did expect that you would enter into consideration of the lamentable state of our poor country, most tyrannically oppressed, and of your own gentle consciences, in maintaining, relieving and helping the enemies of God and our country in wars infallibly tending to the promotion of heresy : But now seeing you are so obstinate in that which hereunto you continued of necessity, I must use severity against you (whom otherwise I most entirely love) in reclaiming you by compulsion. My tolerance and happy victories by God's particular favour doubtless obtained could work no alteration in your consciences, notwithstanding the great calamity and misery, whereunto you are most likely to fall by persevering in that damnable state in which hereunto you have lived. Having commiseration on you I thought it good to forewarn you, requesting every of you to come and join with me against the enemies of God and our poor country. If the same you do not, I will use means to spoil you of all your goods, but according to the utmost of my power shall work what I may to dispossess you of all your lands, because you are the means whereby wars are maintained against the exaltation of the Catholic faith. Contrariwise, whosoever it shall be that shall join with me, upon my conscience, and as to the contrary I shall answer before God, I will employ myself to the utmost of my power in their defence and for the extirpation of heresy, the planting of the Catholic religion, the delivery of our country of infinite murders, wicked and detestable policies by which this kingdom was hitherto governed, nourished in obscurity and ignorance, maintained in barbarity and incivility, and consequently of infinite evils which were too lamentable to be rehearsed.

And seeing these are motives most laudable before any men of consideration, and before the Almighty most meritorious, which is chiefly to be expected, I thought myself in conscience bound, seeing God hath given me some power to use all means for the reduction of this our poor afflicted country into the Catholic faith, which can never be brought to any good pass without either your destruction or helping hand; hereby protesting that I neither seek your lands or goods, neither do I purpose to plant any in your places, if you will adjoin with me; but will extend what liberties and privileges that heretofore you have had if it shall stand in my power, giving you to understand upon my salvation that chiefly and principally I fight for the Catholic faith to be planted throughout all our poor country, as well in cities as elsewhere, as manifestly might appear by that I rejected all other conditions proffered to me this not being granted. I have already by word of mouth protested, and do now hereby protest, that if I had to be King of Ireland without having the Catholic religion which before I mentioned, I would not the same accept. Take your example by that most Catholic country, France, whose subjects for defect of Catholic faith did go against their most natural king, and maintained wars till he was constrained to profess the Catholic religion, duly submitting himself to the Apostolic See of Rome, to the which doubtless we may bring our country, you putting your helping hand with me to the same. As for myself I protest before God and upon my salvation I have been proffered oftentimes such conditions as no man seeking his own private commodity could refuse; but I seeking the public utility of my native country will prosecute these wars until that generally religion be planted throughout all Ireland. So I rest, praying the Almighty to move your flinty hearts to prefer the commodity and profit of our country, before your own private ends.'

As a crusader, the O'Neill was a worthy disciple of the King of Spain. The Catholics of the south had no wish to engage in a religious war, but the northern chief aspiring to

the sovereignty of the whole island, resolved to reclaim them
by compulsion, seeing that his tolerance and happy victories
had worked no change in their consciences, and they still
persevered in that ' damnable state ' in which they had lived.
From his entire love and commiseration he forewarned them
that if they did not come and join him against the enemies
of God and ' our poor country,' he would not only despoil
them of all their goods, but dispossess them of all their lands.
The extirpation of heresy, the planting of the Catholic
religion, he declared could never be brought to any good
pass without either the destruction or the help of the
Catholics in the towns of the south and west.   He did not
want their lands or goods, nor did he intend to plant others
in their places *if they would adjoin with him.*   Pointing to
the example of France, he vowed that he would prosecute
those wars until the Catholic religion should be planted
throughout all Ireland, praying that God would move their
flinty hearts to join him in this pious and humane enterprise.
In those times when religious wars had been raging on the
continent, when the whole power of Spain was persistently
employed to exterminate Protestants with fire and sword and
every species of cruelty, it is not at all surprising that a
chief like O'Neill, leading such a wild warlike life in Ulster,
should persuade himself that he would be glorifying God
and serving his country by destroying the Catholic inhabitants of the towns, that is all the most civilised portion of the
community, because they would not join him in robbing and
killing the Protestants.   But it is not a little surprising
that an enlightened, learned, and liberal Catholic priest,
writing in Dublin in the year 1868, should give his deliberate sanction to this unchristian and barbarous policy.
Yet Father Meehan writes : ' But no ; not even the dint of
that manifesto, *with the ring of true steel in its every line,*
could strike a spark out of their hearts, for they were chalky.'*

It was very natural that the English Government should
act upon the same principle of intolerance, especially when

* Page 34.

they had the plea of state necessity. They did not yet go the length of exterminating Catholicity by the means with which the O'Neill threatened his peaceable and industrious co-religionists in the towns.

All they required was that the Catholics should cease to harbour their priests, and that they should attend the Protestant churches. Remarking upon the proclamation of Chichester to this effect Mr. Meehan says : —' Apart from the folly of the king, who had taken into his head that an entire nation should, at his bidding, apostatise from the creed of their forefathers, the publishing such a manifesto in Dungannon, in Donegal, and elsewhere was a bitter insult to the northern chieftains, whose wars were *crusades*,—the natural consequence of faith, stimulated by the Roman Pontiffs, assisted by Spain, then the most Catholic kingdom in the world.' Does not Mr. Meehan see that crusading is a game at which two can play ? And if wars which were crusades were the natural consequence of the Catholic faith, were stimulated by the Roman Pontiffs, and assisted by Spain, for the purpose of destroying the power of England, everywhere as well as in Ireland, and abolishing the Reformation,—does it not follow as a necessary consequence that the English Government must in sheer self-defence have waged a war of extermination against the Catholic religion, and have regarded its priests as mortal enemies ? No better plea for the English policy in Ireland was ever offered by any Protestant writer than this language, intended as a condemnation, by a very able priest in our own day. It was no doubt extreme folly for King James I. to expect that a nation, or a single individual, should apostatise at his bidding; but it was equal folly in the King of Spain to expect Protestants to apostatise at his bidding ; and if possible still greater folly for O'Neill to expect the Catholic citizens of Munster to join him in the bloody work of persecution. It was, then, the Spanish policy stimulated by the Sovereign Pontiff that was the standing excuse of the cruel intolerance and rancorous religious animosity which have continued to

distract Irish society down to our own time. Persecution
is alien to the Irish race. The malignant *virus* imported
from Spain poisoned the national blood, maddened the
national brain, and provoked the terrible system of reta-
liation that was embodied in the Penal Code, and which,
surviving to our own time, still defends itself by the old
plea—the intrusion of a foreign power attempting to over-
rule the government of the country.

CHAPTER VI.

THE LAST OF THE IRISH PRINCES.

THE accession of James I. produced a delirium of joy in the Catholics of the south. Their bards had sung that the blood of the old Celtic monarchs circulated in his veins, their clergy told them that as James VI. of Scotland he had received supplies of money from the Roman court, and above all Clement VIII. then reigning, had sent to congratulate him on his accession, having been solicited by him to favour his title to the crown of England, which the Pope guaranteed to do on condition that James promised not to persecute the Catholics. The consequence was that the inhabitants of the southern towns rose *en masse* without waiting for authority, forced open the gates of the ancient churches, re-erected the altars and used them for the public celebration of worship. The lord deputy was startled by intelligence to this effect from Waterford, Limerick, Cork, Lismore, Kilkenny, Clonmel, Wexford, &c. The cathedrals, churches, and oratories were seized by the people and clergy, Father White, Vicar-Apostolic of Waterford, being the leader in this movement, going about from city to city for the purpose of 'hallowing and purifying' the temples which Protestantism had desecrated.

The mayors of the cities were rebuked by Mountjoy as seditious and mutinous in setting up 'the public exercise of the Popish religion,' and he threatened to encamp speedily before Waterford, 'to suppress insolences and see peace and obedience maintained.' The deputy kept his word, and on May 4, 1603, he appeared before Waterford at the head

H

of 5,000 men, officered by Sir R. Wingfield, and others who had distinguished themselves during Tyrone's war. ' There is among the family pictures at Powerscourt,' says Mr. Meehan, ' a portrait of this distinguished old warrior, whose lineal descendant, the present noble lord, has always proved most generous to his Catholic tenantry.' The reverend gentleman gives an amusing sketch of a theological encounter between the old warrior and Father White and a Dominican friar, who came forth to the camp under a safe-conduct, both wearing their clerical habits and preceded by a cross-bearer. The soldiers jeered at the sacred symbol, and called it an idol. Father White indignantly resented the outrage, when Sir Richard Wingfield threatened to put an end to the controversy by running his sword through the Vicar-Apostolic. ' The deputy however was a bookish man, at one period of his life inclined to Catholicity, and he listened patiently to Father White on the right of resisting or disobeying the natural prince; but when the latter quoted some passage thereanent in the works of St. Augustine, Mountjoy caused to be brought to him out of his tent the identical volume, and showed to the amazement of the bystanders, that the context explained away all the priest had asserted.' The noble theologian told Father White that he was a traitor, worthy of condign punishment for bringing an idol into a Christian camp and for opening the churches by the Pope's authority. Father White appeared in the camp a second time that day, making a most reasonable request. He fell on his knees before the deputy, begging liberty of conscience, free and open exercise of religion, protesting that the people would be ready to resist all foreign invasion were that granted; and finally beseeching that some of the ruined churches might be given to the Catholics, who were ready to rebuild them, and pay for them a yearly rent into his majesty's exchequer. But the deputy was inexorable, and all he would grant was leave to wear clerical clothes, and celebrate mass in private houses. Mountjoy entered Waterford, received from the citizens the oath of allegiance, and made over the city churches to the small section of Protestants. At the same time he sent despatches to other towns ordering the authorities to evict the Roman Catholics from the places of worship. And then proceeding to Cork, and thence through Cashel to Dublin, he undid all that the clergy had done with respect to the churches, ' leaving perhaps to future statesmen,' writes Father Meehan, ' living above the atmosphere of effete prejudices, the duty of restoring to the Catholics of Ireland those grand old temples, which were never meant to accommodate a fragment of its people.' *

When Mountjoy returned to Dublin he found that he had been created Lord Lieutenant of Ireland with two-thirds of the deputy's allowance, Sir George Carew, appointed deputy during his absence in England, receiving the other third together with his own pay as treasurer-at-war. Mountjoy was also informed that the royal pardon had been granted to Tyrone under the great seal, and that all other grants made to him by the lord deputy had been confirmed. The king concluded by requesting that he would induce Tyrone to go with him to London, adding, ' as we think it very convenient for our service, and require you so to do; and if not that at least you bring his son.' Along with these instructions came a protection for O'Neill and his retinue. It was supposed that James felt grateful to the Ulster chieftain for the services he had rendered him during the late queen's reign; and it is stated by Craik that after the victory of the Blackwater, he sent his secretary O'Hagan to Holyrood, to signify to his majesty that if he supplied him with money and munitions he would instantly march on Dublin, proclaim him King of Ireland, and set the crown upon his head.

In compliance with the sovereign's request, Mountjoy, with a brilliant suite, accompanied by Tyrone and Rory O'Donel, embarked in May 1603, and sailed for Holyhead. But when they had sighted the coast of Wales, the pinnace was driven back by adverse winds, and nearly wrecked in a

* Page 30.

fog at the Skerries. They landed safe, however, at Beaumaris, whence they rode rapidly to Chester, where they stopped for the night, and were entertained by the mayor. The king's protection for the O'Neill was not uncalled for. Whenever he was recognised in city or hamlet, the populace, notwithstanding their respect for Mountjoy, the hero of the hour, pursued the earl with bitter insults, and stoned him as he passed along. Throughout the whole journey to London, the Welsh and English women assailed him with their invectives. Not unnaturally, for ' there was not one among them but could name some friend or kinsman whose bones lay buried far away in some wild pass or glen of Ulster, where the object of their maledictions was more often victor than vanquished.' * The king, however, gave the Irish chiefs a gracious reception, having issued a proclamation that he had restored them to his favour, and that they should be ' of all men honourably received.' This excited intense disgust amongst English officers who had been engaged in the Irish wars. Thus Sir John Harrington, writing to a bishop, said : ' I have lived to see that damnable rebel, Tyrone, brought to England, honoured and well liked. Oh, what is there that does not prove the inconstancy of worldly matters! How I did labour after that knave's destruction! I adventured perils by sea and land, was near starving, eat horseflesh in Munster, and all to quell that man, who now smileth in peace at those who did hazard their lives to destroy him ; and now doeth Tyrone dare us old commanders with his presence and protection.'

In fact the favour of the king went to an excess fatal to its object, by conceding powers incompatible with his own sovereignty, leading to disorders and violence, and exciting jealousy and mortal enmity in those who were charged with the government in Ireland. The lords of the Privy Council, with the king's consent, gave O'Neill authority for martial law, ' to be executed upon any offenders that shall live under him, the better to keep them in obedience.' It was ordered that the king's garrisons should not meddle

* Father Meehan.

with him or his people. The king also invested O'Donel with all the lands and rights of ancient time belonging to his house, excepting abbeys and other spiritual livings, the castle and town of Ballyshannon, and 1,000 acres adjoining the fishing there. He also received the style and title of Earl of Tyrconnel, with remainder to his brother Caffar, the heirs male apparent being created Barons of Donegal. He was formally installed in Christ Church Cathedral on the 29th of September following, in presence of Archbishop Loftus and a number of high officials. Tyrone, however, was dogged by spies while he was in London, and one Atkinson swore informations to the effect that he was in the habit of entertaining a Jesuit named Archer, who was intriguing with the foreign enemies of England, and who was held by Irish royalists for ' the most bloody and treacherous traitor, who could divert Tyrone and all the rest from the king, and thrust them again into actual rebellion.'

In the meantime, Sir George Carew was pursuing a policy in Ireland which must of necessity involve the north in fresh troubles. In his letters to England, he complained that the country ' so swarmed with priests, Jesuits, seminarists, friars, and Romish bishops, that if speedy means were not used to free the kingdom of this wicked rabble, which laboured to draw the subjects' hearts from their due obedience to their prince, much mischief would burst forth in very short time. For,' he said, ' there are here so many of this wicked crew, that are able to disquiet four of the greatest kingdoms in Christendom. It is high time they were banished from hence, and none to receive, or aid, or relieve them. Let the judges and officers be sworn to the supremacy; let the lawyers go to the church and show conformity, or not plead at the bar; and then the rest by degrees will shortly follow.'

Carew was succeeded as deputy by Sir Arthur Chichester, descended from a family of great antiquity in Devon. He had served in Ireland as governor of Carrickfergus, admiral of Lough Neagh, and commander of the Fort of Mountjoy.

Father Meehan describes him as malignant and cruel, with
a physiognomy repulsive and petrifying; a Puritan of
the most rigid character, utterly devoid of sympathy,
solely bent on his own aggrandisement, and seeking it
through the plunder and persecution of the Irish chieftains.
That is the Irish view of his character. How far he deserved it the reader will be able to judge by his acts. He
was evidently a man of strong will, an able administrator
and organiser ; and he set himself at once, and earnestly, to
the establishment of law and order in the conquered territories of the Irish princes. He sent justices of assize
throughout Munster and Connaught, reducing the ' countries or regions' into shire-ground, abolishing cuttings,
cosheries, spendings, and other customary exactions of the
chiefs, by which a complete revolution was effected. He
issued a proclamation, by the king's order, commanding all
the Catholics, under penalties, to assist at the Church of
England service ; proscribing priests, and other ecclesiastical persons ordained by authority from the see of Rome ;
forbidding parents to send their children to seminaries beyond the seas, or to keep as private tutors other than those
licensed by the Protestant archbishop or bishop. If any
priest dared to celebrate mass, he was liable to a fine of
200 marks, and a year's imprisonment ; while to join the
Romish Church was to become a traitor, and to be subject
to a like penalty. Churchwardens were to make a monthly
report of persons absent from church, and to whet the zeal
of wardens and constables, for each conviction of offending
parties, they were to have a reward of forty shillings, to be
levied out of the recusant's estate and goods. Catholics
might escape these penalties by quitting the country, and
taking the oath of abjuration, by which they bound themselves
to abjure the land and realm of James, King of England, Scotland, France, and Ireland, to hasten towards a certain port
by the most direct highway, to diligently seek a passage,
and tarry there but one flood and ebb. According to one
form, quoted by Mr. Meehan, the oath concluded thus:

' And, unless I can have it (a passage) in such a place, I will go every day into the sea up to my knees, essaying to pass over, so God me help and His holy judgment.'

The deputy found some difficulty in bending the consciences of the Dublin people to the will of the sovereign in matters of faith; but the said will was to be enforced *circa sacra* at all hazards; so he summoned sixteen of the chief citizens and aldermen before the Privy Council, and censured them for their recusancy, imprisoned them in the castle during pleasure, inflicting upon six a fine of 100*l.* each, and upon three 50*l.* each. The king was delighted with this evangelical method of extending reformed religion in Ireland. Congratulating his deputy, he expressed a hope that many, by such means, would be brought to conformity in religion, who would hereafter ' give thanks to God for being drawn by so gentle a constraint to their own good.' The ' gentle constraint ' was imposed in all directions. The Privy Council decreed that none but a member of the Church of England could hold any office under the Crown. The old Catholic families of the Pale humbly remonstrated, and their chief men were flung into prison. Sir Patrick Barnwell, their agent, was sent to London by order of the king, and was forthwith committed to the Tower for contempt. Henry Usher, then Archbishop of Armagh, carried out the system of exclusion in his own diocese, which included the territories of Tyrone. All ' Papists ' were forbidden to assist at mass, on pain of forfeiture of their goods and imprisonment. In a like manner, the Catholic worship was prohibited even in the residence of the Earl of Tyrconnel. He and Tyrone strongly remonstrated against this violation of the royal word, that they and their people might have liberty for their worship in private houses. The answer was decided. His majesty had made up his mind to disallow liberty of worship, and his people, whether they liked it or not, should repair to their parish churches.

In addition to this religious grievance, which excited the bitterest feelings of discontent, the two earls were subjected to the most irritating annoyances. They complained that their people were plundered by sheriffs, under-sheriffs, officers, and soldiers; and that even their domestic privacy was hourly violated, that their remonstrances were unheeded, and their attempts to obtain legal remedies were frustrated. At the same time their vassals were encouraged to repudiate their demands for tribute and rent. Bishop Montgomery of Derry was a dangerous neighbour to O'Neill. Meeting him one day at Dungannon, the earl said: ' My lord, you have two or three bishopricks, and yet you are not content with them, but seek the lands of my earldom.'

' My lord,' replied the bishop, ' your earldom is swollen so big with the lands of the Church, that it will burst if it be not vented.' If he had confined his venting operations to the chiefs, and abstained from bleeding the poor people, it would have been better for Protestantism. For we read that he sent bailiffs through the diocese of Raphoe, to levy contributions for the Church. ' For every cow and plough-horse, 4d.; as much out of every colt and calf, to be paid twice a year; and half-a-crown a quarter of every shoe-maker, carpenter, smith, and weaver in the whole country; and 8d. a year for every married couple.'

This bishop seems to have been greatly impressed with the ' commodities ' of O'Cahan's country, which he describes with much unction in a letter to the Earl of Salisbury. He said that the country was ' large, pleasant, and fruitful; twenty-four miles in length between Lough Foyle and the Bann; and in breadth, from the sea-coast towards the lower parts of Tyrone, 14 miles.' He states that O'Cahan was able to assist the Earl of Tyrone, during his war, with 1,200 foot and 300 horse, the ablest men that Ulster yielded; and, by the confession of gentlemen of the first plantation, had oftener put them to their defence than any enemy they had to do with, not suffering them to cut a bough or build a cabin without blows. When Tyrone was driven to his fastness, Glenconkeine, O'Cahan sent him 100 horse and 300 foot, and yet made good his own country against

the army lying round about him, adding, that his defection
' did undo the earl, who, as he had his country sure behind
him, cared little for anything the army could do to him.'
The bishop was, therefore, very anxious that Tyrone should
not have any estate in O'Cahan's country, ' since he was of
great power to offend or benefit the poor infant city of
Derry, its new bishop and people, cast out far from the
heart and head into the remotest part of Ireland, where life
would be unsafe until the whole region was well settled with
civil subjects. If this be not brought to pass, we may say :
" *fuimus Troes,—fuit Ilium.*" ' *

The defection of O'Cahan was, no doubt, a very serious
matter to O'Neill. Their case was referred for adjudication
to the lord deputy, Chichester, before whom they personally
pleaded. Their contradictory statements, and the eagerness
of each for the support of a ruler whom they regarded as a
common enemy, accounts for the facility with which their
power was ultimately destroyed. They at the same time
throw much light on the condition of Ulster before the confiscation of James I., proving that it was by no means so
poor and wild and barren a region as it is generally represented by modern writers. The two chiefs had a personal
altercation at the council table, and O'Neill so far lost his
temper as to snatch a paper out of the hand of O'Cahan.
Whereupon Sir John Davis remarked : ' I rest assured, in
my own conceit, that I shall live to see Ulster the best reformed province in this kingdom ; and as for yourself, my
lord, I hope to live to see you the best reformed subject in
Ireland.' To this the haughty chief replied with warmth,
that he hoped ' the attorney-general would never see the
day when injustice should be done him by transferring his
lands to the Crown, and thence to the bishop, who was
intent on converting the whole territory into his own
pocket.'

Acting under the advice of the bishop, O'Cahan employed
a skilful hand to draw up a statement of his case, which was

* Meeban, p. 79.

presented on May 2, 1607, in the form of 'the humble petition of Donald Ballagh O'Cahan, chief of his name,' addressed to the lord deputy and council. He declared that for 3,000 years and upwards, he and his ancestors had been possessed of a country called ' O'Cahan's country,' lying between the river Bann and Lough Foyle, without paying any rent, or other acknowledgment thereof to O'Neill, saving that his ancestors were wont to aid O'Neill twice a year if he had need, with risings of 100 horse and 300 foot, for which O'Cahan had in return O'Neill's whole suit of apparel, the horse that he rode upon, and 100 cows in winter. He also paid 21 cows every year in the name of *Cios'righ*, the king's rent, or the king's rent-cess. He alleged that Queen Elizabeth had granted him his country to be held immediately from her majesty at the accustomed rent, by virtue of which he enjoyed it for one whole year without paying, or being craved payment, of any rent or duty, until the Earl of Tyrone, on his return from England, alleged that he had got O'Cahan's country by patent, from the king, who had made him vassal to Tyrone and his heirs for ever, imposing the annual payment of 100 cows, with the yearly rent of 200*l.* He had also claimed the fishing of the Bann; he preyed yearly upon other parts of his country, and drew from him his best tenants. He therefore prayed for the protection of the lord deputy against these unjust demands and usurpations.

On the 23rd of the same month, O'Neill made a counter statement to the following effect: O'Cahan had no estate in the territory that was by a corruption of speech called O'Cahan's country; nor did he or any of his ancestors ever hold the said lands but as tenants at sufferance, servants and followers to the defendant and his ancestors. His grandfather Con O'Neill was seised in fee of those lands before he surrendered to Henry VIII., ' and received yearly, and had thereout, as much rents, cutting, spending and all other duties as of any other lands which he had in demesne,' within the province of Ulster and territory of Tyrone, and that after Con's surrender the territories were all re-granted with the rents, customs, duties, &c. as before. He was ready to prove that the ancestors of O'Cahan never enjoyed the premises at any time, but at the will and sufferance of O'Neill and his ancestors. A few days after, he despatched a memorial to the king setting forth his grievances, in which he stated that there were so many that sought to deprive him of the greatest part of the residue of his territory that without his majesty's special con-sideration he should in the end have nothing to support his ' estate ' or rank. For the Lord Bishop of Derry, not con-tent with the great living the king had bestowed upon him, sought to have the greater part of the earl's lands, to which none of his predecessors had ever laid claim. And he also set on others to question his titles which had never before before doubted. He therefore humbly besought the king to direct that new letters patent should be made out re-conveying to him and his heirs the lands in dispute, being, he said, ' such a favour as is appointed by your majesty to be extended to such of your subjects of this kingdom as should be suitors for the same, amongst whom I will during my life endeavour to deserve to be in the number of the most faithful, whereunto not only duty, but also your majesty's great bounty, hath ever obliged me.'

This was dated at Mellifont on May 26, 1607. It does not appear that any answer was received to his appeals to the king, nor is it likely that it served his cause, for it is seldom safe to appeal from an agent or deputy to the supreme authority. The Privy Council in Dublin, how-ever, made a report confirming to some extent the claims put forth by Tyrone. A jury had been appointed to inquire into the boundaries and limits of the lands granted by Queen Elizabeth, and they found that they extended from the river Fuin to Lough Foyle, and from Lough Foyle by the sea-shore to the Bann, and thence to the east of Lough Neagh. Within these limits they found that there existed the territory called O'Cahan's, Glenconkeine and Killetragh, which were not the lands of the O'Neills, *' but held by tenants having estates in them equivalent to estates of freehold.'* The jury could not determine what rents the tenants of said lands were accustomed to pay, but they found generally that all lands within the limits of Tyrone, except the lands of the church, rendered to O'Neill bonnaght or free quarters for armed retainers, 'rising out, cutting and spending.' The parties, however, did not abide by the decision of the privy council, but kept up their contention in the courts of law. It was quite clear that matters could not remain long in that unsettled state, with so many adventurers thirsting for the possession of land, which was lying comparatively idle. It was thought desirable to appoint a president of Ulster, as there had been a president of Munster. The Earl of Tyrone applied to the king for the office, evidently fearing that if Chichester were appointed, he must share the fate of the Earl of Desmond. On the other hand, it was felt that with his hereditary pretensions, impracticable temper, and vast influence with the people, it would be impossible to establish the English power on a permanent basis until he was got out of the way. This was not difficult, with unprincipled adventurers who were watching for opportunities to make their fortunes in those revolutionary times. Among these was a person named St. Lawrence, Baron of Howth. This man worked cunningly on the mind of the lord deputy, insinuating that O'Neill was plotting treason and preparing for a Spanish invasion. He even went so far as to write an anonymous letter, revealing an alleged plot of O'Neill's to assassinate the lord deputy. It was addressed to Sir William Usher, clerk of the council, and the writer began by saying that it would show him, though far severed from him in religion, how near he came home to him in honesty. He was a Catholic, and professed to reveal what he had heard among Catholic gentlemen, 'after the strictest conditions of secresy.' The conspirators were, in the first place, to murder or poison the lord deputy when he came to Drogheda, 'a place thought apt and secure to act the same.' They thought it well to begin with him, because his authority, wisdom, and valour stood only in the way of their first attempts. Next after him they were to cut off Sir Oliver Lambert, whom for his own judgment in the wars, his sudden resolution, and undertaking spirit, they would not suffer to live. These two lights thus put out, they would neither fear nor value any opposite in the kingdom. The small dispersed garrisons must either through hunger submit themselves to their mercy, or be penned up as sheep to the shambles. They held the castle of Dublin for their own, neither manned nor victualled, and readily surprised. The towns were for them, the country with them, the great ones abroad prepared to answer the first alarm. The Jesuits warranted from the Pope and the Catholic king would do their parts effectually, and Spanish succours would not be wanting. These secrets greatly troubled the sensitive conscience of Lord Howth. From the time he was entrusted with them, he said, ' till I resolved to give you this caveat, my eyelids never closed, my heart was a fire, my soul suffered a thousand thousand torments ; yet I could not, nor cannot persuade my conscience, in honesty, to betray my friends, or spill their bloods, when this timely warning may prevent the mischief.' In conclusion, he said, ' though I reverence the mass and the Catholic religion equal with the devoutest of them, I will make the leaders of this dance know that I prefer my country's good before their busy and ambitious humours.' It is related of this twenty-second baron of Howth, known as Sir Christopher St. Lawrence, that having served in Ulster under Essex, and accompanied him in his flight to England, he proposed to murder Lord Grey de Wilton, lest he should prejudice the queen's mind against her former favourite, if he got access to her presence before him ; that he had commanded a regiment of infantry under Mountjoy, and that when that regiment was disbanded, he became discontented, not having got either pension or employment ; that having gone as a free lance to the Low Countries, and failed to advance

himself there as he expected, through the interest of Irish
ecclesiastics, he returned to England, and skulked about
the ante-chambers of Lord Salisbury, waiting upon Providence, when he hit upon the happy idea of the revelations
which he conveyed under the signature of ' A. B.' *

After some time he acknowledged the authorship of the
letter privately, but refused to come forth publicly as an
informer, nor was he able to produce any corroboration of
the improbable story.   Ultimately, however, when pressed
by Chichester, he induced his friend Baron Devlin to swear
an information to the same effect, revealing certain alleged
conversations of O'Neill.   In the meantime St. Lawrence
cunningly worked upon the fears of the earl, giving him to
understand that his ruin was determined on, and that he
had better consult his safety, by leaving the country.   It
appears that he received intimations to the same effect from
his correspondents in Spain and in London.   At all events,
he lost heart, became silent, moody, and low-spirited, suspecting foul play on the part of the king, who was very
urgent that he should be brought over to London, in which
case Tyrone was led to believe that he would certainly be
sent to the Tower, and probably lose his head.   With such
apprehensions, he came to the conclusion that it was idle to
struggle any longer against the stream.

He had for some weeks been engaged quietly making
preparations for his flight.   He had given directions to his
steward to collect in advance one half of his Michaelmas
rents, leading the lord deputy to think that he did so either
to provide funds for his journey to London, or to defray the
expenses of his son's projected marriage with the daughter
of Lord Argyle.   Meanwhile a vessel had been purchased
by Cu-Connaught Maguire, and Bath, the captain of this
vessel, assured the Earl of Tyrconnel, whom he met at Ballyshannon, that he also would lose his life or liberty if he
did not abandon the country with O'Neill.   On September 8,
Tyrone took leave of the lord deputy, and then spent a

* Meehan, p. 103.

day and night at Mellifont with his friend Sir Garret
Moore, who was specially dear to him as the fosterer of his
son John. The earl took his leave with unusual emotion,
and after giving his blessing according to the Irish fashion
to every member of his friend's household, he and his suite
took horse and rode rapidly by Dundalk, over the Fews to
Armagh, where he rested a few hours, and then proceeded
to Creeve, one of his crannoges or island habitations, where
he was joined by his wife and other members of his family.
Sir Oliver Lambert in a communication to the Irish Government, relating to the affairs of Ulster, made some interesting allusions to O'Neill. He states that he had apologised
for having appealed to the king in the case between him and
O'Cahan, and said that he felt much grieved in being called
upon so suddenly to go to England, when on account of
his poverty he was not able to furnish himself as became
him for such a journey and for such a presence. In all
things else, said Sir Oliver, ' he seemed very moderate and
reasonable, albeit he never gave over to be a general solicitor in all causes concerning his country and people however criminal.' He thought the earl had been much abused
by persons who had cunningly terrified, and diverted him
from going to the king; ' or else he had within him a thousand witnesses testifying that he was as deeply engaged in
these secret treasons as any of the rest, whom they knew or
suspected.' At all events he had received information on
the previous day from his own brother Sir Cormac O'Neill,
from the primate, from Sir Toby Caulfield and others, that
the earl had taken shipping with his lady, the Baron of Dungannon, his eldest son, and two others of his children, John
and Brien, both under seven years old, the Earl of Tyrconnel,
and his son and heir, an infant, not yet a year old, his brother Caffar O'Donel, and his son an infant two years old.
' with divers others of their nearest and trusted followers
and servants, as well men as women, to the number of between thirty and forty persons.'

The Rev. Mr. Meehan gives graphic details of the flight

of his two heroes. Arrived at Rathmullen they found Maguire and Captain Bath laying stores of provisions on board the ship that had come into Lough Swilly under French colours. Here they were joined by Rory, Earl of Tyrconnel. At noon on Friday they all went on board and lifted anchor, but kept close to the shore waiting for the boats' crews, who were procuring water and fuel; but they had to wait till long after sunset, when the boats came with only a small quantity of wood and water. According to a fatality which makes one Irishman's extremity another Irishman's opportunity, the foraging party was set upon by M'Sweeny of Fanad, who churlishly prevented them getting a sufficient supply of these necessaries. This barbarous conduct is accounted for by Mr. Meehan, from the fact, that this M'Sweeny had recently taken a grant of his lands from the crown. At midnight, September 14, 1607, they spread all sail and made for the open sea, intending, however, to land on the Island of Arran, off the coast of Donegal, to provide themselves with more water and fuel. The entire number of souls on board this small vessel, says O'Keenan in his narrative, was ninety-nine, having little sea store, and being otherwise miserably accommodated. Unable to make the island of Arran, owing to a gale then blowing off the land, and fearing to be crossed by the king's cruisers, they steered for the harbour of Corunna in Spain. But for thirteen days, continues O'Keenan, ' the sea was angry, and the tempest left us no rest; and the only brief interval of calm we enjoyed, was when O'Neill took from his neck a golden crucifix containing a relic of the true cross, and trailed it in the wake of the ship. At that moment, two poor merlins with wearied pinions sought refuge in the rigging of our vessel, and were captured for the noble ladies, who nursed them with tenderest affection.' After being tempest-tossed for three weeks, they dropped anchor in the harbour of Quillebœuf in France, having narrowly escaped shipwreck, their only remaining provisions being one gallon of beer and a cask of water.

They proceeded to Brussels and thence to Louvain, where splendid accommodation was provided for them. In several of the cities through which they passed they received ovations, their countrymen clerical and military having prepared for their reception with the greatest zeal and devotion. The King of Spain was of course friendly, but to avoid giving offence to King James he discouraged the stay of the exiles in his dominions, and they found their final resting-place at Rome, where the two earls were placed upon the Pope's civil list, which, however, they did not long continue to burden. Tyrconnel fell a victim to the malaria, and died on July 28, 1608. ' Sorrowful it was,' say the Four Masters, ' to contemplate his early eclipse, for he was a generous and hospitable lord, to whom the patrimony of his ancestors seemed nothing for his feastings and spending.' His widow received a pension of 300*l.* a year out of his forfeited estates. O'Neill survived his brother earl eight years, having made various attempts to induce the King of Spain to aid him in the recovery of his patrimony. He died in 1616, in the seventy-sixth year of his age. Sir Francis Cottington, announcing the event from Madrid, said, ' The Earl of Tyrone is dead at Rome; by whose death this king saves 500 ducats every month, for so much pension he had from here, well paid him. Upon the news of his death, I observed that all the principal Irish entertained in several parts of this kingdom are repaired unto this court.'

CHAPTER VII.

GOVERNMENT APPEALS TO THE PEOPLE.

THE flight of the earls caused great consternation to the Irish Government. Letters were immediately despatched to the local authorities at every port to have a sharp look out for the fugitives, and to send out vessels to intercept them, should they be driven back by bad weather to any part of the coast. At the same time the lord deputy sent a despatch to the Government in London, deprecating censure for an occurrence so unexpected, and so much to be regretted, because of the possibility of its leading to an invasion by the Spaniards. In other respects it was regarded by the principal members of the Irish Government, and especially by the officials in Ulster, as a most fortunate occurrence. For example, Sir Oliver Lambert, in his report to the lords of the council, already referred to, said:—' But now these things are fallen out thus, contrary to all expectation or likelihood, by the providence of God I hope, over this miserable people, for whose sake it may be he hath sent his majesty this rare and unlooked for occasion : whereby he may now at length, with good apprehension and prudent handling, repair an error which was committed in making these men proprietary lords of so large a territory, without regard of the poor freeholders' rights, or of his majesty's service, and the commonwealth's, that are so much interested in the honest liberty of that sort of men, which now, in time, I commend unto your lordships' grave consideration and wisdom, and will come to that which nearest concerns ourselves and the whole.'

According to Sir John Davis, in his letter to the first minister, Lord Salisbury, Tyrone could not be reconciled in his heart to the English Government, because 'he ever lived like a free prince, or, rather, like an absolute tyrant, there. The law of England, and the ministers thereof, were shackles and handlocks unto him.' He states that *after the Irish manner*, he made all the tenants of his land *villeins.* 'Therefore to evict any part of that land from him was as grievous unto him as to pinch away the quick flesh from his body. . . Besides,' the attorney-general added, 'as for us that are here, we are glad to see the day wherein the countenance and majesty of the law, as civil government, hath banished Tyrone out of Ireland, which the best army in Europe, and the expense of two millions of sterling pounds did not bring to pass. And we hope his majesty's happy government will work a greater miracle in this kingdom, than ever St. Patrick did; for St. Patrick did only banish the poisonous worms, but suffered the men full of poison to inhabit the land still; but his majesty's blessed genius will banish all that generation of vipers out of it, and make it, ere it be long, a right fortunate island.'

Again, Sir Geoffry Fenton, writing to Salisbury on the same subject, says, 'And now I am to put your lordship in mind what a door is open to the king, if the opportunity be taken, and well converted, not only to pull down for ever these two proud houses of O'Neill and O'Donel, but also to bring in colonies to plant both countries, to a great increasing of his majesty's revenues, and to establish and settle the countries perpetually in the crown; besides that many well-deserving servitors may be recompensed in the distribution; a matter to be taken to heart, for that it reaches somewhat to his majesty's conscience and honour to see these poor servitors relieved, whom time and the wars have spent, even unto their later years, and now, by this commodity, may be stayed and comforted without charges to his majesty.'

This advice was quite in accordance with the views of the prime minister, who in a letter to Chichester said, 'I do think it of great necessity that those countries be made the king's by this accident; that there be a mixture in the plantation, the *natives* made his majesty's tenants of part, but the rest to be divided among those that will *inhabit*; and in no case any man is suffered to embrace more than is visible he can and will *manure*. That was an oversight in the plantation of Munster, where 12,000 acres were commonly allotted to bankrupts and country gentlemen, that never knew the disposition of the Irish; so as God forbid that those who have spent their blood in the service should not of all others be preferred.' It was because this idea of manuring, i.e. residence and cultivation, was carried out in Ulster, that the plantation has proved so successful. But Davis would allow but small space comparatively to the natives, whom he compared to weeds which, if too numerous, would choke the wheat. With him the old inhabitants were simply a nuisance from the highest to the lowest; and if there were no other way of getting rid of them, he would no doubt have adopted the plan recommended by Lord Bacon, who said, ' Some of the chiefest of the Irish families should be transported to England, and have recompense there for their possessions in Ireland, till they were cleansed from their blood, incontinency, and theft, which were not the lapses of particular persons, but the very laws of the nation.' The Lord Deputy Chichester, however, agreed thoroughly with his attorney-general, for he certainly made no more account of rooting out the ' mere Irish ' from their homes than if they were the most noxious kinds of weeds or vermin. ' If,' said he, writing to Lord Salisbury, ' I have observed anything during my stay in this kingdom, I may say it is not *lenity* and good works that will reclaim the Irish, but *an iron rod*, and severity of justice, for the restraint and punishment of those firebrands of sedition, *the priests*; nor can we think of any other remedy but to proclaim *them, and their relievers and harbourers, traitors.*'

Considering that those Englishmen were professedly Christian rulers, engaged in establishing the reformed religion, the accounts which they give with perfect coolness of their operations in this line, are among the most appalling passages to be met with in the world's history. For instance, the lord deputy writes: ' I have often said and written, it is *famine that must consume the Irish*, as our *swords* and other endeavours worked not that speedy effect which is expected; *hunger* would be a better, because a speedier, weapon to employ against them than the sword.' He spared no means of destruction, but combined all the most fearful scourges for the purpose of putting out of existence the race of people whom God in his anger subjected to his power. Surely the spirit of cruelty, the genius of destruction, must have been incarnate in the man who wrote thus: ' I burned all along the Lough (Neagh) within four miles of Dungannon, and killed 100 people, sparing none, of what quality, age, or sex soever, besides *many burned to death*. We killed man, *woman and child*, horse, beast, and whatsoever we could find.'

At the time of the flight of the earls, however, he was very anxious about the safety of the kingdom. He was aware that the people were universally discontented, he had but few troops in the country, and little or no money in the treasury, so that in case of a sudden invasion, it was quite possible that the maddened population would rise and act in their own way upon his own merciless policy of extermination. He therefore hastened to issue a proclamation for the purpose of reassuring the inhabitants of Ulster, and persuading them that they would not suffer in any way by the desertion of their chiefs. In this proclamation, headed by 'The *Lord Deputy and Counsell*,' it was stated that Tyrone and Tyrconnel and their companions had lately embarked themselves at Lough Swilly and had secretly and suddenly departed out of this realm without license or notice. The Government was as yet uncertain about their purpose or destination. But inasmuch as the manner of their departure, considering the quality of their persons, might raise many doubts in the minds of his majesty's loving subjects in those parts, and especially the common sort of people inhabiting the counties of Tyrone and Tyrconnel, who might suppose they were in danger to suffer prejudice in their *lands* and goods for the contempt or offence of the earls, —they were solemnly assured that they had nothing whatever to fear. The words of the proclamation on this point are : ' We do therefore in his majesty's name declare, proclaim, and publish that all and every his majesty's good and loyal subjects inhabiting those countries of Tyrone and Tyrconnel shall and may quietly and securely possess and enjoy all and singular *their lands and goods* without the trouble or molestation of any of his majesty's officers or ministers or any other person or persons whatsoever as long as they disturb not his majesty's peace, but live as dutiful and obedient subjects. And forasmuch as the said earls to whom his majesty, reposing special trust in their loyalty, had committed the government of the said several countries are now undutifully departed, therefore his Majesty doth graciously receive all and every of his said loyal subjects into his own immediate safeguard and protection, giving them full assurance to defend them and every of them by his kingly power from all violence or wrong, which any loose persons among themselves or any foreign force shall attempt against them. And to that end, we the lord deputy and council have made choice of certain commissioners as well Irish as English, residing in the said several countries, not only to preserve the public peace there, but also to administer speedy and indifferent justice to all his majesty's loving subjects in those parts, which shall have any cause of complaint before them.' All governors, mayors, sheriffs, justices of peace, provost-marshals, bailiffs, constables, and all other his majesty's ministers whatsoever were strictly charged to use their utmost endeavours faithfully and diligently to keep the people in their duty and obedience to his majesty and the laws of the realm.

The assurance thus given that the subjects and tenants of the absconding princes should securely possess and enjoy their lands and be protected from all oppression under the sceptre of King James would have been very satisfactory had the royal promise been realised, but conciliation was then absolutely necessary, for the lord deputy himself stated that ' the kingdom had not been in the like danger these hundred years, as we have but few friends and no means of getting more.' The foregoing proclamation was issued from Rathfarnham on September 10. On November 9 following, another proclamation of a general nature was published and widely circulated in order to justify the course the Government adopted. According to this document it was known to all the world ' how infinitely ' the fugitive earls had been obliged to the king for his singular grace and mercy in giving them free pardon for many heinous and execrable treasons, above all hope that they could in reason conceive, and also in restoring the one to his lands and honours justly forfeited, and in raising the other ' from a very mean estate to the degree and title of an earl, giving him withal large possessions for the support of that honour, before either of them had given any proof of loyalty, or merited the least favour.' Even in the point of religion, which served as a cloak for all their treasons, they got no provocation or cause of grievance. For these and other causes it was announced that his majesty would seize and take into his hands all the lands and goods of the said fugitives. But he would, notwithstanding, extend such grace and favour to the loyal inhabitants of their territories that none of them should be ' impeached, troubled, or molested in *their own lands,* goods, or bodies, they continuing in their loyalty, *and yielding unto his majesty such rents and duties as shall be agreeable to justice and equity.*' This assurance was repeated again emphatically in these words : ' His most excellent majesty doth take all the good and loyal inhabitants of the said countries, together with their wives and children, land and goods, into his own immediate protection, to defend them in general against all rebellions and invasions, and to right them in all their wrongs and oppressions, offered or to be offered unto them by any person whatsoever, &c.'

CHAPTER VIII.

THE CASE OF THE FUGITIVE EARLS.

BEFORE proceeding to notice the manner in which these promises of justice, equity, and protection to the occupiers of the land were fulfilled, it is well to record here the efforts made by King James and his ambassador to discredit the fugitive earls on the Continent, and the case which they made out for themselves in the statement of wrongs and grievances which they addressed to the king soon after. There was great alarm in England when news arrived of the friendly reception accorded to the Irish chiefs by the continental sovereigns through whose dominions they passed, and especially by the King of Spain, who was suspected of intending another invasion of Ireland. Consequently the most active preparations were made to meet the danger. In every street of the metropolis drums were beating for recruits, and large detachments were sent in all possible haste to reinforce the Irish garrisons. Sir Charles Cornwallis was then English ambassador at Madrid; and lest his diplomatic skill should not be up to the mark, James himself sent him special and minute instructions as to the manner in which he should handle the delicate subjects he had to bring before the Spanish sovereign. There has been seldom a better illustration of the saying, that the use of speech is to conceal thought, than in the representations which the ambassador was instructed to make about Irish affairs. Indeed Cornwallis had already shown that he scarcely needed to be tutored by his sovereign. In a preliminary despatch he had sent an account of his conversation with Philip III.'s secretary of state about the fugitive earls. He told him that though they had been guilty of rebellions and treasons they had not only been pardoned, but loaded with dignities such as few or none of the king's ancestors had ever bestowed on any of the Irish nation. He had conferred upon them an absolute and, 'in a manner, unlimited government in their own countries, nothing wanting to their ambitions but the name of kings, and neither crossed in anything concerning their civil government, nor so much as in act or imagination molested, or in any sort questioned with, for their consciences and religion.' He thought therefore that they would never have fled in such a way, unless they had been drawn to Spain by large promises in the hope of serving some future turns.

The secretary listened to this insinuation with much impatience, and declared solemnly, laying his hand on his breast with an oath, that of the departure and intention of the earls there was no more knowledge given to the king or any of his state than to the ambassador himself. He added that there had been much consumption of Spanish treasure by supporting strangers who had come from all parts. In particular they had a bitter taste of those who had come from James's dominions; and they would have suffered much more, 'if they had not made a resolute and determined stop to the running of that fountain and refused to give ear to many overtures.' The ambassador expressed his satisfaction at this assurance, and then endeavoured to show how unworthy those Irish princes were of the least encouragement. Their flight was the result of madness, they departed without any occasion of 'earthly distaste' or offence given them by their sovereign, whose position towards the Irish was very different from that of the late queen. Elizabeth had employed against their revolts and rebellions only her own subjects of England, who were not accustomed either to the diet of that savage country, or to the bogs, and other retreats which that wild people used. But now, the king his master, being possessed of Scotland, had in that country, 'near adjoining to the north part of Ireland, a people of their own fashion, diet, and disposition, that could walk their bogs as well as themselves, live with their food, and were so well practised and accustomed in their own country to the like, that they were as apt to pull them out of their dens and withdrawing places, as ferrets to draw rabbits out of their burrows.' Moreover all other parts of Ireland were now reduced to such obedience, and so civil a course, and so well planted with a mixture of English, that there was not a man that showed a forehead likely to give a frown against his majesty, or his government. Cornwallis went on to plead the incomparable virtues of the king his master, among which liberality and magnificence were not the least. But if he had given largely, it was upon a good exchange, for he had sowed money, which of itself can do nothing, and had reaped hearts that can do all. As for the alleged number of 'groaning Catholics,' he assured the secretary that there were hardly as many hundreds as the fugitives reckoned thousands.

According to his report the minister heard him with great attention, and at the conclusion protested, that he joined with him in opinion that those fugitives were dangerous people and that the Jesuits were turbulent and busy men. He assured him on the word of a caballero, that his majesty and council had fully determined never to receive or treat any more of those 'straying people;' as they had been put to great inconvenience and cost, how to deliver themselves from those Irish vagabonds, and continual begging pretenders.

This despatch, dated October 28, 1607, was crossed on the way by one from the English minister Salisbury, dated the 27th, giving the king's instructions 'concerning those men that are fled into Spain.' Cornwallis was directed not to make matters worse than they really were, because the end must be good, 'what insolencies soever the Jesuits and pack of fugitives there might put on. King James knew that this remnant of the northern Irish traitors had been as full of malice as flesh and blcod could be, no way reformed by the grace received, but rather sucking poison out of the honey thereof.' He knew also that they had absolutely given commission to their priests and others to abandon their sovereign if Spain would entertain their cause. But this he could not demonstrably prove *in foro judicii*, though clear *in foro conscientiæ*, and therefore punishment would savour of rigour. So long as things were in that state his majesty was obliged to suffer adders in his bosom, and give them means to gather strength to his own prejudice, whereas now the whole country which they had possessed would be made of great use both for strength and profit to the king. What follows should be given in his majesty's own words :—

'Those poor creatures who knew no kings but those petty lords, under the burden of whose tyranny they have ever groaned, do now with great applause desire to be protected by the immediate power, and to receive correction only from himself, so as if the council of Spain shall conceive that they have now some great advantage over this state, where it shall appear what a party their king may have if he shall like to support it, there may be this answer : that those Irish without the King of Spain are poor worms upon earth ; and that when the King of Spain shall think it time to begin with Ireland, the king my master is more like than Queen Elizabeth was, to find a wholesomer place of the King of Spain's, where he would be loath to hear of the English, and to show the Spaniards who shall be sent into Ireland as fair a way as they were taught before. In which time the more you speak of the base, insulting, discoursing fugitives, the more proper it will be for you. In the meantime upon their departure, not a man hath moved, neither was there these thirty years more universal obedience than there is now. Amongst the rest of their barbarous lies I doubt not but they will pretend protection for religion, and breach of promise with them; wherein you may safely protest this, that for any, of all those that are gone, there never was so much as an offer made to search their consciences.'

Not content with the labours of his ambassadors at the various continental courts, to damage the cause of the Irish earls, the king issued a proclamation, which was widely dispersed abroad. His majesty said he thought it better to clear men's judgments concerning the fugitives, ' not in respect of any worth or value in these men's persons, being base and rude in their original,' but to prevent any breach of friendship with other princes. For this purpose he declared that Tyrone and Tyrconnel had not their creation or possessions in regard of any lineal or lawful descent from ancestors of blood or virtue, but were only conferred by the late queen and himself for some reasons of state. Therefore, he judged it needless to seek for many arguments ' to confirm whatsoever should be said of these men's corruption and falsehood, whose heinous offences remained so fresh in memory since they declared themselves so very monsters in nature, as they did not only withdraw themselves from their personal obedience to their sovereign, but were content to sell over their native country, to those who stood at that time in the highest terms of hostility with the crowns of England and Ireland.' ' Yet,' adds the king, ' to make the absurdity and ingratitude of the allegation above mentioned so much the more clear to all men of equal judgment, we do hereby profess in word of a king that there was never so much as any shadow of molestation, nor purpose of proceeding in any degree against them for matter concerning religion :—such being their condition and profession, to think murder no fault, marriage of no use, nor any man worthy to be esteemed valiant that did not glory in rapine and oppression, as we should have thought it an unreasonable thing to trouble them for any different point in religion, before any man could perceive by their conversation that they made truly conscience of any religion. The king thought these declarations sufficient to disperse and to discredit all such untruths as these contemptible creatures, so full of infidelity and ingratitude, should discharge against him and his just and moderate proceedings, and which should procure unto them no better usage than they would wish should be afforded to any such pack of rebels born their subjects and bound unto them in so many and so great obligations.'

Such was the case of the English Government presented to the world by the king and his ministers. Let us now hear what the personages so heartily reviled by them had to say for themselves. The Rev. C. P. Meehan has brought to light the categorical narratives, which the earls dictated, and which had lain unpublished among the ' old historic rolls,' in the Public Record Office, London. These documents are of great historic interest, as are many other state-papers now first published in his valuable work.* O'Neill's defence is headed, ' Articles Exhibited by the Earl of Tyrone to the King's Most Excellent Majesty, declaring certain Causes of Discontent offered Him, by which he took occasion to Depart His Country.' The statement is divided into twenty items, of which the following is the substance : It was proclaimed by public authority in his manor of Dungannon, that none should hear mass upon pain of losing his goods and imprisonment, and that no ecclesiastical person should enjoy any cure or dignity without swearing the oath of supremacy and embracing the contrary religion, and those who refused so to do were actually deprived of their benefices and dignities, in proof of which the earl referred to the lord ·deputy's answer to his own petition, and to the Lord Primate of Ireland, who put the persecuting decree into execution. The Earl of Devon, then lord-lieutenant, had taken from him the lands of his ancestors called the Fews, in Armagh, and given them to other persons. He was deprived of the annual tribute of sixty cows from Sir Cahir O'Dogherty's country called Inishowen, which tribute had never been brought into question till James's reign. The same lord-lieutenant had taken from him the fishings of the Bann, which always belonged to his ancestors, and which he was forced to purchase again. Portions of his territory had been taken ' under colour of church-lands, a thing never in any man's memory heard of before.' One

* Page 192.

Robert Leicester an attorney had got some more of the earl's land, which he transferred to Captain Leigh. 'So as any captain or clerk had wanted means, and had no other means or device to live, might bring the earl in trouble for some part or parcel of his living, falsely inventing the same, to be concealed or church-land.' The Archbishop of Armagh and the Bishop of Derry and Clogher claimed the best part of the earl's whole estate, as appertaining to their bishoprics, 'which was never moved by any other predecessors before, other than that they had some *chiefry* due to them, in most part of all his living, and would now have the whole land to themselves as their domain lands, not content with the benefit of their ancient registers, which the earl always offered, and was willing to give without further question. O'Cahan, ' one of the chiefest and principalest of the earl's tenants, was set upon by certain of his majesty's privy council, as also by his highness's counsel-at-law, to withdraw himself and the lands called *Iraght-I-Cahan* from the earl, being a great substance of his living;' and this although O'Cahan had no right to the property except as his *tenant at will,* yielding and paying all such rents, dues, and reservations as the other tenants did. He complained that at the council table in Dublin it was determined to take two-thirds of O'Cahan's country from him; and he perceived by what Sir John Davis said, that they had determined to take the other third also. They further made claim in his majesty's behalf to four other parcels of the earl's land, which he named, being the substance of all that was left, and began their suit for the same in the court of exchequer. In fine he felt that he could not assure himself of anything by the letters patent he had from the king. Whenever he had recourse to law his proceedings were frustrated by the government; so that he could not get the benefit of his majesty's laws, or the possession of his lands ; ' and yet any man, of what degree soever, obtained the extremity of the law with favour against him, in any suit.' Although the king had allowed him to be lieutenant of his country, yet he had no more command there than his boy; the worst man that belonged to the sheriff could command more than he, and that even in the earl's own house. If they wanted to arrest any one in the house they would not wait till he came out, but burst open the doors, and ' never do the earl so much honour in any respect as once to acquaint him therewith, or to send to himself for the party, though he had been within the house when they would attempt these things; and if any of the earl's officers would by his direction order or execute any matter betwixt his own tenants, with their own mutual consent, they would be driven not only to restore the same again, but also be first amerced by the sheriff, and after indicated as felons, and so brought to trial for their lives for the same; so as the earl in the end could scarce get any of his servants that would undertake to levy his rents.' According to law the sheriff should be a resident in the county, have property there, and be elected by the nobility and chief gentlemen belonging to it; but the law was set aside by the lord deputy, who appointed as sheriffs for the counties Tyrone and Armagh Captain Edmund Leigh and one Marmaduke Whitechurch, dwelling in the county of Louth, both being retainers, and very dear friends to the Knight-marshal Bagenal, who was the only man that urged the earl to his last troubles. Of all these things ' the earl did eftsoons complain to the lord deputy, and could get no redress, but did rather fare the worse for his complaints, in respect they were so little regarded.'

The earl understanding that earnest suit had been made to his majesty for the presidentship of Ulster, made bold to write to the king, humbly beseeching him not to grant any such office to any person over himself, ' suspecting it would be his overthrow, as by plain experience he knew the like office to be the utter overthrow of others of his rank in other provinces within the realm of Ireland.' He also wrote to the Earl of Salisbury, who replied that the earl was not to tie his majesty to place or displace officers at his (the earl's) pleasure in any of his majesty's kingdoms.

This was not the earl's meaning, but it indicated to him pretty plainly that he had no favour to expect from that quarter. The office was intended for Sir Arthur Chichester, and he much feared that it would be used for his destruction without his majesty's privity. Therefore, seeing himself envied by those who should be his protectors, considering the misery sustained by others through the oppression of the like government, he resolved to sacrifice all rather than live under that yoke.

The next item is very characteristic. The earl's nephew Brian M'Art happened to be in the house of Turlough M'Henry, having two men in his company. Being in a merry humour, some dispute arose between him and a kinsman of his own, who 'gave the earl's nephew a blow of a club on the head, and tumbled him to the ground; whereupon, one of his men standing by and seeing his master down, did step up with the fellow and gave him some three or four stabs of a knife, having no other weapon, and the master himself, as it was said, gave him another, through which means the man came to his death. Thereupon, the earl's nephew and his two men were taken and kept in prison till the next sessions holden in the county Armagh, where his men were tried by a jury of four innocent and mere ignorant people, having little or no substance, most of them being bare soldiers and not fit, as well by the institution of law in matters of that kind as also through their own insufficiency, to be permitted or elected to the like charge; and the rest foster-brethren, followers, and very dear friends to the party slain, that would not spare to spend their lives and goods to revenge his death. Yet all that notwithstanding were they allowed, and the trial of these two gentlemen committed to them, through which means, and the vigorous threatening and earnest enticements of the judges, they most shamefully condemned to die, and the jury in a manner forced to find the matter murder in each of them, and that, not so much for their own offences, as thinking to make it an evidence against the master, who was in prison in the

Castle of Dublin, attending to be tried the last Michaelmas term, whose death, were it right or wrong, was much desired by the lord deputy.

Again, the earl had given his daughter in marriage to O'Cahan with a portion of goods. After they had lived together for eight years, O'Cahan was induced to withdraw himself from the earl, and at the same time, by the procurement of his setters on, he turned off the earl's daughter, kept her fortune to himself, and married another. The father appealed to the lord deputy for justice in vain. He then took proceedings against O'Cahan, at the assizes in Dungannon. But the defendant produced a warrant from the lord deputy, forbidding the judges to entertain the question, as it was one for the Lord Bishop of Derry. The Bishop of Derry, however, was the chief instigator of the divorce, and therefore no indifferent judge in the case. Thus the earl's cause was frustrated, and he could get no manner of justice therein, no more than he obtained in many other weighty matters that concerned him. The next complaint is about outrages committed by one Henry Oge O'Neill, one Henry M'Felemey and others, who at the instigation of the lord deputy, 'farther to trouble the earl,' went out as a wood-kerne to rob and spoil the earl and his nephew, and their tenants. They committed many murders, burnings, and other mischievous acts, and were always maintained and manifestly relieved amongst the deputy's tenants and their friends in Clandeboye, to whom they openly sold the spoils. They went on so for the space of two years, and the earl could get no justice, till at length they murdered one of the deputy's own tenants. Then he saw them prosecuted, and the result was, that the earl cut them all off within a quarter of a year after. But the lord deputy was not at all pleased with this. Therefore he picked up ' a poor rascally knave ' and brought him to Dublin, where he persuaded him to accuse above threescore of the earl's tenants of relieving rebels with meat, although it was taken from them by force. For the rebels killed their cattle in the fields, and left them dead there, not being able to carry them away; burnt their houses, took what they could of their household stuff, killed and mangled themselves. 'Yet were they, upon report of that poor knave, who was himself foremost in doing these mischiefs, all taken and brought to their trial by law, where they were, through their innocency, acquitted, to their no small cost; so as betwixt the professed enemy, and the private envy of our governors, seeking thereby to advance themselves, there was no way left for the poor subject to live.'

One Joice Geverard, a Dutchman, belonging to the deputy, was taken prisoner on his way from Carrickfergus to Toome, and he was compelled to pay to his captors a ransom of 30*l.* For this the lord deputy assessed 60*l.* on the county, and appointed one-half of it to be taken from O'Neil's tenants, being of another county, and at least twelve miles distant from the scene of the outrage, perpetrated by a wood-kerne, 'and themselves being daily killed and spoiled by the said wood-kerne, and never no redress had to them.' Several outrages and murders perpetrated by the soldiers are enumerated; but they were such as might have been expected in a state bordering on civil war, which was then the condition of the province. If, however, Tyrone is to be believed, the rulers themselves set the example of disorder. Sir Henry Folliott, governor of Ballyshannon, in the second year of his majesty's reign, came with force of arms, and drove away 200 cows from the earl's tenants, 'and killed a good gentleman, with many other poor men, women, and children; and besides that, there died of them above 100 persons with very famine, for want of their goods; whereof the earl never had redress, although the said Sir Henry could show no reasonable cause for doing the same.'

Finally the earl saw that the lord deputy was very earnest to aggravate and search out matters against him, touching the staining of his honour and dignity, scheming to come upon him with some forged treason, and thereby to bereave him of both his life and living. The better to compass this he placed his ' whispering companion,' Captain Leigh, as sheriff in the county, ' so as to be lurking after the earl, to spy if he might have any hole in his coat.' Seeing then that the lord deputy, who should be indifferent, not only to him but to the whole realm, having the rod in his own power, did seek his destruction, he esteemed it a strife against the stream for him to seek to live secure in that kingdom, and therefore of both evils he did choose the least, and thought it better rather to forego his country and lands, till he had further known his majesty's pleasure—to make an honourable escape with his life and liberty only, than by staying with dishonour and indignation to lose both life, liberty, and country, which much in very deed he feared. Indeed the many abuses ' offered ' him by Sir John Davis, ' a man more fit to be a stage player than a counsel,' and other inferior officers, might be sufficient causes to provoke any human creature, not only to forego a country, were it ever so dear to him, but also the whole world, to eschew the like government. And thus he concludes his appeal to his ' most dread sovereign :' ' And so referring himself, and the due consideration of these, and all other his causes, to your majesty's most royal and princely censure, as his only protector and defender, against all his adversaries, he most humbly taketh his leave, and will always, as in bounden duty, pray.'

The Earl of Tyrconnel's statement contains no less than forty-four items under the following heading : ' A note, or brief collection of the several exactions, wrongs, and grievances, as well spiritual as temporal, wherewith the Earl of Tyrconnel particularly doth find himself grieved and abused by the king's law ministers in Ireland, from the first year of his majesty's reign until this present year of 1607 : to be presented to the king's most excellent majesty.'

Imprimis, all the priests and religious persons dwelling within the said earl's territories were daily pursued and persecuted by his majesty's officers. Sir Arthur Chichester told him, in the presence of divers noblemen and gentlemen,

K 2

that he must resolve to go to church, or he would be forced to go. This was contrary to the toleration which had been till then enjoyed, and he resolved rather to abandon lands and living, yea, all the kingdoms of the earth, with the loss of his life, than to be forced utterly against his conscience to any such practice.

When Sir George Carew was lord deputy, Captain Nicholas Pynnar and Captain Basil Brook, officers of the king's forces at Lifford, plundered the earl's tenants there, taking from them 150 cows, besides as many sheep and swine as they pleased. Not satisfied with this spoil, they most tyrannically stripped 100 persons of all their apparel. These outrages the earl complained of ' in humble wise ' to the lord deputy, and could find no remedy ; for the same year the garrisons of Lough Foyle, and Ballyshannon took from the earl's tenants 400 cows for the victualling of the soldiers ; and although the English council wrote to the lord deputy, requiring him to pay for the cattle in English money, the payment was never made. When, in pursuance of a promise made to him by the lord deputy, he appeared before the king, to get new letters patent of his territories, &c., his property, in Sligo, Tyrawly, Moylurg, Dartry, Sir Cahir O'Dogherty's country, and all Sir Nial O'Donel's lands, were excepted and kept from him, together with the castle of Ballyshannon and 1,000 acres of land, and the whole salmon-fishing of the river Erne, worth 800*l.* a year, ' the same castle being one of the earl's chieftest mansion houses.' They also took from him 1,000 acres of his best land, and joined it to the garrison of Lifford for the king's use, without any compensation. There were seven sheriffs sent into Tyrconnel, by each of which there was taken out of every cow and plough-horse 4*d.*, and as much out of every colt and calf twice a year, and half-a-crown a quarter of every shoemaker, carpenter, smith, and weaver in the whole country, and eight pence a year for every married couple.'

Sir Nial O'Donel was committed to prison by Tyrconnel, for usurping the title of O'Donel and taking his herds and tenants. ' He broke loose from prison and killed some of his Majesty's subjects. For this the earl prosecuted him under a special warrant from the lord deputy; but notwithstanding all this, Carew gave warrants to Captains Pynnar, Brook, and Bingley, to make reprisals upon the earl's tenants for the pretender's use. Accordingly three English companies joining with nine score of Sir Nial's men, seized and carried away 500 cows, 60 mares, 30 plough-horses, 13 horses, besides food and drink to support the assailants for six weeks. They were guilty of many other extortions, the country being extremely poor after the wars, and 17 of the earl's tenants were hindered from ploughing that season. A certain horse-boy, who was sentenced to be hanged for killing one Cusack, was promised his life by Sir George Carew, if he accused Tyrconnel as having employed him to commit the murder. The boy did make the accusation, which served no purpose ' but to accelerate his hanging.' Thus betrayed, he declared at the gallows, and in the presence of 400 persons, the sheriff of the county, and the portreve of Trim, he retracted the false confession. A similar attempt was made with an Englishman, who was kept a close prisoner without food, drink, or light, in order to get him to accuse the earl of Cusack's murder. All such, with many other of the said Carew's cruel and tyrannical proceedings, the earl showed to the council in England, which promised to give satisfaction by punishing the said Carew, who at his arrival in England did rather obtain greater favours than any reprehension or check of his doings, so as the earl was constrained to take *patience* for a full satisfaction of his wrongs.

Sir Henry Docwra, governor of Derry, levied 100*l*. off Tyrconnel's tenants for the building of a church in that city, but the money was applied by Sir Henry to his own use. Carew ordered the troops under Sir H. Docwra, Sir H. Folliott, Sir Ralph Constable, Sir Thomas Roper, and Captain Doddington, to be quartered for three months upon Tyrconnel's people, ' where they committed many rapes, and used many extortions, which the earl showed, and could neither get payment for their victuals nor obtain that they should be punished for their sundry rapes and extortions.' Indeed there was never a garrison in Tyrconnel that did not send at their pleasure private soldiers into the country to fetch, now three beeves, now four, as often as they liked, until they had taken all; and when the earl complained, Carew seemed rather to flout him than any way to right him. Sir H. Folliott's company on one occasion took from his tenants thirty-eight plough-horses, which were never restored or paid for; at another time they took twenty-one, and again fourteen. This being done in the spring of the year the tenants were hindered from ploughing as before. During a whole year Folliott took for the use of his own house, regularly every month, six beeves and six muttons, without any manner of payment. Captain Doddington and Captain Cole made free with the people's property in the same manner.

'All these injuries he laid in a very humble manner before the lord deputy, but instead of obtaining redress he was dismissed by him in a scoffing manner, and even a lawyer whom he employed was threatened by Carew in the following terms:—that he and his posterity should smart for his doings until the seventh generation; so that all the earl's business was ever since left at random, and no lawyer dared plead in his cause.'

Tyrconnel killed some rebels, and captured their chief, whom his men carried to Sir H. Folliott to be executed. Sir Henry offered to spare his life if he could accuse the earl of any crime that might work his overthrow. He could not, and he was hanged. In order to settle a dispute between the earl and Sir Nial, the English *protégé* and pretender to the chieftainship, twelve tenants of each were summoned to be examined by the king's officers in the neighbourhood. 'The earl's men were not examined, but locked up in a room; and the vice-governor, upon the false deposition of Sir Nial's men, directed warrants, and sent soldiers to the number of 300, to bring all the earl's tenants unto Sir Nial, to the number of 340 persons, who paid half-a-crown a piece, and 12*d.* for every cow and garron, as a fee unto the captains, whereby they lost their ploughing for the space of twenty-eight days, the soldiers being in the country all the while. One Captain Henry Vaughan, being sheriff in the year 1605, got a warrant to levy 150*l.* to build a sessions house. He built the house of timber and wattles. It was not worth 10*l.*, and it fell in three months. Nevertheless he levied every penny of the money, and the people had to meet a similar demand the next year, to build another house. It was a rule with the governors of the local garrisons to offer his life to every convict about to be executed, and also a large reward, if he could accuse the earl of some detestable crime. No less than twenty-seven persons hanged in Connaught and Tyrone were offered pardon on this condition. He was at the same sessions called to the bar for hanging some wood-kerne, although he had authority from the king to execute martial law. Shortly after, by the lord deputy's orders, the horse and foot soldiers under Docwra and Folliott 'were cessed upon the country, where they for four months remained, and paid nothing for their charges of horse-meat or man's meat.' In the year 1606 the lord deputy came to Ballyshannon, where, being at supper, he demanded of the earl what right he had to the several territories he claimed. He replied that his ancestors had possessed them for 1,300 years, and that the duties, rents, and homages were duly paid during that time. Whereupon the lord deputy said, 'the earl was unworthy to have them, he should never enjoy them, the State was sorry to have left so much in his possession, and he should take heed to himself or else the deputy would make his pate ache.' The matters in dispute between him and Sir Nial being referred on that occasion to the lord deputy, both parties having submitted their papers for examination, every case was decided against Tyrconnel, all his challenges frustrated, 300*l.* damages imposed, and his papers burned; while Sir Nial's papers were privately given back to him. The result was that at the next sessions Sir Nial had the benefit of all his papers, his opponent having nothing to show to the contrary. The fishery of Killybegs, worth 500*l.* a season, had belonged to Tyrconnel's ancestors for 1,300 years. But it was taken from him without compensation, by Sir Henry Folliott and the Bishop of Derry, with the ultimate sanction of the lord deputy, who confirmed the bishop in possession ' both for that season and for all times ensuing.' Sir H. Folliott on one occasion took away for his carriage the horses that served the earl's house with fuel and wood for fire, ' and the soldiers, scorning to feed the horses themselves, went into the earl's house, and forcibly took out one of his boys to lead them, and ran another in the thigh with a pike for refusing to go with him.' He had a number of tenants, who held their lands ' by lease of years for certain rents.' Yet the lord deputy sent warrants to them, directing them to pay no rents, and requiring the Governor of Derry ' to raise the country from time to time, and resist and hinder the earl from taking up his rents.'

To crown all, when Tyrconnel made a journey into the Pale to know the reason why he was debarred from his rents, he lodged on his way in the Abbey of Boyle. He had scarcely arrived there when the constable of the town, accompanied by twenty soldiers, and all the churls of the place, surrounded and set fire to the house where he lay, he having no company within but his page and two other serving men. ' But it befell, through the singular providence of Almighty God, whose fatherly care he hath ever found vigilant over him, that he defended himself and his house against them all the whole night long, they using on the other side all their industry and might to fire it, and throwing in of stones and staves in the earl's face, and running their pikes at him and swords until they had wounded him, besides his other bruisings, with stones and staves in six places; they menacing to kill him, affirming that he was a traitor to the king, and that it was the best service that could be rendered to his majesty to kill him. And that all this is true, Sir Donough O'Conor, who was taken prisoner by the same men, because he would not assist them in their *facinorous* and wicked design of killing the earl, will justify; but in the morning the earl was rescued by the country folk, which conveyed him safely out of the town. And when the earl complained, and showed his wounds unto the lord deputy, he promised to hang the constable and ensign, but afterwards did not once deign so much as to examine the matter or call the delinquents to account, by reason whereof the earl doth verily persuade himself—which his surmise was afterwards confirmed in time, by the credible report of many—that some of the State were sorry for his escape, but specially Sir Oliver Lambert, who had purposely drawn the plot of the earl's ruin.'

* Meehan's Earls of Tyrone and Tyrconnel, pp. 192—224.

CHAPTER IX.

THE CONFISCATION OF ULSTER.

SIR TOBY CAULFIELD, accompanied by the sheriffs of
Tyrone and Tyrconnel, followed quickly the proclamation of
the lord deputy to the people of Ulster, and took possession
of the houses, goods, and chattels of the fugitive earls. Sir
Toby was further empowered to act as receiver over the
estates, taking up the rents according to the Irish usage
until other arrangements could be made. His inventory of
the effects of O'Neill in the castle of Dungannon is a curious
document, showing that according to the ideas of those times
in the matter of furniture 'man wants but little here below.'
The following is a copy of the document taken from the
memorandum roll of the exchequer by the late Mr. Ferguson.
It is headed, ' *The Earl of Tyrone's goods, viz.*' The spell-
ing is, however, modernised, and ordinary figures substituted
for Roman numerals.

The Earl of Tyrone's Goods, viz.

	£	s.	d.
Small steers, 9 at 10*s.*	4	10	0
60 hogs, at 2*s.* 6*d.*	7	10	0
2 long tables, 10*s.*			
2 long forms, 5*s.*; an old bedstead, 5*s.*			
An old trunk, 3*s.*; a long stool, 12*d.*			
3 hogsheads of salt, 28*s.* 6*d.*; all valued at	4	12	6
A silk jacket	0	13	4
8 vessels of butter, containing 4½ barrels	5	17	6
2 iron spikes	0	2	0
A powdering tub	0	0	6
2 old chests	0	4	0
A frying-pan and a dripping-pan	0	3	0

	£	s.	d.
5 pewter dishes	0	5	0
A casket, 2*d.*; a comb and comb case, 18*d.* . . .	0	1	8
2 dozen of trenchers and a basket	0	0	10
2 eighteen-bar ferris	0	6	0
A box and 2 drinking glasses	0	1	3
A trunk 1; a pair of red taffeta curtains 1; other pair of green satin curtains	4	5	0
A brass kettle	0	8	6
'A payer of covyrons'	0	5	0
2 baskets with certain broken earthen dishes and some waste spices	0	2	0
Half a pound of white and blue starch	0	0	4
A vessel with 11 gallons of vinegar	0	3	0
17 pewter dishes	0	15	0
3 glass bottles	0	1	6
2 stone jugs, whereof 1 broken	0	0	6
A little iron pot	0	1	6
A great spit	0	1	6
6 garrons at 30*s.* apiece	9	0	0
19 stud mares, whereof [some] were claimed by Nicholas Weston, which were restored to him by warrant, 30*l.* 9*s.* being proved to be his own, and so remaineth . .	17	0	0

With respect to rents, Sir Toby Caulfield left a memorandum, stating that there was no certain portion of Tyrone's land let to any of his tenants that paid him rent, and that such rents as he received were paid to him partly in money and partly in victuals, as oats, oatmeal, butter, hogs, and sheep. The money-rents were chargeable on all the cows, milch or in calf, which grazed on his lands, at the rate of a shilling a quarter each. The cows were to be numbered in May and November by the earl's officers, and ' so the rents were taken up at said rate for all the cows that were so numbered, except only the heads and principal men of the *creaghts,* as they enabled them to live better than the common multitude under them, whom they caused to pay the said rents, which amounted to about twelve hundred sterling Irish a year.

' The butter and other provisions were usually paid by those styled horsemen—O'Hagans, O'Quins, the O'Donnillys, O'Devolins, and others.' These were a sort of middle men, and to some of them an allowance was made by the Government. ' Thus for example, Loughlin O'Hagan, formerly constable of the castle of Dungannon, received in lieu thereof a portion of his brother Henry's goods, and Henry O'Hagan's wife and her children had all her husband's goods, at the suit of her father Sir G. O'Ghy O'Hanlon, who had made a surrender of all his lands to the crown.'

The cattle were to be all numbered over the whole territory in one day, a duty which must have required a great number of men, and sharp men too; for, if the owners were dishonestly inclined, and were as active in that kind of work as the peasantry were during the anti-tithe war in our own time, the cattle could be driven off into the woods or on to the lands of a neighbouring lord. However, during the three years that Caulfield was receiver, the rental amounted to 12,000l. a year, a remarkable fact considering the enormous destruction of property that had taken place during the late wars, and the value of money at that time.

A similar process was adopted with regard to the property of O'Donel, and guards were placed in all the castles of the two chiefs. In order that their territories might pass into the king's possession by due form of law, the attorney-general, Sir John Davis, was instructed to draw up a bill of indictment for treason against the fugitive earls and their adherents. With this bill he proceeded to Lifford, accompanied by a number of commissioners, clerks, sheriffs, and a strong detachment of horse and foot. At Lifford, the county town of Donegal, a jury was empanelled for the trial of O'Donel, consisting of twenty-three Irishmen and ten Englishmen. Of this jury Sir Cahir O'Dogherty was foreman. He was the lord of Inishowen, having the largest territories in the county next to the Earl of Tyrconnel. The bill being read in English and Irish, evidence was given, wrote the attorney-general, ' that their guilty consciences, and fear of losing their heads, was the cause of their flight.' The jury, however, had exactly the same sort of difficulty that troubled the juries in our late Fenian trials about finding the accused guilty of compassing the death of the sovereign. But Sir John laboured to remove their scruples by explaining the legal technicality, and arguing that, 'whoso would take the king's crown from his head would likewise, if he could, take his head from his shoulders; and whoever would not suffer the king to reign, if it lay in his power, would not suffer the king to live.' The argument was successful with the jury. In all the conflicts between the two races, whether on the field of battle or in the courts of law, the work of England was zealously done by Celtic agents, who became the eager accusers, the perfidious betrayers, and sometimes the voluntary assassins of men of their own name, kindred, and tribe.

The commissioners next sat at Strabane, a town within two or three miles of Lifford, where a similar jury was empanelled for the county Tyrone, to try O'Neill. One of the counts against him was that he had treasonably taken upon him the name of O'Neill. In proof of this a document was produced: ' O'Neill bids M'Tuin to pay 60*l.*' It was also alleged that he had committed a number of murders; but his victims, it was alleged, were criminals ordered for execution in virtue of the power of life and death with which he had been invested by the queen. He was found guilty, however; and Henry Oge O'Neill, his kinsman, who was foreman of the jury, was complimented for his civility and loyalty, although he belonged to that class concerning which Sir John afterwards wrote, ' It is as natural for an Irish lord to be a thief as it is for the devil to be a liar, of whom it was written, he was a liar and a murderer from the beginning.'

True bills having been found by the grand juries, proceedings were taken in the Court of King's Bench to have the fugitive earls and their followers attainted of high treason. The names were:—' Hugh earl of Tyrone, Rory earl of Tyrconnel, Caffar O'Donel, Cu Connaught Maguire, Donel Oge O'Donel, Art Oge, Cormack O'Neill, Henry O'Neill, Henry Hovenden, Henry O'Hagan, Moriarty O'Quinn, John Bath, Christopher Plunket, John O'Punty O'Hagan, Hugh O'Galagher, Carragh O'Galagher, John and Edmund

M'Davitt, Maurie O'Multully, Donogh O'Brien, M'Mahon, George Cashel, Teigue O'Keenen, and many other false traitors, who, by the instigation of the devil, did conspire and plot the destruction and death of the king, Sir Arthur Chichester, &c.; and did also conspire to seize by force of arms the castles of Athlone, Ballyshannon, Duncannon, co. Wexford, Lifford, co. Donegal, and with that intent did sail away in a ship, to bring in an army composed of foreigners to invade the kingdom of Ireland, to put the king to death, and to dispose him from the style, title, power, and government of the Imperial crown.'

The lord deputy and his officers, able, energetic, far-seeing men, working together persistently for the accomplishment of a well-defined purpose, were drawing the great net of English law closer and closer around the heads of the Irish clans, who struggled gallantly and wildly in its fatal meshes. The episode of Sir Cahir O'Dogherty is a romance. On the death of Sir John O'Dogherty, the O'Donel, in accordance with Irish custom, caused his brother Phelim Oge to be inaugurated Prince of Inishowen, because Cahir, his son, was then only thirteen years of age, too young to command the sept. But this arrangement did not please his foster brothers, the M'Davitts, who proposed to Sir Henry Docwra, governor of Derry, that their youthful chief should be adopted as the queen's O'Dogherty; and on this condition they promised that he and they would devote themselves to her majesty's service. The terms were gladly accepted. Sir Cahir was trained by Docwra in martial exercises, in the arts of civility, and in English literature. He was an apt pupil. He grew up strong and comely; and he so distinguished himself before he was sixteen years of age in skirmishes with his father's allies, that Sir Henry wrote of him in the following terms: ' The country was overgrown with ancient oak and coppice. O'Dogherty was with me, alighted when I did, kept me company in the greatest heat of the fight, behaved himself bravely, and with a great deal of love and affection; so much so, that I recommended him at my next meeting with the Lord Deputy Mountjoy, for the honour of knighthood, which was accordingly conferred upon him.' The young knight went to London, was well received at court, and obtained a new grant of a large portion of the O'Dogherty's country. He married a daughter of Lord Gormanstown, a catholic peer of the Pale, distinguished for loyalty to the English throne, resided with his bride at his Castle of Elagh, or at Burt, or Buncranna, keeping princely state, not in the old Irish fashion, but in the manner of an English nobleman of the period; hunting the red deer in his forest, hawking, or fishing in the teeming waters of Lough Foyle, Lough Swilly, and the Atlantic, which poured their treasures around the promontory of which he was the lord. His intimate associates were officers and favourites of the king.

Docwra had given up the government of Derry and retired to England. He was succeeded by Sir George Paulet, a man of violent temper. Sir Cahir had sold 3,000 acres of land, which was to be planted with English; and, in order to perfect the deed of sale, it was necessary to have the document signed before the governor of Derry. It had been reported to the lord deputy that Sir Cahir, not content with his position, intended to leave the country, probably with the design of joining the fugitive earls in an attempt to destroy the English power in Ireland. He was therefore summoned before the lord deputy ; and Lord Gormanstown, Thomas Fitzwilliam of Merrion, and himself, were obliged to give security that he should not quit Ireland without due notice and express permission. This restraint had probably irritated his hot impetuous spirit, and made it difficult for him to exercise due self-control when he came in contact with the English governor of Derry, with whom his relations were not improved by the suspicions now attaching to his loyalty. Accordingly, while the legal forms of the transfer were being gone through, the young chief made a remark extremely offensive to Paulet, which was resented by a blow in the face with his clenched fist. Instead of returning

the blow, young O'Dogherty hurried away to consult the
M'Davitts, whose advice was that the insult he received
must be avenged by blood. The affair having been immediately reported to the lord deputy, who apprehended that
mischief would come of it, he sent a peremptory summons
to Sir Cahir, requiring him to appear in Dublin, 'to free
himself of certain rumours and reports touching disloyal
courses into which he had entered, contrary to his allegiance
to the king, and threatening the overthrow of many of
his majesty's subjects.' His two sureties were also written
to, and required to 'bring in his body.' But O'Dogherty
utterly disregarded the lord deputy's order. Taking counsel
with Nial Garve O'Donel, he resolved to seize Culmore
Fort, Castle Doe, and other strong places ; and then march
on Derry, and massacre the English settlers in the market
square.

Towards the close of April, Sir Cahir invited Captain
Harte, governor of Culmore Castle, on the banks of the
Foyle, about four miles from Derry, with his wife and infant
child, of which he was the godfather, to dine with him at
his Castle of Elagh.

The entertainment was sumptuous, and the pleasures of
the table protracted to a late hour. After dinner the host
took his guest into a private apartment, and told him that
the blow he had received from Paulet demanded a bloody
revenge. Harte remonstrated; O'Dogherty's retainers rushed
in, and, drawing their swords and skeines, declared that they
would kill his wife and child in his presence, unless he delivered up the castle of Culmore. The governor was terri
fied, but he refused to betray his trust. Sir Cahir, commanding the armed men to retire, locked the chamber door, and
kept his guest imprisoned there for two hours, hoping that
he would yield when he had time for reflection. But finding
him still inflexible, O'Dogherty grew furious, and vented his
rage in loud and angry words. Mrs. Harte, hearing the
altercation, and suspecting foul play, rushed into the room,
and found Sir Cahir enforcing his appeal with a naked

sword pointed at her husband's throat. She fell on the floor in a swoon. Lady O'Dogherty ran to her assistance, raised her up, and assured her that she knew nothing of her husband's rash design. The latter then thrust the whole party downstairs, giving orders to his men to seize Captain Harte. Meantime, Lady Harte fell on her knees, imploring mercy, but the only response was an oath that she and her husband and child should be instantly butchered if Culmore were not surrendered. What followed shall be related in the words of Father Meehan : ' Horrified by this menace, she consented to accompany him and his men to the fort, where they arrived about midnight. On giving the pass word the gate was thrown open by the warder, whose suspicions were lulled when Lady Harte told him that her husband had broken his arm and was then lying in Sir Cahir's house. The parley was short, and the followers of Sir Cahir, rushing in to the tower, fell on the sleeping garrison, slaughtered them in their beds, and then made their way to an upper apartment where Lady Harte's brother, recently come from England, was fast asleep. Fearing that he might get a bloody blanket for his shroud, Lady Harte followed them into the room, and implored the young man to offer no resistance to the Irish, who broke open trunks, presses and other furniture, and seized whatever valuables they could clutch. Her thoughtfulness saved the lives of her children and her brother; for as soon as Sir Cahir had armed his followers with matchlocks and powder out of the magazine, he left a small detachment to garrison Culmore, and then marched rapidly on Derry, where he arrived about two o'clock in the morning. Totally unprepared for such an irruption, the townsfolk were roused from their sleep by the bagpipes and war-shout of the Clan O'Dogherty, who rushed into the streets, and made their way to Paulet's house, where Sir Cahir, still smarting under the indignity of the angry blow, satisfied his vow of vengeance by causing that unhappy gentleman to be hacked to death with the pikes and skeines of Owen O'Dogherty and others of his kindred. After plundering the houses of the more opulent inhabitants, seizing such arms as they could find, and reducing the young town to a heap of ashes, Sir Cahir led his followers to the palace of Montgomery the bishop, who fortunately for himself was then absent in Dublin. Not finding him, they captured his wife, and sent her, under escort, to Burt Castle, whither Lady O'Dogherty, her sister-in-law and infant daughter, had gone without warders for their protection.   It was on this occasion that Phelim M'Davitt got into Montgomery's library and set fire to it, thus destroying hundreds of valuable volumes, printed and manuscript, a feat for which he is not censured—we are sorry to have to acknowledge it—by Philip O'Sullivan in his account of the fact.   Elated by this successful raid, Sir Cahir called off his followers and proceeded to beleaguer Lifford, where there was a small garrison of English who could not be induced to surrender, although suffering severely from want of provisions.   Finding all his attempts to reduce the place ineffectual, he sent for the small force he had left in Culmore to join the main body of his partisans, and then marched into M'Swyne Doe's country.'

Meantime news of these atrocities reached Dublin, and the lord deputy immediately sent a force of 3,000 men, commanded by Sir Richard Wingfield, Sir Thomas Roper, and Sir Toby Caulfield, with instructions to pursue the revolted Irish into their fastnesses and deal with them summarily. He himself set out to act with the troops, and on reaching Dundalk published a proclamation, in which he offered pardon to all who laid down their arms, or would use them in killing their associates.   He took care, however, to except Phelim M'Davitt from all hope of mercy, consigning him to be dealt with by a military tribunal.   The English force in the interval had made their way into O'Dogherty's country, and coming before Culmore, found it abandoned by the Irish, who, unable to carry off the heavy guns, took the precaution of burying them in the sea.   Burt Castle surrendered without a blow.   Wingfield immediately liberated the inmates, and sent Bishop Montgomery's wife to her husband, and Lady

O'Dogherty, her infant daughter and sister-in-law, to Dublin Castle. As for Sir Cahir, instead of going to Castle Doe, he resolved to cross the path of the English on their march to that place, and coming up with them in the vicinity of Kilmacrenan, he was shot dead by a soldier. The death of the young chieftain spread panic among his followers, most of whom flung away their arms, betook themselves to flight, and were unmercifully cut down. Sir Cahir's head was immediately struck off and sent to Dublin, where it was struck upon a pole at the east gate of the city.

O'Dogherty's country was now confiscated, and the lord deputy, Chichester, was rewarded with the greatest portion of his lands. But what was to be done with the people? In the first instance they were driven from the rich lowlands along the borders of Lough Foyle and Lough Swilly, and compelled to take refuge in the mountain fastnesses which stretched to a vast extent from Moville westward along the Atlantic coast. But could those ' idle kerne and swordsmen,' thus punished with loss of lands and home for the crimes of their chief, be safely trusted to remain anywhere in the neighbourhood of the new English settlers? Sir John Davis and Sir Toby Caulfield thought of a plan by which they could get rid of the danger. The illustrious Gustavus Adolphus was then fighting the battles of Protestantism against the house of Austria. In his gallant efforts to sustain the cause of the Reformation every true Irish Protestant sympathised, and none more than the members of the Irish Government. To what better use, then, could the ' loose Irish kerne and swordsmen' of Donegal be turned than to send them to fight in the army of the King of Sweden? Accordingly 6,000 of the able-bodied peasantry of Inishown were shipped off for this service. Sir Toby Caulfield, founder of the house of Charlemont, was commissioned to muster the men and have them transported to their destination, being paid for their keep in the meantime. A portion of his account ran thus : ' For the dyett of 80 of said soldiers for 16 daies, during which tyme they were kept in prison in Dungannon till they were sent away, at iiii[d] le peece per diem; allso for dyett of 72 of said men kept in prison at Armagh till they were sent away to Swethen, at iiii[d] le peece per diem,' &c., &c. Caulfield was well rewarded for these services; and Captain Sandford, married to the niece of the first Earl of Charlemont, obtained a large grant of land on the same score. This system of clearing out the fighting men among the Irish was continued till 1629, when the lord deputy, Falkland, wrote that Sir George Hamilton, a papist, then impressing soldiers in Tyrone and Antrim, was opposed by one O'Cullinan, a priest, who was rash enough to advise the people to stay at home and have nothing to do with the Danish wars. For this he was arrested, committed to Dublin Castle, tortured and then hanged.

With regard to the immediate followers of O'Dogherty in his insane course, many of the most prominent leaders were tried by court-martial and executed. Others were found guilty by ordinary course of law. Among these was O'Hanlon, Sir Cahir's brother-in-law. He was hanged at Armagh; and his youthful wife was found by a soldier, 'stripped of her apparel, in a wood, where she perished of cold and hunger, being lately before delivered of a child.' M'Davitt, the firebrand of the rebellion, was convicted and executed at Derry. At Dungannon Shane, Carragh O'Cahan was found guilty by 'a jury of his *kinsmen*' and executed in the camp, his head being stuck upon the castle of that place — the castle from which his brother was mainly instrumental in driving its once potent lord into exile. At the same place a monk, who was a chief adviser of the arch-rebel, saved his life and liberty by tearing off his religious habit, and renouncing his allegiance to the Pope. Father Meehan states that many of the clergy, secular and regular, of Inishown might have saved their lives by taking the oath of supremacy. It was a terrible time in Donegal. No day passed without the killing and taking of some of the dispersed rebels, one betraying another to get his own pardon, and the goods of the party betrayed, according to a proviso in the deputy's proclamation. Among the informers was a noble lady, the mother of Hugh Roe O'Donel and Rory Earl of Tyronnel, who accused Nial Garve, her own son-in-law, of complicity in O'Dogherty's revolt, for which she got a grant of some hundreds of acres in the neighbourhood of Kilmacrenan.

The insurgent leaders and the dangerous kerne having been effectually cleared off in various ways, the whole territory of Inishown was overrun by the king's troops. The lord deputy, Sir Arthur Chichester, with a numerous retinue, including the attorney-general, sheriffs, lawyers, provosts-martial, engineers, and 'geographers,' made a grand ' progress,' and penetrated for the first time the region which was to become the property of his family. It was a strange sight to the poor Irish that were suffered to remain. ' As we passed through the glens and forests,' wrote Sir John Davis, ' the wild inhabitants did as much wonder to see the king's deputy as the ghosts in Virgil did to see Æneas alive in hell.' In this exploring tour a thorough knowledge of the country was for the first time obtained, and the attorney-general could report that ' before Michaelmas he would be ready to present to his majesty a perfect survey of six whole counties which he now hath in actual possession in the province of Ulster, of greater extent of land than any prince in Europe hath in his own hands to dispose of.' A vast field for plantation ! But Sir John Davis cautioned the Government against the mistakes that caused the failure of former settlements, saying, that if the number of the Scotch and English who were to come to Ireland did not much exceed that of the natives, the latter would quickly ' overgrow them, as weeds overgrow corn.'

O'Cahan, who was charged with complicity in O'Dogherty's outbreak, or with being at least a sympathiser, had been arrested, and was kept, with Nial Garve, a close prisoner in Dublin Castle. An anonymous pamphleteer celebrated the victories that had been achieved by the lord deputy, giving to his work the title, ' The Overthrow of an Irish Rebel,' having for its frontispiece a tower with portcullis, and the

O'Dogherty's head impaled in the central embrazure. The spirit of the narrative may be inferred from the following passage : ' As for Tyrone and Co., or Tyrconnel, they are already fled from their coverts, and I hope they will never return; and for other false hearts, the chief of note is O'Cahan, Sir Nial Garve, and his two brothers, with others of their condition. They have holes provided for them in the castle of Dublin, where I hope they are safe enough from breeding any cubs to disquiet and prey upon the flock of honest subjects.'

O'Cahan and his companion, however, tried to get out of the hole, although the lord deputy kept twenty men every night to guard the castle, in addition to the ordinary ward, and two or three of the guards lay in the same rooms with the prisoners. Their horses had arrived in town, and all things were in readiness. But their escape was hindered by the fact that Shane O'Carolan, who had been acquitted of three indictments, cast himself out of a window at the top of the castle by the help of his mantle, which broke before he was half way down; and though he was presently discovered, yet he escaped about supper time. ' Surely,' exclaimed the lord deputy, ' these men do go beyond all nations in the world for desperate escapes !' The prisoners were subsequently conveyed to the Tower, where they remained many years closely confined, and where they ended their days. Sir Allen Apsley, in 1623, made a report of the prisoners then in his custody, in which he said, ' There is here Sir Nial Garve O'Donel, a man that was a good subject during the late queen's time, and did as great service to the state as any man of his nation. He has been a prisoner here about thirteen years. His offence is known specially to the Lord Chichester. Naghtan, his son, was taken from Oxford and committed with his father. I never heard any offence he did.'

While O'Cahan was in prison, commissioners sat in his mansion at Limavaddy, including the Primate Usher, Bishop Montgomery of Derry, and Sir John Davis. They decided that by the statute of 11 Elizabeth, which it was supposed had been cancelled by the king's pardon, all his territory had been granted to the Earl of Tyrone, and forfeited by his flight. It was, therefore, confiscated. Although sundry royal and viceregal proclamations had assured the tenants that they would not be disturbed in their possessions, on account of the offences of their chiefs, it was now declared that all O'Cahan's country belonged to the crown, and that neither he nor those who lived under him had any estate whatever in the lands. Certain portions of the territory were set apart for the Church, and handed over to Bishop Montgomery. ' Of all the fair territory which once was his, Donald Balagh had not now as much as would afford him a last resting-place near the sculptured tomb of Cooey-na-gall. O'Cahan got no sympathy, and he deserved none ; for he might have foreseen that the Government to which he sold himself would cast him off as an outworn tool, when he could no longer subserve their wicked purposes.'* ' Thus were the O'Cahans dispossessed by the colonists of Derry, to whom their broad lands and teeming rivers were passed, *mayhap* for ever. Towards the close of the Cromwellian war in Ireland, the Duchess of Buckingham, passing through Limavaddy, visited its ancient castle, then sadly dilapidated, and, entering one of the apartments, saw an aged woman wrapped in a blanket, and crouching over a peat fire, which filled the room with reeking smoke. After gazing at this pitiful spectacle, the duchess asked the miserable individual her name; when the latter, rising and drawing herself up to her full height, replied, " I am the wife of the O'Cahan." '†

* Meehan, p. 317.

† Father Meehan dedicates his valuable work to the lord chancellor of Ireland, the Right Hon. Thomas O'Hagan,—the first Catholic chancellor since the Revolution. Descended from the O'Hagans, who were hereditary justiciaries and secretaries to the O'Neill, he is, by universal consent, one of the ablest and most accomplished judges that ever adorned the Irish Bench. His ancestors were involved in the fortunes of Tyrone. How strange that the representative of the judicial and literary clan of ancient Ulster should now be the head of the Irish magistracy !

CHAPTER X.

THE PLANTATION OF ULSTER.

IN the account which the lord deputy gave of the flight of Tyrone and Tyrconnel, he referred to the mistake that had been committed in making these men proprietary lords of so large a territory, ' *without regard to the poor freeholders' rights, or of his majesty's service, or the commonwealth's, that are so much interested in the honest liberty of that sort of men.*' And he considered it a providential circumstance that the king had now an opportunity of repairing that error, and of relieving the natives from the exactions and tyranny of their former barbarous lords. How far this change was a benefit to the honest freeholders and the labouring classes may be seen from the reports of Sir Toby Caulfield to the lord deputy, as to his dealings with those people. He complains of his ill success in the prosecution of the wood-kerne. He had done his best, and all had turned to nothing. When the news of the plantation came, he had no hope at all, for the people then said it would be many of their cases to become wood-kerne themselves out of necessity, ' no other means being left for them to keep being in this world than to live as long as they could by scrambling.' They hoped, however, that so much of the summer being spent before the commissioners came down, ' so great cruelty would not be showed as to remove them upon the edge of winter from their houses, and in the very season when they were employed in making their harvest. They held discourse among themselves, that if this course had been taken with them in war time, it had had some colour of justice ; but being pardoned, and their land given them, and they having lived under law ever since, and being ready to submit themselves to the mercy of the law, for any offence they can be charged withal, since their pardoning, they conclude it to be the greatest cruelty that was ever inflicted upon any people.'

It is no wonder that Sir Toby was obliged to add to his report this assurance: ' There is not a more discontented people in Christendom.' It is difficult to conceive how any people in Christendom could be contented, treated as they were, according to this account, which the officer of the Government did not deny ; for surely no people, in any Christian country, were ever the victims of such flagrant injustice, inflicted by a Government which promised to relieve them from the cruel exactions of their barbarous chiefs—a Government, too, solemnly pledged to protect them in the unmolested enjoyment of their houses and lands. How little this policy tended to strengthen the Government appears from a confession made about the same time by the lord deputy himself. He wrote : ' The hearts of the Irish are against us: we have only a handful of men in entertainment so ill paid, that everyone is out of heart, and our resources so discredited, by borrowing and not repaying, that we cannot take up 1,000*l.* in twenty days, if the safety of the kingdom depended upon it. The Irish are hopeful of the return of the fugitives, or invasion from foreign parts.'

But the safety of England, do what she might in the way of oppression, lay then, as it lay often since, and ever will lie, in the tendency to division, and the instability of the Celtic character. The Rev. Mr. Meehan, with all his zeal for Irish nationality, admits this failing of the people with his usual candour. He says : ' These traits, so peculiar to the Celtic character, have been justly stigmatised by a friendly and observant Italian (the Nuncio Rinuccini) who, some thirty years after the period of which we are writing, tells us that the native Irish were behind the rest of Europe in the knowledge of those things that tended to their material improvement—indifferent agriculturists, living from hand to

mouth—caring more for the sword than the plough good
Catholics, though by nature barbarous—and placing their
hopes of deliverance from English rule on foreign intervention. For this they were constantly straining their eyes
towards France or Spain, and, no matter whence the ally
came, were ever ready to rise in revolt. One virtue, however—intensest love of country—more or less redeemed
these vices, for so they deserve to be called ; but to establish
anything like strict military discipline or organisation among
themselves, it must be avowed they had no aptitude.' This,
says Mr. Meehan, ' to some extent, will account for the
apathy of the Northern Catholics, while the undertakers
were carrying on the gigantic eviction known as the plantation of Ulster ; for, since Sir Cahir O'Dogherty's rebellion
till 1615, there was only one attempt to resist the intruders,
an abortive raid on the city of Derry, for which the meagre
annals of that year tell us, six of the Earl of Tyrone's
nearest kinsmen were put to death. Withal the people of
Ulster were full of hope that O'Neill would return with
forces to evict the evicters, but the farther they advanced
into this agreeable perspective, the more rapidly did its
charms disappear.

The proclamations against wood-kerne present a curious
picture of these ' plantation ' times. The lord deputy, in
council, understood that ' many idle kerne, loose and
masterless men, and other disordered persons, did range up
and down in sundry parts of this kingdom, being armed with
swords, targets, pikes, shot, head-pieces, horsemen's staves,
and other warlike weapons, to the great terror of his
majesty's well-disposed subjects, upon whom they had
committed many extortions, murders, robberies, and other
outrages. Hence divers proclamations had been published
in his majesty's name, commanding that no person of what
condition soever, travelling on horseback, should presume
to carry more arms than one sword or rapier and dagger ;
and that no person travelling on foot should carry any
weapons at all. Twenty days were allowed for giving the

arms to the proper officers. If the proclamation was not obeyed within that time, the arms were to be seized for the king's use, and the bearers of them committed to prison.

On July 21, 1609, a commission was issued by the crown to make inquisition concerning the forfeited lands in Ulster after the flight of the Earls of Tyrone and Tyrconnel. The commissioners included the Lord-Deputy Chichester, the Archbishops of Armagh and Dublin, Sir John Davis, attorney-general; Sir William Parsons, surveyor-general, and several other public functionaries. This work done, King James, acting on the advice of his prime minister, the Earl of Salisbury, took measures for the plantation of Ulster, a project earnestly recommended by statesmen connected with Ireland, and for which the flight of O'Neill and O'Donel furnished the desired opportunity. The city of London was thought to be the best quarter to look to for funds to carry on the plantation. Accordingly, Lord Salisbury had a conference with the lord mayor, Humphry Weld, Sir John Jolles, and Sir W. Cockaine, who were well acquainted with Irish affairs. The result was the publication of ' Motives and Reasons to induce the City of London to undertake the Plantation in the North of Ireland.'

The inducements were of the most tempting character. It is customary to speak of Ulster, before the plantation, as something like a desert, out of which the planters created an Eden. But the picture presented to the Londoners was more like the land which the Israelitish spies found beyond Jordan—a land flowing with milk and honey. Among ' the land commodities which the North of Ireland produceth ' were these :—the country was well watered generally by abundance of springs, brooks, and rivers. There was plenty of fuel—either wood, or ' good and wholesome turf.' The land yielded ' store of all necessary for man's sustenance, in such a measure as may not only maintain itself, but also furnish the city of London yearly with manifold provision, especially for their fleets—namely, with beef, pork, fish, rye, bere, peas, and beans.' It was not only fit for all sorts of husbandry, but it excelled for the breeding of mares and the increase of cattle; whence the Londoners might expect ' plenty of butter, cheese, hides, and tallow,' while English sheep would breed abundantly there. It was also held to be good in many places for madder, hops, and woad. It afforded ' fells of all sorts in great quantity, red deer, foxes, sheep, lambs, rabbits, martins and squirrels,' &c. Hemp and flax grew more naturally there than elsewhere, which, being well regarded, would give provision for canvas, cables, cording, besides thread, linen cloth, and all stuffs made of linen yarn, ' which are more fine and plentiful there than in all the rest of the kingdom.' Then there were the best materials of all sorts for building, with ' the goodliest and largest timber, that might compare with any in his majesty's dominions ;' and, moreover, the country was ' very plentiful in honey and wax.'

The sea and the rivers vied with the land in the richness of their produce. ' The sea fishing of that coast was very plentiful of all manner of usual sea fish—there being yearly, after Michaelmas, for taking of herrings, above seven or eight score sail of his majesty's subjects and strangers for lading, besides an infinite number of boats for fishing and killing.'

The corporation were willing to undertake the work of plantation if the account given of its advantages should prove to be correct. With the caution of men of business, they wished to put the glowing representations of the Government to the test of an investigation by agents of their own. So they sent over ' four wise, grave, and discreet citizens, to view the situation proposed for the new colony.' The men selected were John Broad, goldsmith; Robert Treswell, painter-stainer ; John Rowley, draper ; and John Munns, mercer. On their return from their Irish mission they presented a report to the Court of Common Council, which was openly read. The report was favourable. A company was to be formed in London for conducting the plantation. Corporations were to be founded in Derry and Coleraine, everything concerning the colony to be managed and performed in Ireland by the advice and direction of the company in London. It was agreed between the Privy Council and the City that the sum of 20,000*l.* should be levied, 15,000*l.* for the intended plantation, and 5,000*l.* 'for the clearing of private men's interest in the things demanded.' That 200 houses should be built in Derry, and room left for 300 more. ' That 4,000 acres lying on the Derry side, next adjacent to the wherry, should be laid thereunto—bog and barren mountain to be no part thereof, but to go as waste for the city ; the same to be done by indifferent commissioners.'

The royal charters and letters clearly set forth the objects of the plantation. James I., in the preamble of the charter to the town of Coleraine, thus described his intentions in disposing of the forfeited lands to English undertakers : ' Whereas there can be nothing more worthy of a king to perform than to establish the true religion of Christ among men hitherto depraved and almost lost in superstition ; to improve and cultivate by art and industry countries and lands uncultivated and almost desert, and not only to stock them with honest citizens and inhabitants, but also to strengthen them with good institutions and ordinances, whereby they might be more safely defended not only from the corruption of their morals but from their intestine and domestic plots and conspiracies, and also from foreign violence : And whereas the province of Ulster in our realm of Ireland, for many years past, hath grossly erred from the true religion of Christ and divine grace, and hath abounded with superstition, insomuch that for a long time it hath not only been harassed, torn, and wasted by private and domestic broils but also by foreign arms : We therefore, deeply and heartily commiserating the wretched state of the said province, have esteemed it to be a work worthy of a Christian prince, and of our royal office, to stir up and recal the same province from superstition, rebellion, calamity, and poverty, which heretofore have horribly raged therein, to religion, obedience, strength, and prosperity. And whereas our beloved and faithful subjects the mayor and commonalty and citizens of our city of London, burning with a flagrant zeal to promote such our pious intention in this behalf, have undertaken a considerable part of the said plantation in Ulster, and are making progress therein '. . . .

King James, having heard very unsatisfactory reports of the progress of the plantation, wrote a letter to the lord deputy in 1612, strongly complaining of the neglect of the ' Londoners ' to fulfil the obligations they had voluntarily undertaken. He had made ' liberal donations of great proportions of those lands to divers British undertakers and servitors, with favourable tenures and reservations for their better encouragement; but hitherto neither the safety of that country, nor the planting of religion and civility among those rude and barbarous people, which were the principal motives of that project, and which he expected as the only fruits and returns of his bounty, had been as yet any whit materially effected. He was not ignorant how much the real accomplishment of the plantation concerned the future peace and safety of that kingdom ; but if there was no reason of state to press it forward, he would yet pursue and effect that object with the same earnestness, ' merely for the goodness and morality of it ; esteeming the settling of religion, the introducing of civility, order, and government among a barbarous and unsubjected people, to be acts of piety and glory, and worthy also a Christian prince to endeavour.'

The king therefore ordered that there should be a strict inquiry into the work done, because ' the Londoners pretended the expense of great sums of money in that service, and yet the outward appearance of it was very small.' The lord deputy was solemnly charged to give him a faithful account without care or fear to displease any of his subjects, English or Scottish, of what quality soever.'

Sir Josias Bodley was the commissioner appointed for this purpose. He reported very unfavourably, in consequence of which his majesty called upon the Irish society and the several companies to give him an account of their stewardship. He also wrote again to the lord deputy in 1615. The language the king uses is remarkable, as proving the *trusteeship* of the companies. Referring to Bodley's report he said:—

'We have examined, viewed, and reviewed, with our own eye, every part thereof, and find greatly to our discontentment the slow progression of that plantation; some few only of our British undertakers, servitors, and natives having as yet proceeded effectually by the accomplishment of such things in all points as are required of them by the articles of the plantation; the rest, and by much the greatest part, having either done nothing at all, or so little, or, by reason of the slightness thereof, to so little purpose, that the work seems rather to us to be forgotten by them, and to perish under their hand, than any whit to be advanced by them; some having begun to build and not planted, others begun to plant and not built, and all of them, in general, retaining the Irish still upon their lands, the avoiding of which was the fundamental reason of that plantation. We have made a collection of their names, as we found their endeavours and negligences noted in the service, which we will retain as a memorial with us, and they shall be sure to feel the effects of our favour and disfavour, as there shall be occasion. It is well known to you that if we had intended only (as it seems most of them over-greedily have done) our present profit, we might have converted those large territories to our escheated lands, to the great improvement of the revenue of our crown there; but we chose rather, for the safety of that country and the civilizing of that people, to part with the inheritance of them at extreme undervalues, and to make a plantation of them; and since we were merely induced thereunto out of reason of state, we think we may without any breach of justice make bold with their rights who have neglected their duties in a service of so much importance unto us, and by the same law and reason of state resume into

our hands their lands who have failed to perform, according
to our original intention, the articles of plantation, and
bestow them upon some other men more active and worthy
of them than themselves: and the time is long since expired
within which they were bound to have finished to all purposes their plantation, so that we want not just provocation
to proceed presently with all rigour against them.'

He gave them a year to pull up their arrears of work, and
in conclusion said to Chichester : ' My lord, in this service
I expect that zeal and uprightness from you, that you will
spare no flesh, English or Scottish ; for no private man's
worth is able to counterbalance the particular safety of a
kingdom, which this plantation, well accomplished, will
procure.'

Two or three years later, Captain Pynnar was sent to
survey the lands that had been granted to the undertakers,
and to report upon the improvements they had effected.
A few notices from his report will give an idea of the state
of Ulster at the commencement of this great social revolution :—

Armagh was one of the six counties confiscated by
James I.   The territory had belonged to the O'Neills, the
O'Hanlons, the O'Carrols, and M'Kanes, whose people were
all involved more or less in the fortunes of the Earl of Tyrone,
who wielded sovereign power over this portion of Ulster.
The plantation scheme was said to be the work of the Privy
Council of Ireland, and submitted by them for the adoption
of the English Government.   It was part of the plan that
all the lands escheated in each county should be divided into
four parts, whereof two should be subdivided into proportions
consisting of about 1,000 acres a piece ; a third part into
proportions of 1,500 acres ; and the fourth in proportions of
2,000 acres.   Every proportion was to be made into a parish,
a church was to be erected on it, and the minister endowed
with glebe land.   If an incumbent of a parish of 1,000 acres
he was to have sixty ; if of 1,500 acres, ninety ; and if 2,000
acres, he was to have 120 acres ; and the whole tithes and

duties of every parish should be allotted to the incumbent as well as the glebe. The undertakers were to be of several sorts. 1st, English and Scotch, who were to plant their proportions with English and Scotch tenants; 2nd, servitors in Ireland, who might take English or Scotch tenants at their choice; 3rd, natives of the county, who were to be free-holders.

With respect to the disposal of the natives, it was arranged that the same course should be adopted as in the county of Tyrone, which was this: some were to be planted upon two of the small proportions, and upon the glebes; others upon the land of Sir Art O'Neill's sons and Sir Henry Oge O'Neill's sons, 'and of such other Irish as shall be thought fit to have any *freeholds*; some others upon the portions of such servitors as are not able to inhabit these lands with English or Scotch tenants, especially of *such as best know how to rule and order the Irish.* But the swordsmen (that is, the armed retainers or soldiers of the chiefs) are to be transplanted into such other parts of the kingdom as, by reason of the wastes therein, are fittest to receive them, namely, into Connaught and some parts of Munster, where they are to be dispersed, and not planted together in one place; and such swordsmen, who have not followers or cattle of their own, to be disposed of in his majesty's service.' This provision about planting the swordsmen, however, was not carried out. The whole county of Armagh was found to contain 77,300 acres of arable and pasture land, which would make 60 proportions. That county, as well as other parts of ancient Ireland, was divided into ballyboes, or townlands, tracts of tillage land surrounding the native villages unenclosed, and held in *rundale,* having ranges of pasture for their cattle, which were herded in common, each owner being entitled to a certain number of ' collops ' in proportion to his arable land. As these ballyboes were not of equal extent, the English made the division of land by acres, and erected boundary fences.

M

The primate's share in this county was 2,400 acres. The glebes comprised 4,650 acres; the College of Dublin got 1,200, and the Free School at Armagh 720; Sir Turlough M'Henry possessed 9,900 acres, and 4,900 had been granted to Sir Henry Oge O'Neill. After these deductions, there were for the undertakers 55,620 acres, making in all forty-two proportions.

Number one in the survey is the estate of William Brownlow, Esq., which contained two proportions, making together 2,500 acres. Pynar reported as follows: ' Upon the proportion of Ballenemony there is a strong stone house within a good island ; and at Dowcoran there is a very fair house of stone and brick, with good lyme, and hath a strong bawne of timber and earth with a pallizado about it. There is now laid in readiness both lyme and stone, to make a bawne thereof, the which is promised to be done this summer. He hath made a very fair town, consisting of forty-two houses, all which are inhabited with English families, and the streets all paved clean through ; also two water-mills and a wind-mill, all for corn, and he hath store of arms in his house.'

Pynar found 'planted and estated' on this territory 57 families altogether, who were able to furnish 100 men with arms, there not being one Irish family upon all the land. There was, however, a number of sub-tenants, which accounts for the fact that there was 'good store of tillage.' Five of the English settlers were freeholders, having 120 acres each; and there were 52 leaseholders, whose farms varied in size from 420 acres to 5 ; six of them holding 100 acres and upwards. This was the foundation of the flourishing town of Lurgan.

Mr. Obens had 2,000 acres obtained from William Powell, the first patentee. He had built a bawne of sods with a pallizado of boards ditched about. Within this there was a 'good fair house of brick and lyme,' and near it he had built four houses, inhabited by English families. There were twenty settlers, who with their under-tenants were able to furnish forty-six armed men. This was the beginning of Portadown.

The fourth lot was obtained from the first patentee by Mr. Cope, who had 3,000 acres. ' He built a bawne of lyme and stone 180 feet square, 14 feet high, with four flankers; and in three of them he had built very good lodgings, which were three stories high.' He erected two water-mills and one wind-mill, and near the bawne he had built fourteen houses of timber, which were inhabited by English families. This is now the rich district of Lough Gall.

It should be observed here that, in all these crown grants, the patentees were charged crown rents only for the *arable* lands conveyed by their title-deeds, bogs, wastes, mountain, and unreclaimed lands of every description being thrown in gratuitously; amounting probably to ten or fifteen times the quantity of demised ground set down in acres. Lord Lurgan's agent, Mr. Hancock, at the commencement of his evidence before the Devon Commission, stated that ' Lord Lurgan is owner of about 24,600 acres, with a population of 23,800, under the census of 1841 '—that is, by means of original reclamation, drainage, and other works of agricultural improvement, Mr. Brownlow's 2,500 acres of the year 1619, had silently grown up to 24,600 acres, and his hundred swordsmen, or pikemen, the representatives of 57 families, with a few subordinates, had multiplied to 23,800 souls. Now Mr. Hancock founds the tenant-right custom upon the fact that few, if any, of the ' patentees were wealthy; ' we may therefore fairly presume that the *settlers built their own houses, and made their own improvements at their own expense,* contrary to the English practice.' As the population increased, and ' arable ' land became valuable, bogs, wastes, and barren land were gradually reclaimed and cultivated, through the hard labour and at the cost of the occupying tenantry, until the possessions of his descendants have spread over ten times the area nominally demised by the crown to their progenitor. This process went on all over the province.

Sixteen years passed away, and in the opinion of the Government the London companies and the Irish Society, instead of reforming as Irish planters, went on from bad to worse. Accordingly, in 1631, Charles I. found it necessary to bring them into the Star Chamber. In a letter to the lords justices he said : —

'Our father, of blessed memory, in his wisdom and singular care, both to fortify and preserve that country of Ireland from foreign and inward forces, and also for the better establishment of true religion, justice, civility, and commerce, found it most necessary to erect British plantations there; and, to that end, ordained and published many politic and good orders, and for the encouragement of planters gave them large proportions and privileges. Above the rest, his grace and favour was most enlarged to the Londoners, who undertook the plantation of a considerable part of Ulster, and were specially chosen for their ability and professed zeal to public works ; and yet advertisements have been given from time to time, not only by private men, but by all succeeding deputies, and by commissioners sent from hence and chosen there, and being many of them of our council, that the *Londoners for private lucre* have broken and neglected both their general printed ordinances and other particular directions given by us and our council here, so as if they hall escape unpunished all others will be heartened to do the like, and in the end expose that our kingdom to former confusions and dangers; for prevention whereof we have, upon mature advice of our councillors for those causes, caused them to be questioned in our high court of Star-chamber here, whence commission is now sent to examine witnesses, upon interrogatories, for discovery of the truth; and because we understand that the Londoners heretofore prevailed with some, from whom we expected better service, that in the return of the last commission many things agreed under the hands of most commissioners were not accordingly certified : Now that our service may not suffer by like partiality, we will and require you to have an especial eye to this business ; and take care that this commission be faithfully executed, and that no practice or indirect means be used, either to delay the return or to frustrate the ends of truth in every interrogatory.'

This proceeding on the part of the crown was ascribed to the influence of Bishop Bramhall, who had come over with Lord Strafford as his chaplain. The result was, that in 1632 the whole county of Londonderry was sequestrated, and the rents levied for the king's use, the Bishop of Derry being appointed receiver and authorised to make leases. The lord chancellor, with the concurrence of the other judges, decreed that the letters patent should be surrendered and cancelled. This decree was duly executed.

Cromwell reinstated the companies in their possessions, and Charles II., instead of reversing the forfeiture, granted a new charter. This charter founded a system of protection and corporate exclusiveness, the most perfect perhaps that ever existed in the three kingdoms. He began by constituting Londonderry a county, and Derry city a corporation —to be called Londonderry. He named the aldermen and burgesses, who were to hold their offices during their natural lives. He placed both the county and city under the control of ' the Irish Society,' which was then definitely formed. He appointed Sir Thomas Adams first governor, and John Saunders, deputy governor. He also appointed the twenty-four assistants, all citizens of London. He invested the society with full power ' to send orders and directions from this kingdom of England into the said realm of Ireland, by letters or otherwise, for the ordering, directing, and disposing of all and all manner of matters and things whatsoever of and concerning the same plantation, or the disposition or government thereof. The grant of property was most comprehensive :—

' We also will, and, by these presents for us, our heirs and successors, do give, grant, and confirm to the said society of the governor and assistants [London] of the new plantation in Ulster within the realm of Ireland, and their successors:

'All that the city, fort, and town of Derry, and all edifices
and structures thereof, with the appurtenances, in the county
of the city of Derry aforesaid, in the province of Ulster, in
our realm of Ireland ; and also the whole island of Derry,
with the appurtenances, and all lands and the whole ground
within the island of Derry aforesaid, in the said county of
the city of Derry, otherwise Londonderry, within the province of Ulster, in our aforesaid realm of Ireland. And
also all those lands next adjacent to the said city or town of
Derry, lying and being on or towards the west part of the
river of Loughfoyle, containing by estimation four thousand
acres, besides bog and barren mountains, which said bog and
barren mountains may be had and used as waste to the same
city belonging. And also all that portion and proportion of
land by the general survey of all the lands in the aforesaid
late county of Coleraine, now Londonderry, heretofore taken,
called the great proportion of Boughtbegg, lying and being
in the barony or precinct of Coleraine, now Londonderry,
within the province of Ulster aforesaid, in our said realm of
Ireland; that is to say, all lands, tenements, and other hereditaments, called and known by the names, and situate,
lying, and being in or within the several towns, villages,
hamlets, places, balliboes, or parcels of land following, that
is to say : Hacketbegg, being two balliboes of land; Agla-
kightagh, being two balliboes of land; Altybryan, being one
balliboe of land ; Bratbooly, being one balliboe of land;
Hackmoore, being one balliboe of land; Tirecurrin, being one
balliboe of land; Edermale, being one balliboe of land;
Lennagorran, being one balliboe of land; Knockmult, being
one balliboe of land; Boughtmore, being one balliboe of land;
Boughtbegg, being one balliboe of land, &c.

'We will also, and by these presents for us, our heirs and
successors, do grant and confirm to the said society of the
governor and assistants [London] of the new plantation in
Ulster, and their successors, that they and their successors,
and also all their assigns, deputies, ministers, and servants
shall and may have full liberty of fishing, hawking, and

fowling in all the places, tenements, shores, and coasts aforesaid, at their will and pleasure.

'And that it shall and may be lawful to and for them and every of them to draw and dry their nets, and pack the fishes there taken upon any part of the shores and coasts aforesaid where they shall fish ; and the salmons and other fishes there taken to take thence and carry away without any impediment, contradiction, or molestation of us or others whomsoever, wheresoever it shall happen to be done.

'And that in like manner they may have the several fishings and fowlings within the city of Londonderry aforesaid, and in all lands and tenements before mentioned to be granted and confirmed to the said society of the governor and assistants [London] of the new plantation in Ulster and their successors, and in the river and water of Loughfoile, to the ebb of the sea, and in the river or water of Bann to Loughneagh.'

The grants were made without any reservation in favour of the tenants or the old inhabitants, saving some portions of land given by letters patent by his grandfather to 'certain *Irish gentlemen* in the said county of Londonderry, heretofore inhabiting and residing, and who were heretofore made freeholders, and their successors, under a small yearly rent,' which was to be paid to the Irish Society. Even the Irish gentlemen were not allowed to hold their ancient inheritance directly under the crown. I am informed that there is but one Roman Catholic landed gentleman now remaining in the whole province of Ulster.

The Londoners had extraordinary privileges as traders. They had free quarters in every port throughout the kingdom, while they treated all but the members of their own body as 'foreigners.' They knew nothing of reciprocity :—

' And further we will, and, by these presents for us, our heirs and successors, do grant and confirm to the said mayor and commonalty and citizens of our city of Londonderry aforesaid, that all citizens of the said city of Londonderry and liberty of the same (as much as in us is) be for ever quit

and free, and all their things throughout all Ireland, of all
tolls, wharfage, murage, anchorage, beaconage, pavage,
pontage, piccage, stallage, passage, and lestage, and of all
other tolls and duties.'

The 'foreigners,' including all his majesty's subjects but
the favoured few within the walls of Derry, were forbidden
to buy or sell, or practise any trade in this sanctuary of freedom and head-centre of 'civility.' 'And that merchants
and others which are not of the freedom of the city of
Londonderry aforesaid shall not sell by retail any wines or
other wares whatsoever within the same city of Londonderry,
the suburbs, liberties, or franchises of the same, upon pain
of forfeiture for the things so bought, or the value thereof, to
the use of the mayor and commonalty and citizens of the
city of Londonderry aforesaid. And also that no person
being a foreigner from the freedom of the city aforesaid
shall use or exercise within the same city, liberties or suburbs
of the same, any art, mystery, or manual occupation whatsoever, to make his gain and profit thereof, upon pain of forfeiture of forty shillings for every time wherein such person
shall use or exercise within the said city of Londonderry,
liberties, and suburbs of the same, any art, mystery, or
manual occupation as aforesaid.'

Foreigners were not allowed to buy from or sell to
foreigners, and there was to be no market for the accommodation of the unprivileged inhabitants within seven miles
of the city.

Similar exclusive privileges were conferred upon the
corporation of Coleraine. Such was the system established
by the City of London in its model communities in Ireland
normal schools of freedom, fountains of civilising and Chris-
tianising influences which were to reclaim and convert the
barbarous and superstitious natives into loyal subjects and
enlightened Protestants! What the natives beheld in
Londonderry was, in fact, a royal organisation of selfishness, bigotry, and monopoly, of the most intensely exclusive
and repulsive character. In one sense the Londoners in

Derry showed that they peculiarly prized the blessings of civilisation, for they kept them all to themselves. The fountain was flowing in the most tempting manner before the thirsty Irish, but let them dare to drink of it at their peril! A fine which no Irishman was then able to pay must be the penalty for every attempt at civilisation!

The representatives of Derry and Coleraine were not only elected without cost, but paid for their attendance in Parliament.

From the very beginning, the greatest possible care was taken to keep out the Irish. The society, in 1615, sent precepts to all the companies requiring each of them to send one or two artisans, with their families, into Ulster, to settle there; and directions were also given, in order that Derry might not in future be peopled with Irish, that twelve Christ's Hospital and other poor children should be sent there as apprentices and servants, and the inhabitants were to be prohibited from taking Irish apprentices. Directions were also given to the companies, to repair the churches on their several proportions, and furnish the ministers with a bible, common-prayer book, and a communion cup. The trades which the society recommended as proper to introduce into Ulster were, weavers of common cloth, fustians, and new stuffs, felt-makers and trimmers of hats, and hat-band makers, locksmiths and farriers, tanners and fellmongers, iron makers, glass-makers, pewterers, coast fishermen, turners, basket-makers, tallow-chandlers, dyers, and curriers.

The Christ's Hospital children arrived safe, and became the precious seed of the 'prentice boys.

In 1629 the following return was made of the total disbursements by the Londoners in Derry from January 2, 1609, to this year:—

					£
For 77½ houses at 140*l.* a house	.	.	.	.	10,850
For 33 houses at 80*l.* a house	.	.	.	.	2,680
For the Lord Bishop's house	.	.	.	.	500
For the walls and fortifications	.	.	.	.	8,357

		£
For digging the ditch and filling earth for the rampire	.	1,500
For levelling earth to lay the rampire	. . .	500
For building a faggot quay at the water-gate	. .	100
For two quays at the lime kilns	. . . .	10
For the building of the town house	. . .	500
For the quays at the ferry	. . . . .	60
For carriage and mounting the ordnance	. . .	40
For arms	. . . .	558
For a guardhouse	. . . . . .	50
For the platforms for bulwarks	. . . .	300
For some work done at the old church	. . .	40
For some work done at the town pike	. . .	6
For sinking 22 cellars, and sundry of the houses not done at first, at 20s. a cellar, one with another	. .	440
For the building of lime kilns	. . . .	120
		26,611

Sum total, as given in the Commissioners' account　　. 27,197

The exclusive and protective system utterly failed to accomplish its purpose in keeping out the Irish.

Sir Thomas Phillips made a muster-roll in 1622, in which he gives 110 as the number of settlers in the city of Derry capable of bearing arms. There are but two Irish names in the list—Ermine M'Swine, and James Doherty. The first, from his Christian name, seemed to have been of mixed blood, the son of a judge, which would account for his orthodoxy. But his presence might have reminded the citizens unpleasantly of the Irish battle-axes. Never were greater pains taken to keep a community pure than within the sacred precincts of the Derry walls; and never was Protestantism more tenderly fostered by the state—so far as secular advantages could do it. The natives were treated as 'foreigners.' No trade was permitted except by the chartered British. They were free of tolls all over the land, and for their sake restrictions were placed on everybody that could in any way interfere with their worldly interests. So complete was the system of exclusion kept up by the English Government and the London corporation, in this grand experiment for planting religion and civility among a barbarous people, that, so late as the year 1708, the Derry corporation considered itself nothing more or less than *a branch of the City of London*! In that year they sent an address to the Irish Society, to be presented through them to the queen. ' In this address they stated themselves to be a branch of the City of London. The secretary was ordered to wait upon the lord lieutenant of Ireland with the address and entreat the favour of his lordship's advice concerning the presenting of the same to her majesty.' A few days after it was announced that the address had been graciously received, and published in the *Gazette.*

The Irish were kept out of the enclosed part of the city till a late period. In the memory of the present generation there was no Catholic house within the walls, and I believe it is not much longer since the Catholic servants within the sacred enclosure were obliged to go outside at night to sleep among their kinsfolk. The English garrison did not multiply very fast. In 1626 there were only 109 families in the city, of which five were families of soldiers liable to be removed. Archbishop King stated that in 1690 the whole of the population of the parish, including the Donegal part, was about 700.

But the irrepressible Irish increased and multiplied around the walls with alarming rapidity. The tide of native population rose steadily against the ramparts of exclusion, and could no more be kept back than the tide in the Foyle. In the general census of 1800 there were no returns from Derry. But in 1814 it was stated in a report by the deputation from the Irish Society, that the population amounted at that time to 14,087 persons. This must have included the suburbs. In the census of 1821 the city was found to have 9,313 inhabitants. The city and suburbs together contained 16,971.

The report of the commissioners of public instruction in 1831 made a startling disclosure as to the effect of the system of exclusion in this ' branch of the City of London.' In the parish of Templemore (part of) there were—

Members of the Established Church	.	.	,	.	3,166
Presbyterians	.	.	.	.	5,811
Roman Catholics	.	.	.	.	9,838

The report of 1834 gave the Roman Catholics, 10,299; the Presbyterians, 6,083; and the Church only 3,314.

The figures now are—Catholics	.	.	.	12,036
Protestants of all denominations	.	.	.	8,839
Majority of Irish and Catholics in this 'branch of the City of London'	.	.	.	.	.	3,197

This majority is about equal to the whole number which the exclusive system, with all its ' protection' and ' bounties,' could produce for the Established Church in the course of two centuries! If the Irish had been admitted to the Pale of English civilisation, and instructed in the industrial arts by the settlers, the results with respect to religion might have been very different. In the long run the Church of Rome has been the greatest gainer by coercion. Derry has been a miniature representation of the Establishment. The 'prentice boys, like their betters, must yield to the spirit of the age, and submit with the best grace they can to the rule of religious equality.

The plantation was, however, wonderfully successful on the whole. In thirty years, towns, fortresses, factories, arose, pastures, ploughed up, were converted into broad corn-fields, orchards, gardens, hedges, &c. were planted. How did this happen? ' The answer is that it sprang from the security of tenure which the plantation settlement supplied. The landlords were in every case bound to make fixed estates to their tenants at the risk of sequestration and forfeiture. Hence their power of selling their plantation rights and improvements. This is the origin of Ulster tenant-right.'

Yet the work went on slowly enough in some districts. The viceroy, Chichester, was not neglected in the distribution of the spoils. He not only got the O'Dogherty's country, Innishown, but a large tract in Antrim, including the towns of Carrickfergus and Belfast. An English tourist travel-

ling that way in 1635 gives a quaint description of the
country in that transition period :—

On July 5 he landed at Carrickfergus, where he found that
Lord Chichester had a stately house, ' or rather like a
prince's palace.' In Belfast, he said, my Lord Chichester
had another *daintie*, stately palace, which, indeed, was the
glory and beauty of the town. And there were also *daintie*
orchards, gardens, and walks planted. The Bishop of
Dromore, to whom the town of Dromore entirely belonged,
lived there in a ' little timber house.' He was not given to
hospitality, for though his chaplain was a Manchester man,
named Leigh, he allowed his English visitor to stop at an
inn over the way. ' This,' wrote the tourist, ' is a very dear
house, 8*d.* ordinary for ourselves, 6*d.* for our servants, and
we were overcharged in *beere*.' The way thence to Newry
was most difficult for a stranger to find out. ' Therein he
wandered, and, being lost, fell among the Irish *touns*.'
The Irish houses were the poorest cabins he had seen,
erected in the middle of fields and grounds which they
farmed and rented. ' This,' he added, ' is a wild country,
not inhabited, planted, nor enclosed.' He gave an Irishman
' a groat ' to bring him into the way, yet he led him, like a
villein, directly out of the way, and so left him in the lurch.

Leaving Belfast, this Englishman said : ' Near hereunto,
Mr. Arthur Hill, son and heir of Sir Moyses Hill, hath a
brave plantation, which he holds by lease, and which has
still forty years to come. The plantation, it is said, doth
yield him 1,000*l.* per annum. Many Lancashire and
Cheshire men are here planted. They sit upon a rack-
rent, and pay 5*s.* or 6*s.* for good ploughing land, which now
is clothed with excellent good *corne*.'

According to the Down survey, made twenty-two years
later, Dromore had not improved : ' There are no buildings
in this parish ; only Dromore, it being a market town, hath
some old thatched houses and a ruined church standing in
it. What other buildings are in the parish are nothing but
removeable *creaghts*.'

To the economist and the legislator, the most interesting portions of the state papers of the 16th and 17th centuries are, undoubtedly, those which tell us how the people lived, how they were employed, housed, and fed, what measure of happiness fell to their lot, and what were the causes that affected their welfare, that made them contented and loyal, or miserable and disaffected. Contemporary authors, who deal with social phenomena, are also read with special interest for the same reason. They present pictures of society in their own time, and enable us to conceive the sort of life our forefathers led, and to estimate, at least in a rough way, what they did for posterity.

Harris was moved to write his ' History of Down ' by indignation at the misrepresentations of the English press of his day. They had the audacity to say that ' the Irish people were uncivilised, rude, and barbarous; that they delighted in butter *tempered* with oatmeal, and sometimes flesh without bread, which they ate raw, having first pressed the blood out of it; and drank down large draughts of usquebaugh for digestion, reserving their little corn for the horses; that their dress and habits were no less barbarous; that cattle was their chief wealth; that they counted it no infamy to commit robberies, and that in their view violence and murder were in no way displeasing to God; that the country was overgrown with woods, which abounded in wolves and other voracious animals,' &c. It was, no doubt, very provoking that such stories should be repeated 130 years after the plantation of Ulster, and Harris undertook, with laudable patriotism, to show ' how far this description of Ireland was removed from the truth, from the present state of only one county in the kingdom.' The information which the well-informed writer gives is most valuable, and very much to the purpose of our present inquiry.

More than half the arable ground was then (in 1745) under tillage, affording great quantities of oats, some rye and wheat, and ' plenty of barley,' commonly called English or spring barley, making excellent malt liquor, which of late, by means of drying the grain with Kilkenny coals, was exceedingly improved. The ale made in the county was distinguished for its fine colour and flavour. The people found the benefit of ' *a sufficient tillage,* being not obliged to take up with the poor unwholesome diet which the commonalty of Munster and Connaught had been forced to in the late years of scarcity; and sickness and mortality were not near so great as in other provinces of the kingdom.'

Yet the county Down seemed very unfavourable for tillage. The economists of our time, perhaps our viceroys too, would say it was only fit for bullocks and sheep. It was ' naturally coarse, and full of hills; the air was sharp and cold in winter, with earlier frosts than in the south, the soil inclined to *wood,* unless constantly ploughed and kept open, and the low grounds degenerated into morass or bog where the drains were neglected. Yet, by the constant labour and industry of the inhabitants, the morass grounds had of late, by burning and proper management, produced surprisingly large crops of rye and oats. Coarse lands, manured with lime, had answered the farmers' views in wheat, and yielded a great produce, and wherever marl was found there was great store of barley. The staple commodity of the county was linen, due care of which manufacture brought great wealth among the people. Consequently the county was observed to be 'populous and flourishing, though it did not become amenable to the laws till the reign of Queen Elizabeth, nor fully till the reign of James I.' The English habit, language, and manners almost universally prevailed. ' Irish,' says Harris, ' can be heard only among the inferior rank of *Irish Papists,* and even that little diminishes every day, by the great desire the poor natives have that their children should be taught to read and write in the English tongue in the Charter, or other English Protestant schools, to which they willingly send them.' The author exults in the progress of Protestantism. There were but two Catholic gentlemen in the

county who had estates, and their income was very moderate. When the priests were registered in 1704 there were
but thirty in the county. In 1733 the books of the hearth-
money collectors showed—

Protestant families in the county Down	. . .	14,060
Catholic families	. . . . . .	5,210
Total Protestants, reckoning five a family	. .	70,300
Total Catholics	. . . . . .	26,050
Protestant majority	. . . . .	44,250

Our author, who was an excellent Protestant of the 18th
century type, with boundless faith in the moral influence of
the Charter schools, would be greatly distressed if he could
have lived in these degenerate days, and seen the last religious census, which gives the following figures for the
county of Down:—

Protestants of all denominations	. . .	202,026
Catholics	. . . . . .	97,240
Total population	. . . .	299,266

The total number of souls in the county in the year 1733
was 96,350. These figures show that the population was
more than trebled in 130 years, and that the Catholics have
increased nearly fourfold.

The history of the Hertfort estate illustrates every phase
of the tenant-right question. It contains 66,000 acres,
and comprises the barony of Upper Massereene, part of the
barony of Upper Belfast, in the county of Antrim, and part
of the baronies of Castlereagh and Lower Iveagh, in the
county of Down; consisting altogether of no less than 140
townlands. It extends from Dunmurry to Lough Neagh,
a distance of about fourteen miles as the crow flies. When
the Devon commission made its inquiry, the population
upon this estate amounted to about 50,000. It contains
mountain land, and the mountains are particularly wet,
because, unlike the mountains in other parts of the country,
the substratum is a stiff retentive clay. At that time there
was not a spot of mountain or bog upon Lord Hertfort's

estate that was not let by the acre. About one-third of the
land is of first-rate quality; there are 15,000 or 16,000
acres of mountain, and about the same quantity of land of
medium quality.

In the early part of Elizabeth's reign this property formed
a section of the immense territory ruled over by the O'Neills.
One of these princes was called the Captain of *Kill-Ultagh.*
In those times, when might was right, this redoubtable chief
levied heavy contributions on the settlers, partly in retalia-
tion for aggressions and outrages perpetrated by the English
upon his own people. The queen, with the view of effecting
a reconciliation, requested the lord deputy, Sir H. Sidney,
to pay the Irish chief a visit. He did so, but his welcome
was by no means gratifying. In fact, O'Neill would not
condescend to receive him at all. His reason for exhibiting
a want of hospitality so un-Irish was this:—He said his
' home had been pillaged, his lands swept of their cattle, and
his vassals shot like wild animals.' The lord deputy, in his
notes of the northern tour, written in October, 1585, says:—
' I came to Kill-Ultagh, which I found rich and plentiful,
after the manner of these countries. But the captain was
proud and insolent; he would not come to me, nor have I
apt reason to visit him as I would. But he shall be paid
for this before long; I will not remain in his debt.' The
' apt reason' for carrying out this threat soon occurred.
Tyrone had once more taken the field against the queen;
the captain joined his relative; all his property was consequently forfeited, and handed over to Sir Fulke Conway, a
Welsh soldier of some celebrity. Sir Fulke died in 1626,
and his brother, who was a favourite of Charles I., succeeded
to the estate, to which his royal patron added the lands of
Derryvolgie, thus making him lord of nearly 70,000 statute
acres of the broad lands of Down and Antrim. The Conways brought over a number of English and Welsh families,
who settled on the estate, and intermarrying with the
natives, a race of sturdy yeomen soon sprang up. The
Conways were good landlords, and greatly beloved by the

N

people.   With the addition made to the property the king
conferred upon the fortunate recipient of his bounty the
title of Baron.   At the close of 1627, Lord Conway began
the erection of a castle (finished in 1630) on a picturesque
mount overlooking the Lagan, and commanding a view of
the hills of Down.   During the struggles of 1641 the castle
was burned down, together with the greater part of the
town, which up to this time was called Lisnagarvah, but
thenceforth it received the name of Lisburn.   Very little,
however, had been done by the settlers when the outbreak
occurred, for an English traveller in 1635 remarked that
' neither the town nor the country thereabouts was *planted*,
being almost all woods and moorish.'   About a month after
the breaking out of the rebellion the king's forces, under
Sir George Rawdon, obtained a signal victory over the Irish
commanded by Sir Phelim O'Neill, Sir Con M'Guinness,
and General Plunket.   In 1662 the town obtained a charter
of incorporation from Charles II., and sent two members to
the Irish parliament, the church being at the same time
made the cathedral for Down and Connor.   The Conway
estates passed to the Seymours in this way.   Popham
Seymour, Esq., was the son of Sir Edward Seymour, fourth
baronet, described by Bishop Burnet as ' the ablest man of
his party, the first speaker of the House of Commons that
was not bred to the law; a graceful man, bold and quick,
and of high birth, being the elder branch of the Seymour
family.'   Popham Seymour inherited the estates of the
Earl of Conway, who was his cousin, under a will dated
August 19, 1683, and assumed in consequence the surname
of Conway.   This gentleman died unmarried, and was
succeeded by his brother Francis, who was raised to the
peerage in 1703 by the title of Baron Conway, of Kill-Ultagh,
county Antrim.   His eldest son, the second baron, was
created Viscount Beauchamp and Earl of Hertfort in 1750.
In 1765 he was Viceroy of Ireland, and in 1793 he was
created Marquis of Hertfort.   The present peer, born in
the year 1800, is the fourth marquis, having succeeded his
father in 1842.

Lisburn is classic ground. It represents all sorts of historic interest. On this hill, now called the Castle Gardens, the Captain of Kill-Ultagh mustered his galloglasse. Here, amid the flames of the burning town, was fought a decisive battle between the English and the Irish, one of the Irish chiefs in that encounter being the ancestor of the restorer of St. Patrick's Cathedral. The battle lasted till near midnight, when the Irish were put to flight, leaving behind them dead and wounded thrice the number of the entire garrison. Here, on this mount, stood William III. in June, 1690. I saw in the church the monument of Jeremy Taylor, and the pulpit from which the most eloquent of bishops delivered his immortal sermons. I saw the tablet erected by his mother to the memory of Nicholson, the young hero of Delhi, and those of several other natives of Lisburn who have contributed, by their genius and courage, to promote the fame and power of England. Among the rest Lieutenant Dobbs, who was killed in an encounter with Paul Jones, the American pirate, in Carrickfergus Bay.

I received a hospitable welcome from a loyal gentleman in the house which was the residence of General Munroe, the hero of '98, and saw the spot in the square where he was hanged in view of his own windows. But I confess that none of the monuments of the past excited so much interest in my mind as the house of Louis Crommelin, the Huguenot refugee, who founded the linen manufacture at Lisburn. That house is now occupied by Mr. Hugh M'Call, author of ' Our Staple Manufactures,' who worthily represents the intelligence, the public spirit, and patriotism of the English and French settlers, with a dash of the Irish ardour, a combination of elements which perhaps produces the best 'staple' of character. I stood upon the identical oak floor upon which old Crommelin planned and worked, and in the graveyard Mr. M'Call deciphered for me the almost obliterated inscriptions, recording the deaths of various members of the Crommelin family. Their leader, Louis himself, died in July, 1727, aged 75 years.

The revocation of the Edict of Nantes drove three quarters of a million of Protestants out of France. A great number settled in London, where they established the arts of silk-weaving in Spitalfields and of fancy jewellery in St. Giles's. About 6,000 fled to Ireland, of whom many settled in Dublin, where they commenced the silk manufacture, and where one of them, La Touche, opened the first banking establishment. Wherever they settled they were missionaries of industry, and examples of perseverance and success in skilled labour, as well as integrity in commerce. Many of those exiles settled in Lisburn, and the colony was subsequently joined by Louis Crommelin, a native of Armandcourt near St. Quentin, where for several centuries his forefathers had carried on the flaxen manufacture on their own extensive possessions in the province of Picardy. Foreseeing the storm of persecution, the family had removed to Holland, and, at the personal request of the Prince of Orange, Louis came over to take charge of the colonies of his countrymen, which had been established in different parts of Ireland. The linen trade had flourished in this country from the earliest times. Linen formed, down to the reign of Elizabeth, almost the only dress of the population, from the king down—saffron-coloured, and worn in immense flowing robes, occasionally wrapped in various forms round the body. Lord Strafford had exerted himself strenuously to improve the fabric by the forcible introduction of better looms; but little had been done in this direction till the Huguenots came and brought their own looms, suited for the manufacture of fine fabrics. Mark Dupre, Nicholas de la Cherois, Obre, Rochet, Bouchoir, St. Clair, and others, whose ashes lie beside the Lisburn Cathedral and in the neighbouring churchyards, and many of whose descendants still survive among the gentry and manufacturers of Down and Antrim, were, with Crommelin, the chief promoters of the linen trade which has wrought such wonders in the province of Ulster. Lord Conway granted the Lisburn colonists a site for a place of worship, which was known as the French Church, and stood on the ground now occupied by the Court-house in Castle Street. The Government paid 60*l.* a year to their first minister, Charles de la Valade, who was succeeded by his relative, the Rev. Saumarez du Bourdieu, distinguished as a divine and a historian. His father was chaplain to the famous Schomberg, and when he fell from his horse mortally wounded the reverend gentleman carried him in his arms to the spot on which he died a short time after. Talent was hereditary in this family, the Rev. John du Bourdieu, rector of Annahilt, was author of the Statistical Surveys of Down and Antrim, published by the Royal Dublin Society. Referring to his ancestors he says that his father had been fifty-six years minister of the French Church in Lisburn. Mr. M'Call states that, for some time before his death in 1812, he held the living of Lambeg, the members of the French Church having by that time merged into union with the congregation of the Lisburn Cathedral. A similar process took place in Dublin, Portarlington, and elsewhere, the descendants of the Huguenots becoming zealous members of the Established Church.

Du Bourdieu informs us that Louis Crommelin obtained a patent for carrying on and improving the linen manufacture, with a grant of 800*l.* per annum, as interest of 10,000*l.*, to be advanced by him as a capital for carrying on the same; 200*l.* per annum for his trouble; 120*l.* per annum for three assistants; and 160*l.* for the support of the chaplain. Mr. M'Call, in his book, copies the following note of payments made by the Government from 1704 to 1708 :—

	£	s.	d.
Louis Crommelin, as overseer of linen manufacture .	470	19	0
W. Crommelin, salary and rent of Kilkenny factory .	451	6	7
Louis Crommelin, to repay him for sums advanced to flax dressers and reed makers, and for services of French ministers	2,225	0	0
Louis Crommelin, for individual expenses and for sums paid Thomas Turner, of Lurgan, for buying flax-seed and printing reports	993	4	0
Louis Crommelin, three years' pension . .	600	0	0
French minister's two years' pension . . .	120	0	0
Total . . .	£4,860	9	7

It should be mentioned, that when the owner of Lisburn, then Earl of Hertfort, held the office of lord lieutenant in 1765, with his son, Viscount Beauchamp, as chief secretary, he rendered very valuable services to the linen trade, and was a liberal patron of the damask manufacture, which arrived at a degree of perfection hitherto unequalled, in the hands of Mr. William Coulson, founder of the great establishment of that name which still flourishes in Lisburn, and from whom not only the court of St. James's but foreign courts also received their table linen. Du Bourdieu mentions that Lisburn and Lurgan were the great markets for cambrics— the name given to cloth of this description, which was then above five shillings a yard; under that price it was called lawn. In that neighbourhood cambric had been made which sold for 1*l.* 2*s.* 9*d.* a yard unbleached. The principal manufacturing establishments in addition to Messrs. Coulsons' are those of the Messrs. Richardson and Co. and the Messrs. Barbour.

Lord Dufferin has written the ablest defence of the Irish landlords that has ever appeared. In that masterly work he says : ' But though a dealer in land and a payer of wages, I am above all things an Irishman, and as an Irishman I rejoice in any circumstance which tends to strengthen the independence of the tenant farmer, or to add to the comfort of the labourer's existence.' If titles and possessions implied the inheritance of religion and blood, Lord Dufferin ought indeed to be ' Irish of the Irish ' as the men of Ulster in the olden times proudly called themselves. On the railroad from Belfast to Bangor there is a station constructed with singular beauty, like the castellated entrance to a baronial hall, and on the elaborately chiselled stone we read ' Clandeboye.' Under the railway from Graypoint on Belfast Lough runs a carriage-drive two miles long, to the famous seat of the O'Neills, where his lordship's mansion is situated, enclosed among aged trees, remembrancers of the past. Perhaps there is no combination of names in the kingdom more suggestive of the barbaric power of the middle ages and the most refined culture of modern civilisation. The avenue, kept like a garden walk, with a flourishing plantation on each side, was cut through some of the best farms on the estate, and must have been a work of great expense. Taking this in connection with other costly improvements, among which are several picturesque buildings for the residence of workmen—model lodging-houses resembling fancy villas at the seaside—we can understand how his lordship, within the last fifteen years, has paid away in wages of labour the immense sum of 60,000*l.*, at the rate of 4,000*l.* a year.

The Abbot of Bangor never gave employment like that. William O'Donnon, the last of the line, was found in the thirty-second year of Henry VIII. to be possessed of thirty-one townlands in Ards and Upper Clandeboye, the grange of Earbeg in the county Antrim, the two Copeland Islands, the tithes of the island of Raghery, three rectories in Antrim, three in Down, and a townland in the Isle of Man. The abbey, some of the walls of which still remain, adjoining the parish church, was built early in the twelfth century. We are informed by Archdall, that it had so gone to ruin in 1469 through the neglect of the abbot, that he was evicted by order of Pope Paul II., who commanded that the friars of the third order of St. Francis should immediately take possession of it, which was accordingly done, says Wadding, by Father Nicholas of that order. The whole of the possessions were granted by James I. to James Viscount Clandeboye.

Bangor was one of the most celebrated schools in Ireland when this island was said to have been ' the *quiet* abode of learning and sanctity.' As to the quiet, I could never make out at what period it existed, nor how the ' thousands ' of students at Bangor could have been supported. The Danes came occasionally up the lough and murdered the monks *en masse*, plundering the shrines. But the greatest scourges of the monasteries in Down and elsewhere were, not the foreign pagans and pirates, but the professedly Christian chiefs of their own country. It appears, therefore, that neither the Irish clergy nor the people have much reason to regret the flight of the Celtic princes and nobles, who were utterly unable to fulfil the duties of a government; and who did little or nothing but consume what the industry of the peasants, under unparalleled difficulties, produced. The people of Clandeboye and Dufferin might have been proud that their chief received 40*l.* a year as a tribute or blackmail from Lecale, that he might abstain from visiting the settlers there with his galloglasse; but Lord Dufferin, the successor of the O'Neill of Clandeboye, spends among the peasantry of the present day 4,000*l.* a year in wages. And how different is the lot of the people! Not dwelling in wattled huts under the oaks of the primeval forest, but in neat slated houses, with whitewashed walls, looking so bright and pretty in the sunshine, like snowdrops in the distant landscape. On the hill between Bangor and Newtownards, Lord Dufferin has erected a beautiful tower, from which, reclining on his couch, he can see the country to an immense extent, from the mountains of Antrim to the mountains of Mourne, Strangford Lough, Belfast Lough, the Antrim coast, and Portpatrick at the other side of the Channel, all spread out before him like a coloured map.

CHAPTER XI.

THE REBELLION OF 1641.

THE Rebellion of 1641—generally called a 'massacre'—was undoubtedly a struggle on the part of the exiled nobles and clergy and the evicted peasants to get possession of their estates and farms, which had been occupied by the British settlers for nearly a generation. They might probably have continued to occupy them in peace, but for the fanaticism of the lords justices, Sir John Parsons and Sir John Borlace. It was reported and believed that, at a public entertainment in Dublin, Parsons declared that in twelve months no more Catholics should be seen in that country. The English Puritans and Scottish Covenanters were determined never to lay down their arms till they had made an end of Popery. Pym, the celebrated Puritan leader, avowed that the policy of his party was not to leave a priest alive in the land. Meantime, the Irish chiefs were busy intriguing at Rome, Madrid, Paris, and other continental capitals, clamouring for an invasion of Ireland, to restore monarchy and Catholicity—to expel the English planters from the forfeited lands. Philip III. of Spain encouraged these aspirations. He had an Irish legion under the command of Henry O'Neill, son of the fugitive Earl of Tyrone. It was reported that in 1630 there were in the service of the Archduchess, in the Spanish Netherlands alone, 100 Irish officers able to command companies, and 20 fit to be colonels. There were many others at Lisbon, Florence, Milan, and Naples. They had in readiness 5,000 or 6,000 stand of arms laid up at Antwerp, bought out of the deduction of their monthly pay. The banished ecclesiastics formed at every court a most efficient diplomatic corps, the chief of these intriguers being the celebrated Luke Wadding. Religious wars were popular in those times, and the invasion of Ireland would be like a crusade against heresy. But with the Irish chiefs the ruling passion was to get possession of their homes and their lands. The most active spirit among these was Roger, or Rory O'Moore, a man of high character, great ability, handsome person, and fascinating manners. With him were associated Conor Maguire, Costelloe M'Mahon, and Thorlough O'Neill, Sir Phelim O'Neill, Sir Con Magennis, Colonel Hugh M'Mahon, and the Rev. Dr. Heber M'Mahon. O'Moore visited the country, went through the several provinces, and, by communicating with the chiefs personally, organised the conspiracy to expel the British and recover the kingdom for Charles II. and the Pope.

The plan agreed upon by the confederates was this:— A rising when the harvest was gathered in; a simultaneous attack on all the English fortresses; the surprise of Dublin Castle, said to contain arms for 12,000 men; and to obtain for these objects all possible aid, in officers, men, and arms, from the Continent. The rising took place on the night of October 22, 1641. It might have been completely successful if the Castle of Dublin had been seized. It seemed an easy prey, for it was guarded only by a few pensioners and forty halberdiers, who would be quickly overpowered. But the plot was made known to the lords justices by an informer when on the eve of execution.

Sir Phelim O'Neill was one of those ' Irish gentlemen ' who, by royal favour, were permitted to retain some portions of their ancient patrimonies. At this time he was in possession of thirty-eight townlands in the barony of Dungannon, county Tyrone, containing 23,000 acres, then estimated to be worth 1,600*l.* a-year, equal to some 10,000*l.* of our money. Charles Boulton held by lease from the same chief 600 acres, at a yearly rent of 29*l.* for sixty years, in consideration of a fine of 1,000*l.* In 1641 this property yielded a profit rent of 150*l.* a year. Three townlands in the same barony were claimed by George Rawden of Lisnagarvagh, as leased to him by Sir Phelim under the rent of 100*l.*, estimated to be worth 50*l.* per annum.

Sir Phelim might, therefore, have been content, so far as property was concerned. But, setting aside patriotism, religion, and ambition, it is likely enough that he distrusted the Government, and feared the doom pronounced in Dublin Castle against all the gentlemen of his creed and race. At all events he put himself at the head of the insurrection in Ulster. He and the officers under his command, on the night of the 22nd, surprised and captured the forts of Charlemont and Mountjoy. The towns of Dungannon, Newry, Carrickmacross, Castleblancy, Tandragee fell into the hands of the insurgents, while the O'Reillys and Maguires overran Cavan and Fermanagh. Sir Conor Magennis wrote from Newry to the Government officers in Down : ' We are for our lives and liberties. We desire no blood to be shed ; but, if you mean to shed our blood, be sure we shall be as ready as you for that purpose.' And Sir Phelim O'Neill issued the following proclamation :—

' These are to intimate and make known unto all persons whatsoever, in and through the whole country, the true intent and meaning of us whose names are hereunto subscribed : 1. That the first assembling of us is nowise intended against our sovereign lord the king, nor hurt of any of his subjects, either English or Scotch ; but only for the defence and libertie of ourselves and the Irish natives of this kingdom. And we further declare that whatsoever hurt hitherto hath been done to any person shall be presently repaired ; and we will that every person forthwith, after proclamation hereof, make their speedy repaire unto their own houses, under paine of death, that no further hurt be done unto any one under the like paine, and that this be proclaimed in all places.

' PHELIM O'NEILL.

' At Dungannon, the 23rd October, 1641.'

It is easy for an insurgent chief to give such orders to a tumultuous mass of excited, vindictive, and drunken men, but not so easy to enforce them. The common notion among Protestants, however, that a midnight massacre of all the Protestant settlers was intended, or attempted, is certainly unfounded. Though horrible outrages were committed on both sides, the number of them has been greatly exaggerated. Mr. Prendergast quotes some contemporary authorities, which seem to be decisive on this point. In the same year was published by ' G. S., minister of God's word in Ireland,' ' A Brief Declaration of the Barbarous and Inhuman Dealings of the Northern Irish Rebels . . .; written to excite the English Nation to relieve our poor Wives and Children that have escaped the Rebels' savage Cruelties.'

This author says, it was the intention of the Irish to massacre all the English. On Saturday they were to disarm them; on Sunday to seize all their cattle and goods; on Monday, at the watchword ' Skeane,' they were to cut all the English throats. The former they executed; the third only (that is the massacre) they failed in.

That the massacre rested hitherto in intention only is further evident from the proclamation of the lords justices of February 8, 1642; for, while offering large sums for the heads of the chief northern gentlemen in arms (Sir Phelim O'Neill's name heading the list with a thousand pounds), the lords justices state that the massacre had failed. Many thousands had been robbed and spoiled, dispossessed of house and lands, many murdered on the spot; but the chief part of their plots (so the proclamation states), and amongst them a universal massacre, had been disappointed.

But, says Mr. Prendergast, after Lord Ormond and Sir Simon Harcourt, with the English forces, in the month of April, 1642, had burned the houses of the gentry in the Pale, and committed slaughters of unarmed men, and the Scotch forces, in the same month, after beating off Sir Phelim O'Neill's army at Newry, drowned and shot men, women, and priests, in that town, who had surrendered on condition of mercy, then it was that some of Sir Phelim O'Neill's wild followers in revenge, and in fear of the advancing army, massacred their prisoners in some of the towns in Tyrone. The subsequent cruelties were not on one side only, and were magnified to render the Irish detestable, so as to make it impossible for the king to seek their aid without ruining his cause utterly in England. The story of the massacre, invented to serve the politics of the hour, has been since kept up for the purposes of interest. No inventions could be too monstrous that served to strengthen the possession of Irish confiscated lands.

' A True Relation of the Proceedings of the Scots and English Forces in the North of Ireland,' published in 1642, states that on Monday, May 5, the common soldiers, without direction from the general-major, took some eighteen of the Irish women of the town [Newry], stripped them naked, threw them into the river, and drowned them, shooting some in the water. More had suffered so, but that some of the common soldiers were made examples of.

' A Levite's Lamentation,' published at the same time, thus refers to those atrocities : ' Mr. Griffin, Mr. Bartly, Mr. Starkey, all of Ardmagh, and murdered by these bloudsuckers on the sixth of May. For, about the fourth of May, as I take it, we put neare fourty of them to death upon the bridge of the Newry, amongst which were two of the Pope's pedlers, two seminary priests, in return of which they slaughtered many prisoners in their custody.'

A curious illustration of the spirit of that age is given in the fact that an English officer threw up his commission in disgust, because the Bishop of Meath, in a sermon delivered in Christ Church, Dublin, in 1642, pleaded for mercy to Irish women and children.

The unfortunate settlers fled panic-stricken from their homes, leaving behind their goods, and, in many cases, their clothes; delicate women with little children, weary and footsore, hurried on to some place of refuge. In Cavan they

crowded the house of the illustrious Bishop Bedell, at Kilmore. Enniskillen, Derry, Lisburn, Belfast, Carrickfergus,
with some isolated castles, were still held by the English
garrisons, and in these the Protestant fugitives found succour
and protection.   Before their flight they were in such terror
that, according to the Rev. Dr. Maxwell, rector of Tynan,
for three nights no cock was heard to crow, no dog to bark.
The city of London sent four ships to Londonderry with all
kinds of provisions, clothing, and accoutrements for several
companies of foot, and abundance of ammunition.   The
twelve chief companies sent each two pieces of ordnance.
No doubt these liberal and seasonable supplies contributed
materially to keep the city from yielding to the insurgent
forces by which it was besieged.

Meantime the Government in Dublin lost not a moment in
taking the most effectual measures for crushing the rebellion.
Lord Ormond, as lieutenant-general, had soon at his disposal
12,000 men, with a fine train of field artillery, provided by
Strafford for his campaign in the north of England.   The
king, who was in Scotland, procured the dispatch of 1,500
men to Ulster; and authorised Lords Chichester and Clandeboye to raise regiments among their tenants.   Thus the
'Scottish army' was increased to about 5,000 foot, with
cavalry in proportion.   The Irish, on the other hand, were
ill-provided with arms and ammunition.   They were not
even provided with pikes, for they had not time to make
them.   The military officers counted upon did not appear,
though they had promised to be on the field at fourteen
days' notice.   Rory O'Moore, like ' Meagher of the sword '
in 1848, had never seen service ; and Sir Phelim O'Neill,
like Smith O'Brien, was only a civilian when he assumed
the high-sounding title of ' Lord General of the Catholic
army in Ulster.' He also took the title of ' the O'Neill.'
The massacre of a large number of Catholics by the Carrickfergus garrison, driving them over the cliffs into the sea at
the point of the bayonet, madly excited the Irish thirst for
blood.   Mr. Darcy Magee admits that, from this date for-

ward till the arrival of Owen Roe O'Neill, the war assumed a ferocity of character foreign to the nature of O'Moore, O'Reilly, and Magennis. 'That Sir Phelim permitted, if he did not in his gusts of stormy passion instigate, those acts of cruelty which have stained his otherwise honourable conduct, is too true; but he stood alone among his confederates in that crime, and that crime stands alone in his character. Brave to rashness and disinterested to excess, few rebel chiefs ever made a more heroic end out of a more deplorable beginning.' The same eulogy would equally apply to many of the English generals. Cruelty was their only crime. The Irish rulers of those times, if not taken by surprise, felt at the outbreak of open rebellion much as the army feels at the breaking out of a war, in some country where plenty of prize money can be won, where the looting will be rich and the promotion rapid. Relying with confidence on the power of England and the force of discipline, they knew that the active defenders of the Government would be victorious in the end, and that their rewards would be estates. The more rebellions, the more forfeited territory, the more opportunities to implicate, ruin, and despoil the principal men of the hated race. The most sober writer, dealing with such facts, cannot help stirring men's blood while recording the deeds of the heroes who founded the English system of government in Ireland, and secured to themselves immense tracts of its most fertile soil. What then must be the effect of the eloquent and impassioned denunciations of such writers as Mr. Butt, Mr. A. M. Sullivan, and Mr. John Mitchell, not to speak of the 'national press'? Yet the most fiery patriot utters nothing stronger on the English rule in Ireland than what the Irish may read in the works of the greatest statesmen and most profound thinkers in England. The evil is in the facts, and the facts cannot be suppressed because they are the roots of our present difficulties. Mr. Darcy Magee, one of the most moderate of Irish historians, writing far away from his native land, not long before he fell by the bullet of the assassin—a martyr to his loyalty sketches the preliminaries of confiscation at the commencement of this civil war.

In Munster, their chief instruments were the aged Earl of Cork, still insatiable as ever for other men's possessions, and the president, St. Leger: in Leinster, Sir Charles Coote. Lord Cork prepared 1,100 indictments against men of property in his province, which he sent to the speaker of the Long Parliament, with an urgent request that they might be returned to him, with authority to proceed against the parties named as outlaws. In Leinster, 4,000 similar indictments were found in the course of two days by the free use of the rack with witnesses. Sir John Read, an officer of the king's bedchamber, and Mr. Barnwall of Kilbrue, a gentleman of threescore and six, were among those who underwent the torture. When these were the proceedings of the tribunals in peaceable cities, we may imagine what must have been the excesses of the soldiery in the open country. In the south, Sir William St. Leger directed a series of murderous raids upon the peasantry of Cork, which at length produced their natural effect. Lord Muskerry and other leading recusants, who had offered their services to maintain the peace of the province, were driven by an insulting refusal to combine for their own protection. The 1,100 indictments of Lord Cork soon swelled their ranks, and the capture of the ancient city of Cashel, by Philip O'Dwyer, announced the insurrection of the south. Waterford soon after opened its gates to Colonel Edmund Butler; Wexford declared for the Catholic cause, and Kilkenny surrendered to Lord Mountgarret. In Wicklow, Coote's troopers committed murders such as had not been equalled since the days of the pagan Northmen. Little children were carried aloft writhing on the pikes of these barbarians, whose worthy commander confessed that ' he liked such frolics.' Neither age nor sex was spared, and an ecclesiastic was especially certain of instant death. Fathers Higgins and White of Naas, in Kildare, were given up by Coote to these ' lambs,' though each had been granted a safe-conduct by his superior officer, Lord Ormond. And these murders were taking place at the very time when the Franciscans and Jesuits of Cashel were protecting Dr. Pullen, the Protestant chancellor of that cathedral and other Protestant prisoners ; while also the castle of Cloughouter, in Cavan, the residence of Bishop Bedell, was crowded with Protestant fugitives, all of whom were carefully guarded by the chivalrous Philip O'Reilly.'

In Ulster, by the end of April, there were 19,000 troops, regulars and volunteers, in the garrison or in the field. Newry was taken by Monroe and Chichester. Magennis was obliged to abandon Down, and McMahon Monaghan ; Sir Phelim was driven to burn Armagh and Dungannon, and to take his last stand at Charlemont. In a severe action with Sir Robert and Sir William Stewart, he had displayed his usual courage with better than his usual fortune, which, perhaps, we may attribute to the presence with him of Sir Alexander McDonnell, brother to Lord Antrim, the famous *Colkitto* of the Irish and Scottish wars. But the severest defeat which the confederates had was in the heart of Leinster, at the hamlet of Kilrush, within four miles of Athy. Lord Ormond, returning from a second reinforcement of Naas and other Kildare forts, at the head, by English account, of 4,000 men, found on April 13 the Catholics of the midland counties, under Lords Mountgarrett, Ikerrin, and Dunboyne, Sir Morgan Cavenagh, Rory O'Moore, and Hugh O'Byrne, drawn up, by his report 8,000 strong, to dispute his passage. With Ormond were the Lord Dillon, Lord Brabazon, Sir Richard Grenville, Sir Charles Coote, and Sir T. Lucas. The combat was short but murderous. The confederates left 700 men, including Sir Morgan Cavenagh and some other officers, dead on the field; the remainder retreated in disorder, and Ormond, with an inconsiderable diminution of numbers, returned in triumph to Dublin. For this victory the Long Parliament, in a moment of enthusiasm, voted the lieutenant-general a jewel worth 500*l.* If any satisfaction could be derived from such an incident, the violent death of their most ruthless enemy, Sir Charles Coote, might have afforded the Catholics some consolation.   That merciless soldier, after the combat at Kilrush, had been employed in reinforcing Birr and relieving the castle of Geashill, which the Lady Letitia of Offally held against the neighbouring tribe of O'Dempsey.   On his return from this service he made a foray against a Catholic force, which had mustered in the neighbourhood of Trim; here, on the night of the 7th of May, heading a sally of his troop, he fell by a musket shot—not without suspicion of being fired from his own ranks.   His son and namesake, who imitated him in all things, was ennobled at the Restoration by the title of the Earl of Mountrath.

The Long Parliament would not trust the king with an army in Ireland.   They consequently took the work of subjugation into their own hands.   Having confiscated 2,500,000 acres of Irish land, they offered it as security to 'adventurers' who would advance money to meet the cost of the war.   In February, 1642, the House of Commons received a petition ' of divers well affected ' to it, offering to raise and maintain forces at their own charge ' against the rebels of Ireland, and afterwards to receive their recompense out of the rebels' estates.'   Under the act ' for the speedy reducing of the rebels ' the adventurers were to carry over a brigade of 5,000 foot and 500 horse, and to have the right of appointing their own officers.   And they were to have estates given to them at the following rates: 1,000 acres for 200l. in Ulster, for 300l. in Connaught, for 450l. in Munster, and 600l. in Leinster.   The rates per acre were 4s., 6s., 8s., and 12s. in those provinces respectively.

The nature of the war, and the spirit in which it was conducted, may be inferred from the sort of weapons issued from the military stores.   These included scythes with handles and rings, reaping-hooks, whetstones, and rubstones.   They were intended for cutting down the growing corn, that the people might be starved into submission, or forced to quit the country.   The commissary of stores was ordered to issue Bibles to the troops, one Bible for every file, that they might learn from the Old Testament the sin and danger of sparing idolaters.

The rebellion in Ulster had almost collapsed before the end of the year. The tens of thousands who had rushed to the standard of Sir P. O'Neill were now reduced to a number of weak and disorganised collections of armed men taking shelter in the woods. The English garrisons scoured the neighbouring counties with little opposition, and where they met any they gave no quarter. Sir William Cole, ancestor of the Earl of Enniskillen, proudly boasted of his achievement in having 7,000 of the rebels famished to death within a circuit of a few miles of his garrison. Lord Enniskillen is an excellent landlord, but the descendants of the remnant of the natives on his estate do not forget how the family obtained its wealth and honours. The Government, however, seemed to have good reason to congratulate itself that the war was over with the Irish. To these Sir Phelim O'Neill had shown that there is something in a name; but if the name does not represent real worth and fitness for the work undertaken, it is but a shadow. It was so in Sir Phelim's O'Neill's case. Though he had courage, he was a poor general. But another hero of the same name soon appeared to redeem the honour of his race, and to show what the right man can do. At a moment when the national cause seemed to be lost, when the Celtic population in Ulster were meditating a wholesale emigration to the Scottish Highlands—' a word of magic effect was whispered from the sea-coast to the interior.' Colonel Owen Roe O'Neill had arrived off Donegal with a single ship, a single company of veterans, 100 officers, and a quantity of ammunition. He landed at Doe Castle, proceeded to the fort of Charlemont, met the heads of the clans at Clones in Monaghan, was elected general-in-chief of the Catholic forces, and at once set about organising an army. The Catholics of the whole kingdom had joined a confederation, which held its meetings at Kilkenny.

A general assembly was convened for October 23, 1642. The peerage was represented by fourteen lords and eleven bishops. Generals were appointed for each of the other provinces, Preston for Leinster, Barry for Munster, and Burke for Connaught. With the Anglo-Irish portion of the confederacy the war was Catholic, and the object religious liberty. With them there was no antipathy or animosity to the English. There was the Pope's Nuncio and his party, thinking most of papal interests, and there was the national party, who had been, or were likely to be, made landless. The king, then at Oxford, was importuned by the confederation on the one side and the Puritans on the other; one petitioning for freedom of worship, the other for the suppression of popery. Pending these appeals there was a long cessation between the Irish belligerents.

Ormond had amused the confederates with negotiations for a permanent peace and settlement, from spring till midsummer, when Charles, dissatisfied with these endless delays, dispatched to Ireland a more hopeful ambassador. This was Herbert, Earl of Glamorgan, one of the few Catholics remaining among the English nobility, son and heir to the Marquis of Worcester, and son-in-law to Henry O'Brien, Earl of Thomond. Of a family devoutly attached to the royal cause, to which it is said they had contributed not less than 200,000*l.*, Glamorgan's religion, his rank, his Irish connections, the intimate confidence of the king which he was known to possess, all marked out his embassy as one of the utmost importance.

The earl arrived in Dublin about August 1, and, after an interview with Ormond, proceeded to Kilkenny. On the 28th of that month, preliminary articles were agreed to and signed by the earl on behalf of the king, and by Lords Montgarrett and Muskerry on behalf of the confederates. It was necessary, it seems, to get the concurrence of the Viceroy to these terms, and accordingly the negotiators on both sides repaired to Dublin. Here Ormond contrived to detain them ten long weeks in discussions on the articles relating to religion; it was the 12th of November when they returned to Kilkenny, with a much modified treaty. On the next day, the 13th, the new Papal Nuncio, a prelate who, by his rank, his eloquence, and his imprudence, was destined to exercise a powerful influence on the Catholic councils, made his public entry into that city.

This personage was John Baptist Rinuccini, Archbishop of Fermo in the marches of Ancona, which see he had preferred to the more exalted dignity of Florence.

From Limerick, borne along on his litter, such was the feebleness of his health, he advanced by slow stages to Kilkenny, escorted by a guard of honour, despatched on that duty by the supreme council.

The pomp and splendour of his public entry into the Catholic capital was a striking spectacle. The previous night he slept at a village three miles from the city, for which he set out early on the morning of November 13, escorted by his guard and a vast multitude of the people. Five delegates from the supreme council accompanied him. A band of fifty students, mounted on horseback, met him on the way, and their leader, crowned with laurel, recited some congratulatory Latin verses. At the city gate he left the litter and mounted a horse richly housed; here the procession of the clergy and the city guilds awaited him: at the market cross, a Latin oration was delivered in his honour, to which he graciously replied in the same language. From the cross he was escorted to the cathedral, at the door of which he was received by the aged bishop, Dr. David Rothe. At the high altar he intonated the *Te Deum*, and gave the multitude the apostolic benediction. Then he was conducted to his lodgings, where he was soon waited upon by Lord Muskerry and General Preston, who brought him to Kilkenny Castle, where, in the great gallery, which elicited even a Florentine's admiration, he was received in stately formality by the president of the council—Lord Mountgarrett. Another Latin oration on the nature of his embassy was delivered by the Nuncio, responded to by Heber, Bishop of Clogher, and so the ceremony of reception ended.*

* Darcy Magee, vol. ii. p. 128.

After a long time spent in negotiations, the celebrated Glamorgan treaty was signed by Ormond for the king, and Lord Muskerry and the other commissioners for the confederates. It conceded, in fact, all the most essential claims of the Irish—equal rights as to property, in the army, in the universities, and at the bar ; gave them seats in both houses and on the bench; authorised a special commission of oyer and terminer, composed wholly of confederates ; and declared that ' the independency of the parliament of Ireland on that of England ' should be decided by declaration of both houses ' agreeably to the laws of the kingdom of Ireland.' In short, this final form of Glamorgan's treaty gave the Irish Catholics, in 1646, all that was subsequently obtained, either for the church or the country, in 1782, 1793, or 1829. ' Though some conditions were omitted, to which Rinuccini and a majority of the prelates attached importance, Glamorgan's treaty was, upon the whole, a charter upon which a free church and a free people might well have stood, as the fundamental law of their religious and civil liberties.'

General O'Neill was greatly annoyed at these delays. Political events in England swayed the destiny of Ireland then as now. The poor vacillating, double-dealing king was delivered to the Puritans, tried, and executed. But before Cromwell came to smash the confederation and everything papal in Ireland, the Irish chief gladdened the hearts of his countrymen by the glorious victory of Benburb, one of the most memorable in Irish history.

In a naturally strong position, the Irish, for four hours, received and repulsed the various charges of the Puritan horse. Then as the sun began to descend, pouring its rays upon the enemy, O'Neill led his whole force—five thousand men against eight—to the attack. One terrible onset swept away every trace of resistance. There were counted on the field 3,243 of the Covenanters, and of the Catholics but 70 killed and 100 wounded. Lord Ardes, and 21 Scottish officers, 32 standards, 1,500 draught horses, and all the guns and tents, were captured. Monroe fled to

Lisburn and thence to Carrickfergus, where he shut himself up till he could obtain reinforcements. O'Neill forwarded the captured colours to the Nuncio at Limerick, by whom they were solemnly placed in the choir of St. Mary's Cathedral, and afterwards, at the request of Pope Innocent, sent to Rome. The *Te Deum* was chanted in the confederate capital; penitential psalms were sung in the northern fortresses. 'The Lord of Hosts,' wrote Monroe, 'has rubbed shame on our faces till once we are humbled.' O'Neill emblazoned the cross and keys on his banner with the Red Hand of Ulster, and openly resumed the title originally chosen by his adherents at Clones, 'the Catholic Army.'

The stage of Irish politics now presented the most extraordinary complications political and military. The confederation was occupied with endless debates and dissensions. Commanders changed positions so rapidly, the several causes for which men had been fighting became so confused in the unaccountable scene-shifting, giving glimpses now of the king, now of the commonwealth, and now of the pope, that no one knew what to do, or what was to be the end. The nuncio went home in disgust that his blessings and his curses, which he dispensed with equal liberality, had so little effect.

At length appeared an actor who gave a terrible unity to the drama of Irish politics. Cromwell left London in July 1649, 'in a coach drawn by six gallant Flanders mares,' and made a grand progress to Bristol. He landed at Ring's End, near Dublin, on August 14. He entered the city in procession and addressed the people from 'a convenient place,' accompanied by his son Henry, Blake, Jones, Ireton, Ludlow, Hardress, Waller, and others. The history of Cromwell's military exploits in Ireland is well known. I pass on, therefore, to notice the effects of the war on the condition of the people.

As usual, in such cases, the destruction of the crops and other provisions by the soldiers, brought evil to the conquerors as well as to their victims. There had been a fifteen years' war in Ulster, when James I. ascended the throno, and it left the country waste and desolate. Sir John Davis, his attorney-general, asserted the unquestionable fact that perpetual war had been continued between the two nations for ' four hundred and odd years,' and had always for its object to ' root out the Irish.' James was to put an end to this war, and, as we have seen, the lord deputy promised the people ' estates ' in their holdings. The effect of this promise, as recorded by Davis, is remarkable. ' He thus made it a year of jubilee to the poor inhabitants, because every man was to return to his own house, and be restored to his ancient possessions, and they all went home rejoicing.'

Poor people ! they soon saw the folly of putting their trust in princes. Now, after a seven years' war, the nation was again visited with famine, and the country converted into a wilderness. Three-fourths of the cattle had been destroyed ; and the commissioners for Ireland reported to the council in England in 1651, that four parts in five of the best and most fertile land in Ireland lay waste and uninhabited, stating that they had encouraged the Irish to till the land, promising them the enjoyment of the crops. They had also given orders ' for enforcing those that were removed to the mountains to return.' The soldiers were employed to till the lands round their posts. Corn had to be imported to Dublin from Wales. So scarce was meat that a widow was obliged to petition the authorities for permission to kill a lamb ; and she was 'permitted and lycensed to kill and dresse so much lambe as shall be necessary for her own eating, not exceeding three lambes for this whole year, notwithstanding any declaration of the said Commissioners of Parliament to the contrary.'* This privilege was granted to Mrs. Buckley in consideration of ' her old age and weakness of body.' In 1654 the Irish revenue from all sources was only 198,000*l.*, while the cost of the army was 500,000*l.* A sort of conditional amnesty was granted from necessity, pending the decision of Parliament, and on May 12, 1652,

* Prendergast, the Cromwellian Settlement, p. 16.

the Leinster army of the Irish surrendered on terms signed at Kilkenny, which were adopted successively by the other principal armies between that time and the September following, when the Ulster forces surrendered. By these Kilkenny articles, all except those who were guilty of the first blood were received into protection on laying down their arms ; those who should not be satisfied with the conclusions the Parliament might come to concerning the Irish nation, and should desire to transport themselves with their men to serve any foreign state in amity with the Parliament, should have liberty to treat with their agents for that purpose. But the Commissioners undertook faithfully to mediate with the Parliament that they might enjoy such a remnant of their lands as might make their lives comfortable at home, or be enabled to emigrate.

The Cromwellian administration in Ireland effected a revolution unparalleled in history. Its proceedings have been well summarised by Mr. Darcy Magee :—

The Long Parliament, still dragging out its days under the shadow of Cromwell's great name, declared in its session of 1652 the rebellion in Ireland ' subdued and ended,' and proceeded to legislate for that kingdom as a conquered country. On August 12 they passed their Act of Settlement, the authorship of which was attributed to Lord Orrery, in this respect the worthy son of the first Earl of Cork. Under this act there were four chief descriptions of persons whose status was thus settled: 1. All ecclesiastics and royalist proprietors were exempted from pardon of life or estate. 2. All royalist commissioned officers were condemned to banishment, and the forfeit of two-thirds of their property, one-third being retained for the support of their wives and children. 3. Those who had not been in arms, but could be shown, by a parliamentary commission, to have manifested ' a constant, good affection' to the war, were to forfeit one-third of their estates, and receive ' an equivalent' for the remaining two-thirds west of the Shannon. 4. All husbandmen and others of the inferior sort, 'not possessed of lands or goods exceeding the value of 10l.,' were to have a free pardon, on condition also of transporting themselves across the Shannon.

This last condition of the Cromwellian settlement distinguished it, in our annals, from every other proscription of the native population formerly attempted. The great river of Ireland, rising in the mountains of Leitrim, nearly severs the five western counties from the rest of the kingdom. The province thus set apart, though one of the largest in superficial extent, had also the largest proportion of waste and water, mountain and moorland. The new inhabitants were there to congregate from all the other provinces before the first day of May, 1654, under penalty of outlawry and all its consequences; and when there, they were not to appear within two miles of the Shannon, or four miles of the sea. A rigorous passport system, to evade which was death without form of trial, completed this settlement, the design of which was to shut up the remaining Catholic inhabitants from all intercourse with mankind, and all communion with the other inhabitants of their own country.

A new survey of the whole kingdom was also ordered, under the direction of Dr. William Petty, the fortunate economist who founded the house of Lansdowne. By him the surface of the kingdom was estimated at 10,500,000 plantation acres, three of which were deducted for waste and water. Of the remainder, above 5,000,000 were in Catholic hands, in 1641; 300,000 were church and college lands; and 2,000,000 were in possession of the Protestant settlers of the reigns of James and Elizabeth. Under the Protectorate, 5,000,000 acres were confiscated; this enormous spoil, two-thirds of the whole island, went to the soldiers and adventurers who had served against the Irish, or had contributed to the military chest, since 1641—except 700,000 acres given in 'exchange' to the banished in Clare and Connaught; and 1,200,000 confirmed to 'innocent Papists.' Such was the complete uprooting of the ancient tenantry or clansmen from their original holdings, that, during the survey, orders of parliament were issued to bring back individuals from Connaught to point out the boundaries of parishes in Munster. It cannot be imputed among the sins so freely laid to the historical account of the native legislature, that an Irish parliament had any share in sanctioning this universal spoliation. Cromwell anticipated the union of the kingdoms by 150 years, when he summoned, in 1653, that assembly over which ' Praise-God Barebones ' presided; members for Ireland and Scotland sat on the same benches with the commons of England. Oliver's first deputy in the government of Ireland was his son-in-law Fleetwood, who had married the widow of Ireton; but his real representative was his fourth son Henry Cromwell, commander-in-chief of the army. In 1657, the title of lord deputy was transferred from Fleetwood to Henry, who united the supreme civil and military authority in his own person until the eve of the restoration, of which he became an active partisan. We may thus properly embrace the five years of the Protectorate as a period of Henry Cromwell's administration.

In the absence of a parliament, the government of Ireland was vested in the deputy, the commander-in-chief, and four commissioners, Ludlow, Corbett, Jones, and Weaver. There was, moreover, a high court of justice, which perambulated the kingdom, and exercised an absolute authority over life and property greater than even Strafford's Court of Star Chamber had pretended to. Over this court presided Lord Lowther, assisted by Mr. Justice Donnellan, by Cooke, solicitor to the parliament on the trial of King Charles, and the regicide Reynolds. By this court, Sir Phelim O'Neill, Viscount Mayo, and Colonels O'Toole and Bagnall were condemned and executed; children of both sexes were captured by thousands, and sold as slaves to the tobacco-planters of Virginia and the West Indies. Sir William Petty states that 6,000 boys and girls were sent to those islands. The number, of all ages, thus transported, was estimated at 100,000 souls. As to the ' swordsmen ' who had been trained to fighting, Petty, in his *Political Anatomy,* records that ' the chiefest and most eminentest of the nobility and many of the gentry had taken conditions from the King of Spain, and had transported 40,000 of the most active, spirited men, most acquainted with the dangers and discipline of war.' The chief commissioners in Dublin had despatched assistant commissioners to the provinces. The distribution which they made of the soil was nearly as complete as that of Canaan among the Israelites; and this was the model which the Puritans had always before their minds. Where a miserable residue of the population was required to till the land for its new owners, they were tolerated as the Gibeon-ites had been by Joshua. Irish gentlemen who had obtained pardons were obliged to wear a distinctive mark on their dress on pain of death. Persons of inferior rank were distinguished by a black spot on the right cheek. Wanting this, their punishment was the branding-iron or the gallows.

No vestige of the Catholic religion was allowed to exist. Catholic lawyers and schoolmasters were silenced. All ecclesiastics were slain like the priests of Baal. Three bishops and 300 of the inferior clergy thus perished. The bedridden Bishop of Kilmore was the only native clergyman permitted to survive. If, in mountain recesses or caves, a few peasants were detected at mass, they were smoked out and shot.

Thus England got rid of a race concerning which Mr. Prendergast found this contemporary testimony in a MS. in Trinity College library, Dublin, dated 1615 :—

' There lives not a people more hardy, active, and painful . . . neither is there any will endure the miseries of warre, as famine, watching, heat, cold, wet, travel, and the like, so naturally and with such facility and courage that they do. The Prince of Orange's excellency uses often publiquely to deliver that the Irish are souldiers the first day of their birth. The famous Henry IV., late king of France, said there would prove no nation so resolute martial men as they, would they be ruly and not too headstrong. And Sir

John Norris was wont to ascribe this particular to that nation above others, that he never beheld so few of any country as of Irish that were idiots and cowards, which is very notable.'

At the end of 1653, the parliament made a division of the spoil among the conquerors and the adventurers; and, on September 26, an act was passed for the new planting of Ireland by English. The Government reserved for itself the towns, the church lands, and the tithes, the established church, hierarchy and all, having been utterly abolished. The four counties of Dublin, Kildare, Carlow, and Cork were also reserved. The amount due to the adventurers was 360,000*l.* This they divided into three lots, of which 110,000*l.* was to be satisfied in Munster, 205,000*l.* in Leinster, and 45,000*l.* in Ulster, and the moiety of ten counties was charged with their payment—Waterford, Limerick, and Tipperary, in Munster; Meath, Westmeath, King's and Queen's Counties, in Leinster; and Antrim, Down, and Armagh, in Ulster. But, as all was required by the Adventurers Act to be done by lot, a lottery was appointed to be held in Grocers' Hall, London, for July 20, 1653, to begin at 8 o'clock in the morning, when lots should be first drawn in which province each adventurer was to be satisfied, not exceeding the specified amounts in any province; lots were to be drawn, secondly, to ascertain in which of the ten counties each adventurer was to receive his land—the lots not to exceed in Westmeath 70,000*l.*, in Tipperary 60,000*l.*, in Meath 55,000*l.*, in King's and Queen's Counties 40,000*l.* each, in Limerick 30,000*l.*, in Waterford 20,000*l.*, in Antrim, Down, and Armagh 15,000*l.* each. And, as it was thought it would be a great encouragement to the adventurers (who were for the most part merchants and tradesmen), about to plant in so wild and dangerous a country, not yet subdued, to have soldier planters near them, these ten counties, when surveyed (which was directed to be done immediately, and returned to the committee for the lottery at Grocers' Hall), were to be divided, each county by baronies, into two moieties, as equally as might be, without dividing any barony. A lot was then to be drawn by the adventurers, and by some officer appointed by the Lord General Cromwell on behalf of the soldiery, to ascertain which baronies in the ten counties should be for the adventurers, and which for the soldiers.

The rest of Ireland, except Connaught, was to be set out amongst the officers and soldiers for their arrears, amounting to 1,550,000*l.*, and to satisfy debts of money or provisions due for supplies advanced to the army of the commonwealth amounting to 1,750,000*l.* Connaught being by the parliament reserved and appointed for the habitation of the Irish nation, all English and Protestants having lands there, who should desire to remove out of Connaught into the provinces inhabited by the English, were to receive estates in the English parts, of equal value, in exchange.

The next thing was to clear out the remnant of the inhabitants, and the overture to this performance was the following merciful proclamation :—

'The Parliament of the Commonwealth of England having by one act lately passed (entitled an Act for the Settling of Ireland) declared that *it is not their intention to extirpate this whole nation,* but that mercy and pardon for life and estate be extended to all husbandmen, plowmen, labourers, artificers, and others of the inferior sort, in such manner as in and by the said Act is set forth : for the better execution of the said Act, and that timely notice may be given to all persons therein concerned, it is ordered that the Governor and Commissioners of Revenue, or any two or more of them, within every precinct in this nation, do cause· the said Act of Parliament with this present declaration to be published and proclaimed in their respective precincts *by beat of drumme and sound of trumpett,* on some markett day, within tenn days after the same shall come unto them within their respective precincts.

'Dated at the Castle of Kilkenny, this 11th October, 1652.

'EDMUND LUDLOW,   MILES CORBET,
'JOHN JONES,   R. WEAVER.'

A letter from Dublin, dated December 21, 1654, four days before Christmas, says the 'transplantation is now far advanced, the men being gone to prepare their new habitations in Connaught. Their wives and children and dependants have been, and are, packing away after them apace, and all are to be gone by the 1st of March next.' In another letter the writer *naïvely* remarks, ' It is the nature of this people to be rebellious, and they have been so much the more disposed to it, having been highly exasperated to it by the transplanting work.' The temper of the settlers towards the natives may be inferred from a petition to the lord deputy and council of Ireland, praying for the enforcement of the original order requiring the removal of all the Irish nation into Connaught, except boys of fourteen and girls of twelve. ' For we humbly conceive,' say the petitioners, ' that the proclamation for transplanting only the proprietors, and such as have been in arms, will neither answer the end of safety nor what else is aimed at thereby. For the first purpose of the transplantation is to prevent those of natural principles ' (*i.e.* of natural affections) 'becoming one with these Irish, as well in affinity as idolatry, as many thousands did who came over in Elizabeth's time, many of which have had a deep hand in all the late murders and massacres. And shall we join in affinity,' they ask, ' with a people of these abominations ? Would not the Lord be angry with us till He consumes us, having said—" the land which ye go to possess is an unclean land, because of the filthiness of the people who dwell therein. Ye shall not, therefore, give your sons to their daughters, nor take their daughters to your sons," as it is in Ezra ix. 11, 12, 14. " Nay, ye shall surely root them out, lest they cause you to forsake the Lord your God." Deut. c. vii. &c.'

In this way they hoped that ' honest men ' would be encouraged to come and live amongst them, because the other three provinces (that is, all the island but Connaught) would be free of ' tories,' when there was none left to harbour or relieve them. They would have made a clean sweep of Munster, Leinster, and Ulster, so that ' the saints' might inherit the land without molestation. If any Protestant friends of the Irish objected to this thorough mode of effecting the work of Irish regeneration, Colonel Lawrence ' doubted not but God would enable that authority yet in being to let out that dram of rebellious bloud, and cure that fit of sullenness their advocate speaks of.'

The commissioners appointed to effect the transplantation were painfully conscious of their unworthiness to perform so holy a work, and were overwhelmed with a sense of their weakness in the midst of such tremendous difficulties, so that they were constrained to say: ' The child is now come to the birth, and much is desired and expected, but there is no strength to bring forth.' They therefore fasted and humbled themselves before the Lord, inviting the officers of the army to join them in lifting up prayers, ' with strong crying and tears, to Him to whom nothing is too strong, that His servants, whom He had called forth in this day to act in these great transactions, might be made faithful, and carried on by His own outstretched arm, against all opposition and difficulty, to do what was pleasing in His sight.'

It is true they had this consolation, ' that the chiefest and eminentest of the nobility and many of the gentry had taken conditions from the king of Spain, and had transported 40,000 of the most active, spirited men, most acquainted with the dangers and discipline of war.' The priests were all banished. The remaining part of the whole nation was scarce one-sixth of what they were at the beginning of the war, so great a devastation had God and man brought upon that land; and that handful of natives left were poor labourers, simple creatures, whose sole design was to live and maintain their families.'

Of course there were many exceptions to this rule. There were some of the upper classes remaining, described in the certificates which all the emigrants were obliged to procure, like Sir Nicholas Comyn, of Limerick, ' who was numb at one side of his body of a dead palsy, accompanied only by his lady, Catherine Comyn, aged thirty-five years, flaxen-haired, middle stature; and one maid servant, Honor M'Namara, aged twenty years, brown hair, middle stature, having no substance,' &c. From Tipperary went forth James, Lord Dunboyne, with 21 followers, and having 4 cows, 10 garrons, and 2 swine. Dame Catherine Morris, 35 followers, 10 cows, 16 garrons, 19 goats, 2 swine. Lady Mary Hamilton, of Roscrea, with 45 persons, 40 cows, 30 garrons, 46 sheep, 2 goats. Pierce, Lord Viscount Ikerrin, with 17 persons, having 16 acres of winter corn, 4 cows, 5 garrons, 14 sheep, 2 swine, &c. There were other noblemen, lords of the Pale, descended from illustrious English ancestors, the Fitzgeralds, the Butlers, the Plunkets, the Barnwells, the Dillons, the Cheevers, the Cusacks, &c., who petitioned, praying that their flight might not be in the winter, or alleging that their wives and children were sick, that their cattle were unfit to drive, or that they had crops to get in. To them dispensations were granted, provided the husbands and parents were in Connaught building huts, &c., and that not more than one or two servants remained behind to look after the respective herds and flocks, and to attend to the gathering in and threshing of the corn. And some few, such as John Talbot de Malahide, got a pass for safe travelling from Connaught to come back, in order to dispose of their corn and goods, giving security to return within the time limited. If they did not return they got this warning in the month of March—that the officers had resolved to fill the jails with them, 'by which this bloody people will know that they (the officers) are not degenerated from English principles. Though I presume we should be very tender of hanging any except leading men, yet we shall make no scruple of sending them to the West Indies,' &c. Accordingly when the time came, all the remaining crops were seized and sold; there was a general arrest of all ' transplantable persons. All over the three provinces, men and women were hauled out of their beds in the dead hour of night to prison, till the jails

P

were choked.' In order to further expedite the removal
of the nobility and gentry, a court-martial sat in St. Patrick's
Cathedral, and ordered the lingering delinquents, who shrunk
from going to Connaught, to be hanged, with a placard on
the breast and back of each victim—'*For not transplanting.*'

Scully's conduct at Ballycohy, was universally execrated.
But what did he attempt to do? Just what the Cromwellian
officers did at the end of a horrid civil war 200 years ago, with
this difference in favour of Cromwell, that Scully did not
purpose to 'transplant.' He would simply uproot, leaving
the uprooted to perish on the highway. His conduct was
as barbarous as that of the Cromwellian officers. But what
of Scully? He is nothing. The all-important fact is, that, in
playing a part worse than Cromwellian, he, *acting according
to English law, was supported by all the power of the state;*
and if the men who defended their homes against his attack
had been arrested and convicted, Irish judges would have
consigned them to the gallows; and they might, as in the
Cromwellian case, have ordered a placard to be put on their
persons :—

'FOR NOT TRANSPLANTING !'

In fact the Cromwellian commissioners did nothing more
than carry out fully the *principles* of our present land
code. Nine-tenths of the soil of Ireland are held by tenants
at will. It is constantly argued in the leading organs of
English opinion, that the power of the landlords to resume
possession of their estates, and turn them into pastures,
evicting all the tenants, is *essential* to the rights of property.
This has been said in connection with the great absentee
proprietors. According to this theory of proprietorship, the
only one recognised by law, Lord Lansdowne may legally
spread desolation over a large part of Kerry; Lord Fitzwilliam may send the ploughshare of ruin through the
hearths of half the county Wicklow; Lord Digby, in the
King's County, may restore to the bog of Allen vast tracts re-

claimed during many generations by the labour of his tenants;
and Lord Hertfort may convert into a wilderness the district
which the descendants of the English settlers have converted
into the garden of Ulster.   If any or all of those noblemen
took a fancy, like Colonel Bernard of Kinnitty or Mr. Allen
Pollok, to become graziers and cattle-jobbers on a gigantic
scale, the Government would be compelled to place the
military power of the state at their disposal, to evict the
whole population in the queen's name, to drive all the
families away from their homes, to demolish their dwellings,
and turn them adrift on the highway, without one shilling
compensation.   Villages, schools, churches would all disappear from the landscape; and, when the grouse season
arrived, the noble owner might bring over a party of
English friends to see his *' improvements ! '*   The right of
conquest so cruelly exercised by the Cromwellians is in this
year of grace *a legal right;* and its exercise is a mere
question of expediency and discretion.   There is not a
landlord in Ireland who may not be a Scully if he wishes.
It is not law or justice, it is not British power, that
prevents the enactment of Cromwellian scenes of desolation
in every county of that unfortunate country.   It is self-
interest, with humanity, in the hearts of good men, and the
dread of assassination in the hearts of bad men, that prevent
at the present moment the immolation of the Irish people
to the Moloch of territorial despotism.   It is the effort to
render impossible those human sacrifices, those holocausts
of Christian households, that the priests of feudal landlordism denounce so frantically with loud cries of *' confiscation.'*
   The ' graces' promised by Charles I. in 1628 demonstrate
the real wretchedness of the country to which they were
deceitfully offered, and from which they were treacherously
withdrawn.   From them we learn that the Government
soldiers were a terror to more than the king's enemies, that
the king's rents were collected at the sword's point, and
that numerous monopolies' and oppressive taxes impoverished
the country.   There was little security for estates in any

part of Ireland, and none at all for estates in Connaught.
No man could sue out livery for his lands without first
taking the oath of the royal supremacy. The soldiers en
joyed an immunity in the perpetration of even capital
crimes, for the civil power could not touch them. Those
who were married, or had their children baptized, by
Roman Catholic priests, were liable to fine and censure.
The Protestant bishops and clergy were in great favour and
had enormous privileges. The patentees of dissolved religious houses claimed exemption from various assessments.
The ministers of the Established Church were entitled to
the aid of the Government in exacting reparation for clan-
destine exercises of spiritual jurisdiction by Roman Catholic
priests, and actually appear to have kept private prisons of
their own. They exacted tithes from Roman Catholics of
everything titheable. The eels of the rivers and lakes, the
fishes of the sea paid them toll. The dead furnished the
mortuary fees to the ' alien church ' in the shape of the best
clothes which the wardrobe of the defunct afforded. The
government of Wentworth, better known as the Earl of
Strafford, is highly praised by high churchmen and admirers
of Laud, but was execrated by the Irish, who failed to
appreciate the mercies of his star-chamber court, or to
recognise the justice of his fining juries who returned dis-
agreeable verdicts. The list of grievances, transmitted by
the Irish House of Peers in 1641 to the English Government, cannot be regarded as altogether visionary, for it was
vouched by the names of lords, spiritual and temporal,
whose attachment to the English interest was undoubted.
The lord chancellor (Loftus), the archbishop of Dublin
(Bulkeley), the bishops of Meath, Clogher, and Killala
were no rebels, and yet they protested against the grievances
inflicted on Ireland by the tyranny of Strafford. According
to these contemporary witnesses, the Irish nobles had been
taxed beyond all proportion to the English nobles; Irish
peers had been sent to prison although not impeached of
treason or any capital offence; the deputy had managed to

keep all proxies of peers in the hands of his creatures, and thus to sway the Upper House to his will; the trade of the kingdom had been destroyed; and the 'graces' of 1628 had been denied to the nation, or clogged by provisoes which rendered them a mockery.   And yet, in the face of such evidence of misery and misgovernment, the Archbishop of Dublin asserted in a charge to his clergy, that 'all contemporary writers agree in describing the flourishing condition of the island, and its rapid advance in civilisation and wealth, when all its improvement was brought to an end by the catastrophe of the Irish rebellion of 1641 '—the very year in which the Irish Houses of Lords and Commons agreed in depicting the condition of Ireland as utterly miserable!

But Archbishop Trench not only contradicts the authentic contemporary records, in picturing as halcyon days one of the most wretched periods of Irish history, but also wrongfully represents one of the saddest episodes of that history.   He reminded his clergy 'that the number of Protestants who were massacred by the Roman Catholics during the rebellion was, by the most moderate estimate, set down as 40,000.'   His grace seems to have been unacquainted with the contemporary evidence collected by the Protestant historian Warner, who examined the depositions of 1641, on which the story of the massacre was based, and found the estimate of those who perished in the so-called massacre to have been enormously exaggerated.   He calculated the number of those killed, 'upon evidence collected within two years after the rebellion broke out,' at 4,028, besides 8,000 said to have perished through bad usage. The parliament commissioners in Dublin, writing in 1652 to the commissioners in England, say that, 'besides 848 families, there were killed, hanged, burned, and drowned 6,062.   Thus there were two estimates—one of 12,000, the other of 10,000—each of which was far lower than the estimate of 40,000, which his grace calls 'the most moderate.'   It turns out, moreover, that the argument based by

Archbishop Trench on the false estimate of those said to have been massacred, is wholly worthless for the purpose intended by his grace.   The disproportion of Protestants to Roman Catholics, which appears by the census of 1861, cannot be accounted for by the statistics of 1641—be those statistics true or false.   For the proportion of Protestants to Roman Catholics was higher in 1672—thirty years after the alleged massacre—than in 1861.   The Protestants in 1672, according to Sir W. Petty, numbered 300,000, and the Roman Catholics 800,000; while in 1861 there were found in Ireland only 1,293,702 Protestants of all denominations to 4,505,265 Roman Catholics.   It follows from these figures, as has been already remarked by Dr. Maziere Brady, that there has been a relative decrease of Protestants, as compared with Roman Catholics, of 395,772 persons.   And this relative decrease was in no way affected —inasmuch as it took place since the year 1672—by the alleged massacre of 1641.

CHAPTER XII.

THE PURITAN PLANTATION.

IT is a fearful thing to undertake the destruction of a nation by slaughter, starvation, and banishment. When we read of such enormities, perpetrated by some 'scourge of God,' in heathen lands and distant ages, we are horrified, and we thank Providence that it is our lot to be born in a Christian country. But what must the world think of our Christianity when they read of the things that, in a most Bible-reading age, Englishmen did in Ireland?

The work of transplanting was slow, difficult, and intensely painful to the Irish, for Connaught was bleak, sterile, and desolate, and the weather was inclement. The natural protectors of many families had been killed or banished, and the women and children clung with frantic fondness to their old homes. But for the feelings of such afflicted ones the conquerors had no sympathy. On the contrary, they believed that God, angry at their lingering, sent his judgments as a punishment. Mr. Prendergast has published a number of letters, written at the time by the English authorities and others, from which some interesting matters may be gleaned. The town of Cashel had got a dispensation to remain. 'But,' says the writer, 'the Lord, who is a jealous God, and more knowing of, as well as jealous against their iniquity than we, by a fire on the 23rd inst. hath burned down the whole town in little less than a quarter of an hour, except a few houses that a few English lived in,' &c. In consequence of the delay, the Irish began to break into 'torying' (plundering). 'The tories fly out and increase. What strange people, not to starve in peace.' To be inclined to plunder under such circumstances, with so gracious a Government, must be held to be a proof of great natural depravity, as well as of a peculiar incapacity to respect, or even to understand, the rights of property.

At length, however, the land was ready for the enjoyment of the officers and soldiers. On August 20, 1655, the lord deputy, Fleetwood, thus addressed one of the officers :—

'Sir,—In pursuance of his highness's command, the council here with myself and chief officers of the army having concluded about disbanding part of the army, in order to lessening the present charge, it is fit that your troope be one. And, accordingly, I desire you would march such as are willing to plant of them into the barony of Shelmaliere, in the county of Wexford, at or before the first day of September, where you shall be put into possession of your lands, for your arrears, according to the rates agreed on by the committee and agents. As also you shall have, upon the place wherein you are, so much money as shall answer the present three months' arrear due to you and your men, but to continue no longer the pay of the army than upon the muster of this August. The sooner you march your men the better; thereby you will be enabled to make provision for the winter.' After some sweetening hints that they will be perhaps paid hereafter as a militia he concludes :—

'And great is your mercy, that after all your hardships and difficulties you may sit down, and, if the Lord give His blessing, may reape some fruits of your past services. Do not think it a blemish or underrating of your past services, that you are now disbanded; but look upon it as of the Lord's appointing, and with cheerfulness submit thereunto; and the blessing of the Lord be upon you all, and keep you in His fear, and give you hearts to observe your past experience of signal appearances. And that this fear may be seen in your hearts, and that you may be kept from the sins and pollutions which God hath so eminently witnessed

against in those whose possessions you are to take up, is the
desire of him who is

    ' Your very affectionate friend, to love and serve you,

                ' CHARLES FLEETWOOD.'

He congratulated them that, ' having by the blessing of
God obtained their peace, they might sit down in the enjoyment of the enemies' fields and houses, which they
planted not nor built not.   They had no reason to repent
their services, considering how great an issue God had
given.'   Yet many refused to settle, and sold their de-
bentures to their officers.   What could they do with the
farms?   They had no horses or ploughs, no cattle to stock
the land, no labourers to till it.   Above all, they had no
women.   Flogging was the punishment for amours with
Irish girls, and marriage with the idolatrous race was forbidden under heavy penalties.   Hence the soldiers pretended
that their wives were converted to Protestantism.   But this
was to be tested by a strict examination of each as to the
state of her soul, and the means by which she had been
enlightened.   If she did not stand the test, her husband was
degraded in rank, and, if disbanded, he was liable to be sent
to Connaught with the fair seducer.   The charms of the
Irish women, however, proved irresistible, and the hearts of
the pious rulers were sorely troubled by this danger.

' In 1652, amongst the first plans for paying the army
their arrears in land, it was suggested there should be a law
that any officers or soldiers marrying Irishwomen should
lose their commands, forfeit their arrears, and be made incapable of inheriting lands in Ireland.   No such provision,
however, was introduced into the act, because it provided
against this danger more effectually by ordering the women
to transplant, together with the whole nation, to Connaught.
Those in authority, however, ought never to have let the
English officers and soldiers come in contact with the Irishwomen, or should have ordered another army of young English-
women over, if they did not intend this provision to be

nugatory.   Planted in a wasted country, amongst the former
owners and their families, with little to do but to make
love, and no lips to make love to but Irish, love or marriage
must follow between them as necessarily as a geometrical
conclusion follows from the premises.   For there were but
few who (in the language of a Cromwellian patriot),

> ——'rather than turne
> From English principles, would sooner burne;
> And rather than marrie an Irish wife,
> Would batchellers remain for tearme of life.'

About forty years after the Cromwellian Settlement, and
just seven years after the Battle of the Boyne, the following
was written: 'We cannot so much wonder at this [the quick
" degenerating " of the English of Ireland], when we consider how many there are of the children of Oliver's soldiers
in Ireland who cannot speak one word of English.   And
(which is strange) the same may be said of some of the
children of King William's soldiers who came but t'other
day into the country.   This misfortune is owing to the
marrying Irishwomen for want of English, who come not
over in so great numbers as are requisite.   'Tis sure that no
Englishman in Ireland knows what his children may be as
things are now; they cannot well live in the country without growing Irish; for none take such care as Sir Jerome
Alexander [second justice of the Common Pleas in Ireland
from 1661 to his death in 1670], who left his estate to his
daughter, but made the gift void if she married any Irishman;' Sir Jerome including in this term 'any lord of Ireland,
any archbishop, bishop, prelate, any baronet, knight, es-
quire, or gentleman of Irish extraction or descent, born and
bred in Ireland, or having his relations and means of subsistence there,' and expressly, of course, any 'Papist.'—'True
Way to render Ireland happy and secure ; or, a Discourse,
wherein 'tis shown that 'tis the interest both of England and
Ireland to encourage foreign Protestants to plant in Ireland;
in a letter to the Hon. Robert Molesworth.'*

---

* Cromwellian Settlement, p. 130.

The impossibility of getting a sufficient number of settlers from England to cultivate the land, produce food, and render the estates worth holding, led to some fraudulent transactions for the benefit of the natives who were 'loath to leave.' The officers in various counties got general orders giving dispensations from the necessity of planting with English tenants, and liberty to take Irish, provided they were not proprietors or swordsmen. But the proprietors who had established friendships with their conquerors secretly became tenants under them to parts of their former estates, ensuring thereby the connivance of their new landlords against their transplantation. On June 1, 1655, the commissioners for the affairs of Ireland (Fleetwood, lord deputy, one of them), being then at Limerick, discovered this fraud; and issued a peremptory order revoking all former dispensations for English proprietors to plant with Irish tenants; and they enjoined upon the governor of Limerick and all other officers the removing of the proprietors thus sheltered and their families into Connaught, on or before that day three weeks. But, happily, says Mr. Prendergast, all penal laws against a nation are difficult of execution. The officers still connived with many of the poor Irish gentry and sheltered them, which caused Fleetwood, then commander of the parliament forces in Ireland, upon his return to Dublin, and within a fortnight after the prescribed limit for their removal was expired, to thunder forth from Dublin Castle a severe reprimand to all officers thus offending. Their neglect to search for and apprehend the transplantable proprietors was denounced as a great dishonour and breach of discipline of the army; and their entertaining any of them as tenants was declared a hindrance to the planting of Ireland with English Protestants. ' I do therefore,' the order continued, 'hereby order and declare, that if any officer or soldier under my command shall offend by neglect of his duty in searching for and apprehending all such persons as by the declaration of November 30, 1654, are to transplant themselves into Connaught; or by entertaining them as

tenants on his lands, or as servants under him, he shall be
punished by the articles of war as negligent of his duty,
according to the demerit of such his neglect.'

The English parliament resolved to clear out the population of all the principal cities and seaport towns, though
nearly all founded and inhabited by Danes or English, and
men of English descent. In order to raise funds for the
war, the following towns were offered to English merchants
for sale at the prices annexed:—Limerick, with 12,000
acres contiguous, for 30,000l., and a rent of 625l. payable to
the state ; Waterford, with 1,500 acres contiguous, at the
same rate; Galway, with 10,000 acres, for 7,500l., and a
rent of 520l. ; Wexford, with 6,000 acres, for 5,000l., and a
rent of 156l. 4s.

There were no bidders ; but still the Government adhered
to its determination to clear out the Irish, and supply their
place with a new English population. Artisans were excepted, but strictly limited in number, each case being
particularly described and registered, while dispensations
were granted to certain useful persons, on the petition of
the settlers who needed their services.

On July 8 in the same year, the governor of Clonmel was
authorised to grant dispensations to forty-three persons in a
list annexed, or as many of them as he should think fit,
being artificers and workmen, to stay for such time as he
might judge convenient, the whole time not to exceed
March 25, 1655. On June 5, 1654, the governor of Dublin
was authorised to grant licences to such inhabitants to continue in the city (notwithstanding the declaration for all
Irish to quit) as he should judge convenient, the licences to
contain the name, age, colour of hair, countenance, and
stature of every such person ; and the licence not to exceed
twenty days, and the cause of their stay to be inserted in
each licence. Petitions went up from the old native inhabitants of Limerick ; from the fishermen of Limerick ; from the
mayor and inhabitants of Cashel, who were all ordered to
transplant ; but, notwithstanding these orders, many of them

still clung about the towns, sheltered by the English, who found the benefit of their services.

The deserted cities of course fell speedily into ruins. Lord Inchiquin, president of Munster, put many artisans, menial servants, grooms, &c. in the houses, to take care of them in Cork ; still about 3,000 good houses in that city, and as many in Youghal, out of which the owners had been driven, were destroyed by the soldiers, who used the timber for fuel. The council addressed the following letter to Secretary Thurloe : —

'Dublin Castle, March 4, 1656.

'Right Honourable,—The council, having lately taken into their most serious consideration what may be most for the security of this country, and the encouragement of the English to come over and plant here, did think fitt that all Popish recusants, as wel proprietors as others, whose habitations are in any port-towns, walled-towns, or garrisons, and who did not before the 15th of September 1643 (being the time mentioned in the act of 1653 for the encouragement of adventurers and soldiers), and ever since profess the Protestant religion, should remove themselves and their families out of all such places, and two miles at the least distant therefrom, before the 20th of May next; and being desirous that the English people may take notice, that by this means there will be both security and conveniency of habitation for such as shall be willing to come over as planters, they have commanded me to send you the enclosed declaration, and to desire you that you will take some course, whereby it may be made known unto the people for their encouragement to come over and plant in this country.

'Your humble servant,

'Thomas Herbert, Clerk of the Council.'

On July 23, 1655, the inhabitants of Galway were commanded to quit the town for ever by the 1st of November following, the owners of houses getting compensation at eight years' purchase.

'On October 30, this order was executed. All the inhabitants, except the sick and bedrid, were at once banished, to provide accommodation for English Protestants, whose integrity to the state should entitle them to be trusted in a place of such importance; and Sir Charles Coote, on November 7, received the thanks of the Government for clearing the town, with a request that he would remove the sick and bedrid as soon as the season might permit, and take care that the houses while empty were not spoiled by the soldiery. The town was thus made ready for the English. There was a large debt of 10,000*l.* due to Liverpool for their loss and suffering for the good cause. The eminent deservings and losses of the city of Gloucester also had induced the parliament to order them 10,000*l.*, to be satisfied in forfeited lands in Ireland. The commissioners of Ireland now offered forfeited houses in Galway, rated at ten years' purchase, to the inhabitants of Liverpool and Gloucester, to satisfy their respective debts, and they were both to arrange about the planting of it with English Protestants. To induce them to accept the proposal, the commissioners enlarged upon the advantages of Galway. It lay open for trade with Spain, the Straits, the West Indies, and other places; no town or port in the three nations, London excepted, was more considerable. It had many noble uniform buildings of marble, though many of the houses had become ruinous by reason of the war, and the waste done by the impoverished English dwelling there. No Irish were permitted to live in the city, nor within three miles of it. If it were only properly inhabited by English, it might have a more hopeful gain by trade than when it was in the hands of the Irish that lived there. There never was a better opportunity of undertaking a plantation and settling manufacturers there than the present, and they suggested that it might become another Derry.' *

Some writers, sickened with the state of things in Ireland, and impatient of the inaction of our rulers, and of the

---

* The Cromwellian Settlement.

tedious forms of constitutional government, have exclaimed :
' Oh for one day of Oliver Cromwell ! ' Well, Ireland had
him and his worthy officers for many years. They had opportunities, which never can be hoped for again, of rooting out the Irish and their religion. ' *Thorough* ' was their
word. They dared everything, and shrunk from no consequences. They found Dublin full of Catholics ; and on
June 19, 1651, Mr. John Hewson had the felicity of
making the following report on the state of religion in the
Irish metropolis :—

' Mr. Winter, a godly man, came with the commissioners,
and they flock to hear him with great desire ; besides, there
is in Dublin, since January last, about 750 Papists forsaken
their priests and the masse, and attends the public ordinances, I having appointed Mr. Chambers, a minister, to in-
struct them at his own house once a week. They all repaire to him with much affection, and desireth satisfaction.
And though Dublin hath formerly swarmed with Papists,
I know none (now) there but one, who is a chirurgeon, and
a peaceable man. It is much hoped the glad tidings of salvation will be acceptable in Ireland, and that this savage
people may see the salvation of God.'

Political economists tell us that when population is
greatly thinned by war, or pestilence, or famine, Nature
hastens to fill up the void by the extraordinary fecundity of
those who remain. The Irish must have multiplied very
fast in Connaught during the Commonwealth ; and the
mixture of Saxon and Celtic blood resulting from the union
of the Cromwellian soldiers with the daughters of the land,
must have produced a numerous as well as a very vigorous
breed in Wexford, Kilkenny, Tipperary, Waterford, Cork,
East and West Meath, King's and Queen's Counties, and
Tyrone. But these were not ' wholly a right seed.' This
was to be found only in the union of English with English,
newly arrived from the land of the free. The more precious this seed was, the more care there should be in bringing it into the field. This matter constituted one of the

great difficulties of the plantation. There were plenty of Irish midwives: they might have been affectionate and careful, possibly skilful; but if they had any good quality, the council could not see it. On the contrary, it gave them credit for many bad qualities, the worst of all being their idolatry and disloyalty. It was really dreadful to think of English mothers and their infants being at the mercy of Irish nurses. Consequently, after much deliberation, and ' laying the matter before the Lord ' in prayer, it was resolved to bring over a state nurse from England, and to her special care were to be entrusted all the *accouchements* in the city of Dublin. Endowed with such a monopoly, it was natural enough that she should be an object of envy and dislike to those midwives whom she had supplanted. She was therefore annoyed and insulted while passing through the streets. To put a stop to these outrages, a proclamation was issued from Dublin Castle for her special protection, which began thus :—

By the Commissioners of Parliament for the Affairs of Ireland.

' Whereas we are informed by divers persons of repute and godliness, that Mrs. Jane Preswick hath, through the blessing of God, been very successful within Dublin and parts about, through the carefull and skillfull discharge of her midwife's duty, and instrumental to helpe sundry poore women who needed her helpe, which hathe abounded to the comfourte and preservation of many English women, who (being come into a strange country) had otherwise been destitute of due helpe, and necessitated to expose their lives to the mercy of Irish midwives, ignorant in the profession, and bearing little good will to any of the English nation, which being duly considered, we thought fitt to evidence this our acceptance thereof, and willingness that a person so eminently qualified for publique good and so well reported of for piety and knowledge in her art should receive encouragement and protection,' &c.

Cromwell and his ministers did not hesitate about applying heroic remedies for what they conceived to be grievances. The Irish parliament was abolished, like the Irish churches, the Irish cities, and everything else that could be called Irish, except the thing for which they fought—*the land*, which was to be Irish no more. The new England which the Protector established in the Island of Saints was represented, like Scotland, in the united parliament at Westminster—which first assembled in 1657. In that parliament, Major Morgan represented the county of Wicklow. In speaking against some proposed taxation for Ireland, he said, among other things, the country was under very heavy charges for rewards paid for the destruction of three beasts—the wolf, the priest, and the tory. ' We have three beasts to destroy,' he said, ' that lay burdens upon us. The first is a wolf, on whom we lay 5*l.* a head if a dog, and 10*l.* if a bitch. The second beast is a priest, on whose head we lay 10*l.* ; if he be eminent, more. The third beast is a tory, on whose head, if he be a public tory, we lay 20*l.* ; and 40*s.* on a private tory. Your army cannot catch them: the Irish bring them in ; brothers and cousins cut one another's throats.'

In May, 1653, the council issued the following printed declaration. ' Upon serious consideration had of the great multitudes of poore swarming in all parts of this nacion, occasioned by the devastation of the country, and by the habits of licentiousness and idleness which the generality of the people have acquired in the time of this rebellion ; insomuch that frequently some are found feeding on carrion and weeds,—some starved in the highways, and many times poor children who have lost their parents, or have been deserted by them, are found exposed to and some of them fed upon *by ravening wolves and other beasts and birds of prey.'*

No wonder the wolves multiplied and became very bold, when they fed upon such dainty fare as Irish children ! By what infatuation, by what diabolical fanaticism were those rulers persuaded that they were doing God a service, or dis-

charging the functions of a Government, in carrying out
such a policy, and consigning human beings to such a fate !

By a printed declaration of June 29, 1653, published
July 1, 1656,* the commanders of the various districts were
to appoint days and times for hunting the wolf; and persons
destroying wolves and bringing their heads to the commissioners of the revenue of the precinct were to receive for
the head of a bitch wolf, 6*l*; of a dog wolf, 5*l*; for the head
of every cub that preyed by himself, 40*s*. ; and for the head
of every sucking cub, 10*s*.   The assessments on several
counties to reimburse the treasury for these advances became, as appears from Major Morgan's speech, a serious
charge.   In corroboration it appears that in March, 1655,
there was due from the precinct of Galway 243*l*. 5*s*. 4*d*. for
rewards paid on this account.   But the most curious evidence of their numbers is that lands lying only nine miles
north of Dublin were leased by the state in the year 1653,
under conditions of keeping a hunting establishment with a
pack of wolf hounds for killing the wolves, part of the rent
to be discounted in wolves' heads, at the rate in the declaration of June 29, 1653.   Under this lease Captain Edward
Piers was to have all the state lands in the barony of Dunboyne in the county of Meath, valued at 543*l*. 8*s*. 8*d*., at a
rent greater by 100*l*. a year than they then yielded in rent
and contribution, for five years from May 1 following, on
the terms of maintaining at Dublin and Dunboyne three
wolf-dogs, two English mastiffs, a pack of hounds of sixteen
couple (three whereof to hunt the wolf only), a knowing
huntsman, and two men and one boy.   Captain Piers was to
bring to the commissioners of revenue at Dublin a stipulated number of wolf-heads in the first year and a diminish-
ing number every year; but for every wolf-head whereby
he fell short of the stipulated number, 5*l*. was to be defalked
from his salary.†

* $\frac{A}{84}$, p. 255. Republished 7th July, 1656.—'Book of Printed Declarations of the Commissioners for the Affairs of Ireland.'   British Museum.
   † Cromwellian Settlement, p. 154.

Twenty pounds was paid for the discovery of a priest, the second ' burdensome beast,' and to harbour him was death. Again I avail myself of the researches of Mr. Prendergast, to give a few orders on this subject.

' *August* 4, 1654.—Ordered, on the petition of Roger Begs, priest, now prisoner in Dublin, setting forth his miserable condition by being nine months in prison, and desiring liberty to go among his friends into the country for some relief; that he be released upon giving sufficient security that within four months he do transport himself to foreign parts, beyond the seas, never to return, and that during that time he do not exercise any part of his priestly functions, nor move from where he shall choose to reside in, above five miles, without permission. Ordered, same date, on the petition of William Shiel, priest, that the said William Shiel being old, lame, and weak, and not able to travel without crutches, he be permitted to reside in Connaught where the Governor of Athlone shall see fitting, provided, however, he do not remove one mile beyond the appointed place without licence, nor use his priestly function.'

At first the place of transportation was Spain. Thus:— ' *February* 1, 1653. Ordered that the Governor of Dublin take effectual course whereby the priests now in the several prisons of Dublin be forthwith shipped with the party going for Spain; and that they be delivered to the officers on shipboard for that purpose : care to be taken that, under the colour of exportation, they be not permitted to go into the country.'

' *May* 29, 1654.—Upon reading the petition of the Popish priests now in the jails of Dublin; ordered, that the Governor of Dublin take security of such persons as shall undertake the transportation of them, that they shall with the first opportunity be shipped for some parts in amity with the Commonwealth, provided the five pounds for each of the said priests due to the persons that took them, pursuant to the tenor of a declaration dated January 6, 1653, be first paid or secured.'

The commissioners give reasons for this policy, which are identical with what we hear constantly repeated at the present day in Ireland and England and in most of the newspapers conducted by Protestants. For two centuries the burden of all comments on Irish affairs is 'the country would be happy but for priests and agitators.' 'Hang or banish the priests!' cry some very amiable and respectable persons, 'and then we shall have peace.' 'We can make nothing of those priests,' says the improving landlord, or agent, 'they will not look us straight in the face.'

On December 8, 1655, in a letter from the commissioners to the Governor of Barbadoes, advising him of the approach of a ship with a cargo of proprietors deprived of their lands, and then seized for not transplanting, or banished for having no visible means of support, they add that amongst them were three priests; and the commissioners particularly desire they may be so employed as they may not return again where that sort of people are able to do much mischief, having so great an influence over the Popish Irish, and alienating their affections from the present Government. 'Yet these penalties did not daunt them, or prevent their recourse to Ireland. In consequence of the great increase of priests towards the close of the year 1655, a general arrest by the justices of the peace was ordered, under which, in April, 1656, the prisons in every part of Ireland seem to have been filled to overflowing. On May 3, the governors of the respective precincts were ordered to send them with sufficient guards from garrison to garrison to Carrickfergus, to be there put on board such ship as should sail with the first opportunity for the Barbadoes. One may imagine the pains of this toilsome journey by the petition of one of them. Paul Cashin, an aged priest, apprehended at Maryborough, and sent to Philipstown on the way to Carrickfergus, there fell desperately sick, and, being also extremely aged, was in danger of perishing in restraint for want of friends and means of relief. On August 27, 1656, the commissioners, having ascertained the truth of his petition, ordered him sixpence a day during his sickness ; and (in answer probably to this poor prisoner's prayer to be spared from transportation) their order directed that it should be continued to him in his travel thence (after his recovery) to Carrickfergus, in order to his transportation to the Barbadoes.'

At Carrickfergus the horrors of approaching exile seem to have shaken the firmness of some of them ; for on September 23, 1656, Colonel Cooper, who had the charge of the prison, reporting that several would under their hands renounce the Pope's supremacy, and frequent the Protestant meetings and no other, he was directed to dispense with the transportation, if they could give good Protestant security for the sincerity of their professions.

As for the third beast—the tory, the following extract gives an idea of the class to which he belonged, or, rather, from which he sprang.

' And whereas the children, grandchildren, brothers, nephews, uncles, and next pretended heirs of the persons attainted, do remain in the provinces of Leinster, Ulster, and Munster, having little or no visible estates or subsistence, but living only and coshering upon the common sort of people who were tenants to or followers of the respective ancestors of such persons, waiting an opportunity, as may justly be supposed, to massacre and destroy the English who, as adventurers or souldiers, or their tenants, are set down to plant upon the several lands and estates of the persons so attainted,' they are to transplant or be transported to the English plantations in America.' *

No wonder that Mr. Prendergast exclaims :—

' But how must the feelings of national hatred have been heightened, by seeing everywhere crowds of such unfortunates, their brothers, cousins, kinsmen, and by beholding the whole country given up a prey to hungry insolent soldiers and adventurers from England, mocking their wrongs, and triumphing in their own irresistible power ! '

* Act for Attainder of the Rebels in Ireland, passed 1656. Scobell's ' Acts and Ordinances.'

Every possible mode of repression that has been devised
at the present time as a remedy for Ribbonism was then
tried with unflinching determination.   John Symonds, an
English settler, was murdered near the garrison town of
Timolin, in the county Kildare.   All the Irish inhabitants
of the town and neighbourhood were immediately transported to Connaught as a punishment for the crime.   A few
months after two more settlers were murdered at Lackagh.

'All the Irish in the townland of Lackagh were seized;
four of them by sentence of court-martial were hanged
for the murder, or for not preventing it; and all the rest,
thirty-seven in number, including two priests, were on
November 27 delivered to the captain of the "Wexford"
frigate, to take to Waterford, there to be handed over to
Mr. Norton, a Bristol merchant, to be sold as bond slaves to
the sugar-planters in the Barbadoes.   Among these were
Mrs. Margery Fitzgerald, of the age of fourscore years, and
her husband, Mr. Henry Fitzgerald of Lackagh; although
(as it afterwards appeared) the tories had by their frequent
robberies much infested that gentleman and his tenants—
a discovery that seems to have been made only after the
king's restoration.'

The penalties against the tories themselves were to
allow them no quarter when caught, and to set a price upon
their heads.   The ordinary price for the head of a tory was
40s.; for leaders of tories, or distinguished men, it varied
from 5l. to 30l.

'But,' continues Mr. Prendergast, 'a more effective way
of suppressing tories seems to have been to induce them,
as already mentioned, to betray or murder one another—a
measure continued after the Restoration, during the absence
of parliaments, by acts and orders of state, and re-enacted
by the first parliament summoned after the Revolution,
when in that and the following reigns almost every provision of the rule of the parliament of England in Ireland
was re-enacted by the parliaments of Ireland, composed of
the soldiers and adventurers of Cromwell's day, or new

English and Scotch capitalists. In 1695 any tory killing two other tories proclaimed and on their keeping was entitled to pardon—a measure which put such distrust and alarm among their bands on finding one of their number so killed, that it became difficult to kill a second. Therefore, in 1718, it was declared sufficient qualification for pardon for a tory to kill one of his fellow-tories. This law was continued in 1755 for twenty-one years, and only expired in 1776. Tory-hunting and tory-murdering thus became common pursuits. No wonder, therefore, after so lengthened an existence, to find traces of the tories in our household words. Few, however, are now aware that the well-known Irish nursery rhymes have so truly historical a foundation :—

> ' Ho ! brother Teig, what is your story ? '
> ' I went to the wood and shot a tory : '
> ' I went to the wood, and shot another ; '
> ' Was it the same, or was it his brother ? '

> ' I hunted him in, and I hunted him out,
> Three times through the bog, and about and about ;
> Till out of a bush I spied his head,
> So I levelled my gun and shot him dead.'

After the war of 1688, the tories received fresh accessions, and, a great part of the kingdom being left waste and desolate, they betook themselves to these wilds, and greatly discouraged the replanting of the kingdom by their frequent murders of the new Scotch and English planters ; the Irish ' choosing rather ' (so runs the language of the act) ' to suffer strangers to be robbed and despoiled, than to apprehend or convict the offenders.' In order, therefore, for the better encouragement of strangers to plant and inhabit the kingdom, any persons presented as tories, by the gentlemen of a county, and proclaimed as such by the lord lieutenant, might be shot as outlaws and traitors ; and any persons harbouring them were to be guilty of high treason.* Rewards were offered for the taking or killing of them ; and the inhabitants of the barony, of the ancient native race,

* The Cromwellian Settlement, p. 163, &c.

were to make satisfaction for all robberies and spoils. If persons were maimed or dismembered by tories, they were to be compensated by 10*l.*; and the families of persons murdered were to receive 30*l.*'

The Restoration at length brought relief and enlargement to the imprisoned Irish nation. They rushed across the Shannon to see their old homes; they returned to the desolated cities, full of hope that the king for whom they had suffered so much would reward their loyalty, by giving them back their inheritances—the ' just satisfaction' promised at Breda to those who had been unfairly deprived of their estates. The Ulster Presbyterians also counted on his gratitude for their devotion to his cause, notwithstanding the wrongs inflicted on them by Strafford and the bishops in the name of his father. But they were equally doomed to disappointment. Coote and Broghill reigned in Dublin Castle as lords justices. The first parliament assembled in Dublin for twenty years, contained an overwhelming majority of undertakers, adventurers, and Puritan representatives of boroughs, from which all the Catholic electors had been excluded. ' The Protestant interest,' a phrase of tremendous potency in the subsequent history of Ireland, counted 198 members against 64 Catholics in the Commons, and in the Lords 72 against 21 peers. A court was established under an act of parliament in Dublin, to try the claims of ' nocent' and ' innocent' proprietors. The judges, who were Englishmen, declared in their first session that 168 were innocent to 19 nocent. The Protestant interest was alarmed; and, through the influence of Ormond, then lord lieutenant, the duration of the court was limited, and when it was compelled to close its labours, only 800 out of 3,000 cases had been decided. If the proportions of nocent and innocent were the same, an immense number of innocent persons were deprived of their property. In 1675, fifteen years after the Restoration, the English settlers were in possession of 4,500,000 acres, while the old owners retained 2,250,000 acres. By an act passed in 1665, it was declared that no Papist, who had not already been adjudged innocent, should ever be entitled to claim any lands or settlements.'

Any movement on the part of the Roman Catholics during this reign, and indeed, ever since, always raised an alarm of the ' Protestant interest ' in danger.   While the panic lasted the Catholics were subjected to cruel restrictions and privations.   Thus Ormond, by proclamation, prohibited Catholics from entering the castle of Dublin, or any other fortress ; from holding fairs or markets within the walls of fortified towns, and from carrying arms to such places.   By another proclamation, he ordered all the *relatives* of known ' tories ' to be arrested and banished the kingdom, within fourteen days, unless such tories were killed or surrendered within that time.   There was one tory for whose arrest all ordinary means failed.   This was the celebrated Redmond O'Hanlon, still one of the most popular heroes with the Irish peasantry. He was known on the continent as Count O'Hanlon, and was the brother of the owner of Tandragee, now the pretty Irish seat of the Duke of Manchester.   As no one would betray this outlaw, who levied heavy contributions from the settlers in Ulster, it was alleged and believed that the viceroy hired a relative to shoot him.   ' Count O'Hanlon,' says Mr. D. Magee, ' a gentleman of ancient lineage, as accomplished as Orrery, or Ossory, was indeed an outlaw to the code then in force ; but the stain of his cowardly assassination must for ever blot the princely escutcheon of James, Duke of Ormond.' *

* See ' The Tory War of Ulster,' by John P. Prendergast, author of 'The Cromwellian Settlement.'   This pamphlet abounds in the most curious information, collected from judicial records, descriptive of Ireland from the Restoration to the Revolution—A.D. 1660–1690.

CHAPTER XIII.

THE PENAL CODE, A NEW SYSTEM OF LAND-WAR.

THE accession of James II. was well calculated to have an intoxicating effect on the Irish race.   He was a Catholic, he undertook to effect a counter-reformation.   He would restore the national hierarchy to the position from which it had been dragged down and trampled under the feet of the Cromwellians.   He would give back to the Irish gentry and nobility their estates ; and to effect this glorious revolution, he relied upon the faith and valour of the Irish.   The Protestant militia were disarmed, a Catholic army was formed ; the corporations were thrown open to Catholics. Dublin and other corporations, which refused to surrender their exclusive charters, were summarily deprived of their privileges ; Catholic mayors and sheriffs, escorted by troops, went in state to their places of worship.   The Protestant chancellor was dismissed to make way for a Catholic, Baron Rice.   The plate of Trinity College was seized as public property.   The Protestants, thoroughly alarmed by these arbitrary proceedings, fled to England in thousands.   Many went to Holland and joined the army of the Prince of Orange.   Dreadful stories were circulated of an intended invasion of England by wild Irish regiments under Tyrconnel.   There was a rumour of another massacre of the English, and of the proposed repeal of the act of settlement.   Protestants who could not cross the channel fled to Enniskillen and to Derry, which closed its gates and prepared for its memorable siege.   James, who had fled to France, plucked up courage to go to Ireland, and make a stand there in defence of his crown.   His progress from Kinsale to Dublin was an ovation.   Fifteen royal chaplains scattered blessings around him; Gaelic songs and dances amused him; he was flattered in Latin orations, and conducted to his capital under triumphal arches. In Dublin the trades turned out with new banners; two harpers played at the gate by which he entered; the clergy in their robes chanted as they went: and forty young girls, dressed in white, danced the ancient *rinka*, scattering flowers on the newly sanded streets. Tyrconnell, now a duke, the judges, the mayor and the corporation, completed the procession, which moved beneath arches of evergreens, and windows hung with 'tapestry and cloth of arras.' The recorder delivered to his majesty the keys of the city, and the Catholic primate, Dominick Maguire, waited in his robes to conduct him to the royal chapel, where the *Te Deum* was sung. On that day the green flag floated from the main tower of the castle, bearing the motto, ' Now or never—now and for ever.'

The followers of James, according to Grattan, ' though papists, were not slaves. They wrung a constitution from King James before they accompanied him to the field.' A constitution wrung from such a man was not worth much. His parliament passed an act for establishing liberty of conscience, and ordering every man to pay tithes to his own clergy only, with some other measures of relief. But he began to play the despot very soon. The Commons voted him the large subsidy of 20,000*l*. He doubled the amount by his own mere motion. He established a bank, and by his own authority decreed a bank monopoly. He debased the coinage, and fixed the prices of merchandise by his own will. He appointed a provost and librarian in Trinity College without the consent of the senate, and attempted to force fellows and scholars on the university contrary to the statutes. The events which followed are well known to all readers of English history. Our concern is with their effects on the land question.

One of the measures passed by this parliament was an act repealing the act of settlement. But, soon after the Revolution, measures were taken to render that settlement firmer than ever.

A commission was appointed to enquire into the forfeited estates; and the consequence was that 1,060,792 acres were declared escheated to the crown. In 1695 King William, in his speech, read to the Irish parliament, assured them that he was intent upon the firm settlement of Ireland upon a Protestant basis. He kept his word, for when he died there did not remain in the hands of Catholics one-sixth of the land which their grandfathers held, even after the passing of the act of settlement. The acts passed for securing the Protestant interest formed the series known as the penal code, which was in force for the whole of the eighteenth century. It answered its purpose effectually; it reduced the nation to a state of poverty, degradation, and slavishness of spirit unparalleled in the history of Christendom, while it made the small dominant class a prodigy of political and religious tyranny. Never was an aristocracy, as a body, more hardened in selfishness, more insolent in spirit; never was a church more negligent of duty, more intensely and ostentatiously secular. Both church and state reeked with corruption.

The plan adopted for degrading the Catholics, and reducing all to one plebeian level, was most ingenious. The ingenuity indeed may be said to be Satanic, for it debased its victims morally as well as socially and physically. It worked by means of treachery, covetousness, perfidy, and the perversion of all natural affections. The trail of the serpent was over the whole system. For example, when the last Duke of Ormond arrived as lord lieutenant in 1703, the Commons waited on him with a bill 'for discouraging the further growth of Popery,' which became law, having met his decided approval. This act provided that if the son of a Catholic became a Protestant, the father should be incapable of selling or mortgaging his estate, or disposing of any portion of it by will. If a child ever so young professed to be a Protestant, it was to be taken from its parents, and placed under the guardianship of the nearest Protestant relation.

The sixth clause renders Papists incapable of purchasing

any manors, tenements, hereditaments, or any rents or profits arising out of the same, or of holding any lease of lives, or other lease whatever, for any term exceeding thirty-one years. And with respect even to such limited leases, it further enacts, that if a Papist should hold a farm producing a profit greater than *one-third of the amount of the rent*, his right to such should immediately cease, and pass over entirely to the first Protestant who should discover the rate of profit. The seventh clause prohibits Papists from succeeding to the properties or estates of their Protestant relations. By the tenth clause, the estate of a Papist, not having a Protestant heir, is ordered to be gavelled, or divided in equal shares between *all* his children. The sixteenth and twenty-fourth clauses impose the oath of abjuration, and the sacramental test, as a qualification for office, and for voting at elections. The twenty-third clause deprives the Catholics of Limerick and Galway of the protection secured to them by the articles of the treaty of Limerick. The twenty-fifth clause vests in the crown all advowsons possessed by Papists.

A further act was passed, in 1709, imposing additional penalties. The first clause declares that no Papist shall be capable of holding an annuity for life. The third provides, that the child of a Papist, on conforming, shall at once receive an annuity from his father ; and that the chancellor shall compel the father to discover, upon oath, the full value of his estate, real and personal, and thereupon make an order for the support of such conforming child or children, and for securing such a share of the property, after the father's death, as the court shall think fit. The fourteenth and fifteenth clauses secure jointures to Popish wives who shall conform. The sixteenth prohibits a Papist from teaching, even as assistant to a Protestant master. The eighteenth gives a salary of 30*l.* per annum to Popish priests who shall conform. The twentieth provides rewards for the discovery of Popish prelates, priests, and teachers, according to the following whimsical scale :—For discovering an archbishop,

bishop, vicar-general, or other person, exercising any foreign ecclesiastical jurisdiction, 50*l.* ; for discovering each regular clergyman, and each secular clergyman, not registered, 20*l.* ; and for discovering each Popish schoolmaster or usher, 10*l.*

In judging the Irish peasantry, we should try to estimate the effects of such a system on any people for more than a century. It will account for the farmer's habit of concealing his prosperity, and keeping up the appearance of poverty, even if he had not reason for it in the felonious spirit of appropriation still subsisting under legal sanction. We are too apt to place to the account of race or religion the results of malignant or blundering legislation. We are not without examples of such results in England itself.

In the winter of 1831–2, a very startling state of things was presented. In a period of great general prosperity, that portion of England in which the poor laws had their most extensive operation, and in which by much the largest expenditure of poor-rates had been made, was the scene of daily riot and nightly incendiarism. There were ninety-three parishes in four counties, of which the population was 113,147, and the poor-law expenditure 81,978*l.*, or 14*s.* 5*d.* per head ; and there were eighty parishes in three other counties, the population of which was 105,728, and the poor-law expenditure 30,820*l.*, or 5*s.* 9*d.* a head. In the counties in which the poor-law expenditure was large, the industry and skill of the labourers were passing away, the connection between the master and servant had become precarious, the unmarried were defrauded of their fair earnings, and riots and incendiarism prevailed. In the counties where the expenditure was comparatively small, there was scarcely any instance of disorder ; mutual attachment existed between the workman and his employer; the intelligence, skill, and good conduct of the labourers were unimpaired, or increased. This striking social contrast was only a specimen of what prevailed throughout large districts, and generally throughout the south and north of England, and it proved that, either through the inherent vice of the system, or gross mal-administration in the southern counties, the poor-law had the most demoralising effect upon the working classes, while it was rapidly eating up the capital upon which the employment of labour depended. This fact was placed beyond question by a commission of enquiry, which was composed of individuals distinguished by their interest in the subject, and their intimate knowledge of its principles and details. Its labours were continued incessantly for two years. Witnesses most competent to give information were summoned from different parts of the country. The commissioners had before them documentary evidence of every kind calculated to throw light on the subject. They personally visited localities, and examined the actual operation of the system on the spot; and when they could not go themselves, they called to their aid assistant commissioners, some of whom extended their enquiries into Scotland, Guernsey, France, and Flanders; while they also collected a vast mass of interesting evidence from our ambassadors and diplomatic agents in different countries of Europe and America. It was upon the report of this commission of enquiry that the act was founded for the amendment and better administration of the laws relating to the poor in England and Wales (4 and 5 William IV., cap. 76). A more solid foundation for a legislative enactment could scarcely be found. The importance of the subject fully warranted all the expense and labour by which it was obtained.

One of the most astounding facts established by the enquiry was the wide-spread demoralisation which had developed itself in certain districts. Home had lost its sanctity. The ties that bind parents and children were loosened, and natural affection gave place to intense selfishness, which often manifested itself in the most brutal manner. Workmen grew lazy and dishonest. Young women lost the virtue which is not only the point of honour with their sex, but the chief support of all other virtues. Not only women of the working classes, but in some cases even substantial farmers' daughters, and sometimes those who were themselves the actual owners of property, had their illegitimate children as charges on the parish, regularly deducting the cost of their maintenance from their poor-rate, neither they nor their relatives feeling that to do so was any disgrace. The system must have been fearfully vicious that produced such depravation of moral feeling, and such a shocking want of self-respect.

Dr. Burn has given a graphic sketch of the duties of an overseer under the old poor-law system in England. 'His office is to keep an extraordinary watch to prevent people from coming to inhabit without certificates; to fly to the justices to remove them. Not to let anyone have a farm of 10l. a year. To warn the parishioners, if they would have servants, to hire them by the month, the week, or the day, rather than by any way that can give them a settlement; or if they do hire them for a year, then to endeavour to pick a quarrel with them before the year's end, and so to get rid of them. To maintain their poor as cheaply as they possibly can, and not to lay out twopence in prospect of any future good, but only to serve the present necessity. To bargain with some sturdy person to take them by the lump, who yet is not intended to take them, but to hang over them *in terrorem*, if they shall complain to the justices for want of maintenance. To send them out into the country a begging. To bind out poor children apprentices, no matter to whom, or to what trade; but to take special care that the master live in another parish. To move heaven and earth if any dispute happen about a settlement; and, in that particular, to invert the general rule, and stick at no expense. To pull down cottages: *to drive out as many inhabitants, and admit as few, as they possibly can ; that is, to depopulate the parish, in order to lessen the poor's-rate.* To be generous, indeed, sometimes, in giving a portion with the mother of a bastard child to the reputed father, on condition that he will marry her, or with a poor widow, *always provided that the husband* be settled elsewhere; or if a poor

man with a large family happen to be industrious, they will
charitably assist him in taking a farm in some neighbouring
parish, and give him 10*l.* to pay his first year's rent with,
that they may thus for ever get rid of him and his pro-
geny.'

The effect of this system was actually to depopulate many
parishes. The author of a pamphlet on the subject, Mr.
Alcock, stated that the gentlemen were led by this system
to adopt all sorts of expedients to hinder the poor from
marrying, to discharge servants in their last quarter, to
evict small tenants, and pull down cottages; so that several
parishes were in a manner depopulated, while England complained of a want of useful hands for agriculture, manufac-
tories, for the land and sea service. ' When the minister
marries a couple,' he said, ' he rightly prays that they may
be fruitful in the procreation of children ; but most of the
parishioners pray for the very contrary, and perhaps complain of him for marrying persons, that, should they have
a family of children, might likewise become chargeable.'
Arthur Young also described the operation of the law in
his time, in clearing off the people, and causing universally
' an open war against cottages.' Gentlemen bought them
up whenever they had an opportunity, and immediately
levelled them with the ground, lest they should become
' nests of beggars' brats.' The removal of a cottage often
drove the industrious labourer from a parish where he could
earn 15*s.* a week, to one where he could earn but 10*s.* As
many as thirty or forty families were sent off by removals
in one day. Thus, as among the Scotch labourers of the
present day, marriage was discouraged ; the peasantry were
cleared off the land, and increasing immorality was the necessary consequence.

There was another change in the old system, by which the
interests of the influential classes were made to run in favour
of the ' beggars' nests,' which were soon at a premium. The
labourer was to be paid, not for the value of his labour, but
according to the number of his family; the prices of pro-

visions being fixed by authority, and the guardians making up the difference between what the wages would buy and what the family required.

The allowance scales issued from time to time were framed on the principle that every labourer should have a gallon loaf of standard wheaten bread weekly for every member of his family, and one over. The effect of this was, that a man with six children, who got 9*s.* a week wages, required nine gallon loaves, or 13*s.* 6*d.* a week, so that he had a pension of 4*s.* 6*d.* over his wages. Another man, with a wife and five children, so idle and disorderly that no one would employ him, was entitled to eight gallon loaves for their maintenance, so that he had 12*s.* a week to support him. The increase of allowance according to the number of children acted as a direct bounty upon marriage. The report of the Committee of the House of Commons on labourers' wages, printed in 1824, describes the effect of this allowance system in paralysing the industry of the poor. ' It is obvious,' remarked the committee, ' that a disinclination to work must be the consequence of so vicious a system. He whose subsistence is secure without work, and who cannot obtain more than a mere sufficiency by the hardest work, will naturally be an idle and careless labourer. Frequently the work done by four or five such labourers does not amount to what might easily be performed by a single labourer at task work. A surplus population is encouraged: men who receive but a small pittance know that they have only to marry and that pittance will be increased proportionally to the number of their children. When complaining of their allowance, they frequently say, " We will marry, and then you must maintain us." This system secures subsistence to all; to the idle as well as the industrious; to the profligate as well as the sober; and, as far as human interests are concerned, all inducements to obtain a good character are taken away. The effects have corresponded with the cause: able-bodied men are found slovenly at their work, and dissolute in their hours of relaxation; a father is negligent of his children, the children do not think it necessary to contribute to the support of their parents; the employer and employed are engaged in personal quarrels; and the pauper, always relieved, is always discontented. Crime advances with increasing boldness; and the parts of the country where this system prevails are, in spite of our gaols and our laws, filled with poachers and thieves.' Mr. Hodges, chairman of the West Kent quarter sessions, in his evidence before the emigration committee, said, ' Formerly, working people usually stayed in service till they were twenty-five, thirty, and thirty-five years of age, before they married; whereas they now married frequently under age. Formerly, these persons had saved 40*l.* and 50*l.* before they married, and they were never burdensome to the parish; now, they have not saved a shilling before their marriage, and become immediately burdensome.'

The farmers were not so discontented with this allowance system as might be supposed, because a great part of the burden was cast upon other shoulders. The tax was laid indiscrimately upon all fixed property; so that the occupiers of villas, shopkeepers, merchants, and others who did not employ labourers, had to pay a portion of the wages for those that did. The farmers were in this way led to encourage a system which fraudently imposed a heavy burden upon others, and which, by degrading the labourers, and multiplying their numbers beyond the real demand for them, must, if allowed to run its full course, have ultimately overspread the whole country with the most abject poverty and wretchedness.

There was another interest created which tended to increase the evil. In the counties of Suffolk, Sussex, Kent, and generally through all the south of England, relief was given in the shape of house accommodation, or free dwellings for the poor. The parish officers were in the habit of paying the rent of the cottages; the rent was therefore high and sure, and consequently persons who had small pieces of ground were induced to cover them with those buildings.

On this subject Mr. Hodges, the gentleman already referred
to, remarks: ' I cannot forbear urging again that any
measure having for its object the relief of the parishes from
their over population, must of necessity become perfectly
useless, unless the act of parliament contains some regula-
tions with respect to the erecting and maintaining of cottages.
I am quite satisfied that the erecting of cottages has been a
most serious evil throughout the country. The getting of
the cottage tempts young people of seventeen and eighteen
years of age, and even younger, to marry. It is notorious
that almost numberless cottages have been built by persons
speculating on the parish rates for their rents.'

The evils of this system had reached their height in the
years 1831-2. That was a time when the public mind was
bent upon reforms of all sorts, without waiting for the admission from the Tories that the grievances of which the
nation complained were ' proved abuses.' The reformers
were determined no longer to tolerate the state of things, in
which the discontent of the labouring classes was propor-
tioned to the money disbursed in poor-rates, or in voluntary
charities; in which the young were trained in idleness,
ignorance, and vice—the able-bodied maintained in sluggish
and sensual indolence—the aged and more respectable
exposed to all the misery incident to dwelling in such
society as that of a large workhouse without discipline or
classification—the whole body of inmates subsisting on food
far exceeding both in kind and amount, not merely the diet
of the independent labourer, but that of the majority of the
persons who contributed to their support. The farmer paid
10s. in the pound in poor-rates, and was in addition compelled
to employ supernumerary labourers not required on his farm,
at a cost of from 100l. to 250l. a year; the labourer had no
need to hasten himself to seek work, or to please his master,
or to put a restraint upon his temper, having all the slave's
security for support, without the slave's liability to punishment. The parish paid parents for nursing their little
children, and children for supporting their aged parents,

thereby destroying in both parties all feelings of natural affection and all sense of Christian duty.

I hope I shall be excused in giving, from a former work of my own, these home illustrations to prove that bad laws can degrade and demoralize a people in a comparatively short time, in spite of race and creed and public opinion; and that, where class interests are involved, the most sacred rights of humanity are trampled in the mire of corruption. Even now the pauperism resulting of necessity from the large-farm system is degrading the English people, and threatening to rot away the foundations of society. On this subject I am glad to find a complete corroboration of my own conclusions in a work by one of the ablest and most enlightened Christian ministers in England, the Rev. Dr. Rigg. He says:—

' Notwithstanding a basis of manly, honest, and often generous qualities, the common character of all the uneducated and unelevated classes of the English labouring population includes, as marked and obvious features, improvidence, distrust of their superiors, discontent at their social position, and a predominant passion for gross animal gratification. Of this general character we regard the rude, heavy, unhopeful English peasant, who knows no indulgence or relaxation but that of the ale-house, and lives equally without content and without ambition, as affording the fundamental type, which, like all other things English, possesses a marked individuality. It differs decidedly from the Irish type of peasant degradation. Something of this may be due to the effect of race. The Kelt and the Saxon may be expected to differ. Yet we think but little stress is to be laid upon this. There is, probably, much more Keltic blood in the southern and western counties of England, and, also, more Saxon blood in some of the southern and even western parts of Ireland, than has been generally supposed. We apprehend that a Saxon population, under the same conditions as the southern and western Irish peasantry, would have grown up into very much the same sort of people as the Irish have been; while a Keltic population, exposed to the same influences, through successive generations, as the midland and southern peasantry of England, would not have been essentially different at the present day from the actual cultivators of the soil.

‘ The Irish peasant is poorer and yet more reckless than the Englishman ; but he is not so sullen or so spiritless. His body is not so muscular or so strongly-set as that of the Anglo-Saxon husbandman, on whose frame the hard and unintermitted toil of thirty generations has stamped its unmistakable impress, and, correspondently, he is a less persevering and less vigorous labourer ; but, as a general rule, his stature is taller and his step far more free and elastic than that of the sturdy but slow and stunted labourer of our southern counties. There are wild mountainous districts of the west, indeed, in which the lowest type of the Irish peasantry is found, that must be taken as exceptions to our general statement ; and as many from those regions cross the Channel to tramp through England in the complex character of mendicant labourers, no doubt some have received from them an impression as to the Irish peasantry very different from what our observations are intended to convey. But no one can have travelled through the south of Ireland without having noticed what we state. The Tipperary and Kilkenny peasantry are proverbially tall ; Connemara has been famed for its “ giants,” and many of both sexes throughout the south, are, spite of their rags, fine figures, and graceful in their movements. While looking at them, we have ceased to wonder at what has been regarded as no better than the arch-agitator’s blarney, when he spoke of the Irish as the “ finest pisantry in the world ; ” and we have even felt saddened as we mentally contrasted with what we saw before us the bearing and appearance of our own southern labourers. For the tattered Irish peasant, living in a mud hovel, is, after all, a gentleman in his bearing ; whereas there is generally either a cringing servility or a sullen doggedness in the demeanour of the south Saxon labourer. The Irishman is, besides, far more intelligent and ready-witted than the Saxon husbandman. The fact is that the Irishman, if underfed, has not been overworked. His life has not been one of unceasing and oppressive labour. Nor has his condition been one of perpetual servitude. With all his poverty, he has been, to a considerable extent, his own master. Half-starved, or satisfying his appetite on light and innutritious fare,—far worse housed and clad than the poorest English labourer, often, indeed, almost half-naked,—oppressed by middle-men, exactors of rack-rent; with all this the Irish cottier has been, from father to son, and from generation to generation, *a tenant, and not merely a day labourer.'* *

* 'Essays for the Times, on Ecclesiastical and Social Subjects,' by James H. Rigg, D.D. London, 1866.

CHAPTER XIV.

ULSTER IN THE EIGHTEENTH CENTURY.

LET us, then, endeavour to get rid of the pernicious delusions about race and religion in dealing with this Irish land question. Identity of race and substantial agreement in religion did not prevent the Ulster landlords from uprooting their tenants when they fancied it was their interest to banish them—to substitute grazing for tillage, and cattle for a most industrious and orderly peasantry.

The letters of Primate Boulter contain much valuable information on the state of Ulster in the last century, and furnish apt illustrations of the land question, which, I fancy, will be new and startling to many readers. Boulter was lord primate of Ireland from 1724 to 1738. He was thirteen times one of the lords justices. As an Englishman and a good churchman, he took care of the English interests and of the establishment. The letters were written in confidence to Sir Robert Walpole and other ministers of state, and were evidently not intended for publication. An address ' to the reader' from some friend, states truly that they give among other things an impartial account of ' the distressed state of the kingdom for want of *tillage*, the vast sums of money sent out of the nation for corn, flour, &c., the dismal calamities thereon, the want of trade and the regulation of the English and other coins, to the very great distress of all the manufacturers,' &c. They show that he was a man of sound judgment, public-spirited, and very moderate and impartial for the times in which he lived. His evidence with regard to the relations of landlord and tenant in Ulster is exceedingly valuable at the present moment. Lord Dufferin could not have read the letters when he wrote his book; otherwise I should think his apology for the landlords of the last century would have been considerably modified.

Primate Boulter repeatedly complained to Walpole, the Duke of Newcastle, and other ministers, that the Ulster farmers were deserting the country in large numbers, emigrating to the United States, then British colonies, to the West Indies, or to any country where they hoped to get the means of living, in many cases binding themselves to work for a number of years *as slaves* in payment of their passage out. The desire to quit the country of their birth is described by the primate as a mania. Writing to the Archbishop of Canterbury in 1728 he says :—'We are under great trouble here about a frenzy that has taken hold of very great numbers to leave this country for the West Indies, and we are endeavouring to learn what may be the reasons of it, and the proper remedies.' Two or three weeks later he reported to the Duke of Newcastle that for several years past some agents from the colonies in America, and several masters of ships, had gone about the country 'and deluded the people with stories of great plenty and estates to be had for going for in those parts of the world.' During the previous summer more than 3,000 men, women, and children had been shipped for the West Indies. Of these, not more than one in ten were men of substance. The rest hired themselves for their passage, or contracted with masters of ships for four years' servitude, 'selling themselves as servants for their subsistence.' The whole north was in a ferment, people every day engaging one another to go next year to the West Indies. ' The humour,' says the primate, ' has spread like a contagious distemper, and the people will hardly hear anybody that tries to cure them of their madness. The worst is that it affects only *Protestants*, and reigns chiefly in the North, which is the seat of our linen manufacture.'

As the Protestant people, the descendants of the English and Scotch who had settled in the country in the full assurance that they were building homes for their posterity, were thus deserting those homes in such multitudes, their pastors sent a memorial to the lord lieutenant, setting forth the grievances which they believed to be the cause of the desertion. On this memorial the primate wrote comments to the English Government, and, in doing so, he stated some astounding facts as to the treatment of the people by their landlords. He was a cautious man, thoroughly acquainted with the facts, and writing under a sense of great responsibility. In order to understand some of those facts, we should bear in mind that the landlords had laid down large portions of their estates in pasture, to avoid the payment of tithes, and that this burden was thrown entirely upon the tenants who tilled the land. Now, let my readers mark what the primate states as to their condition. He says :— 'If a landlord takes too great a portion of the profits of a farm for his share by way of rent (as the tithe will light on the tenant's share), the tenant will be impoverished; but then it is not the tithe, but the increased rent that undoes the farmer. And, indeed, in this country, where I fear the tenant hardly ever has more than one-third of the profits he makes of his farm for his share, and too often but a *fourth*, or, perhaps, a *fifth part*, as the tenant's share is charged with the tithe, his case is, no doubt, hard, but it is plain from what side the hardship arises.' What the gentlemen wanted to be at, according to the primate, was, that they might go on raising their rents, and that the clergy should receive their old payments. He admits, however, that the tenants were sometimes cited to the ecclesiastical courts, and if they failed to appear there, they stood excommunicated ; and he adds, 'possibly when a writ *de excommunicato capiendo* is taken out, and they find they have 7*l.* or 8*l.* to pay, *they run away*, for the greatest part of the occupiers of the land here are so poor, that an extraordinary stroke of 8*l.* or 10*l.* falling on them is certain ruin to them.' He further states that, to his own knowledge, many of the clergy had chosen rather to lose their 'small dues' than to be at a certain great expense in getting them, 'and at an uncertainty whether the farmer would not at last *run away without paying anything.'*

Such was the condition of the Protestants of Ulster during the era of the penal code; and it is a curious fact that it was the Presbyterians and not the Catholics that were forced by the exactions of the Protestant landlords and the clergy to run away from the country which their forefathers had been brought over to civilize. But there was another fact connected with the condition of Ulster which I dare say will be almost incredible to many readers. The tenantry, so cruelly rack-rented and impoverished, were reduced by two or three bad seasons to a state bordering upon famine. There was little or no corn in the province. The primate set on foot a subscription in Dublin, to which he himself contributed very liberally. The object was to buy food to supply the necessities of the north, and to put a stop to ' the great desertion' they had been threatened with. He hoped that the landlords would ' do *their* part by remitting some arrears, or making some abatement of their rents.' As many of the tenants had eaten the oats they should have sowed their lands with, he expected the landlords would have the good sense to furnish them with seed; if not, a great deal of land would lie waste that year. And where were the provisions got? Partly in Munster, where corn was very cheap and abundant. But the people of Cork, Limerick, Waterford, and Clonmel objected to have their provisions sent away, although they were in some places ' as cheap again as in the north; but where dearest, at least one-third part cheaper.' Riotous mobs broke open the store-houses and cellars, setting what price they pleased upon the provisions. And, what between those riots and the prevalence of easterly winds, three weeks elapsed before the 3,000*l.* worth of oats, oatmeal, and potatoes could be got down to relieve the famishing people of the north, which then seemed black enough, even to its own inhabitants. Hence the humane primate was obliged to write: ' The humour of going to America still continues, and the scarcity of provisions certainly makes many quit us. There are now seven ships at Belfast that are carrying off 1,000 passengers thither, and if we knew how to stop them, as most of them can neither get victuals nor work at home, it would be cruel to do it.'

The Presbyterian clergy suffered greatly from the impoverishment of their people. Several of them who had been receiving a stipend of 50l. a year, had their incomes reduced to less than 15l. In their distress they appealed to the primate, and, staunch churchman as he was, they found in him a kind and earnest advocate. Writing to Sir Robert Walpole, on March 31, 1729, he pleaded for the restoration of 400l. a year, which had been given to the non-conforming clergy of Ireland from the privy purse, in addition to the 1,200l. royal bounty, which, it appears, had been suspended for two years, owing to the death of the late king. 'They are sensible,' said his grace, ' there is nothing due to them, nor do they make any such claim; but as the calamities of this kingdom are at present very great, and by the desertion of many of their people to America, and the poverty of the greatest part of the rest, their contributions, particularly in the north, are very much fallen off, it would be a great instance of his majesty's goodness if he would consider their present distress.' In our own days a Presbyterian minister would be considered to deserve well of his country if he emigrated to America, and took with him as many of the people as he could induce to forsake their native land. But what was the great plea which Primate Boulter urged on the English Minister on behalf of the Presbyterian clergy of his day ? It was, that they had exerted their influence to prevent emigration. ' It is,' he said, ' but doing them justice to affirm that they are very well affected to his majesty and his royal family, and by the best enquiries I could make, do their best endeavours to keep their congregations from deserting the country, not more than one or two of the younger ministers having anyways encouraged the humour now prevailing here. And his majesty's goodness in giving them some extraordinary

relief on this occasion of their present great distress would undoubtedly make them *more active to retain their people here.*
I cannot help mentioning on this occasion that, what with
scarceness of corn in the north, *and the loss of all credit there,*
and by the numbers that go, or talk of going, to America,
and with the disturbances in the south, this kingdom is at
present in a deplorable condition.'

In a statement previously made to the Bishop of London,
the Irish primate earnestly solicited his correspondent to use
his influence to prevent the Irish landlords from passing a
law to strip the established clergy of their rights with
respect to the tithe of agistment. They had entered into a
general combination, and formed a stock purse to resist the
payment of tithe, except by the poor tenants who tilled the
soil, a remarkable contrast to the zeal of the landlords of our
own time in defending church property against 'spoliation' by the imperial legislature, and to the liberality with
which many of them are now contributing to the Sustenta-
tion Fund. How shall we account for the change? Is it
that the landlords of the present day are more righteous
than their grandfathers? Or is it that the same principle of
self-interest which led the proprietors of past times to grind
the tenantry and rob the Church, now operates in forms more
consistent with piety and humanity, and by its subtle influence illustrates the maxim of the poet—

> Self-love and social is the same.

However that may be, the primate contented himself in
this letter with a defence of the Church, in which he admitted matters of real grievance, merely alluding to other
grievances, 'such as raising the rents unreasonably, the
oppression by justices of the peace, seneschals, and other
officers in the country.'

From the pictures of the times he presents we should not
be surprised at his statement to the Duke of Newcastle, that
the people who went to America made great complaints of
the oppressions they suffered, and said that those oppres-

sions were one reason of their going. When he went on his visitation, in 1726, he 'met all the roads full of whole families that had left their homes to beg abroad,' having consumed their stock of potatoes two months before the usual time. During the previous year many hundreds had perished of famine. What was the cause of this misery, this desolating process going on over the plains of Ulster? The archbishop accounts for it by stating that many persons had let large tracts of land, from 3,000 to 4,000 acres, which were stocked with cattle, and had no other inhabitants on their land than so many cottiers as were necessary to look after their sheep and black cattle, ' *so that, in some of the finest counties, in many places there is neither house nor corn-field to be seen in ten or fifteen miles' travelling,* and daily in some counties many gentlemen, as their leases fall into their hands, tie up their tenants from tillage ; and this is one of the main causes why so many venture to go into foreign service at the hazard of their lives if taken, because they cannot get land to till at home.'

My readers should remember that the industrious, law-abiding, bible-loving, God-fearing people, who were thus driven by oppression from the fair fields of Ulster, which they had cultivated, and the dwellings which they had erected, to make way for sheep and cattle—because it was supposed by the landlords that sheep and cattle paid better—were the descendants of British settlers who came to the country under a royal guarantee of *freeholds and permanent tenures.* Let them picture to their minds this fine race of honest, godly people, rack-rented, crushed, evicted, heart-broken—men, women, and children—Protestants, Saxons, cast out to perish as the refuse of the earth, by a set of landed proprietors of their own race and creed; and learn from this most instructive fact that, if any body of men has the power of making laws to promote its own interest, no instincts of humanity, no dictates of religion, no restraints of conscience can be relied upon to keep them from acting with ruthless barbarity, and doing more to ruin their country than a foreign invader could accomplish by letting loose upon it his brutal soldiers. How much more earnestly would Boulter have pleaded with the prime minister of England on behalf of the wretched people of Ulster if he could have foreseen that ere long those Presbyterian emigrants, with the sense of injustice and cruel wrong burning in their hearts, would be found fighting under the banner of American independence—the bravest and fiercest soldiers of freedom which the British troops encountered in the American war. History is continually repeating itself, yet how vainly are its lessons taught! The same legal power of extermination is still possessed by the Irish landlords after sixty-nine years of imperial legislation. Our hardy, industrious people, naturally as well disposed to royalty as any people in the world, are still crowding emigrant ships in all our ports, deserting their country with the same bitter feelings that animated the Ulster men a century ago, hating our Government with a mortal hatred, and ready to fight against it under a foreign flag! We have no Primate Boulter now in the Protestant hierarchy to plead the cause of an unprotected tenantry; but we have the press, which can concentrate upon the subject the irresistible force of public opinion.

As a churchman, Primate Boulter naturally regarded the land question in its bearings on the interests of the Establishment. Writing to Sir Robert Walpole in 1737 he said that he had in vain represented to the landlords that, by destroying the tithe of agistment, they naturally discouraged tillage, lessened the number of people, and raised the price of provisions. By running into cattle they caused the young men to enlist in foreign service for bread, there being no employment for them at home, 'where two or three hands can look after some hundreds of acres stocked with cattle.' And by this means, said the primate, 'a great part of our churches are neglected; in many places five, six, or seven parishes bestowed on one incumbent, who, perhaps, with all his tithes, scarce gets 100*l.* a year.' But there was at that time a member of the Irish House of Commons who was

capable of taking a more enlarged view of the Irish question,
This was Mr. Arthur Dobbs, who belonged to an old and
honourable Ulster family—the author of a book on the
' North-west Passage to India,' and of a very valuable work
on the ' Trade of Great Britain and Ireland.' He was
intimately acquainted with the working of the Irish land
system, for he had been many years agent of the Hertfort
estate, one of the largest in Ireland. There is among
Boulter's letters an introduction of Mr. Dobbs to Sir Robert
Walpole, recommending him as a person of good sense, who
had applied himself to the improvement of trade, and to the
making of our colonies in America of more advantage than
they had hitherto been. He was afterwards made Governor
of North Carolina. I have mentioned these facts in the
hope of securing the attention of landlords and statesmen to
the following passage from his book accounting for the
deplorable condition of the province of Ulster at that time,
and the emigration of its industrious and wealth-producing
inhabitants. In my humble opinion it furnishes irresistible
arguments in favour of a measure which should settle the
Irish land question in such a manner that it would speak
to the people of Ireland in the words of holy writ: ' And
they shall build houses, and inhabit them; and they shall
plant vineyards and eat the fruit of them. They shall not
build and another inhabit; they shall not plant and another
eat.' Mr. Dobbs says:—

' How can a tenant improve his land when he is convinced
that, after all his care and toil, his improvements will be
overrated, and he will be obliged to shift for himself? Let
us place ourselves in his situation and see if we should
think it reasonable to improve for another, if those improvements would be the very cause of our being removed from
the enjoyment of them. I believe we should not. Industry
and improvements go very heavily on when we think we
are not to have the property in either. What can be expected, then, from covenants to improve and plant, when the
person to do it knows he is to have *no property in them?*

There will be no concern or care taken to preserve them, and they will run to ruin as fast as made or planted. What was it induced so many of the commonalty lately to go to America but high rents, bad seasons, and want of good tenures, or a permanent property in their land? This kept them poor and low, and they scarce had sufficient credit to procure necessaries to subsist or till their ground. They never had anything to store, all was from hand to mouth; so one or two bad crops broke them. Others found their stock dwindling and decaying visibly, and so removed before all was gone, while they had as much left as would pay their passage, and had little more than what would carry them to the American shore.

'This, it may be allowed, was the occasion of the poor farmers going who had their rents lately raised. But it may be objected that was not the reason why rich farmers went, and those who had several years in beneficial leases still unexpired, who sold their bargains and removed with their effects. But it is plain they all went for the same reason; for these last, from *daily examples before them*, saw the present occupiers dispossessed of their lands at the expiration of their leases, and no preference given to them; so they expected it would soon be their own case, to avoid which, and make the most of the years still unexpired, they sold, and carried their assets with them to procure a settlement in a country where they had reason to expect a permanent property.'

It is a curious fact that sentiments very similar were published by one of Cromwell's officers about a century before. The plea which he put forth for the Irish tenant in the dedication of his work on Ireland to the Protector, has been repeated ever since by the tenants, but repeated in vain: Captain Bligh, the officer alluded to, said: 'The first prejudice is, that if a tenant be at ever so great pains or cost for the improvement of his land, he doth thereby but occasion a greater rack-rent upon himself, or else invests his landlord with his cost and labour *gratis*, or at least lies at his land-

lord's mercy for requital; which occasions a neglect of all
good husbandry, to his own, the land, the landlord, and the
commonwealth's suffering. Now, this, I humbly conceive,
might be removed, if there were a law enacted, by which
every landlord should be obliged either to give him reasonable allowance for his clear improvement, or else suffer him
or his to enjoy it so much longer or till he hath had a pro-
portionable requital.'

But although Primate Boulter protested against the conduct of the landlords—all Episcopalians—who were ruining
the church as well as the country, the established clergy,
as a body, were always on the side of the oppressors.

The Test Act placed the Presbyterians, like the Papists,
in the position of an inferior race. 'In the city of Londonderry alone, which Presbyterian valour had defended,
ten out of twelve aldermen, and twenty out of twenty-four
burgesses, were thrust out of the corporation by that act,
which placed an odious mark of infamy upon at least one-
half the inhabitants of the kingdom.' Presbyterians could
not legally keep a common school. The *Edinburgh Review*
says : 'All the settlements, from first to last, had the
effect of making the cause of the church and the cause of
the landlords really one. During the worst days of landlord oppression it never identified itself with the interests of
the people, but uniformly sustained the power and privileges
of the landlords.'

It was vain to expect justice from the Irish parliament.
The people of Ireland never were governed exclusively, or
at all, by her own Sovereign, her own Lords, and her own
Commons. Ireland was 'in the custody of England,' just as
much before the Union as during the last sixty-seven years.
Even during the few brief years of her spasmodic ' independence,' the mass of the nation formed no part of the ' Commons of Ireland.' It was still, as it always had been, a
sham parliament—a body representing the colonial aristocracy—acting as undertakers for the Government of
England, for whose interest exclusively this island was to

be ruled. Provided this result was secured, it did not matter much, at the other side of the Channel, how the Irish people were treated. Indeed, they were not recognised as the people of Ireland, or any part thereof. Even philosophic liberals, like Lord Charlemont, were shocked at the idea of a Papist getting into the Irish House of Commons; and the volunteer system was shattered by this insane animosity of the ruling race against the subject nation. The antipathy was as strong as the antipathy between the whites and the negroes in the West Indies and the United States. Hence the remorseless spirit in which atrocities were perpetrated in 1798. Mr. Daunt has shown that a large proportion of the Irish House of Lords consisted of men who were English to all intents and purposes—many of them by birth, and many by residence, and, no doubt, they always came over with reluctance to what Lord Chancellor Clare called ' our damnable country.' It may be that in some years after the abolition of the Establishment— after some experience of the *régime* of religious equality— the two races in this island will learn to act together so harmoniously as to give a fair promise that they could be safely trusted with self-legislation. But the '*self*' must be one body animated by one spirit; not two bodies, chained together, irritated by the contact, fiercely struggling against one another, eternally reproaching one another about the mutual wrongs of the past, and not unfrequently coming to blows, like implacable duellists shut up in a small room, each determined to kill or be killed. If England were to let go her hold even now, something like this would be the Irish ' situation.' The abiding force of this antipathy, in the full light of Christianity, is awful.

In his ' Life, Letters, and Speeches of Lord Plunket,' the Hon. David Plunket states that, when his grandfather entered the Irish parliament, ' the English Government had nearly abandoned the *sham* of treating the Irish parliament as an independent legislature; the treasury benches were filled with placemen and pensioners. All efforts tending to

reform of parliament or concession to the Catholics had been
given up as useless. Grattan and some of his immediate
followers had seceded from an assembly too degraded to
appreciate their motives, or to be influenced by their example ; and whatever remained of independence in the
House of Commons ministers still laboured to bring under
their control. Scarcely thirty votes appeared in opposition
on the most important divisions, while Government could at
any time readily whip a majority of 100.'

According to a Government return made in 1784, by
Pitt's direction, 116 nomination seats were divided between
some 25 proprietors. Lord Shannon returned no less than
16 members, and the great family of Ponsonby returned 14;
Lord Hillsborough, 9, the Duke of Leinster, 7, and the
Castle itself 12. Eighty-six seats were *let out* by the
owners, in consideration of titles, offices, and pensions. No
less than 44 seats were occupied by placemen, 32 by gentlemen who had promises of pensions, 12 by gentlemen who
stood out for higher prices from Government. The regular
opposition appears to have been limited to 82 votes, of
which 30 belonged to Whig nominees, and the rest to the
popular party.

It is, then, easy to account for the state of public feeling
which Mr. Plunket, with these facts and figures before him,
so well describes. He says truly that if it were possible to
appeal to the country under these circumstances, the people
would not have responded. ' Gloomy and desperate, they
had lost all confidence in their parliament, and looked to
other quarters for deliverance from the *intolerable tyranny*
under which they suffered. There can be no doubt that
this anarchy and disgrace were in a great degree the result
of a misgovernment, ancient and recent, *which seems to have
been always adopted with a view to bring out strongly the
worst elements of the Irish character*; but it was at that
time said, and no doubt believed by the Opposition, that
the ministry of the day had deliberately planned and accomplished the disorganisation of the Irish people and their

parliament, in order to enable them to carry out their favourite project of the Union.'

Mr. Plunket, after describing the classes of 'representatives' that his grandfather had to deal with in the Irish House of Commons, further says : ' It is true that this corrupt assembly cannot fairly be looked upon as the mirror of national character and national honour. The members of the majority who voted for the Union *were not* the representatives of the people, *but the hired servants of the Minister, for the Parliament had been packed for the purpose.*'

Towards the close of the century, however, the French Revolution, the American war, and the volunteer movement, had begun to cause some faint stirring of national life in the inert mass of the Roman Catholic population, which the penal code had ' *dis-boned.*' Up to this time they were not even thought of in the calculations of politicians. According to Dean Swift, Papists counted no more in politics than the women and children. Macaulay uses a still more contemptuous comparison to express the estimate in which they were held in those times, saying, that their lords and masters would as soon have consulted their poultry and swine on any political question. Nevertheless, during the excitement of the volunteer movement, some of the poor Celts began to raise their heads, and presumed to put the question to the most liberal portion of the ruling race—' Are we not men ? Have not we also some rights?' The appeal was responded to in the Irish parliament, and in 1793 the elective franchise was conceded to Roman Catholics. It was the first concession, and the least that could be granted. But the bare proposal excited the utmost indignation in the Tory party, and especially in the Dublin corporation, where the Orange spirit was rampant. That body adopted an address to the Protestants of Ireland, which bears a remarkable resemblance in its spirit and style to addresses lately issued by Protestant Defence Associations. Both speak in the kindest terms of their Roman Catholic fellow-subjects, disclaim all intention of depriving them of any advantages they enjoy under our glorious constitution, declaring that their objects are purely *defensive*, and that they want merely to guard that constitution against the aggressions of the Papacy quite as much for the sake of Roman Catholics as for the sake of Protestants. 'Countrymen and friends,' said the Dublin Tories, seventy-five years ago, 'the firm and manly support which we received from you when we stood forward in defence of the Protestant Ascendancy, deserves our warmest thanks. We hoped that the sense of the Protestants of Ireland, declared upon that occasion, would have convinced our Roman Catholic fellow-subjects that the pursuit of political power was for them a vain pursuit; for, though the liberal and enlightened mind of the Protestant receives pleasure at seeing the Catholic exercise his religion with freedom, enjoy his property in security, and possess the highest degree of personal liberty, yet, experience has taught us that, without the ruin of the Protestant establishment, the Catholic cannot be allowed the smallest influence in the state.'

Those men were as thoroughly convinced as their descendants, who protest against concession to-day, that all our Protestant institutions would go to perdition, if Papists, although then mere serfs, were allowed to vote for members of parliament. They were equally puzzled to know why Roman Catholics were discontented, or what more their masters could reasonably do for them to add to the enviable happiness of their lot. 'We entreat you,' the Dublin corporation said to their Protestant brethren throughout the country—'we entreat you to join with us in using every honest means of persuading the Roman Catholics to rest content with the most perfect toleration of their religion, the fullest security of their property, and the most complete personal liberty; but, by no means, now or hereafter, to attempt any interference in the government of the kingdom, as such interference would be incompatible with the Protestant Ascendancy, which we have resolved with our lives and fortunes to maintain.' Lest any doubt should exist as to what they meant by ' Protestant Ascendancy,' they expressly defined it. They resolved that it consisted in a Protestant King of Ireland; a Protestant Parliament, Protestant electors and Government; Protestant benches of justice ; a Protestant hierarchy ; the army and the revenue, through all their branches and details, Protestant ; and this system supported by a connection with the Protestant realm of Britain.

The power of the political franchise to elevate a degraded people, to convert slaves into men, is exhibited before the eyes of the present generation in the Southern States of America; even where differences of race and colour are most marked, and where the strongest natural antipathies are to be overcome. We may judge from this what must have been the effect of this concession on the Irish Celts. The forty-shilling freeholders very soon became objects of consideration with their landlords, who were anxious to extend their political influence in their respective counties, for the representation of which the great proprietors had many a fierce contest. The abolition of this franchise by the Emancipation Act made that measure a grievance instead of a relief to the peasantry, for the landlords were now as anxious to get rid of the small holders as they had been to increase them so long as they served their political purpose. It was one of the great drawbacks which deprived emancipation of the healing effect it would otherwise have produced. If--as Pitt intended—that measure had formed part of the Union arrangements ; if the forty-shilling freeholders had been spared, and the priesthood had been endowed, we should never have had an agitation for repeal or even for the separation of the church from the state. Pitt's plan of the Union included the abolition of Protestant Ascendancy.

Edmund Burke, in one of his letters on Ireland, said : ' A word has been lately struck in the mint of the castle of Dublin. Thence it was conveyed to the Tholsel, or city hall, where having passed the touch of the corporation, so respectably stamped and vouched, it soon became current in parliament, and was carried back by the speaker of the

House of Commons, in great pomp, as an offering of homage from whence it came. That word is Ascendancy. The word is not absolutely new.' He then gives its various meanings, and first shows what it does *not* signify in the new sense. Not influence obtained by love or reverence, or by superior management and dexterity; not an authority derived from wisdom or virtue, promoting the happiness and freedom of the Roman Catholic people; not by flattering them, or by a skilful adaptation to their humours and passions. It means nothing of all these. Burke then shows what it does mean. ' New ascendancy is old mastership. It is neither more nor less than the resolution of one sect of people in Ireland to consider themselves the sole citizens in the commonwealth, and to keep a dominion over the rest, by reducing them to absolute slavery under a military power; and thus fortified in their power, to divide the public estate, which is the result of general contribution, as a military booty, solely among themselves. This ascendancy, by being a *Protestant* ascendancy, does not better it, from a combination of a note or two more in this anti-harmonic scale. By the use that is frequently made of the term, and the policy that is grafted on it, the name Protestant becomes nothing more or better than the name of a persecuting faction, with a relation of some sort of theological hostility to others, but without any sort of ascertained tenets of its own, upon the ground of which it persecutes other men; for the patrons of this Protestant ascendancy neither do nor can, by anything positive, define or describe what they mean by the word Protestant. . . . The whole is nothing but pure and perfect malice. It is indeed a perfection in that kind, belonging to beings of a higher order than man, and to them we ought to leave it. . . . Let three millions of people but abandon all that they and their ancestors have been taught to believe sacred, and to forswear it publicly in terms the most degrading, and nothing more is required of them. . . . The word *Protestant* is the charm that locks up in a dungeon of servitude three millions of people.

Every thoughtful reader of the debates in parliament on the state of Ireland, must have been struck with the difference of opinion between the Liberals and the Conservatives, as to the facts of the case. A still more violent difference was presented in the British parliament, in the year 1797, when there were great debates in both houses on the subject, and when the facts were still more glaring, one of them being that the reign of terror established by the Irish Government prevented the press from reporting the maddening atrocities which the ruling faction was daily perpetrating against the mass of the king's subjects. The debate arose in the Lords, on a motion by Lord Moira for an address to the king on the state of Ireland. He described the horrors of which he had been recently a witness, but softened the recital, lest he should shock his hearers too much. Orange loyalty was then licensed and let loose upon the defenceless Roman Catholic population in Ulster. Lord Gosford's description of the scenes of desolation in his own county, Armagh, is well known. He did what he could to prevent the burning of Roman Catholic houses, and the personal injuries inflicted upon the unfortunate inhabitants, while their Orange neighbours chased them out of the country, giving them Cromwell's alternative. But his mercy injured his reputation, and he felt obliged to protest solemnly that he was a loyal man, and that he wished to uphold Protestant ascendancy in Ireland as much as any of his accusers. He only asked that the poor Catholic should be allowed to live in peace. In the debate referred to, Lord Moira declared that ninety-one householders had been banished from one of his own estates; and many of them wounded in their persons. The discontent, he said, was not confined to one sect. He ascribed the state of things to the recall of Lord Fitzwilliam, which crushed the hopes of the Catholics, and gave unbounded licence to the yeomanry, who were empowered to act with a vigour beyond the law; to turn out, banish, or kill the king's subjects, on mere suspicion, often prompted by private malice, and having no better warrant than anonymous information. But for all this the Irish parliament and the new reactionary viceroy freely granted acts of indemnity. According to Earl Fitzwilliam 'whole parishes, baronies, and even counties, were declared to be out of the king's peace.'

Mr. Fox brought forward a similar motion in the House of Commons, pleading the cause of justice and humanity in a noble speech, and boldly affirming principles of government for Ireland, which Mr. Gladstone, Mr. Chichester Fortescue, and Mr. Bright are now endeavouring to have carried out by the imperial parliament after seventy years of concession, extorted by three rebellions. Mr. Fox expressed his abhorrence of ' the truly diabolical maxim ' of ' *Divide et impera*,' by which the government of Ireland was conducted. He hoped that the discontent which threatened the separation of Ireland would be dissipated without the necessity of war. ' But now,' he said, ' the extremity of rigour has been tried—the severity of despotism has been let loose—and the Government is driven to that state when the laws are not to be put into execution, but to be superseded.' The motion was seconded by Sir Francis Burdett, who said: ' Whoever has seen Ireland, has seen a country where the fields are desolated, and the prisons overflowing with the victims of oppression—has seen the shocking contrast between a profligate, extravagant Government, and an enslaved and impoverished people.' The motion was rejected by a majority of 136. Lord Moira made a last and an almost despairing appeal on November 22, in the same year. In his speech he said: ' I have seen in that country a marked distinction made between the English and the Irish. I have seen troops that have been sent full of this prejudice, that every inhabitant of that kingdom is a rebel to the British Government. I have seen the most wanton insults practised upon men of all ranks and conditions. I have seen the most grievous oppression exercised, in consequence of a presumption that the person who was the unfortunate object of such oppression was in hostility to the Government; and yet that

has been done in a part of the country as quiet and as free
from disturbance as the city of London. He who states
these things should be prepared with proofs. I am prepared
with them.' He then went into a number of horrifying
details, and concluded as follows : 'You say that the Irish
are insensible to the benefits of the British constitution, and
you withhold all these benefits from them. You goad them
with harsh and cruel punishments, and a general infliction
of insult is thrown upon the kingdom. I have seen, my
lords, a conquered country held by military force ; *but never
did I see in any conquered country such a tone of insult as
has been adopted by Great Britain towards Ireland.* I have
made a last effort. I acquit my conscience ; I have done
my duty.'

In subsequent debates, the following sentiments were
uttered by the leading Whig statesmen of the day : ' The
treatment of Ireland,' said Mr. Fox, ' was such as to harrow
up the soul. It was shocking to think that a nation of
brothers was thus to be trampled on like the most remote
colony of conquered strangers. . . . The Irish people have
been scourged by the iron hand of oppression, and subjected
to the horrors of military execution, and are now in a situation too dreadful for the mind to contemplate without dismay.
After the inhuman dragooning and horrible executions, the
recital of which makes the blood run cold—after so much
military cruelty, not in one, but in almost every part of the
country—is it possible for this administration to procure
unanimity in Ireland?' On March 22, 1798, the Duke of
Bedford moved an address to the king, asking him to change
his ministers, and alluding to the state of Ireland, as it
was before the breaking out of the Rebellion. He said :
'Were I to enter into a detail of the atrocities which have
been committed in Ireland, the picture would appal the
stoutest heart. It could be proved that the most shocking
cruelties have been perpetrated; but what could be expected
if men kept in strict discipline were all at once allowed to
give loose to their fury and their passions ? '

Lord Holland was persuaded that his majesty's ministers could not tranquillise Ireland even by conciliation. ' How could they conciliate whose concessions are always known to be the concessions of weakness and of fear, and who never granted to the Irish—the most generous people upon earth, —anything without a struggle or resistance?' Lord William Russell, in June following, said: 'A man's loyalty was to be estimated by the desire he testified to imbrue his hands in his brother's blood.' Sheridan asked: ' After being betrayed, duped, insulted—disappointed in their dearest hopes, and again thrown into the hands of the rulers they detested and despised, was it impossible they should feel emotions of indignation? The struggle is not one of partial disaffection, but it is a contest between the people and the Government.' Mr. Tierney said: 'It was certain the people were in arms against the Government, nor was it easy to conceive how—having been scourged, burnt, and massacred —they could have any other feeling than aversion to that Government.'

Every motion on the subject in both houses was rejected by overwhelming majorities. So little impression did the reports of the appalling facts which were of daily occurrence in Ireland make upon that Tory Government, that the speeches of ministers read exactly like the speeches of Mr. Disraeli, Mr. Hardy, Lord Mayo, and Mr. Warren, in the past session. Lord Grenville, the home secretary, professed the most profound respect for the independence of the Irish parliament, and he could not think of interfering in the least with its privileges, however the empire might suffer from its excesses. ' The motion of Lord Moira was not only unnecessary, it was highly mischievous.' He dwelt on the improved state of Ireland, and the tranquillity of the people. If there were partial excesses on the part of the military, they were unavoidable, and could only be deplored. 'He was unable to discern what should alienate the affections of Ireland. For the whole space of thirty years his majesty's Government had been distinguished by the same uniform tenderness of regard, by the same undeviating adherence to the mild principles of a conciliatory system. . . If any cruelties had been practised, they must have been resisted by a high-spirited people. Were there no courts of justice? The conduct of the lord lieutenant was highly commendable. The system recommended by Lord Moira would only tend to villify the Irish Government.' Then came the fatal announcement which sounded the death-knell of thousands of the Irish people, and caused the destruction of millions' worth of property. The home secretary said: 'The contrary system must, therefore, be persevered in; and to the spirited exertions of the British military should we owe the preservation of Irish laws, of Irish property, and of Irish lives!'

To this the Marquis of Downshire added 'that he was not afraid of the effects of coercion. Every concession had been made that could be made towards Ireland. Every Catholic was as free as the safety of the state would admit. Were the Catholics to have an equal share in the government with the Protestants, the Government and the country would be lost.'

I will conclude by quoting the remarks of Mr. Fox, referred to above: 'If you do not allay their discontent, there is no way but force to keep them in obedience. Can you convince them by the musket that their principles are false? Can you prove to them by the bayonet that their pretensions are unjust? Can you demonstrate to them by martial law that they enjoy the blessings of a free constitution? No, it is said, but they may be deterred from the prosecution of the objects which you have determined to refuse. But on what is this founded? On the history of Ireland itself? No; for the history of Ireland proves that, though repeatedly subdued, it could not be kept in awe by force; and the late examples will prove the effect which severity may be expected to produce. . . . I would therefore concede; and if I found I had not conceded enough, I would concede more. I know of no way of governing

mankind, but by conciliating them. . . . My wish is
that the whole people of Ireland should have the same principles, the same system, the same operation of government.
. . . I would have the whole Irish government regulated
by Irish notions and Irish prejudices ; and I firmly believe,
according to an Irish expression, the more she is under Irish
government, the more she will be bound to English interests.
. . . I say, therefore, try conciliation, but do not have
recourse to arms.' He warned and implored in vain. The
Union had been determined on ; and it was thought that it
could be effected only after the prostration of civil war, into
which, therefore, the unfortunate people were goaded.

CHAPTER XV.

POVERTY AND COERCION.

WE are now in the nineteenth century, without any relief for the Irish peasantry. The rebellion of '98, so cruelly crushed, left an abiding sense of terror in the hearts of the Roman Catholic population. Their condition was one of almost hopeless prostration. The Union was effected without the promised relief from their religious disabilities which was to be one of its essential conditions. The established church was secured, the rights of property were secured, but there was no security for the mass of the people. Domestic politics were almost forgotten in the gigantic struggle with Napoleon, which exhausted the energies of the empire. Any signs of political life that showed themselves in Ireland were connected with Catholic emancipation, and the visit of George IV., in 1820, held forth promises of relief which excited unbounded joy. The king loved his Irish subjects, and would never miss an opportunity of realising the good wishes for their happiness which he had so often and so fervently expressed to his Whig friends, when he was Prince Regent. O'Connell's agitation commenced soon after, and in nine years after the royal visit emancipation was extorted by the dread of civil war, frankly avowed by the Duke of Wellington and Sir Robert Peel. But this boon left the masses nearly where they had been, only more conscious of their power, and more determined to use it, in the removal of their grievances.

Lord Redesdale, writing to Lord Eldon in 1821, said :—
' In England the machine goes on almost of itself, and there-

fore a bad driver may manage it tolerably well. It is not so in Ireland. The country requires great exertion to bring it into a state of order and submission to law. The whole population—high and low, rich and poor, Catholic and Protestant—must all be brought to obedience to law; all must be taught to look up to the law for protection. The gentry are ready enough to attend grand juries, to obtain presentments for their own benefit, but they desert the quarter-sessions of the peace. The first act of a constable in arresting must not be to knock down the prisoner; and many, many reforms must be made, which only can be effected by a judicious and able Government *on the spot.* Ireland, in its present state, cannot be governed in England. If insubordination compels you to give, how are you to retain by law what you propose to maintain while insubordination remains? It can only be by establishing completely the empire of the law.'

Sir Archibald Alison ascribed the unhappy relations of classes in Ireland to what he calls 'the atrocious system of confiscation, which, in conformity with feudal usages, the victors introduced on every occasion of rebellion against their authority.' Sir George Nicholls has shown, in his valuable history of the Irish poor law, that as early as 1310 the parliament assembled at Kilkenny resolved that none should keep Irish, or kern, in time of peace to live upon the poor of the country; 'but those which will have them shall keep them at their own charges, so that the free tenants and farmers be not charged with them.' And 130 years afterwards, the parliament assembled in Dublin declared that divers of the English were in the habit of maintaining sundry thieves, robbers, and rebels, and that they were to be adjudged traitors for so doing, and suffer accordingly. In 1450, this class of depredators had increased very much, and by their 'thefts and manslaughters caused the land to fall into decay, poverty wasting it every day more and more; whereupon it was ordained that it should be lawful for every liege man to kill or take notorious thieves, and thieves found robbing, spoiling, or breaking houses; and that every man that kills or takes any such thieves shall have one penny of every plough, and one farthing of every cottage within the barony where the manslaughter is done, for every thief.' These extracts show a very barbarous state of society, but Sir George Nicholls remarks that at the same period the condition of England and Scotland was very similar, save only that that of Ireland was aggravated by the civil conflicts between the colonists and the natives. There were some efforts made in Ireland, by various enactments, to put down this evil, and to provide employment for the large numbers that were disposed to prey upon the industry of their neighbours, by robbery, beggary, and destruction of property. But while there was a legal provision made for the poor in England, there was none in Ireland, where the people were, *en masse*, deprived of the means of self-support by the action of the Government. Hence, so late as the year 1836, the poor-law commissioners reported to the following effect : —

It appeared that in Great Britain the agricultural families constituted little more than a fourth, whilst in Ireland they constituted about two-thirds, of the whole population; that there were in Great Britain, in 1831, 1,055,982 agricultural labourers; in Ireland, 1,131,715, although the cultivated land of Great Britain amounted to about 34,250,000 acres and that of Ireland only to about 14,600,000. So that there were in Ireland about five agricultural labourers for every two that there were for the same quantity of land in Great Britain. It further appeared that the agricultural progress of Great Britain was more than four times that of Ireland; in which agricultural wages varied from sixpence to one shilling a day; the average of the country being about eightpence-halfpenny ; and that the earnings of the labourers came, on an average of the whole class, to from two shillings to two and sixpence a week or thereabouts for the year round. Thus circumstanced, the commissioners observed, ' It is impossible for the able-bodied in general to provide

T

against sickness or the temporary absence of employment, or against old age, or the destitution of their widows and children in the contingent event of their own premature decease. A great portion of them are, it is said, insufficiently provided with the commonest necessaries of life. Their habitations are wretched hovels, several of a family sleep together on straw, or upon the bare ground, sometimes with a blanket, sometimes even without so much to cover them; their food commonly consists of dry potatoes, and with these they are at times so scantily supplied as to be obliged to stint themselves to one spare meal in the day. There are even instances of persons being driven by hunger to seek sustenance in wild herbs. They sometimes get a herring or a little milk, but they never get meat except at Christmas, Easter, and Shrovetide. Some go in search of employment to Great Britain, during the harvest; others wander through Ireland with the same view. The wives and children of many are occasionally obliged to beg; but they do so reluctantly and with shame, and in general go to a distance from home, that they may not be known. Mendicity, too, is the sole resource of the aged and impotent of the poorer classes in general, when children or relatives are unable to support them. To it, therefore, crowds are driven for the means of existence, and the knowledge that such is the fact leads to an indiscriminate giving of alms, which encourages idleness, imposture, and general crime.' Such was the wretched condition of the great body of the labouring classes in Ireland; 'and with these facts before us,' the commissioners say, 'we cannot hesitate to state that we consider remedial measures requisite to ameliorate the condition of the Irish poor. What those measures should be is a question complicated, and involving considerations of the deepest importance to the whole body of the people, both in Ireland and Great Britain.'

Sir George Nicholls, who had been an English poor-law commissioner, was sent over to Ireland to make preliminary enquiries. He found that the Irish peasantry had generally an appearance of apathy and depression, seen in their mode of living, their habitations, their dress and conduct; they seemed to have no pride, no emulation, to be heedless of the present and careless of the future. They did not strive to improve their appearance or add to their comforts: their cabins were slovenly, smoky, dirty, almost without furniture, or any article of convenience or common decency. The woman and her children were seen seated on the floor, surrounded by pigs and poultry: the man lounging at the door, which could be approached only through mud and filth: the former too slatternly to sweep the dirt and offal from the door, the latter too lazy to make a dry footway, though the materials were close at hand. If the mother were asked why she did not keep herself and her children clean with a stream of water running near the cabin, her answer invariably was— 'Sure, how can we help it? We are so poor.' The husband made the same reply, while smoking his pipe at the fire or basking in the sunshine. Sir George Nicholls rightly concluded that poverty was not the sole cause of this state of things. He found them also remarkable for their desultory and reckless habits. Though their crops were rotting in the fields from excessive wet, and every moment of sunshine should be taken advantage of, yet if there was a market, a fair, or a funeral, a horse-race, a fight, or a wedding, forgetting everything else, they would hurry off to the scene of excitement. Working for wages was rare and uncertain, and hence arose a disregard of the value of time, a desultory, sauntering habit, without industry or steadiness of application. 'Such,' he proceeds, 'is too generally the character and such the habits of the Irish peasantry; and it may not be uninstructive to mark the resemblance which these bear to the character and habits of the English peasantry in the pauperised districts, under the abuses of the old poor law. Mendicancy and indiscriminate almsgiving have produced in Ireland results similar to what indiscriminate relief produced in England—the like reckless disregard of the future, the like idle and disorderly conduct, and the same proneness to outrage having then characterised the English pauper labourer which are now too generally the characteristics of the Irish peasant. An abuse of a good law caused the evil in the one case, and a removal of that abuse is now rapidly effecting a remedy. In the other case the evil appears to have arisen rather from the want than the abuse of a law; but the corrective for both will, I believe, be found to be essentially the same.'

The expectation that such a neglected people, made wretched by bad land laws, should be loyal, was surely unreasonable. For them, it might be said, there was no Government, no protection, no encouragement. There could not be more tempting materials for agitators to work upon. Lord Cloncurry vividly sketches the state of things resulting from the want of principle and earnestness among politicians in dealing with Irish questions at that time.

' From the Union up to the year 1829, the type of British colonial government was the order of the day. The Protestants were upheld as a superior caste, and paid in power and official emoluments for their services in the army of occupation. During the second viceroyalty of Lord Anglesea, an effort was made by him to evoke the energies of the whole nation for its own regeneration. That effort was defeated by the conjoint influence of the cowardice of the English cabinet, the petulance of Mr. Stanley, and the unseasonable violence and selfishness of the lately emancipated popular leaders. Upon Lord Anglesea's recall the modern Whig model of statemanship was set up and followed: popular grievances were allowed to remain unredressed; the discontent and violence engendered by those grievances were used from time to time for party purposes; the people were hung and bayoneted when their roused passions exceeded the due measure of factious requirement; and the state patronage was employed to stimulate and to reward a staff of demagogues, by whom the masses were alternately excited to madness, and betrayed, according to the necessities of the English factions. When Russells and Greys were out or in danger, there were free promises of equal laws and privileges and franchises for oppressed Ireland; the minister expectant or trembling for his place, spoke loudly of justice and compensation, of fraternity and freedom. To these key-notes the place-hunting demagogue pitched his brawling. His talk was of pike-making, and sword-fleshing, and monster marching. The simple people were goaded into a madness, the end whereof was for them suspension of the Habeas Corpus Act, the hulks, and the gallows ; for their stimulators, silk gowns and commissionerships and seats on the bench. Under this treatment the public mind became debauched ; the lower classes, forced to bear the charges of agitation, as well as to suffer its penalties, lost all faith in their social future ; they saw not and looked not beyond the momentary excitement of a procession or a monster meeting.'

Sir Robert Peel, when introducing the Emancipation Bill, had to confess the utter failure of the coercive policy which had been so persistently pursued. He showed that Ireland had been governed, since the Union, almost invariably by coercive acts. There was always some political organisation antagonistic to the British Government. The Catholic Association had just been suppressed; but another would soon spring out of its ashes, if the Catholic question were not settled. Mr. O'Connell had boasted that he could drive a coach-and-six through the former act for its suppression; and Lord Eldon had engaged to drive 'the meanest conveyance, even a donkey cart, through the act of 1829.' The new member for Oxford (Sir Robert Inglis) also stated that twenty-three counties in Ireland were prepared to follow the example of Clare. 'What will you do,' asked Sir Robert Peel, 'with that power, that tremendous power, which the elective franchise, exercised under the control of religion, at this moment confers upon the Roman Catholics ? What will you do with the thirty or forty seats that will be claimed in Ireland by the persevering efforts of the agitators, directed by the Catholic Association, and carried out by the agency of every priest and bishop in Ireland ? ' If

Parliament began to recede there could be no limit to the retrogression. Such a course would produce a reaction, violent in proportion to the hopes that had been excited. Fresh rigours would become necessary ; the re-enactment of the penal code would not be sufficient. They must abolish trial by jury, or, at least, incapacitate Catholics from sitting on juries. 2,000,000 of Protestants must have a complete monopoly of power and privilege in a country which contained 5,000,000 of Catholics, who were in most of the country four to one—in some districts twenty to one—of the Protestants. True, there were difficulties in the way of a settlement. ' But,' asked Sir Robert Peel, ' what great measure, which has stamped its name upon the era, has ever been carried without difficulty ?

At the present moment there is a loud cry in the English press for the suspension of the Habeas Corpus Act, and for the old remedy, coercion. Those who raise the cry would do well to read Mr. Shiel's speech at the Clare election in 1828. He said :—

' We have put a great engine into action, and applied the entire force of that powerful machinery which the law has placed under our control. We are masters of the passions of the people, and we have employed our dominion with a terrible effect. But, sir, do you, or does any man here, imagine that we could have acquired this formidable ability to sunder the strongest ties by which the different classes of society are fastened, unless we found the materials of excitement in the state of society itself? Do you think that Daniel O'Connell has himself, and by the single powers of his own mind, unaided by any external co-operation, brought the country to this great crisis of agitation ? Mr. O'Connell, with all his talent for excitation, would have been utterly powerless and incapable, unless he had been allied with a great conspirator against the public peace; and I will tell you who that confederate is—it is the law of the land itself that has been Mr. O'Connell's main associate, and that ought to be denounced as the mighty agitator of Ireland. The rod of oppression is the wand of this enchanter, and the book of his spells is the penal code? Break the wand of this political Prospero, and take from him the volume of his magic, and he will evoke the spirits which are now under his control no longer. But why should I have recourse to illustration, which may be accounted fantastical, in order to elucidate what is in itself so plain and obvious? Protestant gentlemen, who do me the honour to listen to me, look, I pray you, a little dispassionately at the real causes of the events which have taken place amongst you. . . . In no other country, except in this, would such a revolution have been effected. Wherefore? Because in no other country are the people divided by the law from their superiors, and cast into the hands of a set of men who are supplied with the means of national excitement by the system of government under which we live. Surely, no man can believe that such an anomalous body as the Catholic Association could exist excepting in a community that has been alienated from the state by the state itself. The discontent and the resentment of 7,000,000 of the population have generated that domestic government which sways public opinion, and uses the national passions as the instruments of its will. It would be utterly impossible, if there were no exasperating distinctions amongst us, to create any artificial causes of discontent. Let men declaim for a century, and if they have no real grievance their harangues will be empty sound and idle air. But when what they tell the people is true—when they are sustained by substantial facts, effects are produced of which what has taken place at this election is only an example. The whole body of the people having been previously excited, the moment any incident such as this election occurs, all the popular passions start simultaneously up, and bear down every obstacle before them. Do not, therefore, be surprised that the peasantry should throw off their allegiance when they are under the operation of emotions which it would be wonderful if they could resist. The feeling by which they are actuated would make them not only vote against their

landlord, but would make them scale the batteries of a
fortress, and mount the breach; and, gentlemen, give me
leave to ask you whether, after due reflection upon the
motives by which your vassals (for so they are accounted)
are governed, you will be disposed to exercise any measure
of severity in their regard?'

The greatest warrior of the age rebuked the men who
cried in that day that the sword should be the arbiter of the
Irish question; and Sir Robert Peel, in his own vindication
of the Emancipation Act, said:—

' I well know that there are those upon whom such considerations as these to which I have been adverting will
make but a faint impression. Their answer to all such
appeals is the short, in their opinion the conclusive, declaration—" The Protestant constitution in church and state
must be maintained at all hazards, and by any means; the
maintenance of it is a question of principle, and every concession or compromise is the sacrifice of principle to a low
and vulgar expediency." This is easily said; but how was
Ireland to be governed? How was the Protestant constitution in church and state to be maintained in that part of
the empire? Again I can anticipate the reply—" By the
overwhelming sense of the people of Great Britain; by the
application, if necessary, of physical force for the maintenance of authority; by the employment of the organised
strength of government, the police and the military, to enforce
obedience to the law." I deliberately affirm that a minister
of the crown, responsible at the time of which I am speaking
for the public peace and the public welfare, would have
grossly and scandalously neglected his duty if he had failed
to consider whether it might not be possible that the fever of
political and religious excitement which was quickening the
pulse and fluttering the bosom of the whole Catholic population—which had inspired the serf of Clare with the resolution
and energy of a free man—which had, in the twinkling of
an eye, made all considerations of personal gratitude, ancient
family connection, local preferences, the fear of worldly

injury, the hope of worldly advantage, subordinate to the all-absorbing sense of religious obligation and public duty— whether, I say, it might not be possible that the contagion of that feverish excitement might spread beyond the barriers which, under ordinary circumstances, the habits of military obedience and the strictness of military discipline opposed to all such external influences.'

The officer who commanded the military force in Clare during the election, testified, as the result of his observation there, that, even in the constabulary and the army, the sympathies of a common cause, political and religious, could not be altogether repressed, and that implicit reliance could not long be placed on the effect of discipline and the duty of obedience. On July 20, Lord Anglesea wrote as follows:— ' We hear occasionally of the Catholic soldiers being ill-disposed, and entirely under the influence of the priests. One regiment of infantry is said to be divided into Orange and Catholic factions. It is certain that, on July 12, the guard at the castle had Orange lilies about them.' On July 26, the viceroy wrote another letter, from which the following is an extract:—' The priests are using very inflammatory language, and are certainly working upon the Catholics of the army. I think it important that the depôts of Irish recruits should be gradually removed, under the appearance of being required to join their regiments, and that whatever regiments are sent here should be those of Scotland, or, at all events, of men not recruited from the south of Ireland. I desired Sir John Byng to convey this opinion to Lord Hill.'

Emancipation was carried, and the people were disaffected still. And why should they not be disaffected still? Emancipation had done nothing for them. The farmers were still at the mercy of the landlords, whose pride they humbled at the hustings of Clare and Waterford. They were still tormented by the tithe-proctor seizing the tenth of all that their labour produced on the land. The labourers were still wretched, deprived of the forty-shilling freehold, which

protected them from the horrors of eviction and of transportation in a floating hell across the Atlantic. I well remember the celebrated anti-tithe war in 1831, as well as
the system by which it was provoked, and I can bear witness
to the accuracy of the following description of the tithe-
proctor by Henry Grattan. He said:—

'The use of the tithe-farmer is to get from the parishioners
what the parson would be ashamed to demand, and so
enable the parson to absent himself from his duty. The
powers of the tithe-farmer are summary laws and ecclesiastical courts; his livelihood is extortion; his rank in
society is generally the lowest; and his occupation is to
pounce on the poor in the name of the Lord! He is a
species of wolf left by the shepherd to take care of the flock
in his absence.' A single tithe-proctor had on one occasion
processed 1,100 persons for tithes, nearly all of the lower
order of farmers or peasants, the expense of each process
being about 8s. They had heard of opinions delivered in
parliament, on the platform, and from the press by Protestant statesmen of the highest consideration, that it was a
cruel oppression to extort in that manner from the majority
of the tillers of the soil the tenth of its produce, in order to
support the clergy of another church, who, in many cases,
had no flocks, or only a few followers, who were well able
to pay for their own religious instruction. The system
would be intolerable even were the state clergy the pastors
of the majority; but as the proportion between the Protestants and the Roman Catholics was in many parts as one
to ten, and in some as one to twenty, the injustice necessarily involved in the mode of levying the impost was
aggravated a hundredfold. It would be scarcely possible
to devise any mode of levying an impost more exasperating,
which came home to the bosoms of men with more irritating, humiliating, and maddening power, and which violated more recklessly men's natural sense of justice. If a
plan were devised for the purpose of driving men into
insurrection, nothing could be more effectual than the tithe-

proctor system. Besides, it tended directly to the impoverishment of the country, retarding agricultural improvement and limiting production. If a man kept all his land in
pasture, he escaped the impost; but the moment he tilled it,
he was subjected to a tax of ten per cent. on the gross produce. The valuation being made by the tithe-proctor—a
man whose interest it was to defraud both the tenant and
the parson—the consequence was, that the gentry and the
large farmers, to a great extent, evaded the tax, and left the
small occupiers to bear nearly the whole burden; they even
avoided mowing the meadows in some cases, because then
they should pay tithe for the hay.

There was besides a tax called church cess, levied by
Protestants in vestry meetings upon Roman Catholics for
cleaning the church, ringing the bell, washing the minister's
surplice, purchasing bread and wine for the communion,
and paying the salary of the parish clerk. This tax was
felt to be a direct and flagrant violation of the rights of conscience, and of the principles of the British constitution;
and against it there was a determined opposition, which
manifested itself in tumultuous and violent assemblages at
the parish churches all over the country on Easter Monday,
when the rector or his curate, as chairman of the meeting,
came into angry collision with flocks who disowned him,
and denounced him as a tyrant, a persecutor, and a robber.

But the tithe impost was the one most grievously felt, and
at last the peasantry resolved to resist it by force.

Nothing could be more violent than the contrasts presented at this time in the social life of Ireland. On the
one side there was a rapid succession of atrocities and
tragedies fearful to contemplate: the bailiffs, constabulary,
and military driving away cattle, sheep, pigs, and geese to
be sold by public auction, to pay the minister who had no
congregation to whom he could preach the gospel; the
cattle-prisons or 'pounds' surrounded by high walls, but
uncovered, wet and dirty, crowded with all sorts of animals,
cold and starved, and uttering doleful sounds; the driving

away of the animals in the night from one farm to another
to avoid seizures; the auctions without bidders, in the midst
of groaning and jeering multitudes; the slaughter of policemen, and in some instances of clergymen, with fiendish
expressions of hatred and yells of triumph; the mingling of
fierce passions with the strongest natural affections; the
exultation in murder as if it were a glorious deed of war;
the Roman Catholic press and platform almost justifying
those deeds of outrage and blood; the mass of the Roman
Catholic population sustaining this insurrection against the
law with their support and sympathy and prayers, as if it
were a holy war, in which the victims were martyrs. On
the other side were presented pictures which excited the
deepest interest of the Protestant community throughout
the United Kingdom. We behold the clergyman and his
family in the glebe-house, lately the abode of plenty, comfort,
and elegance, a model of domestic happiness and gentlemanly
life; but the income of the rector fell off, till he was bereft
of nearly all his means. In order to procure the necessaries
of life for his family, he was obliged to part with the cows
that gave milk for his household, the horse and car, which
were necessary in the remote place where his glebe-house was
situated, and everything that could be spared, till at length
he was obliged to make his greatest sacrifice, and to send
his books—the dear and valued companions of his life—to
Dublin, to be sold by auction. His boys could no longer
be respectably clad, his wife and daughters were obliged to
part with their jewellery and all their superfluities. There
was no longer wine or medicine, that the mother was accustomed to dispense kindly and liberally to the poor around her,
in their sickness and sorrow, without distinction of creed.

The glebe, which once presented an aspect of so much
comfort and ease and affluence, now looked bare and desolate and void of life. But for the contributions of Christian
friends at a distance, many of those once happy little centres
of Christian civilisation—those well-springs of consolation to
the afflicted—must have been abandoned to the overwhelm-

ing sand of desolation swept upon them by the hurricane of the anti-tithe agitation.

During this desperate struggle, force was employed on several occasions with fatal effect. At Newtownbarry, in the county of Wexford, some cattle were impounded by a tithe-proctor. The peasantry assembled in large numbers to rescue them, when they came into collision with the yeomanry, who fired, killing twelve persons. It was a market day, and a placard was posted on the walls : ' There will be an end of church plunder ; your pot, blanket, and pig will not hereafter be sold by auction to support in luxury, idleness, and ease persons who endeavour to make it appear that it is essential to the peace and prosperity of the country and your eternal salvation, while the most of you are starving. Attend to an auction of your neighbours' cattle.' At Carrickshock there was a fearful tragedy. A number of writs against defaulters were issued by the court of exchequer, and entrusted to the care of process-servers, who, guarded by a strong body of police, proceeded on their mission with secrecy and dispatch. Bonfires along the surrounding hills, however, and shrill whistles soon convinced them that the people were not unprepared for their visitors. But the yeomanry pushed boldly on. Suddenly an immense assemblage of peasantry, armed with scythes and pitchforks, poured down upon them. A terrible hand-to-hand struggle ensued, and in the course of a few moments eighteen of the police, including the commanding officer, were slaughtered. The remainder consulted safety and fled, marking the course of their retreat by the blood that trickled from their wounds. A coroner's jury pronounced this deed of death as ' wilful murder' against some persons unknown. A large government reward was offered, but it failed to produce a single conviction. At Castlepollard, in Westmeath, on the occasion of an attempted rescue, the chief constable was knocked down. The police fired, and nine or ten persons were killed. One of the most lamentable of these conflicts occurred at Gurtroe, near Rathcormac, in the county of Cork. Archdeacon Ryder brought a number of the military to recover the tithes of a farm belonging to a widow named Ryan. The assembled people resisted, the military were ordered to fire, eight persons were killed and thirteen wounded; and among the killed was the widow's son.

These disorders appealed with irresistible force to the Government and the legislature, to put an end to a system fraught with so much evil, and threatening the utter disruption of society in Ireland. In the first place, something must be done to meet the wants of the destitute clergy and their families. Accordingly, Lord Stanley brought in a bill, in May 1832, authorising the lord lieutenant of Ireland to advance 60,000*l.* as a fund for the payment of the clergy, who were unable to collect their tithes for the year 1831. This measure was designed to meet the present necessity, and was only a preliminary to the promised settlement of the tithe question. It was therefore passed quickly through both Houses, and became law on June 1. But the money thus advanced was not placed on the consolidated fund.

The Government took upon itself the collection of the arrears of tithes for that one year. It was a maxim with Lord Stanley that the people should be made to respect the law; that they should not be allowed to trample upon it with impunity. The odious task thus assumed, produced a state of unparalleled excitement. The people were driven to frenzy, instead of being frightened by the chief secretary becoming tithe-collector-general, and the army being employed in its collection. They knew that the king's speech had recommended the settlement of the tithe question. They had heard of the evidence of Bishop Doyle and other champions, exposing what they believed to be the iniquity of the tithe system. They had seen the condemnation of it in the testimony of the Protestant Archbishop of Dublin, who declared his conviction that it could not be collected except at the point of the bayonet, and by keeping up a chronic war between the Government and the Roman Catholic people.

They had been told that parliamentary committees had recommended the complete extinction of tithes, and their commutation into a rent-charge. Their own leaders had everywhere resolved:—

' That it was a glaring wrong to compel an impoverished Catholic people to support in pampered luxury the richest clergy in the world—a clergy from whom the Catholics do not experience even the return of common gratitude—a clergy who, in times past, opposed to the last the political freedom of the Irish people, and at the present day are opposed to reform and a liberal scheme of education for their countrymen. The ministers of the God of charity should not, by misapplication of all the tithes to their own private uses, thus deprive the poor of their patrimony ; nor should ministers of peace adhere with such desperate tenacity to a system fraught with dissension, hatred, and ill-will.' The first proceeding of the Government to recover the tithes, under the act of June 1, was therefore the signal for general war. Bonfires blazed upon the hills, the rallying sounds of horns were heard along the valleys, and the mustering tread of thousands upon the roads, hurrying to the scene of a seizure or an auction. It was a bloody campaign ; there was considerable loss of life, and the Church and the Government thus became more obnoxious to the people than ever. Lord Stanley being the commander-in-chief on one side, and Mr. O'Connell on the other, the contest was embittered by their personal antipathies. It was found that the amount of the arrears for the year 1831 was 104,285*l.*, and that the whole amount which the Government was able to levy, after putting forth its strength in every possible way, was 12,000*l.*, the cost of collection being 15,000*l.*, so the Government was not able to raise as much money as would pay the expenses of the campaign. This was how Lord Stanley illustrated his favourite sentiment that the people should be made to respect the law. But the Liberal party among the Protestants fully sympathised with the anti-tithe recusants.

Of course the Government did not persevere in prosecu-
cutions from which no parties but the lawyers reaped any
advantage ; consequently, all processes under the existing
law were abandoned. It was found that, after paying to
the clergy the arrears of 1831 and 1832, and what would
be due in 1833, about a million sterling would be required,
and this sum was provided by an issue of exchequer bills.
The reimbursement of the advance was to be effected by a
land tax. Together with these temporary arrangements to
meet the exigency of the case, for the payment of the clergy
and the pacification of Ireland, an act was passed to render
tithe composition in Ireland compulsory and permanent.
But Ireland was not yet pacified.*

---

* The foregoing sketch of the tithe war was written by the author
seven years ago for Cassell's *History of England,* from which it is now
extracted.

CHAPTER XVI.

THE FAMINE.

It had often been predicted by writers on the state of Ireland, that, owing to the rottenness at the foundation of the social fabric, it would come down with a crash some day. The facts reported by the census commissioners of 1841 showed that this consummation could not be far off. Out of a population of 8,000,000, there were 3,700,000 above the age of five years who could neither read nor write; while nearly three millions and a half lived in mud cabins, badly thatched with straw, having each but one room, and often without either a window or a chimney. These figures indicate a mass of ignorance and poverty, which could not be contemplated without alarm, and the subject was, therefore, constantly pressed upon the attention of parliament. As usual in cases of difficulty, the Government, feeling that something should be done, and not knowing what to do, appointed in 1845 a commission to enquire into the relations between landlords and tenants, and the condition of the working classes. At the head of this commission was the Earl of Devon, a benevolent nobleman, whose sympathies were on the side of the people. Captain Kennedy, the secretary to the commissioners, published a digest of the report of the evidence, which presented the facts in a readable form, and was the means of diffusing a large amount of authentic information on the state of Ireland. The commissioners travelled through the country, held courts of enquiry, and examined witnesses of all classes. As the result of their extensive intercourse with the farming

U

classes, and their own observations, they were enabled to
state that in almost every part of Ireland unequivocal symptoms of improvement, in spite of many embarrassing and
counteracting circumstances, continually presented themselves to the view, and that there existed a very general
and increasing spirit and desire for the promotion of such
improvement, from which the most beneficial results might
fairly be expected.

Indeed, speaking of the country generally, they add:
' With some exceptions, which are unfortunately too notorious, we believe that at no former period did so active a
spirit of improvement prevail; nor could well directed
measures for the attainment of that object have been proposed with a better prospect of success than at the present
moment.'

But this improvement produced no sensible effect upon
the condition of the labouring people. However brightly
the sun of prosperity might gild the eminences of society, the
darkness of misery and despair settled upon the masses below.
The commissioners proceed: ' A reference to the evidence
of most of the witnesses will show that the agricultural labourer of Ireland continues to suffer the greatest privations
and hardships; that he continues to depend upon casual and
precarious employment for subsistence; that he is still badly
housed, badly fed, badly clothed, and badly paid for his
labour. Our personal experience and observation during
our enquiry have afforded us a melancholy confirmation of
these statements; and we cannot forbear expressing our
strong sense of the patient endurance which the labouring
classes have generally exhibited under sufferings greater,
we believe, than the people of any other country in Europe
have to sustain.' It was deeply felt that the well-being of
the whole United Kingdom depended upon the removal of
the causes of this misery and degradation; for if the Irish
people were not elevated, the English working classes must
be brought down to their level. The facility of travelling
afforded by railways and steam-boats caused such constant
intercourse between England and Ireland, that Irish igno-

rance, beggary, and disease, with all their contagion, physical and moral, would be found intermingling with the British population. It would be impossible to prevent the half-starved Irish peasantry from crossing the Channel, and seeking employment, even at low wages, and forming a pestiferous Irish quarter in every town and city. The question, then, was felt to be one whose settlement would brook no further delay.

It was found that the potato was almost the only food of the Irish millions, and that it formed their chief means of obtaining the other necessaries of life. A large portion of this crop was grown under the con-acre system, to which the poorest of the peasantry were obliged to have recourse, notwithstanding the minute subdivision of land. There were in 1841, 691,000 farms in Ireland exceeding one acre in extent. Nearly one half of these were under five acres each. The number of proprietors in fee was estimated at 8,000—a smaller number, in proportion to the extent of territory, than in any other country of Western Europe except Spain. In Connaught, several proprietors had 100,000 acres each, the proportion of small farms being greater there than in the rest of Ireland. The total number of farms in the province was 155,842, and of these 100,254 consisted of from one to five acres. If all the proprietors were resident among their tenantry, and were in a position to encourage their industry and care for their welfare, matters would not have been so bad; bnt most of the large landowners were absentees. It frequently happened that the large estates were held in strict limitation, and they were nearly all heavily encumbered. The owners preferred living in England or on the Continent, having let their lands on long leases, or in perpetuity to 'middlemen,' who sublet them for as high rents as they could get. Their tenants again sublet, so that it frequently happened that two, three, or four landlords intervened between the proprietor and the occupying tenant, each deriving an interest from the land. The head landlord, therefore, though

ever so well disposed, had no power whatever to help the
occupying tenants generally, and of those who had the
power very few felt disposed.   There were extensive districts without a single resident proprietor.

For a few weeks after the blight of the potato crop
in 1846 the cottiers and small farmers managed to eke
out a subsistence by the sale of their pigs and any little
effects they had.   But pigs, fowl, furniture, and clothing soon went, one after another, to satisfy the cravings
of hunger.   The better class of farmers lived upon their
corn and cattle; but they were obliged to dismiss their
servants, and this numerous class became the first victims
of starvation; for when they were turned off, they were
refused admission by their relations, who had not the means
of feeding them.   Tailors, shoemakers, and other artisans
who worked for the lower orders, lost their employment,
and became destitute also.   While the means of support
failed upon every side, and food rose to such enormous
prices that everything that could possibly be eaten was
economised, so that the starving dogs were drowned from
compassion, the famine steadily advanced from the west and
south to the east and north, till it involved the whole population in its crushing grasp.   It was painfully interesting to
mark the progress of the visitation, even in those parts of
the country where its ravages were least felt.   The small
farmer had only his corn, designed for rent and seed: he
was obliged to take it to the mill to ward off starvation.
The children of the poor, placed on short allowance, were
suffering fearfully from hunger.   Mothers, heart-broken
and worn down to skeletons, were seen on certain days proceeding in groups to some distant depôt, where Indian meal
was to be had at reduced prices, but still double that of the
ordinary market.   As they returned to their children, with
their little bags on their heads, a faint joy lit up their
famine-stricken features.

When the visitors entered a village their first question
was: ' How many deaths?'   '*The hunger is upon us*,' was

everywhere the cry ; and involuntarily they found themselves regarding this hunger as they would an epidemic,
looking upon starvation as a disease. In fact, as they
passed along, their wonder was, not that the people died,
but that they lived ; and Mr. W. G. Forster, in his report,
said : 'I have no doubt whatever, that in any other country
the mortality would have been far greater ; and that many
lives have been prolonged, perhaps saved, by the long ap-
prenticeship to want in which the Irish peasant has been
trained, and by that lovely, touching charity which prompts
him to share his scanty meal with his starving neighbour.
But the springs of this charity must be rapidly dried up.
Like a scourge of locusts, *the hunger* daily sweeps over
fresh districts, eating up all before it. One class after
another is falling into the same abyss of ruin.'*

The same benevolent gentleman describes the domestic
scenes he saw in Connaught, where the poor Celts were
carried off in thousands :—

'We entered a cabin. Stretched in one dark corner,
scarcely visible from the smoke and rags that covered them,
were three children huddled together, lying there because
they were too weak to rise, pale and ghastly ; their little
limbs, on removing a portion of the covering, perfectly
emaciated ; eyes sunk, voice gone, and evidently in the last
stage of actual starvation. Crouched over the turf embers
was another form, wild and all but naked, scarcely human
in appearance. It stirred not nor noticed us. On some
straw, soddened upon the ground, moaning piteously, was a
shrivelled old woman, imploring us to give her something,
baring her limbs partly to show how the skin hung loose
from her bones, as soon as she attracted our attention.
Above her, on something like a ledge, was a young woman
with sunken cheeks, a mother, I have no doubt, who
scarcely raised her eyes in answer to our enquiries ; but
pressed her hand upon her forehead, with a look of unutter-
able anguish and despair. Many cases were widows, whose

* Transactions during the Famine in Ireland, Appendix III.

husbands had been recently taken off by the fever, and thus their only pittance obtained from the public works was entirely cut off. In many the husbands or sons were prostrate under that horrid disease—the result of long-continued famine and low living—in which first the limbs and then the body swell most frightfully, and finally burst. We entered upwards of fifty of these tenements. The scene was invariably the same, differing in little but the manner of the sufferers, or of the groups occupying the several corners within. The whole number was often not to be distinguished, until the eye having adapted itself to the darkness, they were pointed out, or were heard, or some filthy bundle of rags and straw was seen to move. Perhaps the poor children presented the most piteous and heart-rending spectacle. Many were too weak to stand, their little limbs attenuated, except where the frightful swellings had taken the place of previous emaciation. Every infantile expression had entirely departed; and, in some reason and intelligence had evidently flown. Many were remnants of families, crowded together in one cabin; orphaned little relatives taken in by the equally destitute, and even strangers—for these poor people are kind to each other, even to the end. In one cabin was a sister, just dying, lying beside her little brother, just dead. I have worse than this to relate; but it is useless to multiply details, and they are, in fact, unfit.'

In December, 1846, Father Mathew wrote to Mr. Trevelyan, then secretary of the treasury, that men, women, and children were gradually wasting away. They filled their stomachs with cabbage-leaves, turnip-tops, &c., to appease the cravings of hunger. There were then more than 5,000 half-starved wretches from the country begging in the streets of Cork. When utterly exhausted, they crawled to the workhouse to die. The average of deaths in that union was then over a hundred a week.

From December 27, in 1846, to the middle of April, in 1847, the number of human beings that died in the Cork

workhouse was 2,130! And in the third week of the following month the free interments in the Mathew cemetery had
risen to 277—as many as sixty-seven having been buried in
one day. The destruction of human life in other workhouses of Ireland kept pace with the appalling mortality in
the Cork workhouse. According to official returns, it had
reached in April the weekly average of twenty-five per
1,000 inmates; the actual number of deaths being 2,706 for
the week ending April 3, and 2,613 in the following week.
Yet the number of inmates in the Irish workhouses was but
104,455 on April 10.

The size of the unions was a great impediment to the
working of the poor law. They were three times the extent
of the corresponding divisions in England. In Munster and
Connaught, where there was the greatest amount of destitution, and the least amount of local agency available for its
relief, the unions were much larger than in the more favoured
provinces of Ulster and Leinster. The union of Ballina
comprised a region of upwards of half a million acres, and
within its desert tracts the famine assumed its most appalling
form, the workhouse being more than forty miles distant
from some of the sufferers. As a measure of precaution, the
Government had secretly imported and stored a large quantity of Indian corn, as a cheap substitute for the potato,
which would have served the purpose much better had the
people been instructed in the best modes of cooking it. It
was placed in commissariat depôts, along the western coast
of the island, where the people were not likely to be supplied
on reasonable terms through the ordinary channels of trade.
The public works consisted principally of roads, on which
the men were employed as a sort of supplement to the
poor law. Half the cost was a free grant from the treasury,
and the other half was charged upon the barony in which
the works were undertaken. The expense incurred under
the 'Labour Rate Act, 9 and 10 Vict. c. 107,' amounted to
4,766,789*l.* It was almost universally admitted, when the
pressure was over, that the system of public works adopted

was a great mistake, and it seems wonderful that such grievous blunders could have been made with so many able statesmen and political economists at the head of affairs and in the service of the Government. The public works undertaken consisted in the breaking up of good roads to level hills and fill hollows, and the opening of new roads in places where they were not required—works which the people felt to be useless, and at which they laboured only under strong compulsion, being obliged to walk to them in all weathers for miles, in order to earn the price of a breakfast of Indian meal. Had the labour thus comparatively wasted been devoted to the draining, sub-soiling, and fencing of the farms, connected with a comprehensive system of arterial drainage, immense and lasting benefit to the country would have been the result, especially as works so well calculated to ameliorate the soil, and guard against the moisture of the climate, might have been connected with a system of instruction in agricultural matters of which the peasantry stood so much in need, and to the removal of the gross ignorance which had so largely contributed to bring about the famine. As it was, enormous sums were wasted. Much needless hardship was inflicted on the starving people in compelling them to work in frost and rain when they were scarcely able to walk, and, after all the vast outlay, very few traces of it remained in permanent improvements on the face of the country. The system of government relief works failed chiefly through the same difficulty which impeded every mode of relief, whether public or private—namely, the want of machinery to work it. It was impossible suddenly to procure an efficient staff of officers for an undertaking of such enormous magnitude—the employment of a whole people. The overseers were necessarily selected in haste ; many of them were corrupt, and encouraged the misconduct of the labourers. In many cases the relief committees, unable to prevent maladministration, yielded to the torrent of corruption, and individual members only sought to benefit their own dependants. The people everywhere flocked to the public works; labourers, cottiers, artisans, fishermen, farmers, men, women, and children—all, whether destitute or not, sought for a share of the public money. In such a crowd, it was almost impossible to discriminate properly. They congregated in masses on the roads, idling under the name of work, the really destitute often unheeded and unrelieved because they had no friend to recommend them. All the ordinary employments were neglected; there was no fishing, no gathering of sea-weed, no collecting of manure. The men who had employment feared to lose it by absenting themselves for any other object; those unemployed spent their time in seeking to obtain it. The whole industry of the country seemed to be engaged in road-making. It became absolutely necessary to put an end to it, or the cultivation of the land would be neglected. Works undertaken on the spur of the moment, not because they were needful, but merely to employ the people, were in many cases ill chosen, and the execution equally defective. The labourers, desirous to protract their employment, were only anxious to give as little labour as possible, in which their overlookers or gangers in many cases heartily agreed. The favouritism, the intimidation, the wholesale jobbing practised in many cases were shockingly demoralising.

In order to induce the people to attend to their ordinary spring work, and put in the crops, it was found necessary to adopt the plan of distributing free rations. On March 20, therefore, a reduction of twenty per cent. of the numbers employed on the works took place, and the process of reduction went on until the new system of gratuitous relief was brought into full operation. The authority under which this was administered was called the 'Temporary Relief Act,' which came into full operation in the month of July, when the destitution was at its height, and three millions of people received their daily rations. Sir John Burgoyne truly describes this as 'the grandest attempt ever made to grapple with famine over a whole country.' Never in the history of the world were so many persons fed in such a manner by the public bounty. It was a most anxious time —a time of tremendous labour and responsibility to those

who had the direction of this vast machinery. A member
of the Board of Works thus describes the feeling which no
doubt pervaded most of those that were officially connected
with the administration of relief: ' I hope never to see such
a winter and spring again. I can truly say, in looking
back upon it even now, that it appears to me not a succession of weeks and days, but one long continuous day,
with occasional intervals of night-mare sleep. Rest one
could never have, when one felt that in every minute lost a
score of men might die.' Mr. Trevelyan was then secre
tary of the treasury, and it was well that a man so enlightened, energetic, and benevolent occupied the post at
such a time. He was indefatigable in his efforts to mitigate
the calamity, and he wrote an interesting account of ' The
Irish Crisis ' in the *Edinburgh Review.* Having presented
the dark side of the picture in faithfully recording the abuses
that had prevailed, it is right to give Mr. Trevelyan's
testimony as to the conduct of the relief committees during
this supreme hour of the nation's agony. ' It is a fact very
honourable to Ireland that among upwards of 2,000 local
bodies to whom advances were made under this act, there is
not one to which, so far as the Government is informed, any
suspicion of embezzlement attaches.'

The following statement of the numbers receiving rations,
and the total expenditure under the act in each of the four
provinces, compared with the amount of population, and the
annual value assessed for poor-rate, may serve to illustrate
the comparative means and destitution of each province:—

	Population	Valuation	Greatest Number of Rations given out	Total Expendi- ture
		£		£
Ulster . .	2,386,373	3,320,133	346,517	170,598
Leinster .	1,973,731	4,624,542	450,606	308,068
Munster .	2,396,161	. 3,777,103	1,013,826	671,554
Connaught .	1,418,859	1,465,643	745,652	526,048
	8,175,124	13,187,421.	2,556,601	1,676,268

Private benevolence did wonders in this crisis. The British Association raised and distributed 269,302*l.* The queen's letter, ordering collections in the English churches, produced 200,738*l.* But the bounty of the United States of America transcended everything. The supplies sent across the Atlantic were on a scale unparalleled in the history of the world.

Meetings were held in Philadelphia, Washington, New York, and other cities, in quick succession, presided over by the first men in the country. All through the States the citizens evinced an intense interest, and a noble generosity worthy of the great Republic. The railway companies carried free of charge all packages marked 'Ireland.' Public carriers undertook the gratuitous delivery of packages intended for the relief of Irish distress. Storage to any extent was offered on the same terms. Ships of war, without their guns, came to the Irish shores on a mission of peace and mercy, freighted with food for British subjects. Cargo after cargo followed in rapid succession, until nearly 100 separate shipments had arrived, our Government having consented to pay the freight of all donations of food forwarded from America, which amounted in the whole to 33,000*l.* The quantity of American food consigned to the care of the Society of Friends was nearly 10,000 tons, the value of which was about 100,000*l.* In addition to all this, the Americans remitted to the Friends' Committee 16,000*l.* in money. They also sent 642 packages of clothing, the precise value of which could not be ascertained. There was a very large amount of remittances sent to Ireland, during the famine, by the Irish in the United States. Unfortunately, there are no records of those remittances prior to 1848 ; but since that time we are enabled to ascertain a large portion of them, though not the whole, and their amount is something astonishing. The following statement of sums remitted by emigrants in America to their families in Ireland, was printed by order of Parliament:—During

the years 1848, 460,180*l.*; 1849, 540,619*l.*; 1850, 937,087*l.*
1851, 990,811*l.*

The arrival of the American ships naturally excited great interest at the various ports. 'On Monday, April 13,' writes Mr. Maguire, 'a noble sight might be witnessed in Cork harbour—the sun shining its welcome on the entrance of the unarmed war-ship Jamieson, sailing in under a cloud of snowy canvas, her great hold laden with bread-stuffs for the starving people of Ireland. It was a sight that brought tears to many an eye, and prayers of gratitude to many a heart. It was one of those things which one nation remembers of another long after the day of sorrow has passed. Upon the warm and generous people to whom America literally broke bread and sent life, this act of fraternal charity, so gracefully and impressively offered, naturally produced a profound and lasting impression, the influence of which is felt at this moment.'

The clergy, Protestant and Roman Catholic, almost the only resident gentry in several of the destitute districts, worked together on the committees with commendable zeal, diligence, and unanimity. Among the Roman Catholic clergy, Father Mathew was at that time by far the most influential and popular. The masses of the peasantry regarded him as almost an inspired apostle. During the famine months, he exerted himself with wonderful energy and prudence, first, in his correspondence with different members of the Government, earnestly recommending and urging the speedy adoption of measures of relief; and next, in commending those measures to the people, dissuading the hungry from acts of violence, and preaching submission and resignation under that heavy dispensation of Providence. Of this there are ample proofs in the letters published by Mr. Maguire, M.P. 'It is not to harrow your feelings, dear Mr. Trevelyan,' he wrote, 'I tell this tale of woe. No; but to excite your sympathy in behalf of our miserable peasantry. It is rumoured that the capitalists in the corn and flour trade are endeavouring to induce the Government not to protect the people from famine, but to leave them at their mercy. I consider this a cruel and unjustifiable interference. I am so unhappy at the prospect before us, and so horror-struck by the apprehension of our destitute people falling into the ruthless hands of the corn and flour traders, that I risk becoming troublesome, rather than not lay my humble opinions before you.' Again : ' I hail with delight the humane, the admirable measures for relief announced by my Lord John Russell; they have given universal satisfaction. But of what avail will all this be, unless the wise precautions of Government will enable the toiling workman, after exhausting his vigour during a long day to earn a shilling, to purchase with that shilling a sufficiency of daily food for his generally large and helpless family?' Father Mathew earnestly pleaded for out-door relief, in preference to the workhouse, foreseeing the danger of sundering the domestic bonds, which operate so powerfully as moral restraints in Ireland. The beautiful picture which he drew of the Irish peasant's home in his native land was not too highly coloured, as applied to the great majority of the people :—' The bonds of blood and affinity, dissoluble by death alone, associate in the cabins of the Irish peasantry, not only the husband, wife, and children, but the aged parents and the married couple and their destitute relatives, even to the third and fourth degree of kindred. God forbid that political economists should dissolve these ties ! should violate these beautiful charities of nature and the gospel ! I have often found my heart throb with delight when I beheld three or four generations seated around the humble board and blazing hearth; and I offered a silent prayer to the great Father of all that the gloomy gates of the workhouse should never separate those whom such tender social chains so fondly link together.'

The following is a tabular view of the whole amount of voluntary contributions during the Irish famine, which deserves a permanent record for the credit of our common humanity :—

	£ s. d.	£ s. d.
Local contributions officially reported in 1846	...	104,689 18 1
Local contributions officially reported in 1847	...	199,569 4 5
British Relief Association, total received	470,041 1 2	
say five-sixths for Ireland .	...	391,700 17 8
General Central Relief Committee, College Green	83,934 17 11	
Less received from British Relief Association	20,190 0 0	
		63,744 17 11
Irish Relief Association, Sackville Street	...	42,446 5 0
Relief Committee of the Society of Friends, London . .	...	42,905 12 0
Central Relief Committee of the Society of Friends, Dublin .	198,313 15 3	
Less received from Committee of the Society of Friends in London, and interest	39,249 19 11	
		159,063 15 4
Indian Relief Fund	...	13,919 14 2
National Club, London . . .	...	19,928 12 2
Wesleyan Methodist Relief Fund, London	...	20,056 14 4
Irish Evangelical Society, London .	...	9,264 9 9
Baptists' Relief Fund, London . .	...	6,141 11 2
Ladies' Irish Clothing Society, London	9,533 4 0	
Less received from British Association, &c.	5,324 12 11	
		4,208 11 1
Ladies' Relief Association for Ireland .	19,584 0 9	
Less received from Irish Relief Association and for sales of manufactures	7,659 6 7	
		11,924 14 2
Ladies' Industrial Society for encouragement of labour among the peasantry	1,968 12 8	
Less received from Irish Relief Association	1,500 0 0	
		468 12 8
Belfast Ladies' Association for the relief of Irish Distress . .	...	2,617 1 6
Belfast Ladies' Industrial Association for Connaught	...	4,615 16 1
There were also two collections in Belfast for general purposes, the amount of which exceeded .	...	10,000 0 0

CHAPTER XVII.

TENANT-RIGHT IN ULSTER.

THE Earl of Granard has taken a leading part in the movement for the settling of the land question, having presided at two great meetings in the counties in which he has large estates, Wexford and Longford, supported on each occasion by influential landlords. He was the first of his class to propose that the question should be settled on the basis of tenant-right, by legalising and extending the Ulster custom. A reference to this custom has been frequently made recently, in discussions on the platform and in the press. I have studied the history of that province with care; and I have during the year 1869 gone through several of its counties with the special object of inquiring how the tenant-right operates, and whether, and to what extent, it affords the requisite security to the cultivators of the soil; and it may be of some service that I should give here the result of my enquiries.

Of the six counties confiscated and planted in Ulster, Londonderry, as I have already remarked, was allotted to the London companies. The aspect of their estates, is on the whole, very pleasing. In the midst of each there is a small town, built in the form of a square, with a market-house and a town-hall in the centre, and streets running off at each side. There are almost invariably three substantial and handsome places of worship—the parish church, always best and most prominent, the presbyterian meeting-house, and the catholic chapel, with nice manses for the ministers, all built wholly or in part by grants from the companies.

Complaints were constantly made against the Irish Society for its neglect of its trust, for refusing to give proper building leases, and for wasting the funds placed at its disposal for public purposes.   The details are curious and interesting, throwing much light on the social history of the times.   The whole subject of its duties and responsibilities, and of its anomalous powers, was fully discussed at a meeting of the principal citizens, most of them strongly Conservative, on the 28th of May, 1866.   There had been a discussion on the subject in the House of Commons, in which Lord Claud Hamilton, then member for the borough, distinguished himself.   Mr. Maguire brought the Society before Parliament in an able speech.   The legislature, as well as the public, were then preoccupied with the Church question.   But, doubtless, the maiden city will make her voice heard next session, and insist on being released from a guardian who always acted the part of a stepmother.

The Irish Society has been before three parliamentary tribunals, the Commissioners of Municipal Corporations for England and Wales, the Royal Commission of Enquiry into the state of the Corporation of London, and the Irish Municipal Commissioners.   The English Commissioners say :—' We do not know of any pretext or 'argument for continuing this municipal supremacy of the Irish Society. A control of this kind maintained at the present day by the municipality of one town in England over another town in Ireland, appears to us so indefensible in principle, that our opinion would not have been changed, even if it were found that hitherto it has been conducted with discretion and forbearance.'

The Irish commissioners affirmed ' that the Irish Society in their original institution were created for the purpose of forwarding the interests and objects of the Plantation, and not for mere private gain ; and that of the large income which they receive from their possessions in Londonderry, a very inadequate and disproportionate share is applied for the public purposes, or other objects connected with the local interests of the districts from which the revenues of the society are drawn.'

The corporation of Derry cannot put a bye-law in force till it receives the approval of the Irish Society. And what is this tribunal whose fiat must stamp the decision of the Derry corporation before it can operate in the smallest matter within the municipal boundary? The members are London traders, totally ignorant of Ireland. They are elected for two years, so that they must go out by the time they acquire any information about their trust, to make way for another batch equally ignorant. Having everything to learn during their term of office, if they have time or capacity to learn anything about the matter, they must submit to the guidance of the governor, who is elected virtually, though not formally, for life; and the members of the Derry corporation believe him to be the autocrat of the society. Mr. James P. Hamilton, now the assistant-barrister for Sligo, at the great meeting of the citizens of Derry already mentioned, pronounced the governors to be ' the most ignorant, the most incompetent, and the most careless governors that ever were inflicted on a people.' Mr. Hamilton quoted from the answer of the corporation of London in 1624 to the Privy Council, which required them to convey 4,000 acres to the citizens of Derry. The corporation replied that they had allotted 1,500 acres for the use of the mayor and other civil officers. That was either true or false. If true, by what right did they recall the grant, and re-possess themselves of those lands? By the articles they were bound to make quays, which were not made. They were bound to give bog and mountain for the city common, which they never gave. The corporation had a tract called the sheriff's mountain, but the city was robbed of it by her cruel stepmother, the Irish Society. The society was bound to give 200 acres for a free school, and if this had been done Derry might have had a rich foundation, rivalling Westminster or the Charter School. Mr. Hamilton, conservative as he is, with the heart of a true Irishman, indignantly asks,

' Why is this national grievance and insult continued for the profit of no one ? Their very name is an insult and a mockery—*The Governor and Assistants, London, of the New Plantation in Ulster !* What do they govern ? They don't govern us in any sense of the word. They merely hold our property in a dead grip, without any profit to themselves, and to our great disadvantage.'

The city is overwhelmed with debt—debt for the new quays, debt for the new bridge, debt for the public works of the corporation, which has struggled to improve the city under the incubus of this alien power, contending with debt, want of tenure, and other difficulties, which would all have been avoided if the city had the lands which these Londoners hold in their possession and use as their own pleasure dictates, half the revenues being spent in the management.

Mr. William Hazlett, a magistrate of Derry, one of its ablest and most respected citizens, stated that from 1818 to 1847 the expenses of management were 60 per cent. The royal commissioners set it down thus—Total expenditure, 219,898*l.* ; management, 133,912*l.* The law expenses were, during the same period, 40,000*l.* ' This item of itself,' says Mr. Hazlett, ' must be considered an intolerable grievance, for it was laid out for the oppression of the people who should have benefited by the funds so squandered in opposing the very parties who supplied the money, with which they were themselves harassed. If a tenant applies for a lease, and the society consents to grant one, it is so hampered with obstructive clauses that his solicitor objects to his signing it, and says that from its nature it could not be made a negotiable instrument on which to raise money. The tenant remonstrates, but the reply of the city is—" That is our form of lease ; you must comply with it or want !" If you go to law with them, they may take you into Chancery, and fight you with your own money.'

Mr. Hazlett gave a remarkable illustration of this, which shows the spirit in which this body thinks proper to fulfil its duties as steward of this property. The Devon Land Commission recommended that leases of lives renewable for ever should be converted into fee-farm grants, which would be a valuable boon to the tenant without any loss to the owner. A bill founded on the recommendation was introduced to parliament. Did the enlightened and liberal Irish Society hail with satisfaction this wise measure of reform? On the contrary, the governor went out of his way to oppose it. Having striven in vain, with all the vast influence of the corporation, to have the bill thrown out, he endeavoured to get the society exempted from its operation. When, in spite of his efforts, the bill became law, the governor utterly refused to act on it, and brought the matter before the Master of the Rolls and the House of Lords. From these renewable leases the society had an income of about 2,500*l.* yearly. And what amount did they demand—these moderate and discreet gentleman, ' The Governor and Assistants, London, of the new Plantation of Ulster '—for their interest in the renewable leases ? Not less than 100,000*l.*, or about 40 years' purchase. In the year 1765, when the city of Derry was fast hastening to decay under this London government, the society was induced by an increase of 37 per cent. on the rent, to grant those renewable leases. ' And but for the granting of those leases,' said Mr. Hazlett, ' we should have no standing-ground in this city, nor should we even have the right to meet in this hall as we do to-day.'

Other striking facts illustrating the paternal nature of this foreign government of the ' New Plantation ' were produced by Mr. Thomas Chambers, a solicitor who had defended the Rev. J. M. Staples in a suit brought by the society, and which cost them 40,000*l.* of the public money to win, after dragging the reverend gentleman from one court to another, regardless of expense. Originally, as we have seen, the city got a grant of 4,000 acres for the support of the corporation; but actually received only 1,500, valued then at 60*l.* a year. This land was forfeited and transferred to the bishop in the reign of Charles I. Ultimately the bishop gave up the land and the fishery, for which the see received, and still receives, 250*l.* a year. The society got hold of the 1,500 acres, and refused to give them back to the city, which, with the alienation of the sheriff's mountain, and the raising of the city rents (in 1820) from 40*l.* to 600*l.* a year, left it 1,000*l.* a year worse than it had been previously. The result of this policy of a body which was established for promoting ' civility ' in Ireland, was, that the credit of the corporation went down rapidly. Executions were lodged against them, and all their property in quays, markets, &c. was swept away, the bridge being saved only by the intervention of a special act of parliament. In 1831, however, the society granted the corporation an allowance of 700*l.* When the reformed corporation came in, and found that they were so far emancipated from the thraldom of the London governor that they could go before parliament themselves, the society was constrained to increase its dole to 1,200*l.* a year.

Mr. Isaac Colhoun, at the meeting referred to, produced from the accounts of the society for the previous year, published in the local papers, the following items :—

	£	s.	d.
Amount of the present increased income . . .	11,091	17	5
Incidental expenses as per general agents'account for 1865	114	3	0½
Law expenses	492	7	11
Salaries to general agent, deputy, vice-admiral, surveyor, and others	926	16	6
Pension to general agent	250	0	0
Visitation expenses, 1865	539	19	6
Surveying expenses	50	0	0
Salary of clerk and porter's wages	197	10	0
Coal, gas, printing, stationery, advertisements . .	449	11	5
Salary to secretary and assistant governor, and 'assistants ' for attendance at 51 meetings . . .	549	1	6
	4,094	1	6

Here, then, is a trust fund amounting to about 12,000*l.* a year, and the trustees actually spend one-third in its management! And what is its management? What do they do with the money? Mr. Pitt Skipton, D. L., a landed proprietor, who has nothing to gain or lose by the Irish Society, asks, 'Where is our money laid out now? Not on the estate of the Irish Society, but on the estates of the church and private individuals—on those of owners like myself who give their tenants perpetuity, because it is their interest to do so. We should wish to see the funds of the society so expended that we could see some memorial of them. But where is there in Derry any monument wholly erected by the society which they were not specially forced to put up by charter, with the exception of a paltry piece of freestone within one of the bastions bearing their own arms.'

Let us only imagine what the corporation of Derry could do in local improvements with this 12,000*l.* a year, which is really their own property, or even with the 4,000*l.* a-year squandered upon themselves by the trustees! Some of these worthy London merchants, it seems, play the *rôle* of Irish landlords when travelling on the Continent, on the strength of this Derry estate, or their *assistantship* in its management. 'I object,' says Mr. J. P. Hamilton, 'if I take a little run in the summer vacation to Paris or Brussels, to meet a greasy-looking gentleman from Whitechapel or the Minories, turned out sleek and shining from Moses', and to be told by him that he has a large property in *Hireland*, in a place called Derry, and that his tenantry are an industrious, thriving set of fellows, quite remarkable for their intelligence, but that it is all owing to his excellent management of his property and his liberality.'

Mr. Hazlett presented a still funnier picture of the Irish 'visitations' of the members of the society, with their wives and daughters every summer. Gentlemen in London regard it as a fine lark to get elected to serve in the Irish Society, as that includes a summer trip to Ireland free of expense, with the jolliest entertainment. One gentleman, being asked by another whether he was ever in Ireland, answered— 'No, but I intend to get on the Irish Society next year and then I'll have a trip. What kind of people are they over there? Do they all speak Irish?'

'Oh, no; they are a very decent, civilised people.'

' Oh, I'm glad they don't speak Irish; for none of us do, of course; but my daughter can speak French.'

' They had a great siege one time over there ? '

' Oh, yes; the Derry people are proud of the siege.'

' Ah, yes, I see; happened in the reign of King John, I believe.'

But the heaviest charge laid at the door of the Irish Society is its persistent refusal to grant proper tenures for building. By this, even more than their reckless squandering of the revenues of a fine estate, which is not their own, they have obstructed the improvement of the city. They might possibly be compelled to refund the wasted property of their ward, but they could never compensate for stunting and crippling her as they have done. Fortunately, there is a standard by which we are able to measure this iniquity with tolerable accuracy. Dr. William Brown, of Derry, testified that it was the universal conviction of the people of Derry, of all classes and denominations, that, by the mismanagement of their trust, the Irish Society had converted the crown grant from the blessing it was intended to be, and which it would have been under a just administration, into something more akin to a curse. For anything that saps the self-reliant and independent spirit of a community must always be a curse. Within the last hundred years Belfast was not in advance of Derry in population, in trade, in capital, or in any other element constituting or conducing to prosperity. Its river was not so navigable, and by no means so well adapted to foreign, especially transatlantic trade. The country surrounding it was not superior in soil, nor the inhabitants in intelligence and enterprise. It had no estate, as Derry had, granted by the crown to assist in the development of civilisation, education, and commerce. Its prospects, then, were inferior to those of Derry. But Belfast had the one thing, most needful of all, that Derry had not. It had equitable building tenures. And of this one advantage, look at the result! ' Belfast is now seven times the size of Derry; and is in possession of a trade and a trade capital which Derry can never hope to emulate, while smothered by the stick-in-the-mud policy of that miserable anachronism the Irish Society.'

The London companies which have estates in the county Derry claimed to be entitled to all the surplus revenue after the cost of management was deducted. This was the question raised by the celebrated ' Skinners' case,' ultimately decided by the House of Lords. The effect of the decision was, that the society was a trustee, not for the companies but for the public objects defined in the charter and the ' articles of agreement.' Lord Langdale's language on the subject is perfectly clear and explicit. He declared that the Irish Society have not, ' collectively or individually,' any beneficial interest in the estates. In a sense they are trustees. They have important duties to perform; but their powers and duties have all reference to the *Plantation,* whose object was purely public and political.

Adverting to this judgment, it is not Derry alone that is interested in the abolition of the Irish Society. Its objects ' affected the general welfare of Ireland and the whole realm.' The city of London, in its corporate capacity, had no beneficial interest in the estates. ' The money which it had advanced was early repaid, and the power which remained, or which was considered to remain, was, like that of the society, an entrusted power for the benefit of the plantation and those interested in it. The Irish Society seems to have been little, if anything, more than the representative or instrument of the city for the purposes of the Plantation.'

I subjoin the text of the concluding part of the judgment in the *Skinners' Case,* the report of which fills a very bulky volume :—

Lord Langdale said : ' The mistaken views which the society may have subsequently taken of its own situation and duties (and I think that such mistaken views have several times been taken) do not vary the conclusion to be deduced from the charter and the circumstances contemporary with the grant of the first charter. I am of opinion that the powers granted to the society and the trusts reposed in them ,vere in part of a general and public nature, independent of the private benefit of the companies of London, and were intended by the crown to benefit Ireland and the city of London, by connecting the city of Londonderry and the town of Coleraine and a considerable Irish district with the city of London, and to promote the general purposes of the Plantation, not only by securing the performance of the conditions imposed on ordinary undertakers, but also by the exercise of powers and the performance of trusts not within the scope of those conditions. The charter of Charles II. expressly recites that the property not actually divided was retained for the general operation of the Plantation.'

CHAPTER XVIII.

TENANT-RIGHT IN DOWN.

IF there are sermons in stones I ought to have learned something from the ruins of the castle built by Sir Arthur Hill, the founder of the house of Downshire, in which they show the chamber occupied by William III. while his army was encamped at Blaris Moor. This was once a royal fort, and among the most interesting memorials of the past are the primitive gates, long laid aside from duty, the timber gradually mouldering away from the huge nails, which once added to their massive strength. Hillsborough was incorporated by Charles II., and sent two members to parliament. The Hills rose rapidly in rank and influence. In 1717, Trevor Hill, Esq., was created Viscount of Hillsborough and Baron Hill. In 1756, Wills, the second viscount, was made Earl of Hillsborough, and in 1789 he became Marquis of Downshire.

Hillsborough is the most perfect picture of a feudal establishment that I know. On one side of the little, quiet, tradeless town are the ruins of the old castle, with its park and its fine ancestral trees, through the thick foliage of which pierces the spire of the church, lofty and beautiful. On the other side, and quite close to the town, is ' the new castle '—an immense building of cut stone, in the Greek style, two storeys high, shut in by high walls from the view of the townsfolk. Then there is the small market-square, with the court-house in the centre, the hotel at the top, and other buildings of a better class on the opposite side. From the hill, which is crowned by these buildings, descend small

streets, in which dwell the inhabitants, all more or less
dependent on the lord of the manor, all cared for by him,
and many of them pensioned when disabled by age or
infirmity.

There is a monument erected to the memory of the late
marquis's father on a hill to the south of the town. The
view from this point is glorious. Belfast lies a little beyond,
enveloped in the smoke emitted from its numerous tall
chimneys. To the left is the range of the Antrim highlands,
continued along the coast of the Lough towards Carrickfergus, and from which the Cave Hill stands out in bold
relief, looking down on the numerous pretty villas with
which the taste of wealthy manufacturers and merchants has
adorned those pleasant suburbs. Westward towards Lough
Neagh, swelling gradually—southward towards Armagh,
and round to Newry, the whole surface of the country
gently undulating, presents a vast picture of quiet beauty,
fertility, and plenty that can be rivalled only in England.
The tall crowded stooks along the ridges of the corn-fields
attested the abundance of the crops—the rich greenness and
warmth of the landscape showing how well the ground has
been drained, manured, and cultivated. The neat, white-
walled houses gleaming amidst the verdure of sheltering trees
and trimmed hedges tell the thoughtful observer that the
people who dwell in this land belong to it, are rooted in it,
and ply their industry under the happy feeling that, so far
as their old landlords are concerned, their lot is one of ' quiet-
ness and assurance for ever.' Nowhere—even on the high
ranges about Newry, where the population is far too dense,
where the patchwork cultivation creeps up the mountain
side, and the hand of industry snatches a precarious return
from a poor, cold, ungrateful soil, amidst desolating tempests
and blighting fogs—not even there did I notice the least
trace of evictions or clearances. No black remnant of a
wall tells that where sheep now browze and lambs frisk
there was once a fireside, where the family affections were
cherished, and a home where happy children played in the

sunshine. This is the field of capital and enterprise; here we have an aristocracy of wealth, chiefs of industry, each of whom maintains an army of ' hands ' more numerous than the swordsmen of Shane O'Neill when he reigned in his castle yonder on the banks of Lough Neagh. But here also is the aristocracy of rank—lords of ancient lineage, descended from heroes—men who have left magnificent monuments of their creative genius. They have not only founded great houses, but they have laid deep and broad the foundations of a social system to whose strength and beauty every age has been adding something, and which now wants only one topmost stone to make it perfect.

I read on the monument to Lord Downshire the expressive motto of the Downshire family—*Per Deum et ferrum obtinui.* No family ever made better use of the power thus obtained. The inscription states that the third marquis was ' alike distinguished for patriotism, rectitude of principle, and honesty of purpose. Upholding his station with becoming dignity, he was also mindful of the wants of others, and practised his duties with benevolence and humility, which won the regard of every virtuous mind, adding lustre to his exalted rank.' Although these words were engraved upon a monument by the friends and admirers of their object, they are perfectly true, and they would be equally true of the late marquis.

Lord Downshire is esteemed as the best of landlords. He charges 33 per cent. less for his land than it is worth—than the tenants would be able to pay. Tenant-right on his property sells for an enormous amount. He never evicts a tenant, nor even threatens to evict those who vote against him. What he has done for the contentment and prosperity of his tenants, with so much honour and happiness to himself, other landlords may do with like results. The late lord, his father, and his grandfather pursued the same course. They let their lands at a low valuation. They encouraged improvements—they allowed the free enjoyment of tenant-right; but they refused to allow sub-letting or subdivision of the land. They consolidated farms only when tenants, unable to retain small, worn-out holdings, wished to sell their tenant-right and depart. The consequence is that there is great competition for land on the Downshire estates. The tenant-right sells easily for 30*l.* to 40*l.* an Irish acre, the rent being on an average about 28*s.* If a tenant is not able to pay his way, he is let run on in arrears perhaps for two or three years. Then he feels the necessity of selling; but the arrears are deducted, and also debts that he may owe to his neighbours, before he departs with the proceeds in his pocket.

The late marquis seems to have been almost idolised by the tenants. On or off the estate, in town or country, I have heard nothing of him but praise of the warmest and most unqualified kind; and, what is more remarkable, his late agent, Mr. Filgate, was universally respected for his fairness in the discharge of his duties. The way in which I heard this spoken of by the people convinces me that there is nothing that wins their confidence so much as strict impartiality, and justice, calmly, kindly, but firmly administered. The people to whom I spoke laid stress on the fact that Mr. Filgate listened quietly to the statements of both sides, carefully enquired into the merits of each, and decided accordingly. There was no favouritism, they said, no partiality; no hasty decision in a fit of anger, or passion, or impatience; no refusal to listen to reason.

I observed to one of the tenants, 'You admit that the rents are much lower than on other estates, much lower than the value of the lands, and that during the last twenty years the tenant-right has increased in value. Suppose, then, that the marquis should raise the rents, say twenty-five per cent., what would be the consequence? Would they pay the increase willingly?' 'Willingly!' he exclaimed, 'no, there would be rebellion! The late lord could do anything with the people; he could raise the country. But you see when they bought the tenant-right they believed they could never be robbed of the value for which they paid by raising the rent.'

What can be better than the social picture which Harris presents of the state of society here 130 years ago ? ' The inhabitants are warm and well clad at church, fairs, and markets. Tillage and the linen manufacture keep them in constant employment; a busy and laborious life prevents excess and breaches of the laws, which in no part of the kingdom are more reverenced. The people are regular in their attendance on public worship. Few breaches of the peace, felonies, burglaries, or murders come before the judges at the assizes ; convictions for capital offences seldom happen. Men travel securely by day, and are afraid of little disturbance at night to keep them on their guard. Every man sits down securely under his vine and his figtree, and enjoys with comfort the fruit of his honest labours.' He ascribes in the main this prosperity to what he calls ' *the spirit of tillage.*' Until that spirit arose in Ulster, the Irish had to send to America for their daily bread, ' which,' he says, ' to the astonishment of all Europe, has been often our weakness.' Viewing the whole social condition of the county, he exclaims, ' Such are the happy effects of a well-peopled country, *extensive tillage, the linen manufacture, and the Protestant religion.*'

In the first year of the present century, the Dublin Society (not yet ' Royal ') employed ' land commissioners ' to enquire into the condition of agriculture in the several counties of Ireland. The Rev. John Dubourdieu, rector of Annahilt, in this county, was their commissioner for Down and Antrim. He states that the rent was then on an average 20*s.* the *Irish* acre (three equal to five English), allowing for the mountains and bogs, which he computed at 44,658 acres. The rental of the county he sets down at 300,000*l.* The net annual value of property assessed under the Tenement Valuation Act is now 743,869*l.* This is considerably under the letting value, it is supposed, 25 per cent. If this be so, the county yields to the proprietors a revenue of about 1,000,000*l.* a year. If we add the value of the tenant-right, and of the fixtures of all sorts—houses, mills, roads, bridges—as well as the movable property and stock, we may get some idea of the enormous aggregate of wealth which the labour of man has created on this strip of wild wooded hills, swampy plains, and bogs.

Now, what has effected this marvellous change? The tenants, with one voice, exclaim, 'our labour, our capital, our skill, our care, and self-denial. It was we that cleared away the woods which it was so difficult to eradicate. It was we who drained away the bogs and morasses, and by the help of lime and marl converted them into rich land. It was we that built the dwelling-houses and offices. It was we that made the fences, and planted the hedge-rows and orchards. It was we that paid for the making of the roads and bridges. The landlords gave us the wild country to work upon; we have done the rest. Our industry enabled them to build their stately mansions, and we have continued to pay to them their princely revenues. Our forefathers came with them as settlers, that they might "plant" the country with a loyal and industrious race of people, and they came on the assurance that they and their children's children were to remain for ever rooted where they were planted. They did their duty faithfully and well by the land, by the landlords, and by the Government. Where the children that inherited their rights failed, their interest in their farms has been purchased dearly by others of the same race who have taken their places. By what right, then, can they be turned out?'

It is not possible, if it were desirable, to introduce the 'high farming system' in this county. But if possible, would it be desirable? In the eye of a scientific agriculturist it might be better that all those comfortable farmhouses, with the innumerable fences crossing the landscape in every possible form, making all sorts of mathematical figures, presenting the appearance of an immense variegated patchwork—were levelled and removed so that the plough and all the modern machinery might range unobstructed over hill and vale. But assuredly it would not seem better to the philanthropist, the Christian, or the statesman. To the chancellor of the exchequer it would make the most serious difference; for a few herds and ploughmen would consume but a very small portion indeed of the excisable articles now used by the tenant farmers of this county. I have taken some notes on the diet of this people which may be instructive.

At the beginning of the present century the small farmers were generally weavers. There was an obvious incompatibility in the two occupations, and the farms were neglected. Gradually this evil has been corrected, especially since the famine. The weavers have become cottiers, and the farmers have devoted themselves to their agricultural operations exclusively with the more energy since railroads have so facilitated the quick sale of produce, particularly that sort of produce which enables the occupiers to supply the markets with the smaller necessaries of life, and with which large farmers would not trouble themselves. Daily labourers working from 6 A.M., to 6 P.M. in large fields with machinery cannot do the hundreds of little matters which the family of the small holder attends to every hour of the day, often in the night—and which give work to women and children as well as the men—work of the most healthful character and most free from demoralizing influences.

On a farm of fifteen to thirty acres there is constant employment of a profitable kind for the members of a household, including women and children. The effect of good drainage is that farming operations can be carried on through winter, in preparing the ground and putting in wheat and other crops early to supply the markets, when prices are high. Oats, barley, potatoes, flax, turnips claim attention in turn, and then come the weeding and thinning, the turf-making, the hay-making, and all the harvest operations. It is by the ceaseless activity of small farmers in watching over their pigs, poultry, lambs, &c., that the markets are kept so regularly supplied, and that towns grow up and prosper. If Down and Antrim had been divided into farms of thousands of acres each, like Lincolnshire, what would

Belfast have become? Little more than a port for the
shipping of live stock to Liverpool and Glasgow. Before
the famine, the food of the small farmers was generally
potatoes and milk three times a day, with a bit of meat
occasionally. But salt herrings were the main reliance for
giving a flavour to the potato, often 'wet' and bad. After
the failure of the potatoes, their place was supplied by oatmeal in the form of 'stirabout.' Indian meal was subsequently found cheaper and more wholesome. But of late
years the diet of the farmers in these parts has undergone a
complete revolution. There is such brisk demand for butter,
eggs, potatoes, and other things that used to be consumed
by the family, that they have got into the habit of taking
tea, with cakes and other home-made bread twice, or even
three times, a day. The demand for tea is, therefore,
enormous. There is one grocer's establishment in Belfast
which has been able to produce a mixture that suits the
taste of the people, and the quantity of tea sold by it is a
ton a day. This is the business of but one out of many
houses in Belfast. Then there is the brisk trade in such
towns as Newtownards, Lisburn, Ballymena, &c. In
pastoral districts the towns languish, the people pine in
poverty, and the workhouses are in request.

In a financial point of view, therefore, it is manifestly the
interest of the state to encourage 'the spirit of tillage.' It
is thus that most will be got out of the ground, that most
revenue will be raised, and that the other elements of
national power will be most fully developed. How can this
encouragement be most effectually given? Security for the
farmer is essential—of what nature should the security be?
The phrase 'unexhausted improvements' is often used.
But should the legislature contemplate, or make provision
for the exhaustion of improvements? Is the improving
tenant to be told that his remedy is to retrograde—to undo
what he has done—to take out of the land all the good he
has put in it, and reduce it to the comparative sterility in
which he, or those whom he represents, first received it?

Should not the policy of the legislature rather be to keep up improvements of the soil, and its productive power at the highest possible point, and make it the interest of the occupier never to relax in his exertions? The rower will not put forth all his strength unless he believes he will win. In other races, though many start, only one or two can receive the prize. In this race of agricultural improvement all competitors might win ample rewards. But will they put forth all their energies—is it in human nature that they should—was it ever done by any people, if the prizes are to be seized, enjoyed, and flaunted before their eyes by others, who may be strangers, and who never helped them by their sympathy in their toilsome course of training and self-denial? It is because the landlords of the county Down have been so often in the same boat with their tenants, and with so much good faith, generous feeling, and cordial sympathy encouraged their exertions, and secured to them their just rewards, that this great county presents to the world such a splendid example of what industry, skill, and capital can accomplish. Is it not possible to extend the same advantages through the whole island without wronging the landlord or degrading the tenant?

The stranger is at first surprised to see so large a town as Newtownards, with its handsome square, its town-hall, its wide, regular streets, its numerous places of worship, and a population of 9,500, in a place without visible factories, and without communication with the sea, within eight miles of Belfast, and three miles of Bangor, which, though a seaport, is but one-fourth of the size. But although there are no great mills sending forth volumes of smoke, Newtownards is really a manufacturing town. Those clean, regular streets, with their two-storey houses, uniform as a district in the east of London, are inhabited by weavers. In each house there is one loom at least, in most two or three, and in some as many as six. The manufacture of woollen and cotton goods of finer qualities than can be produced by the power-loom is carried on extensively. I saw one man working at

Y

a piece of plaid of six colours, a colour on every shuttle, With the help of his wife, who assisted in winding, he was able to earn only 8s. a week by very diligent work from early morning till night. There is a general complaint of the depression of trade at present. Agents, chiefly from Glasgow houses, living in the town, supply the yarn and pay the wages. I was struck with the number of public-houses in all the leading streets. How far they are supported by the weavers I cannot say, but whether or not they can dispense with the glass, they must have their tobacco, and when this luxury is deducted, and a shilling a week for the rent of the cottage, it is hard to understand how a family of six or eight can be supported on the weekly wages. The trade of muslin embroidery once flourished here, and in the pretty little neighbouring town of Comber; but it has so fallen off that now the best hands, plying the needle unceasingly during the long, long day, can earn only three or four shillings a week. Before the invention of machinery for flax-spinning, the manufacture of fine thread by hand-labour was a most profitable employment. Wonders were wrought in this way by female fingers. The author of 'Our Staple Manufactures' states that in 1799, out of a pound and a half of flax, costing 10s., a woman produced yarn of the value of 5l. 2s. 6d. Miss M'Quillan, of Comber, spun 94 hanks out of one pound of flax, splitting the fibre with her needles to give this degree of fineness.

> But alas! what a change to the cottage hearth!
> The song of the wheel's no more—
> The song that gladdened with guileless mirth
> The hearths and homes of the poor!

But here, and in all the small towns about, they have still the weaving, and it is carried on to a considerable extent by persons who hold a few acres of land, throwing aside the shuttle while putting in the crops and doing the harvest work. Thus combining the two pursuits, these poor people are able, by extraordinary industry, to earn their daily bread; but they can do little more. The weavers, as a class, appear to be feeble and faded specimens of humanity, remarkably quiet, intelligent, and well-disposed—a law-abiding people, who shrink from violence and outrage, no matter what may be their grievances. It is cruel to load them too heavily with the burdens of life, and yet I am afraid it is sometimes done, even in this county, unnecessarily and wantonly. What I have said of the Downshire and Londonderry estates, holds good with respect to the estates of the other large proprietors, such as Lord Roden, the kindest of landlords, almost idolised, even by his Catholic tenants; Lord Annesley; the trustees of Lord Kilmurray; Sir Thomas Bateson, and others. But I am sorry to learn that even the great county Down has a share of the two classes which supply the worst species of Irish landlords—absentees who live extravagantly in England, and merchants who have purchased estates to make as large a percentage as possible out of the investment. It is chiefly, but not wholly, on the estates of these proprietors that cases of injustice and oppression are found. In the first class it is the agent that the tenants have to deal with; and whether he be humane or not matters little to them, for, whatever may be his feelings, the utmost penny must be exacted to keep up the expensive establishments of the landlord in England, to meet the cost of a new building, or the debt incurred by gambling on the turf and elsewhere. Every transaction of the kind brings a fresh demand on the agent, and even if he be not unscrupulous or cruel, he must put on the screw, and get the money at all hazards. I have been assured that it is quite usual, on such estates, to find the tenantry paying the highest rent compatible with the maintenance of bare life. There is in the county of Down a great number of small holders thus struggling for existence. As a specimen let us take the following case:—A man holds a dozen acres of land, for which he pays 2*l.* 10*s.* per acre. He labours as no slave could be made to work, in the summer time from five o'clock in the morning till six in the evening. He can hardly scrape together a pound beyond the rent and taxes. If a bad season comes, he is at starvation point : he falls into arrears with the landlord, and he is forced by the bailiff to sell off his small stock to pay the rent.

Without the excuse of pecuniary difficulties, the merchant landlord is not a whit less exacting, or more merciful. He looks upon the tenants as he would on so many head of cattle, and his sole consideration is what is the highest penny he can make out of them. Not far from Belfast lived a farmer who cultivated a few acres. Sickness and the support of a widowed sister's family forced him into arrears of rent. Ejectment proceedings were taken, and one day when he returned to his house, he found his furniture thrown out on the road, the sister and family evicted, and the door locked. He was offered as much money as would take him to America, but he would not be allowed to sell the tenant-right. Here is another case illustrative of the manner in which that right is sometimes dealt with :— A respectable man purchased a farm at 10*l*. an acre. It was very poor land, much of it unfit for cultivation. Immediately on getting possession a surveyor came and added two acres to the former measurement. The incoming tenant was at the same time informed that the rent was raised to an extent that caused the possession to be a dead loss. On threatening to throw up the concern, some reduction was made, which brought the rent as close as possible to the full letting value.

I have been told by a well-informed gentleman, whose veracity I cannot doubt, that it is quite common in the county of Down (and indeed I have been told the same thing in other counties) to find an *improving* tenant paying 2*l*. to 3*l*. an acre for land, which he has at his own expense brought up to a good state of cultivation, while the adjoining land of his lazy neighbour—originally of equal value—yields only 20*s*. to 35*s*. an acre. The obvious tendency of this unjust and impolitic course on the part of landlords and agents, is to discourage improvements, to dishearten the

industrious, and to fill the country with thriftless, despond-
ing, and miserable occupiers, living from hand to mouth.
There are circumstances under which even selfish men will
toil hard, though others should share with them the benefit of
their labours ; but if they feel that this partnership in the
profits of their industry is the result of a system of legalised
injustice, which enables unscrupulous men to appropriate
at will the whole of the profits, their moral sense so revolts
against that system that they resolve to do as little as they
possibly can.

The consequence of these painful relations of landlord
and tenant, even in this comparatively happy county, is a
perceptible degeneracy in the manhood of the people. Talk
to an old inhabitant, who has been an attentive observer of
his times, and he will tell you that the vigorous and
energetic, the intelligent and enterprising, are departing to
more favoured lands, and that this process has produced a
marked deterioration in the population within his memory.
He can distinctly recollect when there were more than
double the present number of strong farmers in the country
about Belfast. He declares that, with many exceptions of
course, the land is getting into the hands of a second or
third class of farmers, who are little more than servants to
the small landlords. Even where there are leases, such
intelligent observers affirm that they are so over-ridden
with conditions that the farmer has no liberty or security to
make any great improvements. Were it otherwise he
would not think a thirty-one years' lease sufficient for the
building of a stone house, that would be as good at the end
of a hundred years as at the end of thirty. All the information that I can gather from thoughtful men, who are
really anxious for a change that would benefit the landlords
as well as themselves, points to the remedy which Lord
Granard has suggested, as the most simple, feasible, and
satisfactory—the legalisation and extension of the tenant-
right custom. They rejoice that such landlords now
proclaim the injustice which the tenant class have so long

bitterly felt namely, the presumption of law that all the improvements and buildings on the farm belong to the lord of the soil, although the notorious fact is that they are all the work of the tenant.

And here I will take the opportunity of remarking that the legislature were guilty of strange oversight, or deliberate injustice, in the passing of the Incumbered Estates Act. Taking advantage of an overwhelming national calamity, they forced numbers of gentlemen into a ruinous sale of their patrimonial estates, in order that men of capital might get possession of them. But they made no provision whatever for the protection of the tenants, or of the property which those tenants had created on these estates. Many of those were tenants at will, who built and planted in perfect and well-grounded reliance on the honour and integrity of their old landlords. But in the advertisements for the sale of property under the Landed Estates Court, it was regularly mentioned as an inducement to purchasers of the Scully type that the tenants had no leases. The result of this combination of circumstances bearing against the cultivators of the soil—the chief producers of national wealth—is a deep, resentful sense of injustice pervading this class, and having for its immediate objects the landlords and their agents. The tenants don't speak out their feelings, because they dare not. They fear that to offend the *office* in word or deed is to expose themselves and their children to the infliction of a fine in the shape of increased rent, perhaps at the rate of five or ten shillings an acre in perpetuity.

One unfortunate effect of the distrust thus generated, is that when enlightened landlords, full of the spirit of improvement, like Lord Dufferin and Lord Lurgan, endeavour, from the most unselfish and patriotic motives, to make changes in the tenures and customs on their estates, they have to encounter an adverse current of popular opinion and feeling, which is really too strong to be effectually resisted. For example: In order to correct the evils resulting from the undue competition for land among the tenants, they limit the amount per acre which the outgoing tenant is permitted to receive; but the limitation is futile, because the tenants understand one another, and do what they believe to be right behind the landlord's back. The market price is, say, 20*l.* an acre. The landlord allows 10*l.*; the balance finds its way secretly into the pocket of the outgoing tenant before he gives up possession. As a gentleman expressed it to me emphatically, ' The outgoing tenant *must* be satisfied, and he *is* satisfied.' Public opinion in his own class demands it; and on no other terms would it be considered lucky to take possession of the vacant farm.

CHAPTER XIX.

TENANT-RIGHT IN ANTRIM.

I FIND from the Antrim Survey, published in 1812, that at that time leases were general on the Hertfort estate. There were then about 3,600 farmers who held by that tenure, each holding, on an average, twenty English acres, but many farms contained 100 acres or more. Mr. Hugh M‘Call, of Lisburn, the able author of ' Our Staple Manufactures,' gives the following estimates of the rental. In 1726, it was 3,500*l.*; in 1768, it was 12,000*l.*; and for 1869, his estimate is 63,000*l.* Taking the estimate given by Dean Stannus, as 10*l.* or 12*l.* an acre, the tenant-right of the estate is worth 500,000*l.* at the very least, probably 600,000*l.* is the more correct figure. This vast amount of property created by the .industry and capital of the tenants, is held at the will of an absentee landlord, who has on several occasions betrayed an utter want of sympathy with the people who lie thus at his mercy. There are tenant farmers on the estate who hold as much as 100 to 200 acres, with handsome houses built by themselves, whose interest, under the custom, should amount to 1,500*l.* and 2,500*l.* respectively, which might be legally swept away by a six months' notice to quit. The owners of this property might be regarded as very independent, but in reality, unless the spirit of martyrdom has raised them above the ordinary feelings of human nature, they will take care to be very humble and submissive towards Lord Hertfort's agents. If words were the same as deeds, if professions were always consistent with practice, the tenants would certainly have nothing to fear; for great pains have been taken from time to time, both by the landlord and agent, to inspire them with unbounded confidence.

In the year 1845, the tenants presented an address to Lord Hertfort, in which they said :—' It is a proud fact, worthy to be recorded, that the tenant-right of the honest and industrious man on your lordship's estate is a certain and valuable tenure to him, so long as he continues to pay his rent.' To this his lordship replied in the following terms :—
' I am happy to find that the encouragement I have given to the improvement of the land generally has been found effectual, and I trust that the advantage to the tenant of the improved system of agriculture will be found to increase ; and I beg to assure you that with me the right of the improving tenant shall continue to be as scrupulously respected as it has been hitherto by my ancestors. Your kindness alone, independent of the natural interest which I must ever feel as to everything connected with this neighbourhood, affords a powerful inducement to my coming among you, and I hope to have the pleasure of often repeating my visit.'

Twenty-four years have since elapsed, and during all that time the marquis has never indulged himself in a repetition of the exquisite pleasure he then enjoyed. At a banquet given in his honour on that occasion, he used the following language, which was, no doubt, published in the *Times*, and read with great interest in London and Paris :—' This is one of the most delightful days I ever spent. Trust me, I have your happiness and welfare at heart, and it shall ever be my endeavour to promote the one and contribute to the other.'
The parting scene on this occasion must have been very touching ; for, in tearing himself away, his lordship said :
' I have now come to the concluding toast. It is, " Merry have we met, and merry may we *soon* meet again ! " '

The tenants could scarcely doubt the genuineness of their landlord's feelings, for on the same occasion Dean Stannus said : ' I feel myself perfectly justified in using the term " a good landlord ; " because his lordship's express wish to me often was, " I hope you will always keep me in such a position that I may be considered the friend of my tenants." ' But as he did not return to them, a most respectable deputation waited upon him in London in the year 1850, to present a memorial praying for a reduction of rent on account of the potato blight and other local calamities which had befallen the tenantry. The memorialists respectfully showed ' that under the encouraging auspices of the Hertfort family, and on the faith of that just and equitable understanding which has always existed on this estate—that *no advantage would be taken of the tenant's improvements in adjusting the letting value of land,* they had invested large sums of money in buildings and other improvements on their farms, and that this, under the name of tenant-right, was a species of sunk capital that was formerly considered a safe repository for accumulated savings, which could be turned to account at any time of difficulty by its sale, or as a security for temporary advances.' In his reply, Lord Hertfort said, ' I seek not to disturb any interest, much less do I wish to interfere by any plan or arrangement of mine with the tenant-right which my tenants have hitherto enjoyed, and which it is my anxious wish to preserve to them.'

The faith and hope inspired by these assurances of the landlord were repeatedly encouraged and strengthened by the public declarations of his very reverend agent, Dean Stannus. At a meeting of the Killultagh and Derryvolgie Farming Society, in 1849, he stated that he had great pleasure in subscribing to almost everything said by Mr. M'Call. He had taken great pains to convince the late Lord Hertfort that tenant-right was one of the greatest possible boons, *as well to the landlords themselves as to the* tenants. So advantageous did he regard it to the interest of Lord Hertfort and the tenants, that if it were not preserved, he would not continue agent to the estate. Tenant-right was his security for the Marquis of Hertfort's rent, and he would not ask a tenant to relinquish a single rood of land without paying him at the rate of 10*l.* to 12*l.* an acre for it.

Firmly believing in the statements thus emphatically and

solemnly made to them from time to time, that on this estate tenant-right was as good as a lease, the tenants went on building houses, and making permanent improvements in Lisburn and elsewhere, depending on this security. And, indeed, the value of such security could scarcely be presented under more favourable circumstances. The absentee landlord receiving such a princely revenue, and absorbed in his Parisian pursuits, seemed to leave everything to his agent. The agent was rector of the parish of Lisburn, a dignitary of the Church, a gentleman of the highest social position, with many excellent points in his character, and pledged before the world, again and again, to respect rigidly and scrupulously the enormous property which a confiding tenantry had invested in this estate. If, under these circumstances, the security of tenant-right fails, where else can it be trusted? If it be proved, by open and public proceedings, that on the Hertfort estate, the distinctly recognised property of the tenant is liable to be seized and wrested from him by the agent, it is clear to demonstration that such property absolutely requires the protection of law. This proof, I am sorry to say, is forthcoming. Let my readers reflect for a moment on what might have been done for Lisburn and the surrounding country if the Marquis of Hertfort had rebuilt his castle and resided among his people. What an impulse to improvement of every kind, what employment for tradesmen of every class, what business for shops might have resulted from the local expenditure of 50,000*l.* or 60,000*l.* a year! What public buildings would have been erected—how local institutions would have flourished! The proverb that ' absence makes the heart grow fonder ' does not apply to the relations of landlord and tenant. But there is another proverb that applies well—' Out of sight, out of mind.' Of this I shall now give two or three illustrations. Some years ago, it was discovered that no lease of the Catholic chapel at Lisburn could be found, and in the recollection of the oldest member of the congregation no rent had been paid. Rent, however, was now demanded, and the parish priest agreed to pay a nominal amount, which places the congregation at the mercy of the office.   Ground was asked some time ago to build a Presbyterian Church, but it was absolutely refused.   A sum of money was subscribed to build a literary institute, but, though a sort of promise was given for ground to build it on, it was never granted, and the project fell through.   Lord Hertfort spends no portion of his vast income where it is earned.   His estate is like a farm to which the produce is never returned in the shape of manure, but is all carted off and applied to the enrichment of a farm elsewhere.   One might suppose that where such an exhausting process has been going on for so long a time an effort would be made at some sort of compensation, especially at periods of calamity.   Yet, when the weavers on his estate were starving, owing to the cotton famine during the American war, his lordship never replied to the repeated applications made to him for help to save alive those honest producers of his wealth.   The noble example of Lord Derby and other proprietors in Lancashire failed to kindle in his heart a spark of humanity, not to speak of generous emulation.   The sum of 3,000*l.* was raised in Lisburn, and by friends in Great Britain and America, which was expended in saving the people from going *en masse* to the workhouse.   Behold a contrast!   While the great peer, whose family inherited a vast estate for which they never paid a shilling, was deaf to the cries of famishing Christians, whom he was bound by every tie to commiserate and relieve, an American citizen, who owed nothing to Ireland but his birth—Mr. A. T. Stewart, of New York— sent a ship loaded with provisions, which cost him 5,000*l.* of his own money, to be distributed amongst Lord Hertfort's starving tenants, and on the return of the ship he took out as many emigrants as he could accommodate, free of charge.

The tourist in Ireland is charmed with the appearance of Lisburn—the rich and nicely cultivated town parks, the fields white as snow with linen of the finest quality, the busy mills, the old trees, the clean streets, the look of comfort in the population, the pretty villas in the country about. Mrs. S. C. Hall says that there is, probably, no town in Ireland where the happy effects of English taste and industry are more conspicuous than at Lisburn. 'From Drumbridge and the banks of the Lagan on one side, to the shores of Lough Neagh on the other, the people are almost exclusively the descendants of English settlers. Those in the immediate neighbourhood of the town were mostly Welsh, but great numbers arrived from the northern English shires, and from the neighbourhood of the Bristol Channel. The English language is perhaps spoken more purely by the populace of this district than by the same class in any other part of Ireland. The neatness of the cottages, and the good taste displayed in many of the farms, are little, if at all, inferior to aught that we find in England, and the tourist who visits Lough Neagh, passing through Ballinderry, will consider it to have been justly designated *the garden of the north*. The multitude of pretty little villages, scattered over the landscape, each announcing itself by the tapering tower of a church, would almost beguile the traveller into believing that he was passing through a rural district in one of the midland counties of England.'

We have seen that after General Conway got this land, it was described by an English traveller as still uninhabited—'all woods and moor.' Who made it the garden of the north? The British settlers and their descendants. And why did they transform this wilderness into fruitful fields? Because they had permanent tenures and fair rents. The rental 150 years ago was 3,500*l.* per annum. Allow that money was three times as valuable then as it is now, and the rental would have been about 10,500*l.* It is now nearly six times that amount. By what means was the revenue of the landlord increased? Was it by any expenditure of his own? Did any portion of the capital annually abstracted from the estate return to it, to fructify and increase its value? Did the landlord drain the swamps, reclaim the moors, build the dwellings and farmhouses, make the fences, and plant the orchards? He did nothing of the kind. Nor was it agricultural industry alone that increased his revenue. He owes much of the beauty, fertility, and richness of his estate to the linen manufacture, to those weavers to the cries of distress from whose famishing children a few years ago the most noble marquis resolutely turned a deaf ear.

But, passing from historical matters to the immediate purpose of our enquiry, let it suffice to remark that from Lisburn as a centre the linen trade in all its branches—flax growing, scutching, spinning, weaving and bleaching—spread over the whole of the Hertfort estate, giving profitable employment to the tenants, circulating money, enabling them to build and improve and work the estate into the rich and beautiful garden described by Mrs. Hall;—all this work of improvement has been carried on, all or nearly all the costly investments on the land have been made, without leases and in dependence on tenant-right. We have seen what efforts were made by landlord and agent to strengthen the faith of the tenants in this security. We have seen also from the historical facts I have adduced the sort of people that constitute the population of the borough of Lisburn. If ever there was a population that could be safely entrusted with the free exercise of the franchise it is the population of this town—so enlightened, so loyal, so independent in means, such admirable producers of national wealth, so naturally attached to British connection. Yet for generations Lisburn has been a pocket borough, and the nominee of the landlord, often a total stranger, was returned as a matter of course. The marquis sent to his agent a *congé d'élire*, and that was as imperative as a similar order to a dean and chapter to elect a bishop. In 1852 the gentleman whom the Lisburn electors were ordered to return was Mr. Inglis, the lord advocate of Scotland. They, however, felt that the time was come when the borough should be opened, and they should be at liberty to exercise their constitutional rights. A meeting of the inhabitants was therefore held, at which Mr. R. Smith was nominated as the popular candidate. The contest was not political; it was simply the independence of the borough against the *office.* Dean Stannus, as agent to an absentee landlord, was the most powerful personage in the place, virtually the lord of the manor. Before the election that gentleman published a letter in a Belfast paper contradicting a statement that had appeared to the effect that Lord Hertfort took little interest in the approaching contest, in which letter he said: ' I have the best reason for knowing that his lordship views with intense interest what is passing here, and that he is most anxious for the return of Mr. Inglis, feeling that the election of such a representative (which I am now enabled to say is *certain*) will do much credit to the borough of Lisburn, and that this *unmeaning* contest will, at all events, among its other effects, prove to his lordship whom he may regard as his *true* friends in his future relations with this town.'

Notwithstanding this warning, so significantly emphasized, the candidate whom the voters selected as their real representative was returned. Now no one can blame the marquis or his agent for wishing that the choice had fallen upon Mr. Inglis. So far as politics were concerned, the contest *was* unmeaning; but so far as the rights of the people and the loyal working of the British constitution were concerned, the contest was full of meaning, and if the landlord and his agent respected the constitution more than their own personal power they would have frankly acquiesced in the result, feeling that this Protestant and Conservative constituency had conscientiously done its duty to the state. But who could have imagined, after all the solemnly recorded pledges I have quoted, that they would have instantly resolved to punish the independent exercise of the franchise by inflicting an enormous and crushing fine amounting to nothing less than the whole tenant-right property of every adverse voter who had not a lease! Immediately after the election ' notices to quit ' were served upon every one of them. In consequence of this outrageous proceeding a public meeting was held, at which a letter from John Millar, Esq., a most respectable and wealthy man (who was unable to attend) was read by the secretary. He said : ' I have at various times purchased places held from year to year, relying on the custom of the country, and on the declared determination of the landlord and his agent to respect such customary rights of property, for the continued possession of it. I have besides taken under the same landlord several fields as town parks, which were in very bad order. These fields I have drained and very much improved. I have always punctually paid the rent charged for the several holdings, and, I think I may venture to say, performed all the duties of a good tenant. At the last election, however, I exercised my right as a citizen of a free country, by giving my votes at Hillsborough and Lisburn in favour of the tenant-right candidates, without reference to the desires or orders of those who have no legal or constitutional right to control the use of my franchise. I have since received from the office a notice to quit, desiring me to give up possession of all my holdings, as tenant from year to year, in the counties of Down and Antrim, without any intimation that I shall receive compensation, and without being able to obtain any explanation of this conduct towards me except by popular rumour.' At the same meeting Mr. Hugh M'Call said that he had looked over some documents and found that the individuals in Lisburn who had received notices to quit held property to the value of 3,000*l*., property raised by themselves, or purchased by them with the sanction of the landlord. In one case the agent himself went into the premises where buildings were being erected, and suggested some changes. In fact the improvements were carried out under his inspection as an architect. Yet he served upon that gentleman a notice to quit. Some of the tenants paid the penalty for their votes by surrendering their holdings ; others contested the right of eviction on technical points, and succeeded at the quarter sessions. One of the points was, as already mentioned, that a dean and rector could not be legally a land agent at the same time. It was, indeed, a very ugly fact that the rector of the parish should be thus officially engaged, not only in nullifying the political rights of his own Protestant parishioners, but in destroying their tenant-right, evicting them from their holdings, which *they* believed to be legal robbery and oppression, accompanied by such flagrant breach of faith as tended to destroy all confidence between man and man, and thus to dissolve the strongest bonds of society. Sad work for a dignitary of the church to be engaged in!

In April, 1856, there was another contested election. On that occasion the marquis wrote to a gentleman in Lisburn that he would not interfere ' directly or indirectly to influence anybody.' Nevertheless, notices to quit, signed by Mr. Walter L. Stannus, assistant and successor to his father, were extensively served upon tenants-at-will, though it was afterwards alleged that they were only served as matters of form. But what, then, did they mean? They meant that those who had voted against the office had, *ipso facto, forfeited their tenant-right property.* Many other incidents in the management of the estate have been constantly occurring more recently, tending to show that the most valuable properties created by the tenants-at-will are at the mercy of the landlord, and that tenant-right, so called, is not regarded by him as a matter of *right* at all, but merely as a *favour*, to be granted to those who are dutiful and submissive to the office in all matters, political and social. For instance, one farmer was refused permission to sell his tenant-right till he consented to sink 100*l.* or 200*l.* in the shares of the Lisburn and Antrim railway, so that, as he believed, he was obliged to throw away his money in order to get his right.

The enormous power of an office which can deal with property amounting to more than half a million sterling, in such an arbitrary manner, necessarily generates a spirit of wanton and capricious despotism, except where the mind is

z

very well regulated and the heart severely disciplined by
Christian duty.   Of this I feel bound to give the following
illustration, which I would not do if the fact had not been
made public, and if I had not the best evidence that it is
undeniable.   George Beattie, jun., a grocer's assistant in
Lisburn, possessed a beautiful greyhound which he left in
charge of George Beattie, sen., his uncle, on departing for
America.   This uncle possessed a farm on the Hertfort
estate, the tenant-right of which he wanted to sell.   Having
applied to Mr. Stannus for permission, the answer he received was that he would not be allowed to sell until the
head of the greyhound was brought to the office.   The
tenant remonstrated and offered to send the dog away off the
estate to relatives, but to no effect.   He was obliged to kill
the greyhound, and to send its head in a bag to Lord
Hertfort's office.   It was a great triumph for the agent.
What a pretty sensational story he had to tell the young
ladies in the refined circles in which he moves.   How edifying
the recital must have been to the peasantry around him!
How it must have exalted their ideas of the civilising
influence of land agency.   ' It is quite a common thing,'
says a gentleman well acquainted with the estate, ' when a
tenant becomes insolvent, that his tenant-right is sold and
employed to pay those of his creditors who may be in favour.
I know a lady who made application to have a claim against
a small farmer registered in the office, which was done, and
she now possesses the security of the man's tenant-right for
her money.'

The case of the late Captain Bolton is the last illustration
I shall give in connection with this estate.   Captain Bolton
resided in Lisburn, and he was one of the most respected of
its inhabitants.   He was the owner of four houses in that
town, a property which he acquired in this way :—The site
of two of them was obtained by the late James Hogg, in
lieu of freehold property surrendered.   On this ground, his
son, Captain Bolton's uncle, built the two houses entirely at
his own expense.   Two other houses, immediately adjoining,

came into the market, and he purchased the out-going tenant's 'good-will' for a sum of about 40*l.* These houses were thatched, and in very bad condition. He repaired them and slated them, and thus formed a nice uniform block of four workers' houses. Captain Bolton inherited these from his uncle and retained uninterrupted possession till 1852, when he voted for Johnston Smyth at the election of that date. Immediately afterwards he received a notice to quit, an ejectment was brought in due time, the case was dismissed at the quarter sessions, an appeal was lodged, but it was again dismissed at the assizes. Undaunted by these two defeats, the persistent agent served another notice to quit. The captain was a man of peace, whose nerves could not stand such perpetual worrying by litigation, and he was so disgusted with the whole affair that he tied up the keys, and sent them to Lord Hertfort's office. In his ledger that day he made the following entry :—' Plundered, this 20th December 1854, by our worthy agent to the marquis, because I voted for Smyth and the independence of the borough.—J. B.'

The houses remained in the hands of the agent till the next election, when Captain Bolton voted for Mr. Hogg, the office candidate. The conscientious old gentleman—as good a conservative as Dean Stannus—voted from principle in both cases and not to please the agent or anyone else. The agent, however, thought proper to regard it as a penitent act, and as the tenant had ceased to be naughty, and had, it was assumed, shown proper deference to his political superiors, he received his houses back again, retaining the possession of them till his death. The profit rent of the houses is 20*l.* a year. Either this rent belonged to Captain Bolton or to Lord Hertfort. If to Captain Bolton, by what right did Dean Stannus take it from him and give it to the landlord ? If to the landlord, by what right did Dean Stannus take it from Lord Hertfort and give it to Captain Bolton ?

However, the latter gentleman having no doubt whatever, first or last, that the property was his own, bequeathed the

houses to trustees for the support of a school which he had
established in Lisburn. The school, it appears, had been
placed in connection with the Church Education Society,
and as it did not go on to his satisfaction, he placed it in
connection with the National Board of Education, having
appointed as his trustees John Campbell, Esq., M.D.,
William Coulson, Esq., and the Rev. W. J. Clarke,
Presbyterian minister, all of Lisburn. Dr. Campbell died
soon after, and Mr. Coulson refused to act, so that the
burden of the trust fell upon Mr. Clarke, who felt it to be
his duty to carry it out to the best of his ability. Dean
Stannus, however, was greatly dissatisfied with the last will
and testament of Captain Bolton. Yet the dying man had
no reason to anticipate that his affectionate pastor would
labour with all his might to abolish the trust. Dean
Stannus paid the captain a visit on his deathbed, and while
administering the consolations of religion he seemed moved
even to tears. To a friend who subsequently expressed
doubt, the simple-minded old Christian said : ' I will trust
the dean that he will do nothing in opposition to my will.
He was here a few days ago and wept over me. He loves
me, and will carry out my wishes.' The captain died in
April, 1867. He was scarcely cold in his grave when the
agent of Lord Hertfort took proceedings to eject his trustees,
and deprive the schools of the property bequeathed for their
support. Not content with this, he took proceedings to get
possession of the schoolhouse also, deeming it a sufficient
reason for this appropriation of another man's property, this
setting aside of a will, this abolition of a trust, that, in his
opinion, the schools ought to be under the patronage of the
rector, and in connection with the Church Education Society.
He had a perfect right to think and say this, and it might
be his conscientious conviction that the property would be
thus better employed ; but he ought to know that the end
does not sanctify the means ; that he had no right to substitute his own will for that of Captain Bolton, and that he
had no right to take advantage of the absence of an act of

parliament to possess himself of the rightful property of other people. Unfortunately, too, he was a judge in his own case, and he did not find it easy to separate the rector of the parish from the agent of the estate. It is a significant fact that when his son, Mr. Stannus, handed his power of attorney to Mr. Otway, the assistant-barrister, that gentleman refused to look at it, saying, ' I have seen it one hundred times; ' and the Rev. Mr. Clarke, while waiting in the court for the case to come on, observed that all the ejectment processes were at the suit of the Marquis of Hertfort. The school-house was built by Mr. Bolton, at his own expense twenty-eight years ago, and he maintained it till his death. The Rev. W. J. Clarke, the acting trustee, bravely defended his trust and fought the battle of tenant-right in the courts till driven out by the sheriff. He was then called on to perform the same duty with regard to the school-house. He has done it faithfully and well, and deserves the sympathy of all the friends of freedom, justice, and fair dealing. ' I shall never accept a trust,' he says, in a letter to the *Northern Whig*—' I shall never accept a trust, and permit any man, whether nobleman, agent, or bailiff, to alienate that trust, without appealing to the laws of my country ; and if the one-sidedness of such laws shall enable Dean and Mr. Stannus to confiscate this property, and turn it from the purpose to which benevolence designed it, then, having defended it to the last, I shall retire from the field satisfied that I have done my duty to the memory of the dead and the educational interests of the living.' Nor can we be surprised at the strong language that he uses when he says: ' The history of the case rivals, for blackness of persecution, anything that has happened in the north of Ireland for many years. But such a course of conduct only recoils on the heads of those who are guilty of it, and it shall be so in this case. The Marquis of Hertfort will not live always, and the power of public opinion may be able to reach his successor, and be felt even in Lisburn.'

Dean Stannus, in his evidence before the Devon commission,

stated that only a small portion of the estate was held by
lease.   The leases were obtained in a curious way.   In
1823 a system of fining commenced.   If a tenant wanted
a lease he was required to pay in cash a fine of 10*l.* an acre,
which was equal to an addition of ten shillings an acre to
the rent for twenty years, not counting the interest on the
money thus sunk in the land.   Yet, such was the desire of
the tenants to have a better security than the tenant-right
custom, always acknowledged on the estate, that ' every
man who had money took advantage of it.'   Mr. Gregg, the
seneschal of the manor, gave an illustration of the working of
this fining system.   A tenant sold his farm of fourteen acres
for 205*l.*, eight of the fourteen acres being held at will.   The
person who bought the farm was obliged to take a lease of
the eight acres, and to pay a proportional fine in addition to
the sum paid for the tenant-right.   Dean Stannus said ' he
would wish to see the tenant-right upheld upon the estate of
Lord Hertfort, as it always had been.   It is that,' he said,
' which has kept up the properties in the north over the
properties in other parts of Ireland.   It is a security for the
rent in the first instance, and reconciles the tenants to much
of what are called grievances.   If you go into a minute
calculation of what they have expended, they are not more
than paid for their expenditure.'   It transpired in the
course of the examination that a man who had purchased
tenant-right, and paid a fine of 10*l.* an acre on getting a
lease, would have to pay a similar fine over again when
getting the lease renewed.   The result of these heavy
advances was that the middle-class farmers lived in constant
pecuniary difficulties.   They were obliged to borrow money
at six per cent. to pay the rent, but they borrowed it under
circumstances which made it nearly 40 per cent., for it was
lent by dealers in oatmeal and other things, from whom they
were obliged to purchase large quantities of goods at such a
high rate that they sold them again at a sacrifice of 33
per cent.

Mr. Joshua Lamb, another witness, stated that the effect

of the fining system had been to draw away a great deal of the accumulated capital out of the hands of the tenantry, as well as their anticipated savings for years to come, by which the carrying out of improved methods of agriculture was prevented. Still, the existence of a lease for 31 years doubled the value of the tenant-right. This witness made a remarkable statement. With respect to this custom he said : The ' effect of this arrangement, when duly observed, is to prevent all disputes, quarrels, burnings, and destruction of property, so common in those parts of Ireland where this practice does not prevail. Indeed, so fully are farmers aware of this, that very few, except the most reckless, would venture on taking a farm without obtaining the outgoing tenant's " good-will." Such a proceeding as taking land " over a man's head," as it is termed, is regarded here as not merely dishonourable, but as little better than robbery, and as such held in the greatest detestation.' He added that the justice of this arrangement was obvious—' because all the buildings, planting, and other improvements, being entirely at the tenant's expense, he has a certain amount of capital sunk in the property, for which, if he parts with the place, he expects to be repaid by the sale of the tenant-right. He knew no case in the county in which the tenant, or those from whom he purchased, had made no improvements.'

The first marquis occasionally visited the estate, and was proud of the troops of yeomanry and cavalry which had been raised from his tenantry. The second marquis, who died in 1822, was only once in that part of Ireland. The third marquis—he of Prince Regent notoriety—never set foot on the property ; and the present, who has been reigning over 140 townlands for nearly thirty years, has never been among his subjects except during a solitary visit of three weeks in October, 1845, when, it is said, he came to qualify for his ribbon (K.G.) that he might be able to say to the prime minister that he was a resident landlord. He has resided almost entirely in Paris, cultivating the friendship of

Napoleon instead of the welfare of the people who pay him a revenue of 60,000*l.* a year. Bagatelle, his Paris residence, has, it is said, absorbed Irish rents in its ' improvements,' till it has been made worth three quarters of a million sterling. If the residence cost so much, fancy may try to conceive the amount of hard-earned money squandered on the luxuries and pleasures of which it is the temple—the most Elysian spot in the Elysian fields.

The following curious narrative appeared in a Belfast newspaper, and was founded on a speech made by Dean Stannus at a public meeting.

The venerable Dean of Ross and his son, Mr. W. T. Stannus, had been deputed to go to Paris to wait on Lord Hertfort, and urge him to assist in the expense of finishing the Antrim Junction Railway. The dean is in his eighty-first year ; fifty-one years of his life have been spent in the management of the Hertfort estate, and whatever difference of opinion may exist as to his arrangements with the tenantry, every one who knows anything of the affair must admit that there never existed a more faithful representative of a landowner. On arriving in Paris he found the marquis ill, so much so that neither the dean nor his son could get an interview. For three days the venerable gentleman danced attendance on his chief, and on Monday the fourth attempt was made, the dean sent up his name, and had a reply that ' the marquis was too ill to see anyone.' Next day, however, the marquis condescended to receive his agent, and the subject of the railway was introduced. The dean told him that Lord Erne had given 200,000*l.* towards the railway projects on his property—that Lords Lucan, Annesley, and Lifford had contributed largely, and that Lord Downshire had been exceedingly liberal in promoting lines on his estate. But all was vain. The noble absentee, who drains about 60,000*l.* a year from his Irish property, and who often pays 5,000*l.* for a picture, refused to lend 15,000*l.* to aid in finishing a railway, which runs for three-fourths of the mileage through his own estate. During the interview Mr. W. T. Stannus

urged on the marquis that the investment would be the best
that could be made, as preference shares paying five per
cent. would be allocated to him as security for the amount.
All arguments and entreaties, however, were lost on the
noble invalid. Even the appeal of the old gentleman who,
for more than half a century, had managed the estate so
advantageously for the successive owners of that splendid property, was made in vain. ' You never refused me anything
before,' urged the dean, ' and I go away in very bad spirits.'
What a wonderful history lies in this episode of Irish landlordism. Here is an unmarried nobleman whose income
from investments in British and French securities is said to
exceed 30,000*l.* a year, besides the immense revenue of his
English and Irish estates, and yet he refuses to part with
15,000*l.* towards aiding in the construction of a railway on
his own property.

CHAPTER XX.

TENANT-RIGHT IN ARMAGH.

AMONG the undertakers in the county of Armagh were the two Achesons, Henry and Archibald, ancestors of Lord Gosford, who founded Market Hill, Richard Houlston, John Heron, William Stanbowe, Francis Sacheverell, John Dillon, John Hamilton, Sir John Davis, Lord Moore, Henry Boucher, Anthony Smith, Lieutenant Poyntz, and Henry M'Shane O'Neill.

In connection with each of these settlements Pynar uses the phrase, 'I find planted and estated.' What he means is more fully explained in his reference to the precinct of Fews, allotted to Scottish undertakers, where Henry Acheson had obtained 1,000 acres. The surveyor says : 'I find a great number of tenants on this land; but not any that have any estates but by promise, and yet they have been many years upon the land. There are nominated to me two freeholders and seventeen leaseholders, all which were with me, and took the oath of supremacy, and petitioned unto me that they might have their leases, the which Mr. Acheson seemed to be willing to perform it unto them presently. These are able to make thirty men with arms. Here is great store of tillage.' The whole of the reports indicate that the Crown required of the undertakers two things. First, that they should themselves reside on the land, that they should build strong houses, fortified with bawns, and keep a certain number of armed men for the defence of the settlement. Secondly, that the English and Scotch settlers who were expected to reclaim the land and build houses, were to have ' estates ' in their farms, either as freeholders or lessees. The grants were made to the undertakers on these conditions—they should be resident, and they should have around them a number of independent yeomanry to defend the king when called upon to do so. Everything connected with the plantation gives the idea of permanent tenures for the settlers. A curious fact is mentioned about Sir John Davis, who had been so active in bringing about the plantation. He obtained a grant for 500 acres. ' Upon this,' says Pynar, ' there is nothing at all built, nor so much as an English tenant on the land.' It seems his tenants were all of the class for whose extirpation he pleaded, as weeds that would choke the Saxon crop. Henry M'Shane O'Neill got 1,000 acres at Camlagh, ' but he being lately dead, it was in the hands of Sir Toby Caulfield, who intended to do something upon it, for as yet there was nothing built.' Sir Toby was the ancestor of the Earl of Charlemont, always one of the best landlords in Ulster.

It is gratifying to find that both the undertakers and the original tenants are still fairly represented—a considerable number of the former having founded noble houses, and the latter having multiplied and enriched the land to such an extent that, though the population is dense and the farms are generally very small, they are the most prosperous and contented population in the kingdom. Leases were common in this county at the close of the last century, but the terms were short—twenty-one years and one life. Some had leases for thirty-one years or three lives, and there were some perpetuities. Land was then so valuable that when a small estate came into the market—large estates hardly ever did— they brought from twenty-five to thirty years' purchase. The large tracts of church land, which are now among the richest and most desirable in the country, presented at the close of the last century, a melancholy contrast to the farms that surrounded them. The reason is given by Sir Charles Coote. It is most instructive and suggestive at the present time. He says, 'It is very discouraging for a wealthy farmer to have anything to do with church lands, as his improvements cannot even be secured to him during his own life, or the life of his landlord, but he may at any time be deprived of the fruits of his industry, by the incumbent changing his living, as his interest then terminates.' This evil was remedied first by making the leases renewable, on the payment of fines, and, in our own time, an act was passed enabling the tenants to convert their leaseholds into perpetuities. The consequence is, that the church lands now present some of the finest features in the social landscape, occupied by a class of resident gentry, an essential link, in any well-organised society, between the people and the great proprietors. The Board of Trinity College felt so strongly the necessity of giving fixed tenures, if permanent improvements were to be effected on their estates, that, without waiting for a general measure of land reform, they obtained, in 1861, a private act of parliament giving them power to grant leases for ninety-nine years. 'The legislature,' says Dr. Hancock, 'thus gave partial effect in the case of one institution to the recommendation which the Land Occupation Commissioners intended to apply to all estates in the hands of public boards in Ireland.'

Armagh was always free from middlemen. The landlord got what Sir Charles Coote calls a rack rent from the occupying tenant, and it was his interest to divide rather than consolidate farms, because the linen trade enabled the small holder to give a high rent, while the custom of tenant-right furnished an unfailing security for its payment.

The country, when seen from an elevation, is one continuous patchwork of corn, potatoes, clover, and other artificial grasses. Wonders are wrought in the way of productiveness by rotation of crops and house-feeding.

Cattle are not only fattened much more rapidly than on the richest grazing land, but large quantities of the best manure are produced by the practice of house-feeding. The more northern portions of the county, bordering on Down and Lough Neagh, and along the banks of the rivers Bann and Blackwater, are naturally rich, and have been improved to the highest degree by ages of skilful cultivation. But other parts, particularly the barony of Fews, embracing the high lands stretching to the Newry mountains, and bordering on the County Monaghan, were, about the close of the last century, nearly all covered with heather, and absolutely waste. Sir Charles Coote remarked, in 1804, that it had been then undergoing reclamation. Within the last fifteen years the land had doubled in value, and was set at the average rate of 16s. an acre. Mr. Tickell, referring to this county, remarked that the Scotch and English settlers chiefly occupied the lowland districts, and that the natives retired to this poor region, retaining their old language and habits; and he was occasionally obliged to swear interpreters where witnesses or parties came from the Fews, which were 'very wild, and very unlike other parts of the county of Armagh.'

Now let us see what the industry of the people has done in that wild district. The farms are very small, say from three to ten English acres. They have been so well drained, cleared, sub-soiled, and manured, that the occupier is able to support on one acre as many cattle as on three acres when grazed; while affording profitable employment to the women and children. Great labour has been bestowed in taking down crooked and broad fences. Every foot of ground is cultivated with the greatest care, and in the mountain districts, patches of land among rocks, inaccessible to horses, are tilled by the hand. In many cases in the less exposed districts, two crops in the year are obtained from the same ground, viz., winter tares followed by turnips or cabbages, and rape followed by tares, potatoes, turnips, or cabbages.

These crops are succeeded by grain or flax the next year, with which clover is sown for mowing and stall-feeding, yielding two or three cuttings. The green crops are so timed as to give a full supply for house-feeding throughout the year. Nothing is neglected by those skilful and thrifty farmers; the county is famous for orchards, and when I was in the city of Armagh, last autumn, I saw in the market square almost as many loads of apples as of potatoes.

The connection of large grazing farms with pauperism, as cause and effect, has not received sufficient attention from the friends of social progress. I resolved last year to test this matter by a comparison. We have at present no check upon the legally enforced depopulation of this country except the *interest* of the landlords, or what they imagine to be their interest. It is well that the question should be determined whether it is really for the benefit of the owners of the land that they should clear it of Christians and occupy it with cattle—in other words, whether Christians or cattle will pay more rent and taxes. I omit all higher considerations, because some of the most philanthropic and enlightened defenders of the present land system have defended it on this low ground. In order to make the test complete and unexceptionable, I have selected a comparatively poor district for tillage, and one of the richest I could find for grazing, giving all possible natural advantages to Scullyism. But the test would not be fair unless the occupiers of the poorer land had a tolerably secure tenure so long as they paid the highest rent that a reasonable agent could impose. I thought also that possible objections would be obviated if the tenantry were destitute of 'the fostering care of a resident landlord.' Therefore, instead of selecting the tenants of Lord Downshire, or Lord Roden, or Lord Dufferin, I have fixed upon the tenants of Lord Kilmorey, because he and the producers of the rents which he enjoys have never seen one another in the flesh, and they have never received one word of encouragement or instruction from him in the whole course of their lives. Accordingly, with the Union of Kilkeel, which comprises the Mourne district, I have compared the Union of Trim, which comprises some of the richest grazing land in Ireland. Travellers have noted that population always grows thick on rich lands, while it is sparse on poor lands. No one requires to be told the reason of this.

The Unions of Kilkeel and Trim have populations very nearly equal—viz., Kilkeel, 22,614; Trim, 22,918. The total arable land in Kilkeel is 50,000 statute acres, giving $2\frac{1}{3}$ acres on an average for each person, and 14 acres for each holding. Trim contains 119,519 statute acres, giving 5 acres to each person, and 42 to each holding.

In Mourne the area of land under crops is 20,904 acres (nearly half), giving one acre of tillage to each inhabitant, and 6 acres to each holding of 14 acres. In Trim the area under crops is 38,868 acres, giving 2 acres for each inhabitant, and 14 for each holding of 42 acres.

The significance of these figures is shown by the Government valuation in 1867. The valuation of Mourne Union is 40,668*l.*, the average for each person being 2*l.* and for each holding 11*l.* The valuation of Trim is 109,068*l.*, allowing 5*l.* for each person and 38*l.* for each holding. In other words, the capability of the land of Trim to support population is as five to two when compared with Mourne; but whereas in Mourne $2\frac{1}{3}$ acres support one person, in Trim it takes 5 acres to support one person—about double the quantity. As the value of the land in Meath is more than double what it is in Mourne, each acre in Meath ought to maintain its man. That is, if Meath were cultivated like Down, its population ought to be *five times as large as it is!*

But this is not the whole case. The Mourne population may be too large. With so many families crowded on such a small tract of poor land, the Union must be overwhelmed with pauperism. If so, the case for tenant-right and tillage would fall to the ground, and Scullyism would be triumphant. Let us see, then, how stands this essential fact. The number of paupers in the workhouse and receiving outdoor relief in the Union of Trim, in 1866, was 2,474. This large amount of pauperism is not peculiar to Trim. It belongs to other Unions of this rich grazing district, which so fully realises the late Lord Carlisle's ideal of Irish prosperity. Navan Union has 3,820 paupers, and Kells has 1,306. Now, the population of Trim and Mourne being nearly the same, and Trim being twice as rich as Mourne, and not half as thickly peopled, it follows that Mourne ought to have at least four times as many paupers as Trim—that is, it ought to have 9,896. But it actually has only 521 persons receiving relief in and out of the workhouse !

Consequently, Scullyism and grazing produce nearly twenty times the amount of poverty and misery produced by tenant-right and tillage.

I have not overlooked the difference of race and religion. On the contrary, they were uppermost in my mind when rambling among the nice, clean, comfortable, orderly homesteads of Mourne, reminding me strongly of Forth and Bargy in the county Wexford. I said to the owner and driver of my car, who is a Roman Catholic, ' Do the Roman Catholics here keep their houses and farms in as nice order as the Presbyterians?' He answered, ' Why should they not? Are they not the same flesh and blood?'

According to the census of 1861, the Roman Catholics greatly outnumber the Protestants in this Union. The exact figures are :—

Total population of Mourne Union . . .	22,614
Protestants of all denominations	8,080
Roman Catholics	14,534

The result of this comparison may perhaps make a better impression on the reader's mind if cast in the form of tables, as given on succeeding page.

TENANT-RIGHT AND TILLAGE.

Names of Unions	Population in 1861	No. of Holdings in 1864	Total Area	Area under Crops, 1864	Valuation in 1867	No. in Work-house and re-ceiving Out-door Relief, 1866	Protestants of all denominations	Roman Catholics
			Stat. Acres	Stat. Acres	£			
KILKEEL . .	22,614	3,540	50,000	20,904	40,668	521	8,080	14,534
Average for each person . .	...	...	2½	1	2	...	...	...
Average for each holding	...	...	14	6	11	...	...	...

LARGE FARMS AND GRAZING.

TRIM . . .	22,918	2,816	119,519	38,867	109,068	2,474	1,700	21,218
Average for each person . .	...	...	5	2	5	...	...	...
Average for each holding . .	...	...	42	14	38	...	...	...

In Kilkeel Union there were 4,012 acres of flax in 1864, which at 20*l.* an acre would produce 80,000*l.*, considerably more than the rental of the entire district. Trim, in that year, produced only 78 acres of flax.

What everyone wants to know now is this—whether any measure can be devised that will satisfy the cultivators of the soil without wronging the landlords, or militating against the interests of the state. A measure that will not satisfy the tenants and put an end to their discontent, would be manifestly useless. It would be but adding to the numerous legislative abortions that have gone before it. A man engaged in such enquiries as this, is to ascertain what will satisfy the people. It is for the legislature to determine whether it can be rightly or safely granted. I have, there-fore, directed my attention to this point in particular, and I have ascertained beyond question, from the best possible sources of information, that nothing will satisfy the people of this country but what they do not hesitate to name with the most determined emphasis—'Fixity of Tenure.' Whether they are Protestants or Catholics, Orangemen or

A A

Liberals, Presbyterians or Churchmen, this is their unanimous demand, the cry in which they all join to a man. Every case in which tenant-right is disregarded, or in which, while admitted nominally, an attempt is made to evade it, or to fritter it away, excites the bitterest feeling, in which the whole community sympathises.

They deny, however, that the existing tenant-right is a sufficient security :—

Because it depends on the option of the landlord, and cannot be enforced by law.

Because even the best disposed landlord may be influenced to alter his policy by the advice of an agent, by the influence of his family, or by the state of his finances.

Because a good landlord, who knows the tenants and cares for them, may be succeeded by a son who is a 'fast young man,' addicted to the turf and overwhelmed in debt, while the estate gets into the hands of usurers.

Because in such a case the law affords no protection to the property of the tenant, which his family may have been accumulating on the land since the first of them came over from England or Scotland, and settled around their commander, after helping by their swords to conquer the country, and preserve it to the crown of England.

Because it is not in human nature to avoid encroaching on the rights and property of others, if it can be done at will—done legally, and done under the pretext that it is necessary for 'improvement,' and will be a benefit even to those who are despoiled.

Because the custom is no protection to a man's political rights as a British subject. No tenant farmer can vote against his landlord in obedience to his conscience without the risk of ruining his family. The greater his interest in the land, the larger his investments, the heavier his stake; the greater his accumulations in his bank—the farm—the greater will be his dependence, the more complete his political bondage. He has the more to lose. Therefore, if a Conservative, he must vote for a Radical or a Catholic, who would pull down the Church Establishment; or if a Catholic, he must vote for a 'No-popery' candidate, who ignores tenant-right, and against a Liberal statesman, whose life has been devoted to the interests of the country.

It appears to me that the difficulty of settling this question is much aggravated by the importation of opinions from the United States hostile to the aristocracy ; and as this source of discontent and distrust is likely to increase every year, the sooner the settlement is effected the better. What is the use of scolding and reviling the tenant's advocates? Will that weaken one iota the tremendous force of social discontent—the bitter sense of legal injustice, with which the legislature must deal ? And will the legislature deal with it more effectually by shutting its eyes to facts?

CHAPTER XXI.

FARNEY—MR. TRENCH'S 'REALITIES.'

When the six Ulster counties were confiscated, and the natives were all deprived of their rights in the soil, the people of the county Cavan resolved to appeal for justice to the English courts in Dublin. The Crown was defended by Sir John Davis. He argued that the Irish could have no legal rights, no property in the land, because they did not enclose it with fences, or plant orchards. True, they had boundary marks for their tillage ground; but they followed the Eastern custom in not building ditches or walls around their farms. They did not plant orchards, because they had too many trees already that grew without planting. The woods were common property, and the apples, if they had any, would be common property too, like the nuts and the acorns.

The Irish were obliged to submit to the terms imposed by the conquerors, glad in their destitution to be permitted to occupy their own lands as tenants at will. The English undertakers, as we have seen, were bound to deal differently with the English settlers; but their obligations resolved themselves into promises of freeholds and leases which were seldom granted, so that many persons threw up their farms in despair, and returned to their own country.

In the border county of Monaghan, we have a good illustration of the manner in which the natives struggled to live under their new masters. The successors of some of those masters have in modern times taken a strange fancy to the study of Irish antiquities. Among these is Evelyn P.

Shirley, Esq., who has published ' Some Account of the Territory or Dominion of Farney.' The account is interesting, and, taken in connection with the sequel given to the public by his agent, Mr. W. Steuart Trench, it furnishes an instructive chapter in the history of the land war. The whole barony of Farney was granted by Queen Elizabeth to Walter Earl of Essex in the year 1576, in reward for the massacres already recorded. It was then an almost unenclosed plain, consisting chiefly of coarse pasturage, interspersed with low alder-scrub. When the primitive woods were cut down for fuel, charcoal, or other purposes, the stumps remained in the ground, and from these fresh shoots sprang up thickly. The clearing out of these stumps was difficult and laborious; but it had to be done before anything, but food for goats, could be got out of the land. This was ' the M'Mahons' country,' and the tribe was not wholly subdued till 1606, when the power of the Ulster chiefs was finally broken. The lord deputy, the chancellor, and the lord chief justice passed through Farney on their way to hold assizes for the first time in Derry and Donegal. They were protected by a guard of ' seven score foot, and fifty or three score horse, which,' wrote Sir John Davis, ' is an argument of a good time and a confident deputy; for in former times (when the state enjoyed the best peace and security) no lord deputy did ever venture himself into those parts, without an army of 800 or 1000 men.' At this time Lord Essex had leased the barony of Farney to Evor M'Mahon for a yearly rent of 250*l.* payable in Dublin. After fourteen years the same territory was let to Brian M'Mahon for 1,500*l.* In the year 1636, the property yielded a yearly rent of 2022*l.* 18*s.* 4*d.* paid by thirty-eight tenants. A map then taken gives the several townlands and denominations nearly as they are at present. Robert Earl of Essex, dying in 1646, his estates devolved on his sisters, Lady Frances and Lady Dorothy Devereux, the former of whom married Sir W. Seymour, afterwards Marquis of Hertfort, and the latter Sir Henry Shirley, Bart., ancestor of the present proprietor

of half the barony. Ultimately the other half became the
property of the Marquis of Bath.   At the division in 1690,
each moiety was valued at 1313*l.* 14*s.* 4½*d.*   Gradually as
the lands were reclaimed by the tenants, the rental rose.   In
1769 the Bath estate produced 3,000*l.*, and the Shirley
estate 5,000*l.*   The total of 8,000*l.* per annum, from this
once wild and barren tract, was paid by middlemen.   The
natives had not been rooted out, and during the eighteenth
century these sub-tenants multiplied rapidly.   According to
the census in 1841 the population of the barony exceeded
44,000 souls, and they contributed by their industry, to the
two absentee proprietors, the enormous annual revenue of
40,000*l.*, towards the production of which it does not appear
that either of them, or any person for them, ever invested a
shilling.

   Mr. S. Trench was amazed to find ' more than one human
being for every Irish acre of land in the barony, and nearly
one human being for every 1*l.* valuation per annum of the
land.'   The two estates join in the town of Carrickmacross.
When Mr. Trench arrived there, March 30, 1843, to commence his duties as Mr. Shirley's agent, he learned that the
sudden death of the late agent in the court-house of Monaghan had been celebrated that night by fires on almost
every hill on the estate, ' and over a district of upwards of
20,000 acres there was scarcely a mile without a bonfire
blazing in manifestation of joy at his decease.'   Mr. Trench
says, the tenants considered themselves ground down to the
last point by the late agent. As he relates the circumstances,
the people would seem to be a very savage race ; and he
gives other more startling illustrations to the same effect as
he proceeds.   But here, as elsewhere, he does not state all
the facts, while those he does state are most artistically
dressed up for sensational effect, Mr. Trench himself being
always the hero, always acting magnificently, appearing at
the right place and at the right moment to prevent some
tremendous calamity, otherwise inevitable, and by some
mysterious personal influence subduing lawless masses, so

that by a sudden impulse, their murderous rage is converted into admiration, if not adoration. Like the hearers of Herod or of St. Paul, when he flung the viper off his hand, they are ready to cry out, ' He is a god, and not a man.' Of course he, as a Christian gentleman, was always ' greatly shocked,' when these poor wretches offered him petitions 'on their knees. Still he relates every case of the kind with extraordinary unction, and with a picturesqueness of situation and detail so stagey that it should make Mr. Boucicault's mouth water, and excite the envy of Miss Braddon. Not even she can exceed the author of ' Realities of Irish Life,' in prolonging painful suspense, in piling up the agony, in accumulating horrors, in throwing strong lights on one side of the picture and casting deep shade on the other.

It is with the greatest reluctance that I thus allude to the work of Mr. Trench. I do so from a sense of duty, because I believe it is one of the most misleading books on Ireland published for many years. It has made false impressions on the public mind in England, which will seriously interfere with a proper settlement of the land question. The mischief would not be so great if the author did not take so much pains to represent his stories as realities ' essentially characteristic of the country.' It is very difficult to account for the exaggeration and embellishment in which he has permitted himself to indulge, with so many professions of conscientious regard for truth. They must have arisen from the habit of reciting the adventures to his friends during a quarter of a century, naturally laying stress on the most sensational passages, while the facts less in keeping with startling effects dropped out of his memory. Very few of the actors in the scenes he describes now survive. Those who do, and who might have a more accurate memory, are either so lauded that it would be ungrateful of them to contradict—or so artfully discredited as ' virulent ' and base that people would not be likely to believe them if their recollections were different. There is one peculiarity about Mr. Trench's dialogues. There were never any witnesses

present. He always took the wild Irishman, on whom he
operated so magically, into his private office ; or into a private
room in the house of the ' subject ; ' or into a cell alone, if
secrets were to be extracted from a Ribbonman in gaol.
Even conversations with the gentler sex, who knelt before
him as if he were a bishop, were not permitted to reach the
ear of his chief clerk. On some matters, however, others
have spoken since his book appeared. He is very precise
about the trial for an agrarian murder in Monaghan, giving
details from his own actual observation. Mr. Butt, Q.C., who
was engaged in the case, has published a letter, stating that
Mr. Trench was quite mistaken in his account. It seems
strange that he did not refresh his memory by looking at a
report of the trial in some newspaper file.

Mr. Trench ' adds his testimony to the fact that Ireland
is not altogether unmanageable,' that ' justice fully and
firmly administered is always appreciated in the end.' And
at the conclusion of his volume he says :—

' We can scarcely shut our eyes to the fact that the circumstances and feelings which have led to the terrible
crime of murder in Ireland, are usually very different from
those which have led to murder elsewhere. The reader of
the English newspaper is shocked at the list of children
murdered by professional assassins, of wives murdered by
their husbands, of men murdered for their gold. In Ireland
that dreadful crime may almost invariably be traced to a
wild feeling of revenge for the national wrongs, to which so
many of her sons believe that she has been subjected for
centuries.'

There is a mistake here. No murders are committed in
Ireland for ' national wrongs.' The author has gathered together, as in a chamber of horrors, all the cases of assassination that occurred during the years of distress, provoked by
the extensive *evictions* which succeeded the *famine*, and by the
infliction of great hardships on tenants who, in consequence of
that dreadful calamity, had fallen into arrears. People who
had been industrious, peaceable, and well-conducted were thus

driven to desperation; and hence the young men formed
lawless combinations and committed atrocious murders.
But every one of these murders was agrarian, not national.
They were committed in the prosecution of *a war*, not
against the Government, but against the landlords and their
agents and instruments. It was a war *pro aris et focis*, waged
against local tyrants, and waged in the only way possible to
the belligerents who fought for home and family. Mr.
Trench always paints the people who sympathise with their
champions as naturally wild, lawless, and savage. If he
happens to be in good humour with them, he makes them
ridiculous. His son, Mr. Townsend Trench, who did the illustrations for the work, pictures the peasantry as gorillas, always
flourishing shillelaghs, and grinning horribly. With rare
exceptions, they appear as an inferior race, while the ruling
class, and the Trenches in particular, appear throughout
the book as demigods, 'lords of the creation,' formed by
nature to be the masters and guides and managers of such a
silly, helpless people. Nowhere is any censure pronounced
upon a landlord, or an agent, with one exception, and this
was the immediate predecessor of Mr. Trench at Kenmare.
To his gross neglect in allowing God to send so many human
beings into the world, he ascribes the chaos of misery and
pauperism, which he—a heaven-born agent—had to reduce to
order and beauty. But there were other causes of the 'poetic
turbulence' which he so gloriously quelled, that he might
have brought to light, had he thought proper, for the information of English readers. He might have shown—for
the evidence was before him in the report of the Devon
Commission—with what hard toil and constant self-denial,
amidst what domestic privations and difficulties, Mr.
Shirley's tenants struggled to scrape up for him his 20,000*l.*
a year, and how bitterly they must have felt when the landlord sent an order to add one-third to their rack-rent. I
will supply Mr. Trench's lack of service, and quote the
evidence of one of those honest and worthy men, given
before the Devon Commissioners.

Peter Mohun, farmer, a tenant on the Shirley estate, gave the following evidence :—

'What family have you?—I am married, and have two daughters, and my wife, and a servant boy.

'What rent do you pay?—Some time ago I paid 3*l.*19*s.*11*d.* I was doing well at that time; and then my rent was raised to 5*l.* 19*s.* 9*d.*, and sometimes 6*l.*, and one year 5*l.* 19*s.* 6*d.*

'How do you account for the difference?—I do not know; perhaps by the bog rent. We had the bog free before, and we were doing well; and then we were cut down from the bog, and we were raised from 3*l.* 19*s.* 11*d.* to 6*l.* We are beaten down now quite.

'What does the county-cess come to?—Sometimes we pay 1*s.* 6½*d.* an acre, and oftener 1*s.* 7½*d.*, the half-year.

'Have you paid your rent pretty punctually?—Yes, I have done my best so far to pay the rent.

'How much do you owe now?—I believe I shall pay the rent directly after May; I am clear till May. I cannot pay it till harvest comes round.

'How do you get the money to pay the rent? When I had my land cheap, and myself a youth, I was a good workman, and did work by the loom, and I would be mowing in the summer season, and earn a good deal, and make a little store for me, which has stood by me. I buy some oats and make meal of it, and I make money in that way. It was not by my land I was paying my rent, but from other sources.

'How much wheat have you now?—Half an acre, rather above.

'How much oats have you?—Half a rood.

'How much potato land shall you have?—Three and a half roods besides the garden.

'Have you any clover?—Very near a rood of clover.

'What is the smallest quantity of land that you think a man who has no other means of support can subsist and pay rent upon?—I was paying rent well myself when I had three acres, when I was paying 3*l.* 19*s.* 11*d.*

'You weave a little?—Yes, but very little; but there was a good price for the barrel of wheat, and for pigs, and so I made a little store. But as for any man to support himself out of a small farm, at the high price of land, and the price of labour that is going, it is impossible.

'What is the smallest farm upon which a man can support himself at the present rate of rent, taking a man with five or six children?—That is a hard question.

'Supposing a man to pay 35s. an acre, and to have two acres, and to be obliged to live out of the farm, do you think he could do it and pay rent?—He could not; his land must be very good. Unless he lived near a town, and had cheap land, it would be impossible. But a man with five acres, at a moderate rent, he could support his family upon it.

'What should you earn at weaving?—I only weave for my own family. I weave my own shirt.

'Do your family ever spin any wool and weave it?—Yes.

'Do you live upon the Shirley estate?—Yes.

'How much bog do you require to keep your house in fuel?—Half a rood, if it was good; but it is bad bog ground, red mossy turf, white and light; it requires more than the black turf.

'What do you pay for half a rood of turf?—It is 13s. 4d. for a rood—that is, 6s. 8d. for half a rood. There is 4s. 6d. paid for bad bog.

'Do you pay anything for the ticket of leave to cut?— Yes, I do; I have not a ticket unless I pay 6d. for it.

'That is over and above the 4s. 6d.?—Yes.

'Did you ever pay more than 6s. 8d. for the bog in the late agent's time?—He took the good bog off us; we were paying 6s. 8d. for it. They left us to the bad bog, and we do not pay so high for that.

'Was the good bog dearer or cheaper than the bad bog at 4s. 6d.?—Half a rood of the good bog was worth half an acre or an acre of the other. The bad bog smokes so we have often to leave the house: we cannot stay in it unless there is a good draught in the chimney.'

The Rev. Thomas Smollan, P.P., has published a letter to the Earl of Dunraven, a Catholic Peer, to whom Mr. Trench has dedicated his book. In this letter the parish priest of Farney says:—

'In pages 63 and 64 Mr. Trench tells his readers that on the very night the news of the late agent's sudden death, in the county courthouse of Monaghan, reached Carrickmacross, " fires blazed on almost every hill on the Shirley estate, and over a district of more than 20,000 acres there was scarcely a mile without a bonfire blazing in manifestation of joy at his decease." This paragraph, my lord, taken by itself and unexplained in any way, would at once imply that the people were inhuman, almost savages, whom Mr. Trench was sent to tame—that they were insensible to the agent's sudden death, a death so sudden that it would make an enemy almost relent. Mr. Trench assigns no cause for this strange proceeding except what we read in page 64, and what he learned from the chief clerk, viz., " that the people were much excited, that they were ground down to the last point by the late agent, and they were threatening to rise in rebellion against him," &c. One would think that Mr. Trench having learned so much on such authority, would have set to work to try and find out the cause of the discontent and apply a remedy. He does not say in his book that he did so, but seems still unable to understand this to him incomprehensible proceeding. However, I am of opinion that Mr. Trench knew the whole of it, if not then at all events before " The Realities " saw the light, for in a speech of his, when Lord Bath visited Farney (page 383), he said, " A dog could not bark on the estate without it coming to his knowledge." And therefore I say that a man so inquisitive as to find out the barking of a dog on the Bath estate, who had so many sources of information close at hand, could not have been long without knowing the causes of the " excitement, threatened rebellion, bonfires, &c., on the Shirley estate," if he had only wished for the information. Either he knew the cause of all this when he wrote

his book, or he did not. If he did, I say he was bound in
fair play to tell it to the public; if he did not know it his
self-laudation in his speech goes for nought. But, my lord,
with your permission, I will inform your lordship, Mr.
Trench, and the public, as to some of the causes of so
remarkable an occurrence, which could not pass unobserved
by Mr. Trench. At the memorable election of 1826, Evelyn
John Shirley, Esq., and Colonel Leslie, father of the present
M.P., contested the county of Monaghan, and the former
brought all his influence to bear on his tenants to vote for
himself (Shirley) and Leslie, who coalesced against the late
Lord Rossmore. The electors said " they would give one
vote for their landlord, and the other they would give for
their religion and their country ; " the consequence was,
Shirley and Westenra were returned, and Leslie was beaten.
Up to this time Mr. Shirley was a good landlord, and
admitted tenant-right to the fullest extent on the property,
but after that election he never showed the same friendly
feelings towards the people. Soon after the election Mr.
Humphrey Evatt, the agent, died, and was succeeded in the
agency by Mr. Sandy Mitchell, who very soon set about
surveying and revaluing the estate, of course at the instance
of his master, Evelyn John Shirley, Esq. He performed
the work of revaluation, &c., and the result was that the
rents were increased by one-third and in some cases more.
The bog, too, which up to this time was free to the tenants,
was taken from them and doled out to them in small patches
of from twenty-five to forty perches each, at from 4*l.* to 8*l.*
per acre. At the instance of the then parish priest, President
Reilly, Mr. Shirley gave 5*l.* per year to a few schools on his
property, without interfering in any way with the religious
principles of the Catholics attending these schools ; but the
then agent insisted on having the authorised version of the
Bible, without note or comment, read in those schools by
the Catholic children. The bishop, the Most Rev. Dr.
Kernan, could not tolerate such a barefaced attempt at
proselytism, and insisted on the children being withdrawn

from the schools. For obeying their bishop in this, the Catholic parents were treated most unsparingly. I have before me just now a most remarkable instance of the length to which this gentleman carried his proselytising propensities, which I will mention. In the vestry, or sacristy, attached to Corduff Chapel, was a school taught by a man named Rush, altogether independent of the schools aided by Mr. Shirley, and by largely subsidising the teacher, the then agent actually introduced his proselytism into that school too. The priests and people tried legal means to get rid of the teacher, but without success, and in the end the people came by night and knocked down the sacristy, so that in the morning when the teacher came he had no house to shelter him. The Catholics were then without a school, and in order to provide the means of education for them the Rev. F. Keone, administrator, under the Most Rev. Dr. Kernan, applied for aid to the Commissioners of National Education, and obtained it; but where was he to procure building materials? The then agent, in his zeal for " converting " Catholics, having issued an order forbidding the supplying of them from any part of the Shirley estate, which extends over an area of fifteen miles by ten, Father Keone went on the next Sunday to the neighbouring chapels outside the Shirley estate, told his grievances, and on the next day the people came with their horses and carts and left sand, lime, and stones in sufficient quantities to build the house inside the chapel-yard. The priest and people thought it necessary to " thatch " their old chapel, and, though strange it may seem, the agent actually served an ejectment process on the father of the two boys who assisted the priest to make the collection at the chapel door for so absolutely necessary a work. I may add, this man owed no rent. Lastly, the then agent was in the habit of arranging matrimonial alliances, pointing out this girl as a suitable match for that boy, and the boy must marry the girl or give up his farm. These facts being true, my lord, and more which I might state, but that I have trespassed too much already on your lordship's time, I ask you, my Lord Dunraven—I ask any impartial man, Irishman or Englishman—for whom Mr. Trench wrote his " book," is it strange or wonderful that the Catholic people, so treated, would rejoice—would have bonfires on the hill tops at their deliverance from such conduct? I flatter myself that you, my lord—that the learned reading public—that the English people would sympathise with any people so treated for conscience' sake ; and having pronounced the sentence of condemnation against Mr. Trench for not having noticed these facts, that you will direct your name to be erased from the " book." I have the honour to remain, my lord, with the most profound respect, your lordship's faithful servant.'

' Thomas Smollan, P.P.

' Clones, Feb. 15, 1869.'

The electors of Monaghan, in their simplicity, thought they were fairly exercising the rights conferred by the constitution when they gave one vote for the landlord, and one for their religion and their country, thus securing the return of one Liberal. But Mr. Shirley soon taught them that the blessings of our glorious constitution belong not to the tenant, but to the landlord ; and so he punished their mistake by adding one-third to their rent, and depriving them of proper fuel. Not content with this, he carried the war into their chapels and schools, and punished them for their religion. These facts may help to explain the scenes which Mr. Trench describes so poetically.

The persecuting agent died suddenly in the court-house. The landlord and a new agent, Mr. Trench, arrived at Carrickmacross ; and the tenants presented a petition, imploring him to remove the new and intolerable burden that had been put on their shoulders. They were told to come back for an answer on the following Monday :—

' " Monday ! Monday ! " was shouted on all sides. The most frenzied excitement ensued. Hats were thrown in the air, sticks were flourished on all sides, and the men actually

danced with wild delight. After a little time, however, the
crowd cleared away, and the news flew like wildfire over the
town and country, that the whole tenantry were told to
come in on Monday next, that they might know the amount
of the reduction to be granted, and have all their grievances
removed!'

Mr. Shirley quickly repented having given the invitation,
and sent out a circular countermanding it, and requesting
the tenants to stay at home. On Monday, however, a vast
excited mass assembled to hear his *ultimatum*, which was
announced by the new agent. 'He would not reduce their
rents. They might give up their lands if they pleased; but
they had little or no cause of complaint.' They insisted on
his mounting a chair and making a speech. He softened
the message as well as he could. When he had done there
was a dead silence. In describing what follows Mr. Trench
surpasses the wildest romancers in piling up the agony. I
copy the description that the reader may see the difference
between romance and history.

'There was a dead silence when I stopped speaking. It
was broken by a stentorian voice.

'" Then you won't reduce our rents?"

'" I have already given you Mr. Shirley's answer upon
that point," said I. "Stranger as I am, it is impossible for me
to form any opinion as to whether they are too high or not."

'"*Down on your knees, boys!*" shouted the same voice; "we
will ask him once more upon our knees!" and to my horror
and amazement the vast crowd, almost all at least who were
in my immediate vicinity, dropped suddenly on their knees,
and another dead silence ensued.

'It was a dreadful spectacle. Their hats were on their
heads, and their sticks in their hands, some leaning upon
them as they knelt, others balancing and grasping them.
It was fearful to see the attitude of supplication, due only
to a higher power, thus mingled with a wild defiance.

'" *We ask you upon our knees, for God's sake, to get us a
reduction of our rents!*" again the same voice cried aloud.

'I was greatly shocked. I instantly got down off the chair. I entreated them to rise. I told them that I was distressed beyond measure, but that I had given them the only message I was authorised to give; and quite overcome by such a scene, I endeavoured to move again across the crowded space from the office, in order to enter the house, and report proceedings to Mr. Shirley, intending to request that he would himself appear and address his excited tenantry.

' The moment I moved towards the door, the vast crowd leaped again to their feet; I was instantly surrounded, hustled, and prevented from getting near it. I bore this good-humouredly, and the door being quite close to me, I had no doubt they would ultimately let me in. But whilst this scene was going on, a shout was raised by those who were at a distance up the road leading to the town, and who had not heard what had been said. " Bring him up— bring him up, and let us see him ! " In a moment I was seized, and though I resisted to my utmost, I was dragged up the narrow road which led from Shirley House to the town. I was kicked and beaten, and pushed and bruised, my hat knocked off, and my clothes torn; and in this state I was dragged into the main street of Carrickmacross.

' Here a scene of the wildest excitement took place, some cried one thing—some another. I was beaten again, my clothes torn off my back, and sticks whirled over my head. Four or five policemen met me as I was being dragged along, but they might as well have attempted to stop the rushing of an Atlantic wave, as to stem the crowd that had assembled around me; *and they only looked on and let me pass.*'

If the sub-inspector, who was present, and his men acted in this manner, I venture to say it is the only instance in the whole history of the force in which the Royal Irish constabulary were guilty of such a cowardly neglect of duty. However, not only the police, but the best part of the crowd deserted this strange gentleman, and he was ' left in the hands of the vilest and most furious of the mob.'

Where was Mr. Shirley? Where were the clergy and the respectable inhabitants of the town? The mob dragged him along towards Loughfea Castle—a mile and a half—whither they heard Mr. Shirley had fled, still beating, kicking, and strangling their victim, without any object; for how could they serve their cause by killing an agent who had never injured them? And how easy it was to kill him if they wished! But here comes the climax; he asked the murderous multitude to let him stop a few moments to breathe—he then proceeds: 'I shall never forget that moment. I was then about a mile from the town on the broad and open road leading to Loughfea Castle. I turned and looked around me, thinking my last hour was come, and anxious to see if there was one kind face, one countenance, I had ever seen before, who could at least tell my friends how I had died. But I looked in vain. The hills were crowded with people. The long line of road was one mass of human beings, whilst those immediately around me, mad with excitement, seemed only to thirst for my blood.

'Having got a few moments' breathing-time, and seeing all appeal to be vain, I turned again on my way, determined, however, to hold out to the last, as I felt that to fall or to faint must be certain death. Just then I became conscious of an able hand and a stout heart beside me, and I heard a whisper in my ear: "They are determined to have your blood, but hold up, they shall have mine first." The speaker grasped my arm firmly under his own, and walked on steadily by my side.

'By this time I was *completely naked with the exception of my trousers*. My coat, even my shirt, had been torn off, and I walked on, still beaten and ill-treated, like a man to execution; my head bare, and *without any clothes from my waist upwards*. To increase the misery of my situation, I found that my friend had been beaten and dragged away in spite of himself, and again I was left alone in the hands of those merciless men. I felt also I could now go no further, and that a last effort must be made before my senses left me from exhaustion. Stopping therefore once more, I asked to be led towards a high bank at the roadside, and leaning against this I turned and faced those whom I now believed would soon become my murderers.

' " I can go no further," said I; " what have you brought me here for? What do you want me to do? " Again the same voice which I had first heard at the office, though I could not identify the speaker from the shouting and confusion around me, cried aloud, " We want a reduction of our rents, will you promise to get us that? "

' There are times of instant danger, when it is said that the whole of a man's past life rushes before him in the space of a single moment. If ever there be such a time, this was such to me. I stood there, exhausted, without one friendly face on which to rest, and surrounded by *the worst of ten thousand men who seemed determined to have a victim.* I knew and felt all this. So I said very quietly, as a last effort to save my life, and hoping they would name something I could promise to ask,

' " And what reduction will you be content with? "

' Again the same voice replied,

' " We will never pay more than one-half our present rents."

' " Then," said I, " there ends the matter. *I never will promise that.*"

' There was a pause, and a dead silence. I stood *naked and bareheaded before them.* They stood opposite to me, with their sticks clenched in their hands, ready to strike. I looked at them, and they at me. They hesitated; *no one would strike me first.* I saw that they wavered, and instinctively, in a moment I *felt* that I had won. This sudden revulsion of feeling—though I was still externally motionless—sent the blood throbbing to my temples with a rush that became almost oppressive. But the strange pause continued—when at length a shout was raised from the old stentorian voice again, " Stand off, boys—for your lives !

no one shall harm him—he is a good man after all!', and in a moment I was surrounded by a new set of faces, who dashed furiously towards me. They raised me on their shoulders, swept my old enemies away from me, procured me some water to drink, and carried me, now completely overcome, exhausted, and almost fainting, into the demesne of Loughfea.

' Here again these suddenly converted friends desired me to get up on a chair, and speak to the crowd now assembled before the castle. I did so. A reaction for the moment had taken place within me, and I felt some return of strength.

'I told the people I had never injured them. That it was a shame, and a disgrace of which I had not believed any Irishman to be capable, to treat a stranger as they had dealt with me that day. That in my own country I could have as many to fight for me as were now against me, and in short I abused them right heartily and soundly. They bore it without a murmur. My new friends cheered me vociferously, and I was carried, now quite unable to walk, into the Castle of Loughfea. Mr. Shirley's architect here appeared upon the scene, and perceiving that the people were much exasperated at not finding Mr. Shirley at the castle, and that some of the most violent were disposed in consequence to make a fresh attack upon me as I was being carried exhausted inside the gates, he promised to speak to Mr. Shirley in their favour, and in some degree calmed their feelings. The excitement was past. Mr. Shirley had not been there, and the people at last quietly dispersed.

' In the evening I was conveyed in a covered carriage to Carrickmacross, blackened with bruises, stiff and sore, and scarcely able to stand—musing over the strange transactions which had happened that day—and wrapped in a country-man's frieze coat which had been borrowed to cover *my nakedness.*' *

When the reader recovers his breath after this, I will ask

* Realities of Irish Life, chap. v.

him to turn to the history of this transaction—bad enough in itself—and see what fancy and art can do in dressing up a skeleton so that it becomes 'beautiful for ever.' Mr. Trench himself shall be the historian, writing to the authorities when the occurrences were all fresh in his mind. The narrative was handed in to the Devon commissioners as his *sworn evidence*:

' *William Steuart Trench, esq., agent.*

' Have there been any agrarian outrages, and in what have they originated?—There have been none, except *during a late short period of peculiar local excitement.*

' Will you state the particulars of that excitement, and what then occurred?—I think my best mode of doing so will be by handing in the copy of a letter which I addressed to a local magistrate for the information of government.— [*The witness read the following letter:—*]

' Dear Sir—In reply to your communication, enclosing a letter from Mr. Lucas, requesting that I should give a statement of the particulars which occurred to me in Carrickmacross, on Monday last, I beg leave to lay before you the facts, as follows :—

'Mr. Shirley has recently appointed me to the agency over his Monaghan estate. We both arrived here on Thursday, the 30th of March, and on the following morning we went together into the office; and having remained there about an hour, we were much surprised, on our return, to find an immense mass of people outside the door, who immediately presented a petition to Mr. Shirley, requesting a reduction of rent.

' Mr. Shirley declined giving an immediate answer to such an unexpected request; but having read the petition, he told them he would give an answer to it on the Monday following. By Saturday, however, he had arrived at a full conclusion upon the point, and, anxious to avoid any unpleasant altercation with his tenants, he thought it advisable to let his determination be known as soon as possible, and accordingly, on Saturday, he issued and circulated a printed notice, stating the determination at which he had arrived, and declining any further communications upon the subject. I enclose a copy of the notice.

'Notwithstanding this notice, the people came in on Monday in immense numbers; and at about 11 o'clock in the forenoon, the upper part of the street opposite to Shirley House, where we were residing, was filled with dense masses of men. I then thought it my duty to go out, and repeat to them in my capacity as agent, the determination at which their landlord had arrived. I did so in the mildest terms. I told them I had been able to go over only a part of the estate; but that from what I had seen, I was of opinion that a better system of farming and of general management of their land, was in my judgment much more required than a reduction of the rent. That I knew Mr. Shirley had the kindest feeling towards them, and that I was myself quite prepared and willing to render them any assistance—to go to every man's farm, if possible, and to assist them by my counsel and advice. But that as Mr. Shirley had come to a determination to make no present reduction in his rental, I did expect that all who were able to pay their rents would come in and do so; that the utmost leniency would be extended towards those who could not pay; but that my duty was plain, and if those who really were able to pay, refused to come forward and do so, that I had no alternative left but to take advantage of the power which the law afforded for the recovery of the rent—and this I was fully prepared and determined to do, if driven to that unpleasant necessity. I also made some further observations, of less importance; but my manner towards them was quiet and calm, and I expressed myself most anxious to do everything in my power to promote their welfare and comfort.

'*I then attempted to return to the house, across the street; but the mob closed in upon me, and prevented my doing so, and with much violence dragged me up into the town, where I was repeatedly struck and kicked, and nearly strangled, and my coat torn to pieces.*

'*The mob continued thus to ill-treat me for about a mile along the road to Lough Fea, Mr. Shirley's residence, repeatedly kicking me, especially when I showed symptoms of exhaustion, and pressing their hands violently upon my throat, till I was almost overcome by fatigue, heat and pain.*

'*All this appeared to be done for the purpose of forcing me to promise to induce Mr. Shirley to lower the rents to* 10s. *per acre (upwards of fifty per cent.). This I refused to do. They then brought me on to Lough Fea, where they thought Mr. Shirley was; and upon not finding him, they appeared much exasperated. Mr. Shirley's architect then appeared, and by promising to speak to Mr. Shirley in their favour, and by requesting them to send a deputation, instead of coming in a manner like the present, he induced them to desist from further injury to me.*

'Believe me, dear Sir, very truly yours,

'(Signed) 'WILLIAM STEUART TRENCH.

'Carrickmacross, April 8, 1844.

'What has been the general demeanour of the people towards you since that time?—Though they resisted my measures for the recovery of the rent, *to myself they have been perfectly civil; nor have I*·*received any personal insult or unpleasantness, arising from the above cause since that period.*

'How long did this kind of combination exist?—For about six months.'

Setting aside the embellishments, let us note one or two differences as to facts. In the book the suddenly converted friends placed him on a chair and asked him to make a speech before the castle door. He did so, and there is a grand statuesque picture of the hero, naked to the waist, and standing on the chair as lofty pedestal. In the torn coat the artist could never have made him look like Apollo. Even the shirt would have been too commonplace; so off went the shirt. Three or four times attention is directed to the fact of the nakedness by the hero himself, while the pencil of the filial illustrator has rendered him immortal in this primitive costume. In his speech he ' abused them heartily and soundly.' Yet they cheered him vociferously, and then carried him into the castle, where he could get nothing to cover his nakedness but a countryman's frieze coat. It was when he had been cheered vociferously, and kindly carried in, that Mr. Shirley's architect appeared on the scene. Mr. Trench has not been just to that gentleman, for he really came to his rescue, and perhaps saved his life, by giving the people the only sensible advice they got that day. In his sworn statement, made twenty-five years ago, Mr. Trench said: ' Mr. Shirley's architect then appeared, and by promising to speak to Mr. Shirley in their favour, and by requesting them to send a deputation, instead of coming in a manner like the present, *he induced them to desist from further injury to me.*'

If we had contemporary accounts of all the other romantic scenes which have fascinated so many readers, the ' Realities ' would lose much of their gilding. Indeed, in most cases the internal evidence is sufficient to convince us that the sensationalist has been laying on his colours pretty heavily. In the sketch of the Farney rent campaign, however, I am willing to accept Mr. Trench as a faithful historian. It is a most suggestive narrative, because it shows what mischief could be done by driving the agricultural population to desperation. A general strike against the payment of rent would convulse society. If the war which raged in Farney had spread all over the island, the landlords would be in serious difficulty. The British army might then have become rent collectors, as they had been tithe collectors in 1831.

Mr. Shirley resolved, after much deliberation, to enforce his legal rights to the utmost. The bailiff was sent to warn the backward tenants to come in with the rent, and he everywhere received the same answer—' We will pay no rent till our grievances are redressed.' Now all the missiles of the law were showered on the recusants—notices to quit, *latitats*, processes for arrears, &c. Grippers, process-servers, keepers, drivers, were in full requisition. The grippers were to arrest all tenants against whom decrees had been obtained at the quarter-sessions; the keepers were employed to watch the crops that had been seized; and the drivers were to bring the cattle, sheep, horses, or pigs to pound. These constituted the landlord's army, having the police as a reserve, and the military if necessary.

On the other hand, the tenants organised a body called the ' Molly Maguires'—stout young men dressed up in women's clothes, their faces disguised and besmeared in the most fantastic manner. These men waylaid and maltreated the officers of the law so severely, that in a short time no money could induce a gripper, process-server, driver or bailiff to show his nose on the estate. In this dilemma, Mr. Shirley, as commander-in-chief, ordered his lieutenant and his subordinates to go forth, with a body of police, and drive in all the cattle they could seize on the lands of the defaulting tenants. The expedition started one fine morning, led on by the mounted bailiff, a fat man, trembling like a hare at the thought of encountering the ' Molly Maguires.'

Mr. Trench's description of this foray is very graphic:—
' No sooner had this formidable party appeared upon the roads in the open country, than the people rushed to the tops of the numerous hills with which the district abounds; and as we moved forward, they ran from one hill to another shouting and cheering with wild defiant cries, and keeping a line parallel to that in which our party was travelling.

' The object of our expedition was clearly understood by the people; and the exact position of our company was indicated to those in the lowlands by the movements of the parties on the hills; and accordingly, as we advanced, every beast belonging to every tenant who owed rent was housed or locked up, or driven somewhere away. Thus, as we had no legal right to break open any door, or take any cattle out of any house, but only to seize those we might find in the open fields and upon the lands of the defaulting tenants, we soon perceived (as we might have known before we started) that we were likely to return without success. The bailiff declared with a sigh, " that not a hoof nor a horn was left in the whole country-side."

' At length when about to return home, without having secured any booty whatever, we came unexpectedly upon a poor little heifer calf, browsing quietly on the long grass beside a hedge. The bailiff having ascertained that she was grazing on the land of a tenant who was a defaulter, we seized upon the unhappy little beast, and drove it ingloriously home to the pound at Carrickmacross, a distance of about two miles, amidst the jeers and laughter of the populace, at the result of our formidable day's driving.'

Thus baffled, Mr. Shirley resolved to try another move.

He applied to the authorities in Dublin for an order for ' substitution of service.' That is, instead of delivering the legal notices at the houses of the parties, which was impracticable, they were to be posted up on the chapel-door. To effect this object, a large police force was necessary, and it was accompanied by a stipendiary magistrate. ' As soon as the party came near the chapel grounds a shout of defiance was raised by the peasantry, who began to crowd into the chapel yard, and with uplifted sticks and threatening gestures swore that they would never allow the walls of the chapel to be desecrated by such a notice. The bailiff, a most respectable and temperate man, did his utmost to pacify the excited mob. He reasoned with them as best he could; and assured them that no desecration was intended —that he was only carrying out the law, which required that the notice should be posted on the chapel walls. But his voice had no more power than if he had spoken to a storm of wind; they leaped and danced madly about, whirling their sticks over their heads, and shouting that they would never allow him to touch the sacred edifice.

'The stipendiary magistrate now ordered him to do his duty, and that he would be protected in doing it by the police, and he, trembling with fear, as well he might, at length approached with the notice in his hand to post it in due form. No sooner had he approached towards the chapel than a volley of stones sent him staggering back, though none actually struck him. The police were now ordered to advance. They did so amidst another shower of stones. The storm of missiles still continuing and several of the police having been struck and injured, they were at length ordered to fire. They aimed low, and directing their fire straight into the crowd of stone-throwers, they soon checked the vigour of the assault—six or seven men fell under the volley and rolled upon the ground. There was a short pause, a dead silence ensued—but it was only for a moment, and before the police could recover themselves and load again, a furious rush was made upon them by the enraged populace. Stones were seen flying as thick as hail; and finally the police, apprehending that they must be annihilated if they remained, ran to their cars, which were waiting at a little distance, and drove into Carrickmacross as fast as the horses could gallop, accompanied by the stipendiary magistrate!

'The field thus quickly won, remained in the possession of the insurgents. One of the rioters was killed upon the spot—shot through the body. The others who fell were only slightly injured; one had his ear taken off, another was wounded in the finger, another shot in the arm.'

This was 'the battle of Magheracloon.' Mr. Trench wisely recommended a cessation of hostilities till the harvest was gathered in, promising the landlord that he would then by quiet means, acting on the tenants individually and privately, induce them to pay their rents. He succeeded, but as Mr. Shirley declined to adopt his plans for the better management of the estate, he resigned.

He came back, however, after some years, as agent to the Marquess of Bath—a post which he occupies still, being manager-in-chief at the same time of the large estates of the Marquess of Lansdowne, in Kerry, and Lord Digby, in the King's County. In all these undertakings, ably assisted by his sons and his nephew, he has been pre-eminently successful. If the Farney men had been driven off in 1843, or swept away by the famine, it would have been said that their fate was inevitable, nothing could be made of them. They were by nature prone to disorder and rebellion. Well, Lord Bath visited his estate in 1865. On that occasion a banquet was given to the tenants, at which Mr. Trench made an eloquent speech. Referring to the outbreak in 1848, he said : ' And yet never, my Lord, never even in the worst of times, did I bate one jot of heart or hope in the noble people of Farney, never for one moment did I doubt their loyalty to their Queen, their loyalty to their country, their respect for their landlord, and above all, that they would be true and loyal to themselves.' So much for the incurable perversity of the Celtic race, for the ' black morass of Irish nature ' that can never be drained !

The people of Farney got justice, and they were contented and orderly. They got security, and they were industrious and thriving. They got protection under the constitution, and they were loyal. Densely peopled as the estate is, the agent could not coax one of them to emigrate ; and after his former experience at Farney, he did not venture on eviction, though, no doubt, he would gladly repeat the Kenmare experiment in thinning the masses with which he has had to deal. Mr. Horsman, a prophet of the same school of economists, says that Providence sent the famine to relieve the landlords, by carrying away a third of the population, and he seems to think it desirable that another third should be got rid of somehow.

CHAPTER XXII.

BELFAST AND PERPETUITY.

BELFAST, not being blessed with a cathedral like Armagh nd Derry, is not called a 'city.' It is only a 'town ;' but it is the capital of Ulster, and surpasses all other places in Ireland in the rapidity of its progress and in its prosperity. It can boast but little of its antiquity. There is probably not a house in the borough more than 150 years old. The place is first noticed by history in 1178, merely as the site of a fort of the O'Neills, which was destroyed by John De Courcy. It was only a poor village at the time of Bruce's invasion, in 1315, though Spencer erroneously calls it 'a very good town.' It was so insignificant in 1586 that Holinshed does not mention it among the towns and havens of Down and Antrim. Whatever town existed there had been destroyed by the Earl of Kildare when lord-deputy. In 1552 it was repaired and garrisoned, and shortly after it was granted by the crown to Hugh O'Neill of Clandeboye. In 1571 the castle, with a large portion of territory adjoining it, was bestowed upon Sir Thomas Smith and his son. The latter was assassinated by the 'wicked, barbarous, and uncivil people ;' and the former, not being able to fulfil the conditions of his tenure, the district reverted with the whole earldom of Ulster to the crown in the reign of James I. Belfast was then surrounded by extensive forests, abounding in fine timber for building. The best specimen—perhaps the only one in the kingdom—of a forest like what covered the country at that time, still exists at Shane's Castle, the magnificent demesne of Lord O'Neill, where may be seen enormous oaks decaying with age, under whose shade probably the famous Shane marshalled his galloglasse.

In 1613 the castle and manor of Belfast were granted to Sir Arthur Chichester, lord-deputy, ancestor of the Marquis of Donegal, who did so much to effect the final conquest of Ulster. He may be said to be the founder of the town. From the estates of his family, in Devonshire, and from Scotland, many families came over and made a strong settlement here. Ultimately it became a corporation sending two members to the Irish Parliament. The chief magistrate was called ' the sovereign ;' and the first who held the office was Thomas Pottinger, ancestor of the celebrated Sir Henry Pottinger. In 1758 the population was 8,549; in 1821, it was 37,000; in 1831, it was 53,000; in 1841, it had increased to 75,000; in 1851, it amounted to 103,000; and the last census shows it to be 121,602. About 1,500 houses are built annually in the borough, and the present population is estimated at 150,000. The rateable property is more than 394,000*l.* The sum of 560,000*l.* has been spent on the harbour improvements, to which is to be added 250,000*l.* for building new docks. I remember the quays when they were small, irregular, inconvenient, dirty, and when the channel worked its doubtful course through shifting masses of liquid mud, at low water. Now there are quays which extend in a line about a mile, covered with spacious sheds for the protection of the goods being shipped and unshipped. There are docks of all sorts, and great shipbuilding establishments standing on ground created out of the floating chaos of mud. ' Year by year,' as one of its poets has said, ' Belfast is changing its aspect and overstepping its former boundaries, climbing the hill-side, skirting the river margin, and even invading the sea's ancient domain.

' Ambition's mistress of the fertile land,
Shuts out the ocean and usurps the strand.'

Among the ' usurpations ' is Queen's Island, a beautiful people's park, standing in the midst of the Lough. The people of Belfast have effected all these vast improvements from their own resources, without a shilling from the lord of the soil, without any help from Government, except a loan of 100,000*l.* from the Board of Works. Belfast is the ' linen capital' of the empire, as Manchester is the ' cotton capital.' The linen trade was fostered in its infancy there by Strafford, and encouraged by William III., as a set-off against the abolition of the woollen trade. The first spinning of flax by steam power was commenced in 1830, by the Messrs. Mulholland, who employ 2,000 hands, principally females. Mills have sprung up in every direction, and it is estimated that they give employment to 15,000 persons. To supply the consumption of flax, in addition to the home produce, about 50,000 tons are imported every year. Linen is the staple manufacture; but industrial arts of every kind flourish, with all the usual manifestations of wealth.

We have seen in a former chapter that the people of Londonderry, vexed that the maiden city has been left so far behind her younger sister, ascribe the difference to the fact that the Belfast manufacturers were favoured with long building tenures. We hear it said often that the Marquis of Donegal gave his tenants perpetuity leases, implying that he acted very liberally in doing so. If, however, you speak to persons acquainted with the local history, they will ascribe this advantage to ' Lord Donegal's necessities.' If you ask an explanation of this phrase, you will be told that towards the end of last century, and later, Lord Donegal was obliged to adopt extraordinary methods for raising money, and that the perpetuity leases in question were purchased, and at a very high rate too. You will further learn that the tenants were compelled to take the leases, and pay heavy fines for them in lump sums, and that if unable to produce the money they were evicted, and their farms were given to others who were able to pay. It is alleged that his agent got leases in blank, ready to be filled up when the cash was forthcoming, and that all the cash did not reach the landlord's hands. At any rate, attempts have been made to break some of the leases. There has been long pending litigation

on the subject. Whatever may be the defects of title on the
part of the landlord, the tenant must suffer. Dr. Hancock
alludes to this fact in his first report. Referring to Sir John
Romilly's Leasing Powers Bill, he says :—

'The details of these Bills it is not necessary now to refer
to ; but there was one principle provided for in them which
has been neglected in subsequent measures. In the ordinary
course of business a tenant does not investigate his landlord's
title; the cost of doing so would be nearly always too great;
besides, the landlord would not think of consenting to the
investigation on every occasion of granting a lease. It
follows from this that it is a great hardship, if a flaw should
be discovered in a landlord's title, that leases granted before
the tenants had any notice of the litigation should be bad.
Take the case of the estate which the late Duke of Wellington and Mr. Leslie recovered from Lord Dungannon
after he had been for years in possession ; or the case which
is now pending for so many years between the Marquis of
Donegal and Viscount Templemore. Is it not a great
hardship that leases which tenants took, trusting in the title
of Lord Dungannon or Viscount Templemore, who were
then visible owners of great estates, should afterwards turn
out to be worthless on some point of law in title-deeds which
they never had the opportunity of seeing; and which may
be so subtle as to take Courts of Law years to decide ?'

Dr. Hancock says the principle that in such cases the
tenant should be protected, was neglected in subsequent
measures. Now, what must the tenants think of legislation
that subjects them to be robbed of their dearly-bought leases
because of flaws, frauds or blunders with which they could
have nothing to do ? The leases granted to the tenants of
Lord Donegal, however, in Belfast and the neighbourhood
were generally valid, and to these perpetuities we must
undoubtedly ascribe the existence of a middle class of remarkable independence of character, and the accumulation
of capital for manufactures and commerce. Had Lord
Donegal been able to hold the town in a state of tutelage

and dependence—had he been an 'improving landlord' of the modern type, with an agent like Mr. Trench, so vigilant and curious that a dog could not bark on the estate without his knowledge and consent, Belfast might have been far behind Derry to-day—as stationary as Bangor, Hillsborough, Antrim, or Randalstown. Under such paternal care as Mr. Trench bestows upon tenants, with his omnipresent surveillance, there could be no manly self-reliance, no freedom of speech or action, no enterprise. The agent would take care that no interests should grow up on the estate, which his chief could not control or knock down. It is not likely that Lord Donegal would have suffered the landscape to be spoiled, the atmosphere of the deer park and gardens to be darkened and tainted by the smoke of factory chimneys, which could add nothing to his rental, while crowding around him the race which his great progenitor did so much to extirpate. So Belfast may well be thankful that the Marquis of Donegal, for some generations, could not afford to be 'an improving landlord,' fond of paternal intermeddling with other people's affairs, playing the part of Providence to an inferior race.

But there is one memorable fact connected with those perpetuity leases which applies more immediately to our purpose. The tenants who were evicted to make way for the men who had money to advance to the lord of the soil, feeling themselves seriously aggrieved, formed the first of the more modern agrarian combinations under the title of 'the Hearts of Oak;' which continued for a long time to disturb the peace in Antrim and Down. The farms being extensively turned into pasture by the landlords and large graziers, there was no employment for the houseless wanderers, no provision of any kind for their support. They consequently had no respect for the rights of property, in the vindication of which their homes had been demolished and their families sacrificed, because they were not able to purchase fixity of tenure.

It was, however, very fortunate for Belfast that the land-

C C

lord was obliged to sell it; that the head of the great house founded by the conqueror of Ulster, enriched with territory so vast, should have been under the necessity of giving a perpetual property in the soil to some of the sons of industry.   By that simple concession he did more to advance the prosperity of the town, than could have been accomplished by centuries of fostering care, under the shadow of feudalism. Belfast shows, on a grand scale, what might be done on many an estate in Ireland, in many a town and village where the people are pining away in hopeless misery, if the iron bonds of primogeniture and entail which now cramp landed property were struck off.   The Greek philosopher declared that if he had a standing-place he could move the earth. Give to capital the ground of perpetuity of tenure, whereon to plant its machinery, and it will soon lift this island from the slough of despond.   Then may it be said more truly than Grattan said it in 1782, that Ireland had got nearer to the sun.

CHAPTER XXIII.

LEASE-BREAKING—GEASHILL.

THE history of the Manor of Geashill in the King's County
furnishes another instructive illustration of the land question
and of the effect upon the people of the system of management, under the new school of agents, of which Mr. Steuart
Trench may be regarded as the brightest ornament, if not
the apostle. The epoch was favourable for his mission, and
he was the man for the epoch; he had been quietly training
himself for the restoration of disordered estates, and the
critical emergencies of the times thrust him into the front
rank of social reformers. When he describes the wonderful
revolutions wrought by his instrumentality, the whirlwinds
on which he rode, the storms which he directed and quelled,
the chaos out of which he evoked order, he assumes that the
hurricane and the chaos were the normal state of things. A
mysterious pestilence had blighted the principal food of
the people for two or three years, and brought on a
desolating famine. Millions perished by that visitation
chiefly because the legislature had persistently refused up to
that period to make any provision for the Irish poor such as
it had made centuries before for the English poor, and
because no care had been taken to distribute the population
over the waste lands which their labour would have reclaimed
and fertilized; or to improve their position, so that they
might not be wholly dependent on one sort of food, and that
the most precarious and perishable. Mr. Sadler, in his
work on Population, had proved that, even in the case of
Ireland before the famine, there was really no 'surplus
population;' that if the resources of the country had been

developed by a wise Government, sympathising with the people, the text which he adopted would have been applicable there : 'Dwell in the land, and verily ye shall be fed.' There was hasty legislation to meet the emergency, but in all the haste, the heartless economists found time to devise clauses and provisions, by means of which, when the small farmers had consumed all their stock to keep their families alive, they were compelled to relinquish their holdings in order to get food for their famishing children. They must submit to the workhouse test, they must not hold more than a quarter of an acre of land, if they would get relief. Under the dire instigation of hunger, in the stupor and recklessness of their misery, they accepted any terms the landlords chose to impose, and so whole villages disappeared from the landscape, swept off with the besom of destruction.

The political economists (all the new school of land-agents are rigid political economists), taught by their prophet Malthus, ascribed the famine and every other social evil to surplus population, and to the incurably lazy and thriftless habits of the Celtic race. According to them the potato blight had only hastened an inevitable catastrophe. Therefore they set to work with all their agencies and all their might to get rid of the too prolific race, and to supplant the native cultivators by British settlers and wealthy graziers.

This has been done ever since by a quiet and gradual process, steadily, systematically, inexorably, propelled by many powerful tendencies of the age, and checked only by assassination. What are the agrarian outrages which have become so terribly rife of late, but the desperate struggles of a doomed race to break the instruments which pluck them out of their native soil ? A generation of instruction in the national schools and a generation of intercourse with the free citizens of the United States, who call no man 'master' under heaven—have taught them that it is an enormous iniquity to sacrifice humanity to property, to make the happiness, the freedom, the very existence of human beings, secondary to the arbitrary power and self-interest of a small class called landlords. They regard the 'improving land-lord' system as nothing but a legal and civilised continua-tion of the barbarous policy of extermination by fire and sword which we have seen pursued so ruthlessly in the seventeenth century. It is still the land-war, conducted according to modern tactics, aiming with deadly effect at the same object, the slow but sure destruction of a nuisance called the 'Celtic race.' This may be a delusion on their part; but it is the deep-rooted conviction of priests and people, and hence the utter inadequacy of any enactment which will not render such a policy impossible, by making the tenure of the occupiers independent of the will of the landlords. Until such time the peasantry will continue to offer a bloody resistance to the legal attempts to crush them out of the country.

In this self-defensive war, they cannot cope with the armed power of England in the open field; and they are driven upon the criminal resource of the oppressed in all ages and all lands—secret combination and assassination. For this crime they feel no remorse; first, because it is *war* —just as the soldier feels no remorse for killing the enemy in a battle; and, secondly, because their conquerors, and the successors of those conquerors, have taught them too well by repeated examples the terrible lesson of making light of human life. Poor ignorant creatures, they cannot see that, while the most illustrious noblemen in England won ap-plause and honours by shooting down Irish women and children like seals or otters, the survivors of the murdered people should be execrated as cruel, barbarous, and infamous for shooting the men that pull down the rooftrees over the heads of their helpless families and trample upon their house-hold gods. These convictions of theirs are very revolting to our feelings, but they are facts; and as facts the legislature must deal with them. If there be a people, otherwise singularly free from crime, who regard the assassi-nation of the members of a certain class with indifference, or approbation, the phenomenon is one which political phi-

losophy ought to be able to explain, and one which cannot
be got rid of by suspending the constitution and bringing
railing accusations against the nation.

Mr. Trench speaks with something like contempt or pity
of ' good landlords,' a class which he contradistinguishes from
' improving landlords.' But it should be remembered that by
this last phrase he always means agents of the Trench stamp.
For he observes that the landlord himself cannot possibly do
much more than authorize his agent to do what he thinks
best; and it is rather an advantage that the proprietor should
be an absentee, otherwise his good nature might prompt him
to interrupt the work of improvement. Now there is this to
be said of the good landlords, who may be counted by hundreds, and who are found in all the counties of Ireland.
Their estates are free from the ' poetic turbulence ' in which
Mr. Trench is the ' stormy petrel.' They preserved their
tenants through the years of famine, and have them still on
their estates. Nor should the fact be omitted that among
those good landlords, who abhor the idea of evicting their
tenants, are to be found the lineal descendants of some of
the most cruel exterminators of the seventeenth century.
Their goodness has completely obliterated, among their
people, the bitter memories of the past. The present race
of Celts would die for the men whose ancestors shot down
their forefathers as vermin. But the improving landlords
run their ploughshares through the ashes of old animosities,
turning up embers which the winds of agitation blow into
flames. We seldom hear of Ribbonism till the improving
agent comes upon the scene, warring against natural rights,
warring against the natural affections, warring against
humanity, warring against the soul.

These remarks bring us to the case of the barony of
Geashill, the estate of Lord Digby, to which Mr. Trench
became agent in 1857. Lord Digby desired to obtain
his services, but he did not communicate his desire to Mr.
Trench himself, though nothing would seem easier. It was
first conveyed by Lieut.-General Porter, the confidential

friend of Lord Digby, and next by Mr. Brewster, afterwards Lord Chancellor of Ireland. When the police received a notice that the new landlord of Geashill would certainly meet with a ' bloody death ' if he persisted in his threatened dealings with the tenants, there was no more time for diplomatic delicacy in approaching Mr. Trench. The landlord's extremity is Mr. Trench's opportunity. When leases are to be broken, when independent rights are to be extinguished, or ' contracted away,' when an overcrowded estate is to be thinned at the least possible cost to the owner, when a rebellious tenantry are to be subdued, and Ribbonmen are to be banished or hanged, Mr. Trench is the man to do the work of improvement. He admits that he never had before him an uglier job than this at Geashill, and he had the worst apprehensions as to the danger of the enterprise.

It was nothing less than to break 120 leases, which had been granted from time to time by the late Lord Digby during the sixty years that he had enjoyed the property. The value of these leases was 30,600*l.*, for the terms unexpired after his death. Among those 120 leaseholders were the descendants of English settlers, gentlemen farmers, one of them a magistrate, and a number of substantial yeomen, the sort of men the country so much wanted to form an independent middle class. But to an ' improving landlord,' the existence of such a class on his estate is intolerable. At all hazards they must be made tenants-at-will, and brought completely under his control.

They had built houses and planted trees; they had reclaimed the deep bog and converted it into good arable land. They had employed the peasantry, and given them plots of ground, and, more than all, they had allowed a number of families to squat on bits of bog by the roadside, where they lived as well as they could; working when there was a demand for labour, cutting turf and selling it in the neighbouring town of Tullamore, and perhaps carrying on some little dealings. At all events they had survived the famine; and there they were in 1857 with their huts standing on their 'estates,' for they had paid no rent for twenty years, and they had as good a title in law as Lord Digby himself. Mr. Trench seems to have been horrified at not finding the names of these householders in the rent-books of the estate! The idea!—that there should be within the four corners of the King's County, even on the bog of Allen, a number of natives holding land, without a landlord! It was monstrous. But as they could not be evicted for non-title, they were all severally tempted by the offer of money, in sums varying from 5*l*. to 20*l*. each, to sell their freeholds to the landlord. Pity they were not preserved as a remnant of the antediluvian period, ere the ancient tenures were merged in floods of blood. Like a bit of primitive forest, they would be more interesting to some minds than the finest modern plantation.

It was not so easy to deal with the 120 leaseholders. To what extent they had improved their farms before they got the leases, Mr. Trench does not say. But as the absentee landlord had done nothing, and spent nothing, whatever increase to the value had been made was undoubtedly the work of the tenants; and after the leases were obtained, they would naturally feel more confidence in the investment of their savings in the land. However that may be, a professional man, employed by Lord Digby, estimated the value over and above the reserved rent at 30,600*l*., which sum the new landlord proposed to put into his own pocket, by increasing the rent one-third. The plea for this sweeping confiscation was, that the late Lord Digby, cousin to the present, had only a life interest in the Irish estate, and therefore, the leases were all illegal and worthless. Accordingly the new lord commenced proceedings to evict the whole of the tenantry for non-title. They were astounded. They held meetings; they deliberated; they appealed to the landlord; they appealed to the executors of the late peer, who had large estates in England, and died worth a million sterling in the funds, all of which he willed away from the heir of his title and Irish estates. Says Mr. Trench:—

' It may readily be supposed that circumstances so peculiar as these created considerable anxiety in the district. The tenantry, *many* of them large and respectable landholders, now learned, for the first time, that their leases were good for nothing in law. They had been duly 'signed, sealed, and delivered' to them under a full belief on their part that the contract was not only just and honourable, but also perfectly legal; and their feelings may be imagined when they found that they were suddenly threatened with a total loss of the property which they had always looked upon as secure.' *

Pending the ejectment proceedings, they were knocked about from post to pillar, without getting any satisfaction. The landlord referred them to the executors, although he knew well they had no legal claim on them whatever, and that to legal claims only could they pay any attention. The executors again referred them to their landlord, who was determined to break the leases, come what would. Now, if the Irish law regulating the relations of landlord and tenant were based upon justice and equity, the wrong done by the late earl, if any, was a wrong for which the tenants should in no way be held responsible. The wrong was done to the heir-at-law. To him, and not to the tenants, compensation should have been made by the executors. And after all, it was really to him that the money was advanced to buy up the leases, in order to save him from assassination, for the tenants had no legal claim upon them.

The natural, proper, and honest course, then, for the landlord, was to have kept the 30,600*l.* as compensation to himself for the mistake of his predecessor, and to let the leases stand. If he considered the peace of the country, if he wished to inspire in the minds of the people respect for the rights of property, or confidence in the Government, he would not have adopted the desperate course of breaking 120 contracts, kindling the flames of agitation, and planting Ribbon lodges all over a district hitherto peaceful and tran-

* 'Realities of Irish Life,' p. 314.

quill. But he was bent on crushing the independent yeomanry into the abject condition of tenants-at-will. To carry out this purpose, Mr. Trench was indispensable. He knew how to tame the wild Irish. And Mr. Trench was equal to the occasion. He went to reside a few weeks at Tullamore, to reconnoitre the enemy's position. He writes as if this was the first time he made acquaintance with the estate. But his own residence was in the Queen's County, not far off; and there is good reason to believe that he knew all about Geashill long before; and all about every estate belonging to an English absentee in the four provinces; for he had, growing up around him, a young generation of land-agents, trained in all the arts of modern management, and one of the ablest of these, his son, Mr. T. W. Trench, became his partner in this agency. Mr. Trench's tactics are not new, though he excels all men in their skilful application. His plan, adopted on all occasions, is to divide and conquer. Violent measures being dangerous and contrary to his own feelings, he trusts to diplomacy, dealing with individuals, taken separately into a private room, where his irresistible personal fascination invariably brings matters to a satisfactory issue.

In this case, he went over to the English executors, and persuaded them to advance the 30,600*l.* to be distributed among the tenants, under the guarantee of Lord Digby that this sum would cover all possible claims. Thus provided with funds, he summoned the tenants, not all, but ten of the most influential, to meet him at Geashill. He left this meeting, purposely, to the last day and the last hour, as a piece of generalship. He says:—

' They appeared puzzled and anxious, and very uncertain what to do. At length one of them proposed that they should do nothing until they had had an opportunity of consulting the remainder of the leaseholders, of whom there were upwards of 120 upon the estate.

' " No," replied I, " you must come to a decision now; there is a messenger at the door on horseback, to ride to the telegraph station at Portarlington to stop the English witnesses coming over. This must be done within an hour, or they will start for Ireland, and *then* it will be out of my power to stop the lawsuit. You must determine *now*, each man for himself, or the lawsuit must go on."

' " Will you state the amount of money you will give to each of us ? " asked one of the party.

' " Certainly," replied I, " if you will *each come separately with me into another room.*"

' They did so. I named to each an amount something less than the sum set down by the notary, partly as a reserve, lest any tenants holding under these leaseholders should afterwards require to be paid, and partly lest it might be supposed we were yielding to a legal claim already granted. After a little consideration, they all severally signed the consent for judgment.'

The other leaseholders followed. The leases were all surrendered, and the holders became tenants-at-will. I had the pleasure of meeting one of the most influential of them a short time ago at Geashill—a fine tall, patriarchal-looking gentleman, the representative of one of the English settlers. He was waiting about humbly and patiently for an opportunity of speaking to the young agent, who is as courteous and kind as he is efficient. But I could not help reflecting how different would be the bearing of the tenant if he had been still in possession of his lease ! His dwelling-house was not as grand as the stylish villa which the landlord has erected beside it. But every stick and stone about the place were his own property. So also were the old timber trees, which his ancestors planted. But now every stick and stone and tree belong to Lord Digby, and as such the agent exhibits them to visitors—the buildings, the gardens, the trees, the hedges, the rich pasture fields, all having such a look of comfort and independence. I asked, ' Did you ever know a place like this old home of yours to have been made by a tenant-at-will ? ' He answered in the negative.

The tenant on an ' improved estate ' must be very careful

about his speech. An agent has a hundred eyes and a hundred ears. People who seek 'favours' at the office, find it useful to be spies upon their neighbours, to detect violations of the 'rules of the estate.' It is mainly through the spy-system that Mr. Steuart Trench, according to his own avowal, won most of his victories over refractory tenants. For example, on this estate he had a woman acting as a spy at the meetings of the Ribbonmen; and he boasted that a dog could not bark at Farney without his knowledge. I refer to this matter here again for the purpose of saying that I cannot regard as an improvement of the country a system which establishes a despot on every estate, which degrades the tenant into a day-labourer, which—land being limited and scarce—substitutes the old, barbarous, pastoral system for tillage, which banishes the poor and enslaves the rich. Lord Digby levelled cottages, gardens, farms, manured the land, got an enormous crop, which in one year paid all the expenses; and then laid out the land in vast tracts of pasture, for which he gets from 30s. to 40s. an acre. That is improvement for *him*, but not for the people, not for the country, not for the state, not for the Queen. It may crush Ribbonism. But for every Ribbonman crushed, a hundred Fenians spring up; and disaffection becomes not a mere local plague, but an endemic. Mr. Trench gives a significant hint to other landlords to follow the example of Lord Digby, assuring them that it will '*pay*.'

A still more flagrant case of lease-breaking occurred some years ago in the county of Galway. Dr. Hancock has put the facts of this case before the Government in his recent report:—

'The plaintiff was the Rev. Dr. O'Fay, parish priest of Craughwell, in the county of Galway, and the defendant the landlord on whose estate the priest resided. About ten years ago the priest was induced to take a farm that had been held by a former parish priest; the previous proprietor, the father of the defendant, promising a lease for three lives, or thirty-one years. After the priest entered into possession the landlord ascertained that he could not fulfil his promise.

'As he did not possess such a power under the terms of the estate settlement, he offered, instead, a lease for the priest's own life, and 20*l.* to aid in building a house. The priest continued in possession of the farm, and paid the rent agreed on, thus, as he alleged, accepting the arrangement proposed. He was on excellent terms with the landlord, and expended 70*l.* in permanent improvements, and did not ask for the 20*l.* which the landlord had promised. In 1854 the landlord died, and his son, the defendant, succeeded to the property. He gave notice to all his yearly tenants of an intention to raise their rents. The priest claimed to have a promise of a lease, and the agent of the property, during the landlord's absence abroad, admitted this claim, and did not raise the rent. The landlord said he had no notice of his father's promise; he, however, allowed the priest to remain in possession, and the priest expended 400*l.* in buildings, on the faith that he would not be disturbed. A dispute subsequently arose about trespass, and the fences on the boundary between the priest's farm and some land in the possession of the landlord. The landlord served notice to quit, and brought an ejectment. After some delay judgment was given in his favour, subject to an application to the Court of Chancery to compel him to fulfil his father's promise of a lease.'

The Master of the Rolls thus characterised the law which justifies the robbery of the tenants by unscrupulous and vindictive landlords :—

'Even if the Rev. Dr. O'Fay had no claim except as tenant from year to year, I have no hesitation in stating that, although in point of law on the authorities I have referred to, and particularly the case of Pelling *v.* Armitage, the petitioner's suit could not be sustained, *yet nothing can be more repugnant to the principles of natural justice than that a landlord should look on at a great expenditure carried on by a tenant from year to year, without warning the tenant of his intention to turn him out of possession.* The defendant's offer to allow Dr. O'Fay to remove the buildings was a mockery. *I have no jurisdiction to administer equity in the natural sense of that term, or I should have no difficulty whatever in making a decree against the defendant.* I am bound to administer an artificial system, established by the decisions of eminent judges, such as Lord Eldon and Sir William Grant, and *being so bound, I regret much that I must administer injustice in this case, and dismiss the petition,* but I shall dismiss it without costs. *I should be very glad for the sake of justice that my decision should be reversed by the Court of Appeal.'*

Lest it might be supposed that this was the opinion of a single judge, we find in the Court of Appeal equally strong views stated:—It was thrown out that it was a case for amicable settlement, but the respondent's counsel assured the Court that his client 'had resolved to spend his fortune, if necessary, in resisting the claim of the Rev. Dr. O'Fay.' Lord Justice Blackburne pronounced this to be a very irrational determination, although he had to decide that the claim could not be sustained in law or equity.

Lord Chancellor Napier, in concluding his judgment, said:—

'I think I am not overstepping my duty in suggesting to the respondent, that, under all the circumstances of this case, he will best maintain the character and honour of a British officer, satisfy the exigencies of justice, and uphold the rights of property, by making *such an arrangement* with Dr. O'Fay, as to the possession of this farm, *as may leave him the full benefit of an expenditure made in good faith, and with the reasonable expectation of having the full benefit of it sufficiently secured by an undisturbed possession.'*

It is a favourite theory with the new school of agents and improving landlords, that long leases cause bad cultivation; in other words, that industry prospers best where there is no security that you can reap what you have sown, except the honour of a man whose interest it is to appropriate the fruits of your labours, which he can *legally* do. Now, in every class and profession, there are failures,—persons that are good for nothing, indolent, improvident, and thriftless. If such a man has a long lease at a low rent, he may be overwhelmed in debt, and leave his land in very bad condition. Others may imitate their aristocratic superiors in their contempt for labour and their habits of expenditure, and so get into a state of hopeless poverty on a good estate. If there are cases where industrious sober men are the worse for having an old lease, it should be remembered that the most insecure of all tenures is a lease dependent on a single bad life, which may drop at any hour. But there are other causes of the facts urged against long tenures, for which the legislature is responsible, not the unimproving tenant. Dr. Hancock explains this point very satisfactorily :—

' Instances of bad cultivation and neglect of improvements, where long leases exist, are sometimes brought forward to show the inutility of tenure as a security for capital, and the strange economic theory is propounded that a precarious interest is more favourable to the investment of capital than a secure one. As well might the state of landed property in Ireland before the Incumbered Estates Court was established be adduced as an argument against property in land. The remedy, however, which the legislature applied to incumbered estates of large proprietors was not to destroy property in land, but simply to secure its prompt, cheap, and effectual transfer to solvent hands.

' For tenants' interests under leases where the value is small, and where the interests have become complicated, the Landed Estates Court is too expensive, and so these interests remain often for years untransferred, in the hands of some one who has a very limited and often uncertain interest in them. Such a leaseholder is deterred from making improvements by the state of the law which deprives him of the entire value of his improvements if anyone should disturb

him under a prior charge or claim, however obscure or unknown, affecting his interest.   The remedy is to be found in
an extension of the principle of the Record of Title Act to
the local registry of small leasehold interests, and in the
providing for the local sale of such interests in a cheap
manner, with an absolute title.'

CHAPTER XXIV.

THE LAND SYSTEM AND THE WORKING CLASSES.

WE have been told over and over again that the business of Ireland, and all its improvements, requiring education and integrity, are carried on ' by the Protestants, by whose intelligence, and labour, mental and bodily, its prosperity, such as it is, has been produced.' This assertion has been made with great confidence, by many writers and speakers. It is a gross exaggeration, and absurd as it is gross. I say nothing of the unseemly egotism of a dominant caste, thus parading its own merits, flaunting its plumes, strutting and crowing over the common folk—of this pharisaic spirit of the ascendant Protestant, standing close to the altar, reciting to God and the world the number of his resplendent virtues, and scornfully contrasting his excellent moral condition with the degraded Catholic—the vile publican and sinner, overwhelmed with enormous guilt. These monopolising Pharisees, who laboured at such a rate to assert their natural superiority, as the favourites of Heaven, and members of the Sovereign's church, over a race which England enabled them to subjugate and impoverish, have found no trumpeter so loud as Master Fitzgibbon, a chancery judge. In the same spirit the last census has been analysed by one of the ablest defenders of the Irish establishment, the Rev. Dr. Hume, of Liverpool, in order to prove that everything good in Ireland has been done by the Protestants, and everything bad by the Catholics. But he does not state fairly the conditions of the race. He does not state that one of the competitors had been master for centuries, well-fed, well-trained, possessed of all advantages which give strength, skill, courage, and confidence, while the other was ill-fed, untrained, enfeebled, and *over-weighted*, having to work out of himself the slavish spirit which oppression had produced, and to gain, by extra efforts, the skill which the law had forbidden him to acquire. Nevertheless the Catholics have acquired skill, and the extent to which the empire is dependent on their knowledge of the industrial arts is much greater than many people suppose. Of the farming class in Ireland, 76 per cent. are Roman Catholics. But we are indebted to the obnoxious race in other respects than as producers of food.

From the classification of occupations and professions, we learn that the Roman Catholics bear the following proportions to the Protestants of all denominations.

Persons employed in the manufacture of:	Roman Catholics.	
Skin clothing	77	per cent.
Woollen do.	88	„
Flax do.	43	„
Cotton do.	53	„
Straw do.	66	„
Silk do.	66	„
Miscellaneous do.	67	„
In producing furniture	84	„
In unclassed industrial employments	84	„
In amusements	80	„
In architecture	78	„
In making machinery	76	„
In conveyance and travelling	73	„
In literature and education	56	„
In charity and benevolence	52	„
In health	50	„
In science and art	47	„
In justice and government	46	„
In banking and agency	40	„

There are other suggestive figures in the census, bearing on this question. While three-fourths of the farmers are Catholics, three-fourths of the land-agents are Protestants, who, as a rule, have an unconquerable antipathy to the Catholic clergy, as the only obstacle to their absolute power over the tenants, with whom they find it hard to sympathise. Of farm labourers and domestic servants, nine out of ten belong to the race supposed by some to be incapable of virtue and loyalty.   Again, of the whole British army of all ranks, 37 per cent. are Irishmen, and of these Irish soldiers, 67 per cent. are Catholics.   More than three-fourths of the magistrates are Protestants; and they bear about the same proportion on the grand juries.   According to the theory and practice of the constitution, all power, legislative and administrative, must be based on the ownership of land.   The rate-payers have a voice indeed, but it is generally nothing but an echo of the landlord's voice; what else can it be when they are tenants-at-will, depending on the mercy of the proprietor for the means of existence?   In county offices, the Protestants have an overwhelming majority.   It is the same in all the offices filled by government patronage, except the judges of the superior courts.   There Catholics are in the majority, because they had obtained seats in the House of Commons.

On the boards of guardians the mass of the poor might expect that a majority of guardians would be prompted by national and religious feeling to sympathise with them, so that they would find in the master and matron, the doctor and the relieving officer, something like the natural tenderness which a common kindred and creed inspire.   But half the guardians are *ex-officio* members, as magistrates; nearly all landlords and Protestants.   They have in addition ' property votes,' and ' residence votes ; ' so that, with their influence over the elections, they are generally able to pack the board; and in that case the officials are almost invariably Protestants and conservatives.   I know a union in which three-fourths of the rate-payers are Roman Catholics; and yet, with the utmost efforts of the priests, they were not able to elect a single Catholic guardian.   To meet the landlord pressure, some of the rate-payers were required to sign their voting papers in presence of their pastors, yet so terrible was that pressure that they afterwards took them to the agent's office, and, to make assurance doubly sure, tore them up before his face. I have been told by a priest, that such is the mortal dread of eviction, or of a permanent fine in the form of increased rent,. that he had known tenants who, when produced in the witness-box, denied on oath acts of oppression of which they had been bitterly complaining to himself, and which he well knew to be facts.

Thus the land-war rages at every board of guardians, in every dispensary, in every grand jury room, at every petty sessions, in every county court, in every public institution throughout the kingdom. The land-agent is the commanding officer, his office is a garrison, dominating the surrounding district. He is able, in most cases, to defy the confessional and the altar; because he wields an engine of terror generally more powerful over the mind of the peasantry than the terrors of the world to come. Armed with the 'rules of the estate' and with a notice to quit, the agent may have almost anything he demands, short of possession of the farm and the home of the tenant. The notice to quit is like a death warrant to the family. It makes every member of it tremble and agonise, from the grey-headed grandfather and grandmother, to the bright little children, who read the advent of some impending calamity in the gloomy countenances and bitter words of their parents. The passion for the possession of land is the chord on which the agent plays, and at his touch it vibrates with 'the deepest notes of woe.' By the agent of an improving landlord it is generally touched so cunningly, that its most exquisite torture cannot easily be proved to be a grievance. He presents an alternative to the tenant; he does less than the law allows. He could strike a mortal blow, but he lends a helping hand. Resistance entails ruin; compliance secures friendship. Give up the old *status*, and accept a new one: cease to stand upon *right*, consent to hang upon *mercy*, and all may be well.

Passing a cottage by the road-side, one of the kindest and best of those agents said to me, 'See with what infatuation these people cling to their old places! There is a man in that dilapidated cabin, with only one acre of ground. It is an eyesore. I have offered him a nice new slated cottage with ten acres, within a short distance, and he obstinately refuses to quit.'

Why did he refuse? I suppose, because the place was *his own.* The house was probably built by his father; it is the house in which he was born, endeared to him, no doubt, by many powerful associations, little appreciated by those who never condescend to read the 'simple annals of the poor.' He felt that if, like his neighbours, he moved into a house built by the landlord, he would cease to be a free man, and would pass under the yoke of a *master.* I was with some visitors in one of the new cottages. The wife of the cottier with smiles assented to all that was said as to the neatness and comfort of the place. I thought the smiles were forced. I was last in going out, and I heard her heave a heavy sigh. Perhaps she longed for the old home and its freedom, envying the lot of the sturdy peasant to whom I have alluded. Poor fellow! he must give way at last. But his proud manhood is the stuff of which Hampdens are made.

I have devoted much time and attention to personal enquiries from town to town, from village to village, and from house to house, seeking corroborative evidence from men of all ranks and professions, on the effect of the *Improved Land System* on the working classes, and I will here faithfully record as briefly as possible the result of my enquiries. I must premise a few words as to the principles of the system which is called 'English.'

1. There is the principle of *contract,* by which alone any tenant is to be permitted to occupy land. There is to be no foothold in the island, from the centre all round to the sea, from the top of the highest mountain to the shore at low-water-mark, for any Irishman in his native land, unless he obtains it by contract from a landlord and pays for it.

2. There is the principle of *compensation* for unexhausted improvements at the rate of five or six per cent. on the outlay, provided the improvements have been made with

the knowledge and consent of the landlord. A certain number of years is held to be sufficient to recoup the tenant for his outlay. If he is removed before that time he is entitled to the balance of his invested capital; just as if the relation were strictly commercial, and as if he had no further claim than his percentage. If the landlord makes the improvement—which he prefers doing, on the new system—he requires the tenant to pay at the rate of four to six per cent. in the form of rent—a clear gain to the landlord, who can borrow money on much lower terms, and can hardly invest his capital so profitably or so safely elsewhere.

3. *Absenteeism* is no disadvantage or loss to the country. This principle is in great favour with the agents. There is no theme on which they are so eloquent or so argumentative. In the absence of the landlord the agent is all-powerful. What the Irish lord deputy was to the Tudors and Stuarts, the Irish agent now is to the great absentee proprietor residing in London or Paris. He will undertake to demonstrate that the West-end of London would be just as prosperous if the Queen and her court resided constantly at Balmoral or Killarney; if the parliament met alternately in Edinburgh and Dublin, and if the government offices were all at Liverpool. With the blessing of absenteeism, houses in London would be built as fast, and would bring as high rents; trade would be as brisk, artizans of all sorts as well paid, life as happy, and the Londoners as well content. The Irish, however, have, in their ignorance of political economy, conceived the idea, that if the millions sterling sent annually out of the country to London were spent among those by whose labour the money is made, there would be more employment for all sorts of tradesmen, more business for the shopkeepers, more opportunities of advancement for the farmers' sons, more houses built, more trees planted, more land reclaimed, more factories established, more money stirring, more wealth, more life, more enjoyment, an immense increase of national prosperity. The agents say that this is all a delusion.

4. The next principle of the new agents is this—and to carry it out is the aim of all their improvements—that their mission is to produce the greatest amount of rent from the smallest number of tenants.

5. To reduce the population by *emigration* or other means until there is barely a sufficient number of labourers to attend the agricultural machines, and herd the cattle.

6. To discourage *marriage* in every possible way, and to diminish pauperism till there shall be no further use of the workhouses but to serve as lying-in hospitals for the thrifty spinsters, as they do in Cumberland and Westmoreland— where the arrangement seems the most natural thing in the world. It is certainly not an unnatural consequence of the practice of men and women sleeping in the same apartment.

Now let us see the working of this new system in Ireland : for it is at work more or less extensively in all the four provinces. The rules of the estate, when rigidly enforced, as they generally are by the improving agents, tend steadily, powerfully, to break down the small farmers. They are disappearing by thousands every year. Some take their chance across the Atlantic. Others fall into the condition of labourers, and may earn 2s. a day on the estate. This will last for awhile until the land is drained, manured, and turned into permanent pasture. Then their occupation is gone. There is nothing more for them to do. There is no place for them, no room, no support in their native land. The grass will grow without their labour, and the bullocks will fatten without their care.

We are constantly hearing of the immense rise in wages since the famine. Well, they are nominally higher, but in the old times the labourer could get more for 8d. or 10d. than he can now get for 1s. 6d. or 2s. Fuel is now three times as dear as it was, because the ' rules of the estate ' will not allow the tenants to sell turf even on the verge of extensive bogs. Milk, which was formerly abundant and very cheap, is scarcely to be had at all now in the country towns and villages, because the land is devoted to feeding sheep and 'dry cattle.' Under the old system, the cottiers in the small towns and villages, as well as on the roads in the country, were enabled to keep pigs. The pig paid the rent, and made manure which was put out on the ground of some neighbouring farmer, hired as 'conacre.' The crop of potatoes thus obtained was a great help in the winter months, when employment was rarely to be had. This practice still prevails in Ulster. The farmer puts in the crop for the manure, the cottier paying the farmer's rent— 5s. to 10s. a rood, or whatever it may be. With this help the family get over the winter, and feed the pig, without which help, they say, it would be impossible to exist, even with constant employment at a shilling a day. But on the estates of improving landlords in the other provinces, the rules forbid the tenant to give the use of any ground for conacre. He must not, on pain of eviction, take manure for such a purpose, though it would help to enrich his land for the ensuing year. The evicted cottiers and small farmers are forced to go to towns and villages, shut up in unwholesome rooms. When they have been thus so far got rid of, the most ingenious devices are resorted to in order to render it impossible for them to live. By the 'rules of the estate,' the supply of necessaries is cut off on every side. Without fuel, without milk, without potatoes, unless bought at a high rate for ready money, how are they to live? The strong members of the poor man's family emigrate or go to service; the weak ones and the young children pine away in a state of semi-starvation, preferring that to the best fare in the hated workhouse.

The people are fully sensible of the causes of these privations. They know that they have been forced into this condition by the landlords and their improving agents, induced in some cases by the temptation of a few pounds to surrender their little holdings. The lord lieutenant of the King's County has thus cleared an immense district, and has himself become a grazier and a cattle-dealer on a monster scale, attending the markets in person, and driving hard bargains with the farmers and jobbers. By such means the population of that county has been reduced one-third in the last twenty years. The moral aspect of this new system is worthy of consideration. It is thus presented by Archdeacon Redmond of Arklow, one of the most moderate and respected parish-priests in Ireland. When lately presenting an address to Lord Granard from his Wexford tenantry, he said:—

' I have always heard the house of Forbes eulogised for its advocacy of civil and religious liberty, and the name of Grogan Morgan has become a household word through this county as one of the best landlords in Ireland. He never broke down a rooftree during or since the terrible famine. Under his fostering care they have all tided over the calamitous time, and are happy and prosperous in their homes. He did not think his estate overcrowded, nor did he avail himself of the mysterious destruction of the fruits of the earth, to clear off beings made in God's image, and to drive them to the poorhouse, the fever-shed, or the emigrant ship, to whiten the bottom of the sea with their bones, or to face the moral and physical perils of the transatlantic cities. He did not read his bible, like Satan, backwards, nor did he turn out the Son of God in the person of His poor. Hence his name is in benediction, and his estates are more prosperous than the estates of those who forget God in their worldly wisdom, and would seem to have no belief in a judgment to come. What a happiness it is, my Lord and Lady Granard, for you to have such a heritage, and to know that you live in the hearts of your tenantry, who would spill the last drop of their blood to shield you and your dear children from hurt and harm !'

Let it not be supposed that such sentiments are peculiar to the Catholic clergy, or that their causes exist only in the south and west. The Rev. Dr. Drew, a rector in the county Down, an Orange chaplain, a veteran champion of Protestantism and Toryism, but an honourable and humane man, wrote the following letter last autumn :—

If the magnificent lecture of Mr. Butt had done nothing more than elicit this letter from Dr. Drew, it would have been much. But will not the thoughts of many hearts be revealed in the same manner? What a number of plain-speaking Drews we shall have denouncing tyranny when their consciences are relieved from the incubus of the Establishment!

To Isaac Butt, Esq., LL.D.

' My dear Butt—If every other man in the world entertained doubts of my sincerity, you, at least, would give me credit for honesty and just intentions. I write to you accordingly, because my mind has been stirred to its inmost depths by the perusal of your address in my native city of Limerick. I do not regard the subject of your address as a political one. It ought to be regarded solely as a question of humanity, justice, common sense, and common honesty. I wish my lot had never been cast in rural places. As a clergyman I hear what neither landlords nor agents ever hear. I see the depression of the people; their sighs and groans are before me. They are brought so low as often to praise and glorify those who, in their secret hearts, are the objects of abhorrence. All this came out gradually before me. Nor did I feel as I ought to feel in their behalf until, in my own person and purse, I became the victim of a system of tyranny which cries from earth to heaven for relief. Were I to narrate my own story it would startle many of the Protestants of Ireland. There are good landlords—never a better than the late Lord Downshire, or the living and beloved Lord Roden. But there are too many of another state of feeling and action. There are estates in the north where the screw is never withdrawn from its circuitous and oppressive work. Tenant-right is an unfortunate and delusive affair, simply because it is almost invariably used to the landlord's advantage. Here we have an election in prospect, and in many counties no farmer will be permitted to think or act for himself. What right any one man has to demand the surrender of another's vote, I never could see. It is an act of sheer felony—a perfect "stand-and-deliver" affair. To hear a man slavishly and timorously say, " I must give my votes as the landlord wishes," is an admission that the legislature, which bestowed the right of voting on the tenant, should not see him robbed of his right, or subsequently scourged or banished from house and land, because he disregarded a landlord's nod, or the menace of a land agent. At no little hazard of losing the friendship of some who are high and good and kind, I write as I now do.—Yours, my dear Butt, very sincerely,

'THOMAS DREW.

' Dundrum, Clough, County Down,
September 7, 1868.'

Some resident landlords employ a considerable number of labourers, to each of whom they give an excellent cottage, an acre of land, and the grass of a cow, with work all the year round at seven shillings a week. The tenants are most comfortable and most grateful, while the praise of those landlords is in the mouths of the peasantry all round the country. But these considerate landlords are in a minority. As a rule, on the estates where the improvement system is going on, where farms are being consolidated, and grazing supersedes tillage, an iron pressure weighs upon the labouring classes, crushing them out of the country. - It is a cold, hard, calculating, far-reaching system of inhumanity, which makes the peasant afraid to harbour his own flesh and blood. It compels the grandmother to shut the door in the face of the poor homeless orphan, lest the improving agent should hear of the act of sheltering him from the pitiless storm, not more pitiless than the agent himself. The system of terrorism established by the threats of eviction de-humanizes a people remarkable for their hospitality to the poor. Mr. Thomas Crosbie, of Cork, a gentleman whom I believe to be as truthful and honourable as any agent in Ireland, gives

appalling illustrations of this in his account of ' The Lansdowne Estates,' published in 1858.   Mr. Trench has given
the English public several pretty little romances about these
estates; but he omitted some realities that ought to have
impressed themselves upon his memory as deeply as any of
his adventures.   Mr. Crosbie found that the ' rules of the
estate,' which were rigidly enforced, forbid tenants to build
houses for their labourers, ' the consequence of which was
that men and women servants, no matter how great the
number, must live under one roof.'   The rules forbid marriage without the agent's permission.   A young couple got
married, and were chased away to America; and ' the two
fathers-in-law were not merely warned; they were punished
for harbouring their son and daughter, by a fine of a gale
of rent.'   It was a rule ' that no stranger be lodged or harboured in any house upon the estate, lest he should become
sick or idle, or in some way chargeable upon the poor-rates.'
' Several were warned and punished for giving lodging to a
brother-in-law, a daughter,' &c.   ' A poor widow got her
daughter married without the necessary permission; she was
served with a notice to quit, which was withdrawn on the
payment of three gales of rent.'   Mr. Crosbie gives a number of cases of the kind.   The following are the most remarkable.   A tenant, Timothy Sullivan, of Derrynabrack,
occasionally gave lodging to his sister-in-law, whilst her husband was seeking for work.   He was afraid to lodge both
or either; ' but the poor woman was in low fever, and
approaching her confinement.   Even under such circumstances his terror was so great that he removed her to a
temporary shed on Jeremiah Sullivan's land, where she gave
birth to a child.   She remained there for some time.   When
" the office " heard of it, Jeremiah Sullivan was sent for and
compelled to pay a gale of rent (as fine), and to throw down
the shed.   Thus driven out, and with every tenant on the
estate afraid to afford her a refuge, the miserable woman
went about two miles up the mountain, and, sick as she was,
and so situated, took shelter in a dry *cavern,* in which she

lived for several days. But her presence even there was a crime, and a mulct of another gale of rent was levied off Jeremiah Sullivan. Thus, within three weeks he was compelled to pay two gales of 3*l*. 2*s*. 6*d*. each. It was declared also that the mountain being the joint property of Jeremiah Sullivan, Timothy Sullivan, and Thady Sullivan, Timothy Sullivan was a participator in the crime, and should be fined a gale of rent. The third, it appears, escaped.' 'S. G. O.' narrated another horrifying case in the *Times*, at the period of its occurrence, in 1851. Abridged, it runs thus:—' An order had gone forth on the estate (a common order in Ireland) that no tenant was to admit any lodger into his house. This was a general order. It appears, however, that sometimes special orders were given; and one was promulgated that Denis Shea should not be harboured. This boy had no father living. He had lived with a grandmother, who had been turned out of her holding for harbouring him. He had stolen a shilling, a hen—done such things as a neglected twelve-year-old famishing child will do. One night he came to his aunt Donoghue, who lodged with Casey. The latter told the aunt and uncle not to allow him into the house, as the agent's drivers had given orders about him. The aunt beat him away with a pitchfork, the uncle tied his hands with cord behind his back. The poor child crawls to the door of a neighbour, and tries to get in. The uncle is called to take him away, and he does so. He yet returns with hands still tied behind, having been severely beaten. The child seeks refuge in other cabins; but all were forbidden to shelter him. He is brought back by some neighbours in the night, who try to force the sinking child in upon his relation. There is a struggle at the door. The child was heard asking some one to put him upright. In the morning there is blood upon the threshold. The child is stiff dead—a corpse, with its arms tied; around it every mark of a last fearful struggle for shelter—food—the common rights of humanity.' Chief Baron Pigot tried the case, and gave a statement of the facts in his charge which

Mr. Trench ought to have quoted, as a faithful recorder of 'realities.'

'On the western estate, that of Cahirciveen, there was some difference in the rules. If a son or daughter married, the father was obliged to retire with an allowance of 'a cow's grass' or grazing for his support. 'Only the newly married person will be left on the land, or any portion of it, even though the farm should contain 100 acres, or even though there should be two farms. This arbitrary regulation operates injuriously in point of morality, and keeps the land uncultivated. The people have to go to Nedeen, a distance of forty or fifty miles, to get leave to marry.'*

The Kenmare tenantry have recovered from the fearful shock of the famine, after thousands of deaths from hunger, and thousands shipped off to America at 4*l.* 10*s.* a head. Mr. Trench's son, Mr. Townshend Trench, the pictorial illustrator of his father's book, is the acting agent, and an eloquent propagandist of his father's principles. The young marquis paid a visit to his tenantry in 1868, and he was almost worshipped. It is gratifying to know that in a speech on that occasion he promised to see and judge for himself.

'I feel,' he said, 'that my visit to Kenmare has taught me a valuable lesson. As you all know, I was called to my present position at a very young age, and I felt when I came in for my property that I had much to learn; and that is the reason why I was so anxious to travel through the country, and study the desires and comfort of the people. That will afford me occupation for many a year to come, and it will afford me an occupation not only interesting but pleasing. Nothing will do me a more hearty pleasure than to see the marks of civilisation and progress in Kenmare—and not alone in Kenmare, but in the whole country; and I shall hail every manifestation of improvement with delight.'

Lord Lansdowne's system is beautiful, but it is unfinished. Let him 'crown the edifice with *liberty*.' He

* See the 'North British Review,' No. CI. p. 193.

possesses a giant's power, and he uses it like an angel. When he comes to trouble the waters, the multitude gathers around the fountain to be healed. But his visits are, like angels' visits, few and far between. Many of the sick and impotent folk, after long waiting, are not able to get near till the miracle-worker has departed. An absentee landlord, be he ever so good, must delegate his power to an agent. Agents have good memories, and their servants, the bailiffs, are good lookers-on. There is a hierarchy in the heaven of landlordism—the under-bailiff, the head-bailiff, the chief-clerk in the office, the sub-agent, the head-agent. All these must be submissively approached and anxiously propitiated before the petitioner's prayers can reach the ears of Jove himself, seated aloft on his remote Olympian throne. He may be, and for the most part really is—if he belongs to the old stock of aristocratic divinities—generous and gracious, incapable of meanness, baseness, or cruelty. But the tenant has to do, not with the absentee divinity, but with his priest—not with the good spirit, but his medium; and this go-between is not always noble, or disinterested, or unexacting. To him power may be new—a small portion of it may intoxicate him, like alcohol on an empty stomach. He was not born to an inheritance of sycophancy; it comes like an *afflatus* upon him, and it turns his head. It creates an appetite, like strong drink, which grows into a disease. This appetite is as capricious as it is insatiable. Hence, the chief characteristic of landlord power, as felt by the tenant, is *arbitrariness*. The agent may make any rule he pleases, and as many exceptions to every rule as he pleases. He may allow rents to run in arrear; he may suddenly come down upon the defaulter with ' a fell swoop;' he may require the rents to be paid up to the day; he may, without reason assigned, call in ' the hanging gale;' he may abate or increase the rents at will; he may inflict fines for delay or give notices to quit for the sole purpose of bringing in fees to his friend or relative, the solicitor. But whatever he may choose to do, the tenant has nothing for it but to submit; and he must submit with a good grace. Woe to him if the agony of his spirit is revealed in the working of his features, or in an audible groan! Most of the poor fellows do submit, till their hearts are broken—till the hot iron has entered their souls and seared their consciences. When the *slave* is thus finished, the agent and his journeymen are satisfied with their handiwork; their 'honours' can then count on any sort of services they may choose to exact—may bid defiance to the priest and the agitator, and boast of an orderly and deserving tenantry devoted to the best of landlords, who is their natural protector. It would be wicked to interfere with these amicable persons. Why talk about leases? The tenants will not have them; they don't want security or independence by contract. So most of the agents report —but not all. There are noble exceptions which relieve the gloomy picture.

There is certainly one disadvantage connected with a settlement of the land question which would abolish the arbitrary power of proprietors and their agents—it would put an end to the romance of Irish landlordism. The Edgeworths, the Morgans, the Banims, the Carletons, and the Levers would then be deprived of the best materials for their fictions. The fine old family, over-reached and ruined by a dishonest agent; the cruelly evicted farmer, with his wife and children fever-stricken, and his bedridden mother cast out on the roadside on Christmas Eve, exposed to the pelting of the hailstorm, while their home was unroofed and its walls levelled by the crowbar brigade; the once comfortable but now homeless father making his way to London, and trying day after day to present a petition in person to his landlord, repulsed from the gate of the great house, and laughed at for his frieze and brogue by pampered flunkeys. Then he travels on foot to his lordship's country-seat, scores or hundreds of miles—is taken up, and brought before the magistrates as 'an Irish rogue and vagabond.' At length he meets his lordship accidentally, and reveals to him the system of iniquity that prevails on his Irish estate at Castle Squander. Next we have the sudden and unexpected appearance of the god of the soil at his agent's office, sternly demanding an account of his stewardship. He gives ready audience to his tenants, and fires with indignation at bitter complaints from the parents of ruined daughters. Investigation is followed by the ignominious eviction of the tyrannical and roguish agent and his accomplices, a disgorging of their ill-gotten wealth, compensation to plundered and outraged tenants, the liberal distribution of poetical justice right and left.

Many other agents have followed Mr. Trench's example in forbidding to marry, and commanding to abstain from hospitality and charity. An ejectment was lately obtained at the quarter sessions in a southern county against a widow who had married without leave, or married a different person from the one the agent selected. But it is supposed that the threat of assassination prevented a recourse to extremities in this and other cases. For the people seem with one consent to have made a desperate stand against this cruel tyranny. A landlord said to me, ' No one in this part of the country would *presume* to evict a tenant now from fear of assassination. *That* is the tenant's security.'

The wretched outcasts, whom ' improvement ' has swept off the estates, are crowded into cities and towns, without employment, without food. Feeling bitterly their degradation and misery, and taught to blame the Government, they become demoralized and desperately disaffected. From these fermenting masses issues the avenging scourge of Fenianism —' the pestilence that walketh in darkness, and slayeth at noonday.'

For my part, I cannot understand the meaning of improving a country by disinheriting and banishing its inhabitants. I do not understand men who say the population is too dense, and yet give to one family a tract of land large enough to support ten families, turning out the nine to make room for the one. A great deal has been said about

E E

the evils of small farms. But the most disturbed and impoverished parts of Ireland are those in which the farms are largest; while the two most prosperous and best ordered counties—Armagh and Wexford—are the counties in which small farms most abound. I call a reluctant witness, Master Fitzgibbon, to testify that when the Irish tenant, be his holding ever so small, gets common justice and is not subjected to caprice, he gives no trouble. That gentleman informs us that there are 650 estates of all magnitudes, from 100*l.* to 20,000*l.* a-year, under the control and management of the court of chancery; the total rents of these amount to 494,056*l.* a-year payable by 28,581 tenants. These estates are in all parts of Ireland, not only in all the provinces, but in all the counties, without exception; and, according to Master Fitzgibbon, they fairly represent the tenantry of the whole country. He has 452 of the estates under his own jurisdiction, and the rents of these amount to 330,809*l.*, paid by 18,287 tenants. He has now been ten years in the office, during which 'the rents have been paid without murmuring or complaints worth noticing.' 'The pressure of legal remedies for these rents has been very little used; the number of evictions absolutely trifling; and of between 400 and 500 receivers, who collect these rents, *not one has ever been assailed*, or interfered with, or threatened in the discharge of his duty, as far as I have been able to discover; and I am the person to whom the receiver should apply for redress if anything of the kind occurred. It is very well known that my ears are open to any just complaint from any tenant, and yet I am very seldom appealed to, considering the great number of tenants; and whenever a complaint is well-founded, it is promptly and effectually redressed, at scarcely any expense of costs. I believe the other three Masters would make substantially a similar report to this in respect of the estates under their jurisdiction.'

Master Fitzgibbon proceeds to state that 'on one estate there are 2,500 tenants, paying 13,000*l.*,—being an average of 6*l.* a-year. This estate has been sold, and three of the lots fetched over 30 years' purchase of the yearly profit rents. The fourth lot is held by small cottiers, at rents which average only 2*l.*, and this lot fetched 23 years' purchase. This estate has been under a receiver for three years, and there has never been one complaint from a tenant. What is stated of this estate may be said of every one of them in all the four provinces.' He adds: ' Clamour, agitation, or violence of any kind I have never had to deal with amongst the tenantry of any one of these estates since I came into office.'

Another witness of larger views, and free from unhappy prejudices against the majority of his countrymen—Mr. Marcus Keane, agent to the Marquis of Conyngham— in a letter to Colonel Vandeleur, M.P., lately gave the result of his experience for thirty years as agent of several large estates, and as a landlord, on the Irish land question. I submit his suggestions to my readers, as eminently worthy of the consideration of statesmen at the present time :—

' The outline of measures submitted for your consideration combines the very unusual recommendation of meeting, on the one hand, with the approbation of some good landlords of the higher class (who, like yourself, have long been practically acknowledging the just claims of tenants), and, at the same time, of satisfying the claims of many of the warmest advocates of the tenant class. It is calculated to protect the farmers from selfish landlords, whose conduct has tended much to produce the serious disaffection that now prevails.

' I need not burthen you with a lengthened recital of the facts which render such legislation absolutely necessary to the tranquillity of society. In outline, however, they may be briefly stated—

' *First*—The great mass of Irish tenantry have no better title to their holdings than the will of their landlords.

' *Second*—Education is daily rendering the tenant class

more impatient of the condition of dependence which their want of title necessitates.

'*Third*—Every good tenant must improve his land more or less, in order to live in comparative comfort.

'*Fourth*—The rentals of Ireland are steadily following the improvements of the tenants. Some landlords suffer a considerable margin to exist between the actual value and the rent paid; while others lose no opportunity of forcing the rents to the highest amount that circumstances permit.

'*Fifth*—Although good tenants must improve in order to live comfortably, their improvements are not one-fourth of what the condition of the country invites, and are far below what they would be if the occupiers were afforded equitable security.

'*Sixth*—Trade, manufactures, and industrial occupations require local accumulations of surplus capital in order to their prosperity; and such accumulations are hindered by the general want of security of tenure. Society at large is therefore deeply interested in the protection of the tenant class.

'*Seventh*—The increased expense of the governmental establishments, civil and military, which Irish disaffection entails, renders it a matter of imperial importance that the Irish land question should be satisfactorily settled.

'Irish rentals have, in some counties, increased more than tenfold since the beginning of the eighteenth century.'

The next witness shall be a landlord, one of the best and noblest of his class. At a tenant-right meeting of the county Longford, the Earl of Granard said:—'The proposition commences by asserting that which has been acknowledged by successive administrations—that the present state of the land laws of Ireland is highly unsatisfactory. The necessity for their reform has been urged upon parliament since the days of O'Connell up to the present time. The want of reform upon the most vital question which affects the prosperity of Ireland has been the fruitful source of agrarian disturbance, of poverty and of misfortune in every county in Ireland. To take an example near home,—what rendered Ballinamuck a by-word for deeds of violence? Why, that system which permitted a landlord to treat the people of that district with high-handed injustice. And why is that district now amongst the most peaceable in the county? Because it is now administered by its proprietor in a spirit of justice and fair play, and because that proprietor recognises the fact that property has its duties as well as its rights. I believe that similar results are to be obtained everywhere that the warm-hearted and kindly people of this country are treated with justice. In his evidence before Mr. Maguire's committee, Mr. Curling, the excellent agent of an equally excellent landlord—Lord Devon—speaking of his property in Limerick, said that the most warm-hearted and grateful people he had ever met with were the Irish. He was asked, " Grateful for what?" and he replied, " Even for fair play." That is to say, they were grateful for that which in every country save this would have been theirs by law. And it is to a people thus described by, mind you, not an Irishman, but an English gentleman—to a people, I believe, the most religious and affectionate in Europe, that the simple act of justice, of repealing unjust statutes, has been refused. I say it advisedly, that to the system of land laws, which we hope to alter—which at least we are here to protest against—are to be attributed those fearful agrarian outrages which disgrace the fair fame of our country. A celebrated minister of police in France, whenever he heard of a conspiracy, used to ask who was the woman, believing that there was always one mixed up with such organisations, and in a similar spirit, whenever I hear of an outrage in Ireland, I am always inclined to enquire, " Who is the landlord?" For I do not hear of such things occurring on estates where justice and fair play are the rule and not the exception. But brighter days are now in store for us. We have at the head of affairs the most earnest, the most conscientious minister that has ever sat on the treasury bench. He has promised to redress your grievances, and having as

his able lieutenants Mr. Bright, who has ever a kindly word
for Ireland, and Lord Kimberley, whose first act after giving
up the lord-lieutenancy was to say to the House of Lords
that until the church and land questions were settled there
would be neither peace nor contentment in the land—he
must be successful. As to what we want there can be no
doubt. The five points of the Irish charter are—fixity of
tenure at reasonable rents; recognition of right of occupancy
as distinct from right of ownership; standard valuation for
letting purposes; retrospective compensation for 20 years;
and arbitration courts in cases of dispute between owner and
occupier.'

I cannot better express the conclusion of the whole matter
than in the words of a writer in the *Pall Mall Gazette*, who
thoroughly understands the question. Nothing can be more
truthful and accurate than the way in which he puts the
tenants' case :—

' " Morally," they say, " we are part-owners. We have a
moral right to live here. If a great landlord considered
that he could make more of his estate by clearing it of its
inhabitants, and accordingly proceeded to do so, he would
do a cruel act. What we wish is to see our moral rights
converted into legal rights. If you ask us precisely what it
is that we wish, we reply that we wish to be able to live in
moderate comfort in our native land, and to be able to make
our plans upon the assumption that we shall not be interfered with. It is not for us ignorant peasants to draw an
Act of Parliament upon this subject, or to say how our
views are to be reconciled with your English law, which,
on other accounts, we by no means love. You, the English
Government, must find out for yourselves how to do that.
What we want is to be secure and live in reasonable comfort,
and we shall never be at rest, and we will never leave you
at peace, till this is arranged in some way or other." We do
not say whether this feeling is right or wrong, we do not say
how it is to be dealt with, but we do say that it is as intel-
ligible, not to say as natural, a feeling as ever entered into

human hearts, and we say, moreover, that it would be very difficult to exaggerate either its generality, its force, its extent, or the degree to which it has been excited by recent events. We are deeply convinced that to persist in regarding the relation between landlord and tenant as one of contract merely, to repeat again and again in every possible form that all that the Irish peasants have a right to say is that they have made a hard bargain with their landlords which they wish the legislature to modify, is to shut our eyes to the feelings of the people, feelings which it will be difficult and also dangerous to disregard. The very gist and point of the whole claim of the tenants is that their moral right (as they regard it) is as sacred, and ought to be as much protected by law, as the landlords' legal right, and that it is a distinct grievance to a man to be prevented from living in Ireland on that particular piece of land on which he was born and bred, and which was occupied by his ancestors before him.'

The whole drift of this history bears on this point. The policy of the past must be reversed. The tenants must be rooted in the soil instead of being rooted out. ' Improvement ' must include the people as well as the land, and agents must no longer be permitted to arrogate to themselves the functions of Divine Providence.

' *Naturam expellas furcâ, tamen usque recurret.*'

One of the best pamphlets on the Irish Land Question is by Mr. William M'Combie, of Aberdeen. A practical farmer himself, his sagacity has penetrated the vitals of the subject. His observations, while travelling through the country last year, afford a remarkable corroboration of the conclusions at which I have arrived. Of the new method of ' regenerating Ireland,' he says:—

' In it the resources of the soil—to get the most possible out of it by the most summary process—is the great object; the people are of little or no account, save as they can be made use of to accomplish this object. But, indeed, it is not alone by the promoters of the grand culture that the people have been disregarded, but by Irish landlords, generally, of both classes. By the improving landlords—who are generally recent purchasers—they are regarded merely as labourers; by the leave-alone landlords as rent-producers. The one class have ejected the occupiers, the other have applied, harder and harder, the screw, until the " good landlord "—the landlord almost worshipped in Ireland at this hour—is the landlord who neither evicts his tenants nor raises their rents. The consequences are inevitable, and, over a large portion of the island, they are patent to every eye—they obtrude themselves everywhere. The people are poor; they are despondent, broken-spirited. In the south of Ireland decay is written on every town. In the poorer parts you may see every fifth or sixth house tenantless, roofless, allowed from year to year to moulder and moulder away, unremoved, unrepaired. . . . To make room for these large-scale operations, evictions must go on, and as the process proceeds the numbers must be augmented of those who are unfit to work for hire and unable to leave the country. The poor must be made poorer; many now self-supporting made dependent. Pauperism must spread, and the burden of poor rates be vastly increased. If the greatest good of the greatest number be the fundamental principle of good government, this is not the direction in which the state should seek to accomplish the regeneration of Ireland. The development of the resources of the land ought to be made compatible with the improvement of the condition of the people.'

CHAPTER XXV.

CONCLUSION—AN APPEAL TO ENGLISHMEN.

THE difficulty of understanding the case of Ireland is proverbial. Its most enlightened friends in England and Scotland are often charged with 'gross ignorance of the country.' They might excuse themselves by answering, that when they seek instruction from Irishmen, one native instructor is sure to contradict the other. Yet there must be some point of view from which all sides of the Irish question can be seen, some light in which the colours are not confused, the picture is not exaggerated, the features are not distorted. Every nation has its idiosyncrasy, proceeding from race, religion, laws, institutions, climate, and other circumstances; and this idiosyncrasy may be the key of its history. In Ireland three or four nationalities are bound together in one body politic; and it is the conflict of their several idiosyncrasies which perplexes statesmen, and constitutes the main difficulty of the Irish problem. The blood of different races is mingled, and no doubt greatly modified by ages of intercourse. But *religion* is an abiding force. The establishment of religious equality in Ireland is a glorious achievement, enough in itself to immortalise any statesman. It is a far greater revolution than was effected by the Emancipation Act, and more to the credit of the chief actor; because, while Mr. Gladstone did spontaneously what he firmly believed to be right in principle, Sir Robert Peel did, from necessity, what he as firmly believed was wrong in principle. But no reasonable man expected that the disestablishment of the Church would settle all Irish questions; in fact, it but clears the way for the settlement of some of the most important and urgent. It makes It possible for Irishmen of every creed to speak in one voice to the Government. Their respective clergy, hitherto so intent on ecclesiastical claims and pretensions, will no longer pass by on the other side, but turn Samaritans to their bleeding country, fallen among the thieves of Bigotry and Faction. There are many high Protestants—indeed, I may say all, except the aristocracy—who, while firmly believing in the vital importance of the union of the three kingdoms, earnestly wishing that union to be real and perpetual, cannot help expressing their conviction that Ireland has been greatly wronged by England—wronged by the legislature, by the Government, and most of all by the crown. In no country in the world has loyalty existed under greater difficulties, in none has it been so ill requited, in none has so much been done as if of set purpose to starve it to death. In the reign of Elizabeth the capricious will of a despotic sovereign was exerted to crush the national religion, while the greatest military exploits of her ablest viceroys consisted of predatory excursions, in which they slaughtered or carried away the horses and cattle, burned the crops and houses, and laid the country waste and desolate, in order to create famines for the wholesale destruction of the population, thus spoiled and killed as a punishment for the treason of their chiefs, over whom they had no control.

In the reigns of James I. and Charles I. there was a disposition among the remnant of the people—

To fly from petty tyrants to the throne.

But the Stuarts appealed to Irish loyalty merely for the support of their dynasty, and William III. laid the laurels won on the banks of the Boyne upon the altar of English monopoly. In the reigns of Anne and the three Georges, law was made to do the work of the sword, and the Catholics of Ireland, constituting the mass of the nation, knew their sovereign only as the head of an alien power, cruel and unrelenting in its oppression. They were required to love a German prince whom they had never seen. He called himself the father of his subjects; and he had millions of subjects on the other side of a narrow channel, whom he never knew, and never cared to know. When at length the dominant nation relented, and wished to strike the penal chains from the hands of her sister, the king forbade the act of mercy, pleading his conscience and his oath as a bar to justice and to freedom, but yielding at last to English state necessity, and robbing concession of its grace, of all its power to conciliate. From the battle of the Boyne to Catholic emancipation, the king of Ireland had never set foot on Irish soil, except in the case of George IV., whose visit was little better than a melodramatic exhibition, repaid by copious libations of flattery, which however failed to melt his bigotry, or to persuade him to redeem his solemn promises and pledges, until, nine years later, he was compelled to yield by the fear of impending civil war.

Ireland may get from her sister, England, everything but that for which the heart yearns—affection—that which alone ' can minister to a mind diseased, can pluck from the memory its rooted sorrow, and rase out the written troubles from the brain.' That is just what Ireland needs above all things. She wants to be kept from brooding morbidly over the dismal past, and to be induced to apply herself in a cheerful spirit to the business of life. The prescriptions of state physicians cannot fully reach the root of the disease. Say that it is a sentimental malady—a delusion. What is gained by saying *that*, if the sentiment or the delusion makes life wretched, unfits for business, produces suicidal propensities, and renders *keepers* necessary?

In theory, Ireland is one with England; in practice, she is hourly made to feel the reverse. *The Times*, and all the journals which express the instincts of the dominant nation, constantly speak of the Irish people as ' *the subjects of England*,' whom Englishmen have a right to control. They are the subjects of the Queen only in a secondary sense—*as* the Queen of England, and reigning over them through Eng-

land. Every sovereign, from Queen Elizabeth to Queen
Victoria, was sovereign of Ireland merely in this subordinate sense, even when there was an Irish parliament. The
King of *Ireland* could speak to his Irish parliament only as
he was advised by his English ministers; and their advice
was invariably prompted by English interests. Her king
was not *hers* in the true sense. His *heart* and his company
were wholly given to another, to whose pride, power, and
splendour she was made to minister. That state of things
still continues in effect, and while it lasts Ireland can never
be contented. Her heart will always be disquieted within
her. Something bitter will ever be bubbling up from the
bottom of that troubled fountain.

Nor let it be supposed that this is due to a peculiar idiosyncrasy in Ireland—to some unhappy congenital mal-
formation, or some original taint in the blood. It has been
often asked whether England would have submitted to
similar treatment from Ireland if their relations were reversed. Englishmen have not answered that question because they cannot understand it. They find it difficult to
apply the Divine maxim, ' Do as you would be done by,'
in their dealings with other nations. But they can scarcely
conceive its application to their dealings with Ireland, any
more than the American planter could have conceived the
duty of fraternizing with his negroes. If we draw from this
fact the logical inference, we shall be at a loss to discern
whether the Celt or the Saxon suffers more from the moral
perversity of his nature. The truth is, both are perverted
by their unnatural relations, which are a standing outrage
on the spirit of Christianity.

The Emperor of Austria long laboured to govern one
nation through another and for another, in right of conquest,
and we know the result in Italy and Hungary. Lombardy,
though well cultivated and materially prosperous, could
never be reconciled to Austrian rule. Even the nobility
could not be tempted to appear at court. Venetia was more
passionately and desperately hostile, and was consequently

crushed by military repression, till the country was turned into a wilderness, and the capital once so famous for its commerce and splendour, became one of the most melancholy scenes of ruin and desolation to be found in the world. The Austrians, and those who sympathised with Austria as the great conservative power of the Continent, ascribed all this to the perversity of the Italian nature, and to the influence of agitators and conspirators. Austria was bountiful to her Italian subjects, and would be more lenient if she could, but their vices of character and innate propensity to rebellion, rendered necessary a system of coercion. Hence the prisons were full of political offenders; the soldier and the executioner were constantly employed in maintaining law and order. All the Emperor wanted was that his Italian provinces should be so thoroughly amalgamated with Austria, as to form one firmly united empire, and that the inhabitants should be content with their position as *Austrian* subjects, ruled by Austrian officials. But this was precisely what they could not or would not be. 'They smiled at the drawn dagger and defied its point.' They would sacrifice their lives, but they would not sacrifice their nationality at the bidding of an alien power.

This illustrates the force of the national sentiment, and the tremendous magnitude of the calamities to which its persistent violation leads. But the case of Hungary is still more apposite as an illustration of the English policy in Ireland. The Hungarians had an ancient constitution and parliament of their own. The Emperor of Austria was their legitimate king, wearing the crown of Hungary. In this capacity the Hungarians were willing to yield to him the most devoted loyalty. But he wanted to weld his empire into a compact unity, and to centralise all political power at Vienna, so that Austria should be the head and heart of the system, and the other provinces her hands and her feet. Hungary resisted, and revolted. The result was a desolating civil war, in which she was triumphant, till the Czar came to the rescue of his brother despot, and poured his legions in overwhelming numbers into the devoted country. Hungary was now at the feet of her sovereign, and Austria, the dominant state, tried to be conciliatory, in order to bring about the desired amalgamation and consolidation of the empire. She did so, with every apparent prospect of success, and it was generally considered throughout Europe that there was an end of the Hungarian kingdom. But Hungarian nationality survived, and still resisted Austrian centralisation. The Hungarians struggled for its recognition constitutionally, manfully, with admirable self-control, moderation, and wisdom, until at length they achieved a peaceful victory. Their sovereign reigns over them as King of Hungary; he and the empress dwell among them, without Austrian guards. Their children are born among them, and they are proud to call them natives of Hungary. The Hungarians, as subjects of *Austria*, were discontented, miserable, incurably disaffected. As subjects of their own king (though he is also Emperor of Austria) they are intensely loyal. They are prosperous and happy, because they are free. And though they have their distinctions of race and religion, they are united. The Magyars of Hungary correspond very nearly to the Protestants of Ireland. Though a minority, their energy, their education, their natural talent for organisation and government, their love of freedom, their frank recognition of the rights of conscience, enable them to lead without inspiring jealousy, just as the Protestants of Ireland were enabled to lead in 1782, notwithstanding the existence of Protestant Ascendancy. Religious equality is not a cause of tranquillity in itself. It tranquillises simply because it implies the absence of irritation. It takes a festering thorn out of the side of the unestablished community—a thorn which inflames the blood of every one of its members. Let worldly interest, political power, and social precedence cease to be connected with the profession of religion, and religious differences would cease to produce animosity and intolerance. If the Magyars had been the Hungarian party of Protestant ascendancy, and if the Protestant interest had also been the Austrian interest; if the mission of the Magyars had been to act as a garrison to keep down the Roman Catholic majority, their cause could never have triumphed till Protestant ascendancy should be abolished. But Hungarian Protestantism did not need such support, although the Pope has as much authority in Hungary as in Ireland. Of course the cases of Hungary and Ireland are in many respects dissimilar. But they are alike in this : their respective histories establish the great fact that the most benevolent of sovereigns, and the wisest of legislatures, can never produce contentment or loyalty in a kingdom which is ruled *through* and *for* another kingdom.

We can easily understand that when the light of royalty shines upon a country *through a conquering nation still dominant*, the medium is of necessity dense, cold, refracting, and discolouring. Of this the best illustration is derived from the relations between Austria and Hungary, now so happily adjusted to the unspeakable advantage of both nations. Austrian rule was unsympathetic, harsh, insolent, domineering, based upon the arrogant assumption that the Hungarians were incapable of managing their own affairs without the guidance of Austrian wisdom and the support of Austrian steadiness. But the Hungarians, united among themselves, putting their trust, not in boastful, vapouring, and self-seeking agitators, but in honest, truthful, high-minded, and capable statesmen, persevered in a course of firm, but temperate and constitutional, national self-assertion, until the Austrians were compelled to put away from them their supercilious airs of natural superiority, and to concede the principle of international equality and the right of self-government.

What sickens the reader of Irish history most of all is the anarchy of the old clan system, the everlasting alternation of outrages and avenging reprisals. One faction, when it felt strong and had a favourable opportunity, made a sudden raid upon another faction, taken at a disadvantage, plundering and killing with reckless fury. The outraged party treasured up its anger till it had power to retaliate, and then glutted its vengeance without mercy in the same way. When this fatal propensity to mutual destruction was restrained by law, it broke out from time to time in other ways. What was wanted to cure it effectually was a strong, steady, central government, such as England enjoys herself. But the very system which is most calculated to foster factiousness is the one which has reigned for centuries in Dublin Castle. The British sovereign knows no party, and, whatever other sovereigns have done, Queen Victoria has never forgotten this constitutional principle. But the Irish lord-lieutenant is always a party-man, and is always surrounded by party-men. They were Whigs or Tories, Liberals or Conservatives, often extreme in their views and violent in their temper. The vice of the old clan system was its tendency to unsettle, to undo, to upset, to smash and destroy. Instead of counteracting that vice (which still lingers in the national blood), by a fixed, unchanging system of administration, based on principles of unswerving rectitude, which knows no distinction of party, no favouritism, England ruled by the alternate sway of factions.

The Times, referring to the debate on the Irish Church, remarked that the viceroyalty was more and more ' a mere ornament.' It is really nothing more. The viceroy has no actual power, and if he has statesmanship, it is felt to be out of place. He can scarcely give public expression to his sentiments on any political questions without offending one party or the other, whereas the estate of the realm which he represents is neutral and ought to keep strictly to neutral ground. As to the effect of the office in degrading the national spirit among the nobility and gentry, we could not have a better illustration than the fact that the amiable Lord Carlisle was accustomed, at the meeting of the Royal Dublin Society, to tell its members that the true aim, interest, glory, and destiny of Ireland was to be a pasture and a dairy for England,—a compliment which seemed to have been gratefully accepted, or was at all events allowed to pass.

But even as an ' ornament' the viceregal system is a failure. The Viceroy with his family ought to be the head of society in Ireland, just as the Queen is in England. The royal family are the same to all parties and classes, showing no partiality on the ground of politics, but smiling with equal favour and recognition upon all. In Ireland, however, a liberal lord lieutenant is generally shunned by the Conservative portion of the aristocracy, which forms the great majority of the class. On the other hand the Conservatives flock in large numbers to the court of a Tory Viceroy, while Liberals stand aloof. Instead therefore of being a centre of union to all sections of the best society, and bringing them together, so that they may know one another, and enjoy the advantages due to their rank, the viceregal court operates as a source of jealousy and division. So that, looking at the institution as a mere ornament of society, as a centre of fashionable life and refining influences, facilitating intercourse between ranks and classes, bringing the owners of land and the men of commerce more in harmony, it is not worth preserving. On the other hand it produces some of the worst features of conventionalism. It cultivates flunkeyism and servility, while operating as a restraint upon the manly expression of opinion. It fosters a spirit of spurious aristocracy, which shows itself in contempt for men who prefer honest industry to place-hunting and insolvent gentility.

But while I thus speak of the viceregal court as at present constituted, I still maintain that, like Hungary, this country is so peculiarly situated, and is animated by so strong a spirit of nationality, that it ought to have a court of its own, and a sovereign of its own. The case of Hungary shows how easily this great boon might be granted, and how gratifying the results would be to all the parties concerned. The Queen ought to reside in Ireland for some portion of the year. A suitable palace should be provided for the royal family. The Prince of Wales, during her majesty's reign, ought to be the permanent Viceroy,

F F

with the necessary addition to his income. The office would
afford an excellent training for his duties as king. The attraction of the Princess of Wales would make the Irish
court very brilliant. It would afford the opportunity of
contact with real royalty, not the shadowy sort of thing
we have had—reflected through Viceroys very few of whom
were ever *en rapport* with the Irish nation. Not one of
them could so speak to the people as to elicit a spark of
enthusiasm. Of course they could not have the true ring of
royalty, for royalty was not in them. But they could not
play the part well. One simple sentence from the Queen or
the Prince of Wales, or even from Prince Arthur, would be
worth all the theatrical pomp they could display in a generation. Those noblemen had no natural connection with
the kingdom, fitting them to take the first place in it.
They were not hereditary chiefs. They were not elected by
the people. They were mere ' casual' chief-governors ; and
they formed no ties with the nation that could not be broken
as easily as the spider's thread. The *hereditary principle* has
immense force in Ireland. The landlords are now seeking
to weaken it; or rather they are ignoring it altogether, and
substituting the commercial principle in dealing with their
tenants, preferring not the most devoted adherents of the
family, but the man with most money. But I warn them that
they are doing so at the peril of their order. A prince who
was *heir presumptive to the throne as Viceroy*, and who, when
he ascended the throne, should be crowned King of *Ireland*,
as well as King of Great Britain, crowned in his own Irish
palace, and on the *Lia Fail* or stone of destiny, preserved at
Westminster, would save many a million to the British
exchequer, for it would be no longer necessary to support a
large army of occupation to keep the country. If the throne
of Queen Victoria stood in Dublin, there is not a Fenian in
Ireland who would not die in its defence. Standing in
Westminster it is doubtful whether its attraction is sufficient
to retain the hearts even of Orangemen. There, it is the *English* throne. So the *Englishman* regards it with instinctive

jealousy. He feels it is his own; but, say what we may, the Irish loyalist, when he approaches it, is made to feel, by a thousand signs, that he is a stranger and an intruder. He returns to his own bereaved country with a sad heart, and a bitter spirit. Can he be *Anglicised?* Put this question to an English philosopher, and he will answer with Mr. Froude—'Can the Ethiopian change his skin, or the leopard his spots?' We can bridge the channel with fast steamers; but who will bridge the gulf, hitherto impassable, which separates the English Dives from the Irish Lazarus?

'We have,' said Canning, 'for many years been erecting a mound—not to assist or improve, but to thwart nature; we have raised it high above the waters, and it has stood there, frowning hostility and effecting separation. In the course of time, however, the necessities of man, and the silent workings of nature, have conspired to break down this mighty structure, till there remains of it only a narrow isthmus, standing

> Between two kindred seas,
> Which, mounting, viewed each other from afar,
> And longed to meet.

What then, shall be our conduct? Shall we attempt to repair the breaches, and fortify the ruins? A hopeless and ungracious undertaking! Or shall we leave them to moulder away by time and accident—a sure but distant and thankless consummation; or, shall we not rather cut away at once the isthmus that remains, allow free course to the current which has been artificially impeded, and float upon the mingling waves the ark of our glorious constitution?'

Much has been done since Canning's time to remove the narrow isthmus. Emancipation cut deep into it. The disestablishment of the Irish Church submerged an immense portion of it. If Mr. Gladstone's land bill be equally effective, a breach will be made through which the two kindred seas will meet, and, in their commingling flux and reflux, will quickly sweep away all minor obstacles to their perfect union. A just settlement of the land question will reconcile the two races, and close the war of seven centuries.

That is the rock against which the two nationalities have rushed in foaming breakers, lashed into fury by the storms of faction and bigotry. Remove the obstruction, and the world would hear no more the roaring of the waters. Then would float peacefully upon the commingling waves the ark of our common constitution, in which there would be neither Saxon nor Celt, neither English nor Irish, neither Protestant nor Catholic, but one united, free, and mighty people. Then might the Emperor of the French mark the epoch with the announcement—' England has done justice to Ireland!'